Yorkshire Rebel

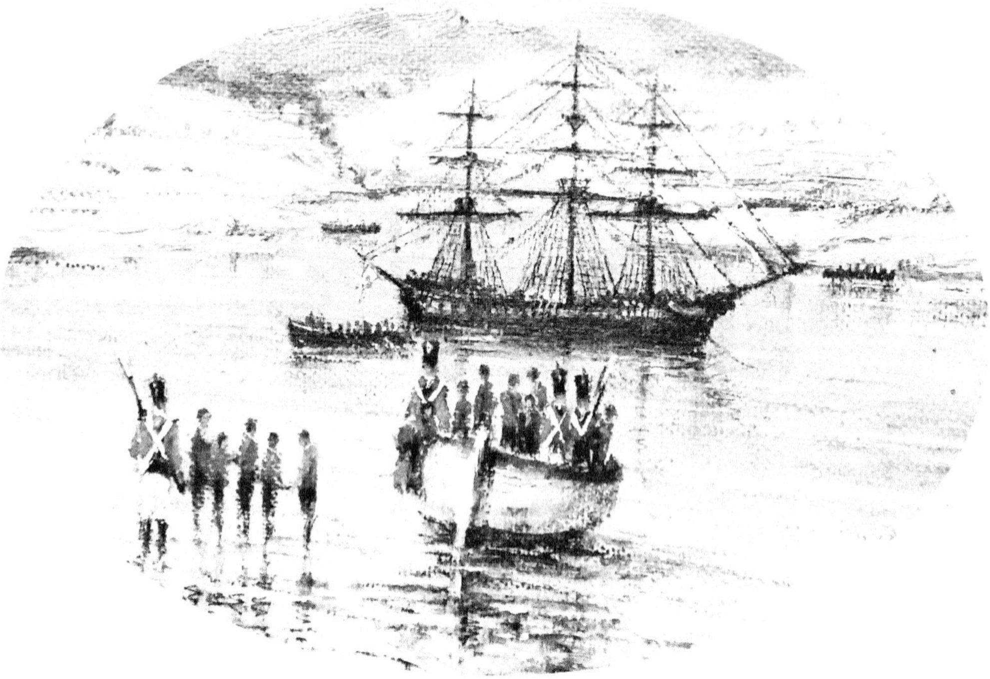

Yorkshire Rebel

The Life and Times of John Lindley 1770 – 1853
Two Hundredth Anniversary Edition

Ron Riley

Yorkshire Rebel
The Life and Times of John Lindley 1770-1853
© Ronald Riley

All rights reserved. No part of this publication may be reproduced, stored in a retrieval system, or transmitted in any form or by any means, electronic mechanical, photocopying recording or otherwise without prior permission of the publisher.

The rights of Ronald Riley to be identified as the author of this work has been asserted by him in accordance with the copyright Design and Patents Act 1998.

Cover painting by John R Henderson FSAA ©
Published by Blue Poppy Publishing, Devon
TWO HUNDREDTH ANNIVERSARY PAPERBACK EDITION
ISBN: 979-8-636944-79-9

This book is dedicated to the memory of my son

Alan J.F.Riley (1957–2015)

ACKNOWLEDGEMENTS

The author wishes to thank the keeper of the National Archives at Kew for permission to quote Crown Copyright Home Office Papers; also the staff at Barnsley Achieves for invaluable help in researching local industry; The staff of the Caird Library in Greenwich for details of naval history; also Frances Stott for her detailed history Looking Back at Mirfield

To Alan Brooke and the late Lesley Kipling for permission to reproduce so much of their work from second edition of Liberty or Death; To the late Harold Taylor for his expertise on Nail Making; Cynthia Dillon for her knowledge of the local history of Barnsley, David Pinder for his expertise on the Luddites; Ros Otzen of Melbourne for visiting and obtaining information from the Tasmanian Archives on my behalf. But particularly the late Margaret Streadwick for proof reading the second edition and Patricia Markham for proof reading the anniversary edition. Finally Joyce Salter for being the driving force behind this anniversary edition.

I am also indebted to Beverley Riley and her late husband Frank Riley for entrusting the 'Lindley Papers' including the front page of the Lindley family Bible to my care.

Front Cover: Van Diemen's Land: The Landing by John R Henderson FSAA ©

This splendid original painting by John Henderson depicts the beauty of the new penal colony in Van Diemen's Land, in contrast to the 'dark satanic mills' that many convicts left behind in England.

Rear Cover: Review by Susannah Long. This is a very sensitive appreciation of the message conveyed by Yorkshire Rebel.

Contents

Foreword by Alan Brooke 1
Prologue - Captain Cook's Discovery of Eastern Australia 1770 2
Introduction – The Life of a Georgian Radical 5
1 Childhood in Darton 1770 - 1775 7
2 Early Years in Darton 1775 - 1802 12
3 The South Yorkshire Iron Industry 23
4 Nail Making in Darton 31
5 Radical Awakening 1760 - 1793 38
6 War with France 1793 - 1802 47
7 The Move to Mirfield 1802 - 1803 56
8 Growth of Radical Politics 1802 - 1810 65
9 Luddite Years 1811 - 1812 72
10 York Castle 1813 89
11 Post War Years 1815 - 1819 93
12 The West Yorkshire Rebellion of 1820 101
13 Transportation 1821 - 1828 118
14 Tasmanian Twelve 126
15 Return to England 1828 132
16 The Great Reform Bill of 1832 137
17 Adult Health 145
18 Chartism 1837 - 1840 154
19 Law and Order in the early Nineteenth Century 163
20 Chartism in the Hungry Forties 1840 - 1842 167
21 Plug Plot of 1842 173
22 Social Reform 1802 - 1850 180
23 Chartist Disillusionment 1848 185
24 The Twilight Years in Mirfield 1838 - 1853 190
Epilogue 195
Lindley Family Trees 196
End Notes 199
Bibliography 213
Chronology 216
Index of Names 218
About the Author 229

FOREWORD

The 'Industrial Revolution' was a time of profound economic social and political change in Great Britain. Yorkshire Rebel recounts how this affected common working people particularly in the industrial areas of the country. This is in stark contrast to the life of the new middle classes, as depicted by Jane Austen, which provides a completely different view of the period.

Ron Riley describes the trials and tribulations of working-class life and work in careful detail, reconstructing conditions in the West Riding communities which shaped John Lindley's view of the world. The reader can almost feel the heat of the nail makers' workshop where John Lindley learned his trade.

The wider backdrop of movements and ideas is also clearly described, bringing to life the political ferment which influenced John Lindley's ideas and set him and hundreds of others on a course of action which could have proved fatal. Although we have no record of John Lindley's personal thoughts, the milieu in which he circulated gives us some idea of what his concerns and ideals must have been. Ron Riley again depicts this with precision – the mounting anticipation of the insurrection, the disillusionment of defeat and the anxiety of the treason trials.

Ron Riley also follows John Lindley on the convict ship and into exile in Van Diemen's Land showing that he was no ordinary convict, but a man with some standing and respect both in the community he left and, as his early return home testifies, the one he was transported to.

The immense changes during John Lindley's remaining lifetime are also brought into the picture. 'Yorkshire Rebel' is not merely the story of one man, but an account of the working class in the West Riding as a whole. Ron Riley has not been content to rest with John Lindley as a small twig on a family tree. He has generated not only a rich foliage and colourful blossoms but also described the ecology in which John Lindley and other working-class radicals flourished. 'Yorkshire Rebel' is an important contribution to our working-class heritage and a valuable reminder of the struggles for freedom which still have a resonance today.

Alan Brooke.
Huddersfield

PROLOGUE

Captain Cook's Discovery of Eastern Australia 1770

Land ahoy! Land ahoy! The loud shout came from an excited Second Lieutenant Hicks (1739–1771) on the bridge of HMS *Endeavour*. He was officer of the watch and second in command of the converted 368-ton Whitby collier on Lieutenant Cook's first expedition round the world. It was about one hour after daybreak, on Thursday 20 April 1770, that *Endeavour* cautiously approached this unexplored coastline. (Note: Cook's Journal records 19 April, since he had made no correction for crossing the 180° longitude, as the international dateline was not agreed for a further one hundred years.) As the first known Europeans to visit the dangerous eastern seaboard of Australia, they prudently exercised extreme care when navigating this uncharted coast with its many hidden reefs. Cook's Journal records:

> *At 5, set the Topsails close reef'd, and 6, saw land extending from North-East to West, distance 5 or 6 Leagues, having 80 fathoms, fine sandy bottom. We continued standing to the Westward with the Wind at South-South-West until 8, at which time we got Topgallant Yards a Cross, made all sail, and bore away along shore North-East for the Eastermost land we had in sight.*[1]

The headland first sighted by the lookout was later named *Point Hicks*. This was an admirable habit of Cook's, who frequently named places after the first man to sight them, regardless of rank. 'From this landfall, *Endeavour* steered a northerly course along the coast of what is now known as New South Wales. Later, he sailed further north, along the Queensland coast, between the Great Barrier Reef and the mainland. The large seas, which rolled in from the south-east, broke ominously and heavily on the beaches and forced *Endeavour* to keep a safe distance from the shore.' Creeping steadily northwards, a suitable anchorage was found in a small bay, a few miles south of where the present-day city of Sydney now stands. And so it was, on 29 April 1770, Lieutenant James Cook, RN (1728–1779) of HM Bark *Endeavour*, stepped ashore at Botany Bay on the eastern seaboard of Australia. He was later to claim the entire eastern coast of New South Wales for the Crown.

> *Notwithstand[ing] I had in the Name of His Majesty taken possession of several places upon this coast, I now once more hoisted English Coulers and in the Name of His Majesty King George the Third took possession of the whole Eastern Coast by the name New South Wales, together with all the Bays, Harbours Rivers and Islands situate upon the said coast, after which we fired three Volleys of small Arms which were Answerd by the like number from the Ship.*[2]

Cook and his crew soon made hesitant contact with the native aboriginal tribe known as Gweagal.

> *Saw, as we came in, on both points of the bay, several of the Natives and a few hutts [sic]; Men, Women, and Children on the South Shore abreast of the Ship, to which place I went in the Boats in hopes of speaking with them, accompanied by Mr Banks, Dr Solander, and Tupia [his Polynesian guide]. As we approached the Shore they all made off, except 2 Men, who seem'd resolved to oppose our landing. As soon as I saw this I order'd the boats to lay upon their Oars, in order to speak to them; but this was to little purpose, for neither us nor Tupia could understand one word they said. We then threw them some nails, beads, etc., a shore, which they took up, and seem'd not ill pleased with, in so much that I thought that they beckon'd to us to come ashore; but in this we were mistaken, for as soon as we put the boat in they again came to oppose us, upon which I fir'd a musquet between the 2, which had no other Effect than to make them retire back, where bundles of their darts lay, and one of them took up a stone and threw at us...*[3]

The *Endeavour* had sailed from Plymouth on 26 August 1768 – a historic journey that had taken twenty months. Prior to reaching Australia, Cook's expedition had fulfilled its prime scientific objective by recording the transit of Venus across the disc of the sun on 3–4 June 1769. From Tahiti, Cook sailed to New Zealand and mapped the entire coastline of both North and South Islands. When he eventually returned to England on 13 July 1771, having successfully circumnavigated the world, he anchored just off Dover and hastened to the Admiralty in London by coach. On arrival, he handed over the logs, journals and charts he had made of the South Pacific; in addition he reported on the success of his anti-scorbutic measures (fruit and vegetables containing vitamin C to prevent scurvy) and the accuracy of the navigation instruments he had been given to evaluate. Cook was presented to George III (1738–1820) and given a warm welcome by the many seafaring officers at the Admiralty, where his extraordinary achievement and nautical contributions to scientific knowledge were fully appreciated by his fellow professionals. He was subsequently promoted to commander in recognition of his fine achievement. But, the public at large reserved popular acclaim for the gentlemen scientists of the expedition, led by Mr Joseph Banks FRS (1743–1820), botanist and chief scientist and his party, which included botanical artists, draughtsmen, naturalists, astronomers and a doctor. Banks was later elected president of the Royal Society and made a baronet in 1781. James Cook, the son of a farm labourer from Marton in Yorkshire, took longer to achieve the full recognition that he deserved.[4]

Cook had been chosen by the Royal Society to lead this three-year voyage of discovery, which circumnavigated the globe, on account of his courage demonstrated at the battle of Quebec, and his surveying skills, particularly his historic survey of Newfoundland. However, it took a second and third voyage to the Pacific to establish his fame as Britain's foremost navigator. Unfortunately, he was killed by natives on 14 February 1779 in Hawaii on the third expedition.

Perhaps Cook's greatest contribution to scientific knowledge was his report on the successful anti-scorbutic measures that he had instituted. It was during this, his first voyage to the Pacific Ocean, that he confirmed the correctness of the principles laid down by Dr James Lind (1716–1794), a naval surgeon, in his paper *A Treatise of the Scurvy*, resulting from experiments on the *Salisbury* in 1747. These experiments demonstrated the effectiveness of oranges and lemons in preventing scurvy. Cook zealously adopted Lind's findings and insisted on including green vegetables, sauerkraut and scurvy grass in the crew's diet. He also included fish whenever possible. Neither Lind, nor Cook, knew how or why the diet worked (all contain vitamin C) but they had practical evidence that it prevented scurvy. Generations of sailors (and John Lindley, who received lemon juice and sugar on the convict ship *Lady Ridley* in 1821) had reason to be grateful to this humane man with an enquiring mind.[5]

In fact, scurvy was a most distressing condition suffered by all long-distance seafarers prior to John Lindley's birth in 1770. The symptoms were easy enough to diagnose and followed a well-known pattern. After eight or nine weeks of eating only dry rations, the men first began to suffer from swollen and bleeding gums, the teeth eventually falling out. Dry rations consisted of: salt beef, cheese often infested with worms, and ships biscuits riddled with weevils, plus dried peas and oatmeal, all washed down with diluted rum. On this diet the connective tissue of their bodies deteriorated, causing bruises to appear for no apparent reason, and the limbs, particularly the legs, became swollen, and wounds failed to heal. Blood would seep into joints and under the skin, causing agonising pain and stiffness. Some men suffered from blurred vision, while others were short of breath and lacked energy as their strength ebbed away. Sudden death occurred due to deterioration of heart muscle and internal bleeding into the heart cavities.[6]

When the Americans finally declared their independence in 1776, they no longer accepted criminals transported from Great Britain and an alternative country, preferably as far as possible from their homeland, had to be found to send not only felons, but an increasing number of British radical political prisoners and vocal Irish Nationalists. A deliberate policy was adopted to remove 'inconvenient' people from sight, and eventually from memory, rather than create martyrs, as occurred with public hangings. Botany Bay in Australia, discovered by Cook, was the destination chosen by England's prime minister, William Pitt the Younger (1759–1806). 'The First Fleet', under Captain Arthur Phillip (1738–1814) in his flagship *Sirius*, 'set sail for Botany Bay on the evening of 12 May 1787, carrying 330 convicts, 203 men and 127 women', and a new chapter in British penal history was about to begin.[7]

INTRODUCTION
The Life of a Georgian Radical

This is the personal story of the late eighteenth century, early nineteenth century radical, John Lindley (1770–1853), an ordinary working man, who lived a far from ordinary life during extraordinary times.

John Lindley's life was contemporaneous with the first seventy-five years of the 'industrial revolution' and, as his story unfolds, it is possible to appreciate how this 'revolution' dramatically changed the lives of working men and women in the manufacturing areas of northern England. John Lindley's story aims to recount his personal history against a background of social and economic change. Ordinary working men of his time did not leave copious written records or correspondence, consequently it has been necessary to assume that he held the views of his contemporaries, perhaps a little stronger than most, as he was prepared to die for his beliefs.

When John was born, in 1770, the West Riding of Yorkshire supported a dual economy of farming and cottage-based industries, of which handloom weaving of woollens was by far the most important. It was essentially a pastoral community, where work was unstructured and people worked at their own pace. Furthermore, 'social and economic units were small, and society was divided into small communities', centred on the local market town.[1]

But the year 1770 also marked the rise of the cotton industry in Lancashire, powered first by Thomas Newcomen's (1663–1729) beam engine and then by the more expensive, but more efficient, double condenser steam engine of James Watt (1736–1819) and his partner Matthew Boulton (1728–1809), who joined forces in 1773. This was the beginning of the factory system, where workers, men, women and children, gathered in multi-storey buildings, owned and run by wealthy manufacturers, employing large and expensive machinery. In these buildings, operatives, working for wages, became 'cogs' in a process that required discipline, and above all good timekeeping. This was totally alien to the traditional working practice of the eighteenth century, which was normally an irregular pattern of work, dictated by the agricultural year. People worked very hard for long hours, an eighteen-hour day was not uncommon, and a twenty-hour day was worked when absolutely necessary – particularly at harvest time – but at other times they took things easy. As Max Webber (1864–1920) the famous sociologist and philosopher observed: 'A man does not by nature wish to earn more and more money, but simply to live as he is accustomed to live and to earn as much as is necessary for that purpose.' The driving force for greater output was hunger and subsistence wages.[2]

It should be remembered, that in the eighteenth century, there was no means available to the labouring classes for saving money for hard times. It was not until the early nineteenth century, with the introduction of penny banks, that banks began to cater for small savers such as craftsmen, household servants and apprentices. These institutions were greatly strengthened by the Savings Bank (England) Act of 1817. Depositors were guaranteed the nominal value of their savings, so that these could be withdrawn at their full value with interest. This was achieved by requiring funds to be invested in government bonds, or deposited at the Bank of England, thereby creating a safe outlet for deposits.

Mechanisation of the cotton industry in Lancashire was soon followed by first the worsted industry, and later the woollen industry in Yorkshire. It was soon recognised that, except for the combing process, spinning yarn from the longer staple wools, used by worsted manufacturers, could easily be adapted to machine production. By 1820, worsted spinning mills used similar methods to those of the cotton factories, with women and children providing much of the labour. The technology of machine spinning woollen yarns proved more difficult and took another three decades to master. In addition, centuries of cultural tradition proved resistant to changes in working methods. The proto-industrial structure of the 'putting out system' had served the woollen industry for centuries and the 'free' workers were not willing to abandon their 'customary practice' without a fight.[3]

When John died, the northern countryside was covered in 'dark satanic mills', crisscrossed with canals and railways, which artificially isolated one section of the community from its neighbour. Many people now worked in factories, obeying the tyranny of the clock. This was part of the hidden cost of transforming 'a green and pleasant land' into an industrial complex that became 'the workshop of the world'. The cultural shock was profound.

From the distance of the twenty-first century, it is difficult to appreciate the daily lives of the vast majority of men, women and children living in the British Isles during the late eighteenth century. For example, John was born in a time before mass transport became commonplace, when most ordinary working people never travelled more than ten miles (sixteen km) from their home village or town – in their entire lifetime! In fact, housewives are recorded as seldom leaving their village except for a visit to the local market town once a year. But, in 1821, John was transported 16,000 miles (25,000 km) to Van Diemen's Land on the far side of the world. Furthermore, he survived in this hostile land for seven years, before making the perilous return journey by sailing ship, to be reunited with his family in Mirfield – a small market town in the West Riding of Yorkshire.[4]

In the days of sailing ships, the journey to Van Diemen's Land, via the Azores, stopping at Rio de Janeiro and rounding the Cape of Good Hope, normally took about four to five months, depending on the season, and whether the trade winds were favourable or unfavourable. On arriving in 1821, John and his fellow prisoners found a raw and very brutal society, founded only eighteen years previously in 1803 (to prevent the French gaining a foothold in Australia), with a population of about 7,400, mostly men, of whom about half were convicts.[5]

How did he come to be sent to Van Diemen's Land? How did he survive the rigours of that primitive country, and how did he live to the great age of eighty-three in his native Yorkshire?

This record of the life and times of John Lindley recounts the many historic events that he experienced during his lifetime, and charts the painful genesis of the Industrial Revolution that in the space of one generation changed the world, and continues to exert its influence today. It recounts the history of the period 1770 to 1853, through the eyes of a nail maker, who became a Yorkshire Rebel.

CHAPTER 1
Childhood in Darton 1770 – 1775

The Parental Home of Robert and Jane Lindley

John Lindley started life in November 1770 in the small parish of Darton, near Barnsley, in the south of Yorkshire. He was christened in the parish church of All Saints, Darton on 5 May 1771, an unusual delay, as it was the custom to christen children within a few days of birth. Ostensibly this was to enrol them in the church of Christ, thereby safeguarding their souls in the event of an early death.[1]

John was the son of Robert Lindley (1745–1831), who was christened in Darton in 1745, and Jane Lindley (born 1746), and the grandson of John Lindley, also christened in Darton, about 1720. As so often happened in the eighteenth century, families and close kin settled in one place and remained there for several generations. In the case of the many Lindley families living in the parish of Darton, this was at Broadroyd Head, a hamlet approximately three miles (five km) to the north-west of Barnsley, part of the 'village' of Mapplewell, comprising the hamlets of Mapplewell, Staincross, Broadroyd Head, Upper Carr Green and Carr Green.

Birth

For many individuals, the period 1770-1853 was a time of short lives and sudden death. Life everywhere was lived under the threat of disease, and in some places up to half of all babies born did not survive infancy. Childhood and adolescence were highly vulnerable periods and, tragically, vast numbers of mothers died in childbirth. To be born successfully, without either deformity or killing the mother, was a major achievement in the eighteenth century and largely depended on the mother's health and lack of post-natal complications. The only anaesthetics available were alcohol for the poor and laudanum (opium dissolved in alcohol) for the more affluent. And, with no knowledge or appreciation of antiseptics and asepsis, it is not surprising that many mothers died of puerperal fever.[2]

Traditionally, childbirth in poor families was attended by midwives, or friends and neighbours, who acquired practical experience by attending such events, but midwives were regarded as dirty and ignorant by qualified doctors. Their knowledge often contained a large amount of folklore and dubious mythology. In fact, 'normal babies' delivered themselves with a variable amount of help from their mothers. Abnormal presentations often resulted in the death of either the baby, or the mother, or both. University trained doctors had more medical knowledge and practised the use of forceps in difficult deliveries – with varying degrees of success. But these so-called accoucheurs (man-midwives) really had no effective treatments for physical injuries and infections suffered by new mothers.

They relied heavily upon the general treatments of sweating, bleeding and purging – the barbaric but universal cures of the age. These treatments were based on an incorrect understanding of illness, that was thought to be caused by a lack of balance in the human system; and treatments, including medication, were prescribed to assist the healing power of nature in restoring balance to the system, not to cure the disease itself.[3]

Infant Nutrition and Health

The first requirement of the newly born baby John was food. Lack of food was by far the largest cause of child mortality. Furthermore, women undernourished during pregnancy caused many foetuses to abort, or produced underweight babies that did not survive. Poor or non-existent breastfeeding caused many more deaths. As the first-born, or perhaps the first surviving child – his parents had been married well over three years when he was born – John could have been expected to have an advantageous start. He would almost certainly have been breastfed for the first six months of his life, ensuring that he imbibed his mother's antibodies to combat infection. It was the custom in labouring families where the 'breadwinner' was involved in heavy work, such as nail making, to ensure that he was adequately nourished, for if the breadwinner was sick and unable to work the whole family starved. With no siblings to compete for food and with a young healthy mother, Jane (nee Stead), who had married Robert Lindley on 3 March 1767 at All Souls Church Darton, John had a good start in life – almost certainly better than his three younger brothers; George born in 1773, Robert born 1776, and Jonathan born 1778.[4]

There was a close relationship between poor nutrition and infectious diseases, especially in infants and young children, that was not recognised at this time. In the eighteenth and nineteenth centuries there were also potential dietary deficiencies, such as the lack of essential vitamins and 'trace' elements, particularly zinc and iodine, all of which were completely unknown. Lack of 'trace' elements in the first two years of life often produced irreversible health problems, which continued for the rest of people's lives. It was known that safe drinking water, drawn from the local well, not polluted river water, was also beneficial in reducing problems of the guts (intestines), and alcohol was often added to drinking water, even for infants.[5]

The science of nutrition was completely unknown to medicine in the eighteenth and early nineteenth centuries, but, with the help of folklore (much of which was untrue but not fatal) and good fortune, children were born and survived in sufficient numbers to produce the next generation. In fact, during John's lifetime, the birthrate began to rise as a result of earlier marriages, an indirect consequence of a wage economy that gave young people earlier independence. As a result, the population increased rapidly.

Having survived the trauma of birth, John Lindley next had to navigate the hazardous years of infancy. At this time, it was generally considered 'unsafe to count one's children until they had reached the age of five.' Certainly, the harvest failure of 1773, which produced widespread hunger when John was only three years old, would have retarded his growth. Poor people, like the Lindleys, had to harden themselves to sickness, pain, disability and premature ageing, and stoicism became second nature to all but a few. As John Locke (1632–1704) was to write in *Some Thoughts Concerning Education* (1693):[6]

Chapter 1

To enjoy a good constitution [as an adult] it was vital to lay a sound foundation in infancy'. [Locke stressed the positive value, indeed the necessity of hardening.] Nothing could be worse than to spoil the new-born infant with cosseting. An overheated birth room was positively harmful, swaddling (whose rationale was to support the limbs) was counter-productive…and the automatic ritualistic dosing of the newborn baby with medicine, and even alcoholic cordials, typically practiced by granny midwives, would equally weaken [the child] by inducing dependency.[7]

It was the custom of labouring classes to sew infants into their clothes for the winter to keep them warm, though that practice was rapidly falling out of favour by 1770. This meant that their tiny bodies were never washed and, as a consequence, they were never examined for the numerous sores and skin diseases that afflicted babies and small children during this period.[8]

The source of childhood diseases was not difficult to find, but it was not until the second half of the eighteenth century that dirt and pollution began to be associated with disease. Perceptions of good hygiene and a clean environment have changed beyond recognition in the last two centuries. 'Georgians accepted a level of dirt and filth that would be intolerable in the twenty-first century': in particular, flies, cockroaches, bedbugs, hair nits and lice were common. All sleeping accommodation had privy-pails, as the earth closet at the bottom of the garden was not an attractive proposition on a cold winter night. Vermin, such as rats and mice, were everywhere, while many people lived in close proximity to domestic animals and pets – a great source of human infection.[9]

The awareness of 'decaying organic matter' as a source of infection, began to produce a decrease in the national death rate of both mothers and their babies from about 1780 onwards, with a resulting increase in population. This message was reinforced by the evangelical preacher John Wesley (1703–1791) who proclaimed that: 'cleanliness is indeed next to godliness.' To reinforce his message, he wrote one of the most popular medical books of the eighteenth century: *Primitive Physick, or an Essay and Natural Method of Curing Most Diseases* (1747). This book was based on common sense and 'curious magical remedies', such as: '*For an Ague,* make six middling pills of cobwebs and take one a little before the cold fit.' By this means, he informed people who could barely read, how to look after themselves with little more than 'a pot of honey, a string of onions, a pitcher of cold water and a prayer'.[10]

Diseases of Childhood

From the preceding paragraph on hygiene, it is not surprising to find that gastric and intestinal problems were endemic both in children and adults. However, small children with their low body weight were particularly susceptible to summer diarrhoea, as it caused rapid dehydration that they were unable to remedy themselves. In addition, the normal injuries of small children, such as bumps, scratches, burns and fractures, often turned septic in the prevailing unhygienic conditions of a labourer's cottage, and those minor injuries often produced complications, which in extreme cases led to death.

There were also a number of infectious diseases, mostly confined to children, which were very common in the eighteenth and nineteenth centuries. They were a complete mystery to doctors and quacks alike and were not brought under control until the second half of the twentieth century. These included scarlet fever, measles, whooping cough, German measles, diphtheria, mumps and chicken pox. It is not surprising that burial registers suggest that one in six children died before they reached their first birthday and it was common for one in four children to die before the age of five. What is more surprising is that it was accepted as 'God's will', a religious interpretation of fatalism. In the spring of 1856, Rev. Archibald Tait (1811–1882), Dean of Carlisle, lost five of his seven children to virulent scarlet fever over a period of five weeks. In 1868, he became Archbishop of Canterbury and obviously retained his faith despite this grievous loss.[11]

Scarlet fever was perhaps the most feared childhood disease, as it was the main cause of death of children throughout the nineteenth century, with ninety-five per cent of all cases being children under the age of ten. In fact, 'epidemics of malignant scarlet fever which broke out in Dublin in 1831 and 1834 caused more deaths than cholera.'[12]

Measles was another acute, highly contagious disease of childhood, which occasionally resulted in encephalitis of the brain. Generally, children exhibited great pain in the eyes and lungs, and many died. Antiquated medical treatments included: bleeding, 'even until fainting comes on' (recommended by medieval physician Rhazes in 910) and purging, recommended by 'the father of English medicine', Doctor Sydenham (1624–1689), at the end of the seventeenth century.[13]

German measles was an acute, highly contagious viral disease, that occurred mostly in older children, particularly adolescents and young adults, which made it a real threat in pregnancy with a high risk of producing serious birth defects and deaths in the next generation.[14]

Whooping cough was the major cause of death in children after smallpox and measles. It was a highly contagious childhood disease for centuries. We now know that it is caused by bacteria. The illness was frightening in the very young, because of the complications of secondary pneumonia and ear infection, both of which often occurred in severe cases.[15]

Diphtheria was principally a disease of young childhood and, during the eighteenth century, ulcerated throats were very common. The *Account of the Sore Throat attended with Ulcers* was described in 1748 by the Yorkshire physician, John Fothergill FRS (1712–1780). This was one of the first descriptions of a streptococcal sore throat in the English language, and he is credited with rejecting ineffective traditional therapies for this disease. Furthermore, in 1751, Fothergill described the characteristics of diphtheria which make it so dangerous. Nevertheless, the American physician Samuel Bard (1742–1821) prescribed treatments that included calomel, opiates, purges, the bark (quinine), blisters on the throat and neck, snake root and poultices, all of which demonstrate the continuing medical ignorance prevailing at that time. To Bard's credit, he did recognise that diphtheria was infectious and recommended removing healthy children from contact with the infected.[16]

Mumps is caused by the mumps virus, but viruses were also unknown during this period. Fortunately, it is not highly contagious, but was a common disease of children between the ages of five and ten years; the symptoms were generally not severe in children.[17]

Chicken pox is a highly contagious, but rarely fatal, disease of childhood. Following the primary infection, it usually produces lifelong protective immunity from further episodes. In John Lindley's day, it was difficult for ordinary people to distinguish innocuous chickenpox from a mild case of the deadly smallpox.[18]

The physical effects of nutritional deficiencies (particularly vitamin deficiencies) were well known and had been for centuries. However, the physiological causes were a mystery. For example, rickets, which is due to a lack of vitamin D (calciferol) or calcium. The condition increased during John Lindley's lifetime, as more people crowded into dark urban living and working conditions. Rickets is caused by a lack of calcium during bone development in young children (which requires vitamin D to control uptake). While deficiency of vitamin B_1 (thiamine) caused beriberi, with the resulting inflammation of the nerves and heart failure. A lack of vitamin B_3 (niacin) caused pellagra, characterised by dermatitis, diarrhoea and mental disorder. John witnessed first-hand, aboard the *Lady Ridley*, the lack of vitamin C (ascorbic acid) that caused scurvy, as described in the Prologue. The exact causes of all these diseases, and many others, were unknown (they are caused by the lack of a specific nutrient in the diet), as most vitamin deficiencies were not recognised as such until the late nineteenth century.[19]

But to young John, at the age of five, living in Mapplewell 'village', all these problems did not concern him. He had successfully negotiated the most dangerous period of his life and, with the optimism of the very young, there is little doubt that his life carried on as it always had for five year olds. He ran errands for his parents, fetching and carrying and making himself useful – for childhood was short in the eighteenth century. In an unchanging world, this was no different from the childhood of his grandfather, John Lindley senior, in 1723, when Daniel Defoe (1660–1731) rode through the West Riding of Yorkshire and recorded 'scarce anything above four years old but its hands were sufficient for its own support.'[20]

Little did John know, at this tender age, that the struggle to compete with machines, and the fight for political recognition of the labouring classes, was to occupy his entire eighty-three years.

CHAPTER 2
Early Years in Darton 1775 – 1802

Housing

Having examined the individual problems of survival, it is now time to look at the type of housing in which John Lindley spent the first thirty-five years of his life.

'In the late eighteenth century…the traditional form of accommodation, for the majority of the labouring classes in pre-industrial west Yorkshire, was the single-storey stone cottage. The evidence of probate inventories indicates that the landless, or low-income labourers, and some more wealthy, lived in single-storey cottages comprising one or two rooms, a house-body and a parlour:' Two-storey houses, with one room on the ground floor and one above, were also known and it is these that have survived. The advantage of the two-storey house was that it required less land and saved on roofing costs.[1]

'Stone was the principal walling material', replacing the timber framed houses of the Stuart period. 'Millstone grit, sandstone or limestone were normally used depending on local availability'. In Mapplewell, this was sandstone from the nearby quarries. 'Poor quality houses' and nail shops 'were often built of quarry waste or other cheap stone', 'with thick walls to ensure stability'. While thatched roofs were still known during this period, increasingly roofs were tiled with overlapping thin slabs of roofing stone, known as thackstone. These tiles were about 1.5 inches (4 cm) thick, fixed to the timber framework by oak pegs.[2]

As the canal system developed, particularly the Barnsley Canal, which opened in 1799, local hardwood began to be replaced by imported softwood. 'Since they were easier to cut and shape, softwood timbers were generally more slender and better finished' than the frequently crooked beams and crudely-shaped hardwood timbers that they replaced. Permanent flooring, in the form of stone flags on the ground-floor, replaced compacted earth of an earlier period, while upper stories had timber floors.

There was only one external door, a front door that opened directly into the living room. Internal doors were made of vertical boards battened with simple wooden or iron latches. Nail shops were often built with split doors, allowing the top half to be opened independently of the bottom half. Windows, made up of a number of small panes of glass, were only fitted in the front of the house, thus saving on construction costs and reducing draughts; it also made them ineligible for window tax (1696-1851). Heating and cooking were carried out on a single coal hearth fire in the main living room. Despite the introduction of chimneys in the previous century, fires generated a great deal of smoke and were notorious for roasting the face while leaving the back cold. The fire also provided the primary source of lighting, because although rushlights, candles and oil lamps were employed, these were generally beyond the means of the labouring classes. Only if the increased output of nails justified the cost of

Chapter 2

lighting (probably a cheap candle in the nail shop) was this expense entertained. Even 'the quality' economised on candles.[3]

There was no provision for water or sanitation in the house, water had to be fetched from the nearest communal spring, well or pump, while privies were usually earth closets at the bottom of the garden or yard. As a consequence, washing in cold water was avoided (warm water had to be heated on the fire) and baths were taken only rarely, if at all, probably in the nearest river.

Nail shops were sometimes built as 'out-shutts' attached to the cottage, but more often comprised a short terrace of single story 'workshops', situated a short distance from the living accommodation.[4]

John Lindley's house was almost certainly built from the sandstone quarried from the nearby Lane End Quarry at Staincross, although there were numerous other quarries in the locality. It is now recognised that the introduction of stone houses, which was taking place at this time, was one of the many factors in improving general hygiene.[5]

Unfortunately, it is not possible to identify the exact site of the house in which John lived, but a good description of a local nail maker's cottage has been recorded by Cynthia Dillon:

> *The cottages [on Haig Head, in the township of Hoylandswaine just five kilometres from Darton] consisted of two rooms one up one down, in each tiny space as many as twelve people, two parents and ten children, lived together. 'The toilet facilities consisted of an earth closet in a little outhouse across Haigh Lane, at the entrance to the garden or allotment, which formed part of each property'... 'There was no water laid on to the houses.' Two wells... provided all the water. ALL water for drinking, cooking and washing had to be carried from these wells'... 'The open fire, or coal fired stove, was the only means of cooking.' Lighting was by means of candles or possibly an oil-lamp. 'A flight of stone steps led up from the ground floor to the bedroom. Where families were large and mixed, a curtain would be drawn across the room to divide the boys' sleeping area from that of the girls.' Mum and dad often shared this room too, though in really big families, parents slept on a makeshift bed in the living room, whilst the children slept head to toe in a variety of beds upstairs.*[6]

The furnishings inside the house would have been sparse and in some cases barely adequate, and oral tradition recounts stories of houses in Mapplewell, in which furniture had been made from old bacon boxes.[7]

By the turn of the century, it was becoming accepted that two bedrooms, as well as a living room were necessary, so that boys and girls could sleep in separate rooms. Even so, well into the Victorian era, complaints were being made of overcrowded and mixed sex sleeping arrangements. For example, Dr Robert Baker expressed the opinion that:

> *It must be manifest that one sleeping room, though it might be quite sufficient for a young couple, must be very inadequate to a family of five persons or more – often eight.*[8]

While George Goodwin, editor of *The Builder*, wrote in 1860:

> *There should always be three bedrooms, so that male and female children may be separated. Cottages for families with only two bedrooms lead to an incredible amount of vice.*[9]

Food

It is difficult to be precise about John's diet as a young man, since conditions gradually became worse as he grew older. Although the decade prior to his birth (1760 to 1769) had seen a series of bad harvests, the failure of the 1766 wheat harvest resulted in greatly increased bread prices, and widespread hunger, with food riots in southern counties. Fortunately for John's parents, 'the oat eating northern counties were less affected than the southern counties of England.' In 1770, the plight of any individual family depended on the local harvest and the yield of their own little plot of ground, because, before the building of canals, there had been no means of distributing large quantities of bulk items except by sea. Mapplewell 'village' was essentially a group of hamlets, surrounded by open fields and Staincross Common. Early inventories from the eighteenth century record local crops in the West Riding of rye (for making rye bread), barley (for brewing) and peas – the soil and climate being unsuitable for wheat. Butter and cheese were also made, but in the days before refrigerators these products had a short shelf life and, in any case, butter gradually became too expensive for common nail makers.[10]

Families who had ancient rights of pasture were able to keep small numbers of cattle and sheep on the extensive local commons. The inventory of John Spark, who was buried in Darton on 13 April 1726, records three cows, a sheep and two lambs, but the number he was allowed to pasture on the common had to comply with the Darton Manor Court ruling of 1674 that decreed: no one was to 'put sheep or other goods on the common of Darton other than such as they can keep in the winter within the manor.' This was to prevent passing drovers fattening their cattle on the way to market. Spark also had four horses at the homestead, 'two load saddles' and 'horse gear and traces', for John Spark was a successful local chapman. A fascinating account of his possessions is to be found in *Aspects of Darton,* by local historian Harold Taylor.[11]

There is no doubt that the children collected edible berries from the hedgerows, in particular blackberries and, from the open moors, that Pennine delicacy – bilberries, all rich in vitamin C. But to John and his friends they were all food and it is well known that growing children can never have enough food! There may also have been rabbits to snare and pigeons to catch. But it is recorded that an incessant war was constantly waged between gamekeepers and 'poachers', and children as young as eleven were hung for poaching. In fact, the theft of any goods over the value of one shilling attracted the death penalty.

Examples of local diets were gathered by Sir Fredrick Eden (1766–1809), who published a report on *The State of the Poor* in 1797. He recorded that at Settle in Craven 'the food used by the labouring poor is oatmeal, tea, milk, butter, potatoes and butchers meat'; at Stokesley in the North Riding, 'bread, milk, tea, potatoes and meat sparingly'; at Great Driffield in the East Riding 'barley bread, potatoes and perhaps 2lb of butchers meat once a week, when they could afford it'. At Halifax in the West Riding, 'butchers meat is very generally used by labourers' and at Leeds, also in the West Riding 'wheaten bread is generally used. Some is made partly of rye and a few people use oatmeal. Animal food forms a considerable part of the diet of the labouring people. Tea is now the ordinary breakfast [beverage], especially [among] women of every description.'[12]

The gradual deterioration in the nail maker's diet really resulted from the ever increasing hours of work, often employing the entire family, which were required to produce enough money to buy bread. There is a general impression that this left little time or energy for growing garden vegetables, but local historian, James Dearnley, records that 'most of the nail makers [in Mapplewell] were very efficient gardeners and took time to work in their gardens.'[13] Bread was the staple diet, baked in four pound loaves; it required one loaf of bread a day to feed a family of five, two adults and three children. Nail making is very strenuous work and consumes a vast amount of energy, so a nail maker required about twice as many calories as a sedentary worker or a member of the gentry. During periods when the price of wheat soared, there are records of bread being baked with other grains and even peas. 'Potatoes, that other staple, were generally rejected as only fit for pigs – or the starving Irish.'

Certainly, by the 1820s and 1830s, meals were reduced to a 'monotonous diet of black bread, treacle, dripping, cheese, 'hasty pudding' (a flour and water gruel), or bread sops made with water, and 'nail makers' tea' made with tea leaves boiled over and over again. Sometimes a weekly joint of meat was purchased and was divided into portions for each day of the week. Many nail makers kept a pig or two in the sties near the nail shops and some had gardens. John Walton, in contrast to Dearnley, claims 'there was little time for gardening'. Later, during the early nineteenth century, there was in general a serious lack of green vegetables, protein, vitamins and very little fresh milk. Since the most calorific food was consumed by the men doing the heaviest work, mothers and young children, who did not contribute to the family income, were seriously undernourished. To compensate they consumed large quantities of beer, which was high in energy. Strangely, beer was regarded as a temperance drink by many reformers, because milk was often infected with tuberculosis bacilli and water was increasingly polluted with industrial effluent, so that beer, and later tea, made with boiled spring water, were the only safe drinks for the poor man and his family.[14]

To overcome the malpractice of shopkeepers, Robert Owen (1771–1887), and others, inspired local people to form Co-operative Societies, and by the 1830s there were about thirty in the Huddersfield area. They provided cheap, unadulterated food for their members. This movement was primarily a northern phenomenon, but the insistence on cash trading limited the spread of outlets as the majority of poor, working people depended on credit to survive.

The modern Cooperative Societies trace their origin to 1844, when the first shop opened in Rochdale, Lancashire, but the movement had been flourishing for some time prior to that date.

Education in Darton

Little is known about John Lindley's early life, but he learnt to read and write, a remarkable achievement for the son of a nail maker under the conditions of this period, and this ability was to play an important role in John's later life. Since the general attitude of the 'gentry' at that time considered 'that to secure the contentment of the poor with their lot, it is requisite that great numbers of them should be ignorant as well as poor'.[15]

How and where John acquired his literacy is unknown, 'but most children before the second half of the eighteenth century were not educated formally' learning their letters from parents and elder siblings or neighbours and friends, who often formed part of a kinship network in a close knit community such as Mapplewell.

This was supplemented in the middle of the eighteenth century with 'dame schools', run by impoverished gentlewomen and disabled men who provided young children, for a few coppers, the most elementary level of learning. The school was frequently the teacher's home, in which children were taught the alphabet and simple reading from the New Testament. They were sometimes given a few domestic chores as a substitute for 'domestic science'. These schools varied enormously in quality, often amounting to no more than child minding services, but, collectively, they laid the foundation of basic literacy among the poor, and this certainly included the majority of nail makers.[16]

Cynthia Dillon recounts the fate of Miss Hannah Shaw, born in Silkstone in 1791, 'Her little school on Mustard Hill, in the township of Hoylandswaine, earned her only a pittance. The 1851 census describes her as a teacher of small children and a pauper. She was already sixty years of age, but with only parish help, she had to try to keep her school open as long as physically possible. The alternative was to enter the workhouse in Penistone.'[17]

The incentive to learn was practical need. Certainly, a nail maker needed to be able to count, as he bought bundles of nail rods, and he produced large numbers of nails for which he was paid a sum of money, depending on the quantity. Perhaps it was this need for basic arithmetic that encouraged the nail makers to acquire numeracy and literacy.

Beyond dame schools were day-schools, which taught more advanced subjects, but these were generally regarded as ineffective, since attendance of pupils was irregular. They were rejected by 'respectable people', because they did not teach Christian values.

Above this level, there were charity schools that resulted from the philanthropic work of Robert Nelson, who founded the Society for Promoting Christian Knowledge in the reign of Queen Anne (1702–1714), which were well established throughout the country by 1775. These schools used the monitor system, where the instructor was often another pupil, only a little advanced on the pupil being taught. The method was unsatisfactory, but it did permit large numbers of children to be taught by a single competent teacher, who was able to concentrate on instructing a small group of the most advanced pupils – the monitors. Again, attendance at schools by pupils was often intermittent, and took second place to domestic requirements dictated by parents. The numerous tasks of fetching and carrying invariably took precedence. In fact, the priority for most families was the 'family income' and schooling could only be indulged in during slack periods when there was no paid work.[18]

However, once children had a simple grasp of the principles of reading and writing they often continued to educate themselves, and the radical literature of this period is full of men who were self-educated. This is in contrast to many agricultural labourers who worked in isolation, with only animals for company, and were renowned for their lack of general education. There was, however, a general mistrust by the labouring classes of formal education, as it concentrated on promoting the doctrines of religion, with its accompanying moral, political and economic control.[19]

At a slightly higher level, there were free schools provided by wealthy benefactors for a specific number of 'poor' boys, and sometimes girls. These aimed to teach religion, reading and writing and, in some cases, practical subjects like carpentry and basket weaving.

Darton was fortunate in having such a free school for poor pupils of both sexes. It was originally endowed by George Beaumont, a merchant of Darton Hall, who, on his death in 1684, bequeathed five hundred pounds for the support of a free school in Darton. This was opened four years later in 1688. It is not known whether John Lindley attended this free school, but it seems unlikely, and certainly by the age of eight or nine he would have been expected to 'earn his keep' and have little time for school or learning.[20]

The free school might also have taken in a few fee-paying pupils, as at Mirfield. The object was to enable children to be able to read the Bible, and most certainly required pupils to learn large passages of scripture by heart, and perhaps write a little – but teaching the labouring classes to write was considered very dangerous. It was also 'expensive', requiring writing materials. To obviate this problem, many eighteenth and nineteenth century children learned to write their letters in a sand box, because even a chalk and slate were considered too expensive. Many 'bright' children were self-taught; for once given the basic principles of reading and writing they were able to learn the rest themselves – often by firelight.

The problem for John and his siblings was that in the latter part of the eighteenth century education was not considered the responsibility of central government. The national policy was to leave education to the administration of unpaid local squires, clergy, lesser gentry and professional people, who then organised schooling as they thought fit. Consequently, it was frequently organised in accordance with the mores of so-called 'respectable society', as expressed in the following passage from *Life and Struggles of William Lovett*:

> *There were people who…had talked of education as a means of light, life, liberty and enjoyment for the whole human family; but these of course were the Utopians of the World; men who failed to perceive that God had made one portion of mankind to rule and enjoy, and others to toil for them, and reverentially obey them.*[21]

William Lovett (1800–1877) was to become a leading Chartist and one of the main architects of 'The People's Charter', written in 1837.

However, much of the formal education of the late eighteenth century was, at best, of an authoritarian and patronising nature. The teachers were invariably members of the Anglican Church who aimed to instil Christian morals, combined with 'the great law of subordination', as exemplified in the following couplet:

> God bless the squire and his relations,
> And keep us in our proper stations.

The Community

It has been assumed that John Lindley was born in the hamlet of Broadroyd Head, on the basis that in the 1841 census (the earliest reliable date) it had a total population of one hundred and thirty-three persons and, of these, forty-one individuals had the surname Lindley, grouped in eight households. They comprised one third of the total inhabitants of this hamlet. The head of all eight Lindley households was a nail maker, including John's younger brother George, who had married his sister-in-law Elizabeth (nee Mellor). George and Elizabeth had at least four children, of whom their son George, also a nail maker, was to follow his uncle to Mirfield. The parish records contain numerous examples of the siblings of one family marrying the siblings of a neighbouring family. In such a small community the choice of suitable marriage partners was very restricted. Parish records also record many apparently unsuitable marriages – obviously made for economic survival, since marriage partnerships were often undertaken for very practical reasons.

Sometimes, this clustering of families was the result of ownership or tenancy of land, but more often in the case of the labouring classes, it was to take advantage of the Elizabethan Poor Relief Act of 1601, amended in the Settlement Act of 1662, that required 'the parish' only to support destitute residents who 'belonged' to that parish.

By 1697 a worker who wished to leave his native village had to obtain from the parish a certificate accepting full responsibility for him if he became a charge on the poor rate of the place to which he was going...An Act of 1795 did indeed allow a man to stay in another parish until he actually became a charge on the poor rate, but the moment that he did so become – the moment he was out of work and destitute – he was immediately sent back to his former home. So a poor man's parish became his prison; he could not leave, for nowhere else would have him.[22]

There was also a strong sense of community and kin support that induced people to remain among friends and relatives, an important consideration before state welfare was introduced.

When John was born in 1770, Broadroyd Head would have been no more than a hamlet of perhaps a dozen cottages, supporting a few nail makers making use of the local open cast coal mines, situated only a few hundred yards from their workshops. Surrounded by fields on three sides, with Silkstone Common to the north, it was really a rural environment and the workshops were considered part of a proto-industry – the forerunner of the factory system.

The community spirit in Mapplewell, whose loss is so mourned by modern politicians, resulted in a long tradition of singing in the village, which was fostered in their chapel choirs. In fact, this leisure activity was very common throughout the West Riding of Yorkshire where, between 1800 and 1914, over 240 choral societies were formed, with the Huddersfield Choral Society, founded in 1836, being the most famous. In the run up to Christmas, they would regularly meet in one of the nail shops and practise their carol singing and glees by candlelight, under a conductor who could teach them all their parts. Then, during the Christmas holidays, they went out to sing, not only in their own village but in the surrounding districts and towns; also, to the big country houses of the local gentry, such as Wooley Hall and Bretton Hall. By this means, any money received helped to supplement their scanty wages, in addition to which they were often given a really good festive supper. 'Other parties went out Morris dancing dressed as characters of St George, Hector, the Doctor, Little Devil Doubt and the rest.'[23]

The background to this parochial history of Darton, was that England in 1770 was a rigidly hierarchical society, run by a landowning oligarchy who believed that they were ordained to rule by virtue of their ancient family bloodlines. They preached obedience and submission to the King, the Anglican Church and a parliament elected by those with a stake in the land, namely themselves and their placemen. The common people had no claim to determine the composition of their parliament. Society was steeped in 'customary practice', but where authority to superiors was paramount, be it the head of the family or the head of the country. As a result, those in power often projected the mythology of benevolence to those beneath them – claiming that England was a free, prosperous and well managed state, where nothing could be improved upon. The truth was different. The reality of rural poverty was to be seen everywhere, with tenants and labourers toiling in the fields trying to scrape a living for themselves and their families; and as we shall see, the nail makers did not fare much better.[24]

With a population of only seven million in England and Wales, dwellings outside the major cities were well spaced in what was overwhelmingly an agricultural landscape, giving an illusion of peace and tranquillity. Here, in the countryside and in small villages, life proceeded at a leisurely pace in tune with the seasons. For example, in autumn the eighteenth-century nail makers ceased sweating in the nail shops to work (but still sweating) in the fields, when all hands were needed to bring in the harvest.[25]

While the aristocracy and great landowners ran the affairs of state, the squires, vicars and lesser gentry were the major political force in villages such as Mapplewell and in market towns, such as Mirfield. It was these 'pillars of society' that held the everyday life of common people in thrall. In the case of Darton, during the late seventeenth and early eighteenth centuries, the Beaumont family of the Oaks was the dominant family, and three generations are buried in the local parish church of All Saints.

While 'everyone knew their place' in society, in Yorkshire there were a large number of cottage industries supporting independent hand loom weavers, craftsmen such as nail makers, blacksmiths and carpenters. It is said that these people 'doffed their cap to no one'. But, despite the superficial air of tranquillity, beneath the surface there was a desperate subsistence economy, totally dependent on the weather and resulting harvest. The state of the harvest determined, more than any other single factor, the level of economic activity and the mood of society. Furthermore, the 1770s saw a major depression in the nailing and textile industries, as trade with the American Colonies declined during the 'War of Independence' (1775–1783).[26]

But the so-called 'Golden Age' (1755 –1775) was about to change, for 1770 marked the beginning of the Industrial Revolution. Utilising the ingenuity of its engineers, the iron and steel of southern Yorkshire and the Midlands, combined with the woollen industry of the West Riding of Yorkshire and the cotton industry of south Lancashire, England became the 'workshop of the world'. During John Lindley's lifetime, Darton rapidly grew into a small township, and Barnsley into a major industrial and coal mining centre.

Population

To gain some idea of the rate of population growth, the most reliable estimate of the population of the parish of Darton, in the middle of the eighteenth century, was taken by Archbishop Herring (1693–1757) in 1743, who estimated one hundred and forty families, representing a population of between six and seven hundred. Fifty-eight years later, this figure had more than doubled to 1,699 at the first national census in 1801. By the 1831 census, it had reached 2,960 – nearly double again in only thirty years.[27]

Religion in Mapplewell 'Village'

Darton had a long history of dissent, going back to Archbishop Herring's visitation of 1743, when he recorded fourteen dissenting families out of the total of about one hundred and forty families. But this marked the beginning of the eighteenth century religious revival, which influenced John's early years.[28]

The most charismatic proponent of the new evangelical message was John Wesley, who was strongly influenced by the Moravians, who believed that God's grace could be experienced by everyone and not just the select few. John Wesley had taken to 'field preaching' in 1739 as a method of circumnavigating the regulations of the Anglican Church, who objected to his use of lay preachers – that is preachers who were not ordained. The message of these preachers was clear and unambiguous; they told the common people in their own language that they possessed spiritual equality with the wealthy and the sanctimoniously upright. In addition, they discarded the orthodox values of submission and reverence and preached a popular religion, with talk of evil spirits and the talismanic salvation for all who accepted Christ. It should be remembered that Wesley himself believed in ghosts.[29]

Methodism spread rapidly, particularly in the northern counties of England, and it was not surprising that a Methodist Society was formed at Staincross in 1760. The society was visited the following year by John Wesley himself, who stayed with John Shaw and his wife Mary in the hamlet of Staincross. Next day, he preached at Carr Green, standing on a sandstone slab, which he employed as a pulpit, before continuing his journey to Rotherham.[30]

No doubt the entire village turned out for this memorable occasion. But the enthusiasm of the crowd should not be interpreted as mass conversion from ritualistic Anglican worship to modern Methodist doctrines. The majority of labouring men and women, while nominally Christian, still lived in fear of evil spirits and witchcraft, a legacy of the seventeenth century (the capital crime of witchcraft had only just been abolished in 1736), and upheld the value of lucky charms and magic potions. Moss from the churchyard, rainwater from the roof, and lead scraped from the church windows, were all thought to have healing properties. These superstitious beliefs were those of people who greatly feared ill health and misfortune and were grafted on to John Wesley's teachings.[31]

Certainly, the Methodist preachers had an uphill struggle; they were persecuted by magistrates who saw large crowds as a threat to 'law and order'; also by Anglican clergymen, since they flouted many regulations of the Church and were seen as a social threat that paid no attention to authority. They were considered rude, crude and intrusive, and worst of all, enthusiastic: Bishop John Butler (1731–1809) told John Wesley that 'pretending to extraordinary revelations and gifts of the Holy Ghost is a horrid thing, a very horrid thing'.[32]

Methodists were attacked in sermons and in print, and at times by organised mobs during open air meetings – for religious intolerance was rife in those days. Nevertheless, Wesley and his followers continued to work among the neglected, needy and rootless. It says much for Wesley's character that when he 'rode over the mountains to Huddersfield' in 1757, only four years before his visit to Mapplewell, he noted 'a wilder people I never saw in England. The men, women and children filled the streets, and seemed just ready to devour us'; nevertheless, he bravely persevered and his honest sincerity and Christian faith won over many of these rough and illiterate people to his new vision of Christianity.[33]

Given this background, it is not surprising that many inhabitants of Mapplewell 'village', predominantly poor nail makers and their families, became Methodists. The fact that the 'village' was on the eastern border of Darton parish and was over a mile (1.5 km) from the influence of the parish church, marooned on the western bank of the river Dearne, helped create fertile conditions for independent beliefs. Nevertheless, some Methodists still found it prudent to meet for prayer in the secrecy of the local quarry. When they attained a position of strength, in 1780, meetings were held openly at Four Lanes End, at the very centre of the village. However, despite what has been said about improvements in hygiene, many nail makers, still in their filthy working clothes, would leave their forge to attend evening prayer meetings and then return directly to their nail-shops to continue working when the meeting was over.[34]

The Methodist movement split when Alexander Kilham, from Sheffield, was expelled from the Wesleyan Methodists in 1796 for criticising the leadership; believing that the Methodist Conference gave too much power to the ministers of the church, at the expense of the ordinary members. Wesleyans responded by accusing Kilham of holding similar views to the political radical Tom Paine (1737–1809), but Kilham's radical sermons appealed to the nail makers of Mapplewell, for, although Methodist teaching was opposed to political radicalism, its spiritual message encouraged a democratic levelling. As a result, Kilham's followers formed a New Connection in 1797, and Providence Chapel, the first Methodist New Connection (or Kilhamite) Chapel, was opened in Pitt Square at Mapplewell in 1800. Not to be outdone, the orthodox Wesleyan Methodists opened their own chapel at Staincross in 1804.[35]

Further rebellion against the Anglican Church in Darton, during the early decades of the nineteenth century, can be found in baptismal registers at Westgate Methodist Chapel and New Street Methodist Chapel, Barnsley. Here, records show that several families of nail makers in Mapplewell took their children all the way to Barnsley for baptism in their 'own' chapels.[36]

What was the attraction that generated the religious revival of the second half of the eighteenth century? No doubt the preaching of John Wesley had a great influence, particularly in the industrial north of England, 'but in general people developed a 'calamity-sensitive' nature that hardened them to the prospect of hunger and disease.' In modern terms 'they were resigned to the will of God' and adopted a stoic attitude to the vagaries of life. Both Anglican and Roman Catholic theology, at that time, regarded undue concern for the welfare of the body as vanity. Concern for the soul was all important. 'Remember the lilies of the fields how they grow'; 'take no concern for the morrow'; 'God will provide'; and 'life's thread depended upon grace and the mysteries of providence'. How else could people bear so much suffering?[37] The zeitgeist of the times is poetically expressed in the hymn by Mrs Cecil Frances Alexander (1818–1895), which starts: 'All things bright and beautiful'. Verse three continues:

> The rich man in his castle,
> The poor man at his gate,
> God made them, high or lowly,
> And order'd their estate.

This was the sincere belief of upper- and middle-class England… [during John Lindley's lifetime]. The order of society was divinely established and any attempt to alter or upset it was an act against God. Furthermore, as far as the rich were concerned, poverty was the consequence of idleness, of drunkenness, or of any other vice you cared to mention. The path of virtue, of course led to wealth.[38]

Gradually, the doctrine of the complacent Anglican Church was rejected and the 1770s and 1780s saw a great spiritual revival of dissenting religious sects, who read the Bible as 'a proclamation of the doctrine of humanity, and the gospel of compassion for the poor and downtrodden.'[39]

After John Wesley's death in 1791, a second Yorkshire revival took place, between 1793 and 1798, led by William Bramwell (1759–1818) of Dewsbury. The social gains of Methodism were also considerable as the popular author and journalist, William Howitt (1792–1879), conceded in 1838:

> *In the manufacturing districts, where the Methodists have gained most influence, it is true enough that they have helped to expel an immense quantity of dog-fighting, cock-fighting, bull-baiting, badger-baiting, boxing and such blackguard amusements.*[40]

John's Own Family

In September 1794, at the age of twenty-four, John Lindley married Hannah Mellor, a Darton girl, the daughter of Joseph Mellor. The marriage took place in Darton, which is hardly surprising given the parochial outlook on life in the eighteenth century, enshrined in the northern saying 'better to wed over the midden [or mixen] than over the moor'. Evidence from parish registers shows that 'marriage partners were overwhelmingly chosen from within a radius of twenty miles'. John's marriage is recorded in the parish register of All Souls, Darton. Lord Hardwicke's Marriage Act (26 Geo. II c.33), which came into force on 25 March 1754, required a formal ceremony of marriage for all denominations to take place in Anglican Churches, except for Jews and Quakers, so this does not disqualify John and Hannah from being Methodists at this time.[41]

John and Hannah had eight children, a normal size for a family at this time, although agricultural families tended to be even larger. The first five children were all born in Darton. The eldest, Jane, was born and baptised in 1795, thirteen months after the marriage. In the days before contraception, it was normal for women to have their first baby within the first year of marriage. The second child, William, was baptised in 1797 and then Phebe in 1798. Three children in three years. All three are known to have died before 1820, as John declared that he had only five children when he arrived in Van Diemen's Land. As noted earlier, this was not an unusual occurrence in the eighteenth and nineteenth centuries, with one in four children failing to reach their fifth birthday. Fortunately, the next five children all survived into adulthood. George was born in 1799 and was alive in 1820, but probably did not marry and certainly left no issue. The line of succession was to reside with the third son, John William, born in 1802, who was to become John's heir, since it was John William's son, also named John Lindley, who was adjudged to be heir to the Knowl property in the county court case (L1254 Lindley vs Lindley) in 1883, on the basis of primogeniture.[42]

In the eighteenth century, many men and women who reached the age of thirty could expect to live for another thirty years, although far more people died in their thirties, forties and fifties than survived into old age. This gave the population a very young appearance by modern standards. Only about six per cent of those who survived childhood to become adults lived beyond the age of eighty. In this, John who lived to the age of eighty-three, and Hannah who lived to the age of eighty-nine, were exceptional; they were also included in that minority of people who lived long enough to know their grandchildren. Of the elderly that did survive, a high proportion were widows, dependent on the Poor Law for the basic necessities of life.[43] Again, Hannah was fortunate, she was looked after by her daughter, Ann, until she died in 1860 at the extraordinary age of eighty-nine. She is buried with her husband at the Knowl in Mirfield.

CHAPTER 3
The South Yorkshire Iron Industry

John Lindley is recorded as a nail maker in all official documents up to the 1851 census, when he is recorded as a retired nail maker. This simple statement is remarkable in itself, as few members of the labouring classes retired; lack of welfare ensured that most people worked until they died. While in the eighteenth century nail maker was a specific occupation, by the middle of the nineteenth century it had become a generic term and implied a maker of small iron objects. The nail trade depended on the development of a thriving local iron industry producing nail rods – the starting point for making nails during John's lifetime.

Historic Location of Iron Industry in South Yorkshire

Iron working has a long history in South Yorkshire. Traditionally, iron has been mined and worked at Wortley near Penistone since Roman times, and it is also possible that the Cistercian monks at Ecclesfield, Rockley, Pilling and Breton, all within a few miles of the Tankersley ironstone seam, may have been making iron in the late twelfth century. But the first documentary evidence for a bloomery relates to Wortley and dates from the Poll Tax Roll of 1379. This historic document records the names of four 'Smyths' (two adults and their sons) and a master. These men worked in a bloomery and employed the simple, direct method of producing malleable iron.[1] A graphic historic account of a bloomery comes from Milnthorpe forge in Furness, Lancashire:

> *The hearth was much the shape of a broad brimmed hat with the crown downwards…it is very much like a blacksmiths, viz a plain open hearth or bottom without any enclosing walls, only where the nose of the bellows comes in through the wall there is a hollow place which they call the furnace made of iron plates. The hollow place they fill and upheap with charcoal, and lay the oar [sic] broken small, all around the charcoal upon the flat hearth, to bake it as it were or heat it and thrust it little by little into the hollow where it is melted by the blast. The glassie Scoriae ran very freely then but the metal is in perfect fusion, but settles as it were in a clod, that they can take out with tongs and turn it under a great hammer, which at the same time beats off a great deal of coarse scoriae and form it after several heats. They use no limestone or other thing to promote the flux.*
> *The process was that known as 'direct' in which the product is not 'pig iron' but a pasty mass of malleable iron capable of being hammered into a bloom. An ironworks always consisted of two hearths, the bloomery in which smelting took place and the smithy in which the bloom was reheated before hammering into shape.*[2]

In Yorkshire, records from 1621 provide evidence that there was a furnace at Wortley in the early seventeenth century, where pigs of iron were heated and hammered into half blooms. In addition to Wortley, which is now being restored by the South Yorkshire Industrial History Society, the remains of an ancient blast furnace survive as an archaeological site at Rockley, near Doncaster.[3]

Raw Materials

The raw materials for extracting iron from ironstone (an oxide of iron with numerous other impurities) are: the ore itself, limestone to assist the removal of slag, and charcoal to act as fuel. After 1750, coke began to replace charcoal as the main fuel. In addition, an abundant supply of mechanical power to augment human muscle power was also needed, if any quantity of iron was to be produced. South Yorkshire was able to supply all these raw materials plus ample water power.

The Tankersley ironstone, known as 'bog-iron' (this occurs beneath moorland turf when iron-bearing waters meet organic material), while not of the highest quality, was however very suitable for making nails and wire. Initially, charcoal did not represent a problem, as there was an abundant supply of woodland in the Pennine valleys for charcoal making. When the wood for making charcoal began to run out, the local outcrops of high quality anthracite – the Barnsley, Silkstone and Ganister coal measures – supplied the necessary fuel for both furnaces and steam engines. Limestone was also in abundant supply from the Jurassic measures that run from Dorset, on the south coast of England, to Flamborough Head near Bridlington, on the east coast of Yorkshire, and this was conveniently available from the adjacent county of Derbyshire. Historically, until the middle of the eighteenth century, power to drive the large mechanical hammers was supplied exclusively by water wheels, fed by the fast-flowing streams of the Pennines. However, in times of drought, or severe frost, the supply proved unreliable. So, in the nineteenth century, steam power generated by the new Boulton and Watt steam engines replaced water power. Unfortunately, the new steam engines were expensive, which resulted in the old water wheels being phased out slowly. In fact, there was a transitional period when the locally manufactured cheap Newcomen-type engines, despite their inefficient use of coal, were employed to pump water back into the dams to ensure that water wheels had a regular supply.[4]

The ironstone was mined from the local outcrops of the Tankersley seam. Initially, this was in the form of opencast mining, but, as the surface ore diminished, it became necessary to dig deeper into the seam, in what is known as a drift mine. The rough ironstone was normally broken into nodules and calcined – burned to remove some of its impurities – close to the source of the ore to minimise transportation of unnecessary waste material.[5]

Limestone was plentiful, but transportation from Derbyshire was costly; so, like ironstone, it was broken into nodules before moving to the south of Yorkshire.

Charcoal was the key ingredient. Since wood did not burn at a high enough temperature to melt ironstone, furnaces and forges originally required charcoal for fuel. As a result, charcoal making was a flourishing industry, using coppiced wood, and a large number of ancient grants of wood and land are recorded in the vicinity of furnaces. In the south of Yorkshire, in the early seventeenth century, it is known that Sir Francis Wortley (1591–1652) owned extensive lands, which produced charcoal, and by 1640 he had built Top Forge at Wortley to capitalise on this asset. In fact, charcoal was so valuable that the

Spencer Syndicate, a local family cartel, purchased whole estates, solely to gain access to charcoal producing woodlands.[6]

For many, charcoal making was a seasonal activity carried out between August and November, using the time-honoured method of dividing the woodlands into small areas, known as 'coupes', where wood was coppiced in rotation. First, a level space about twenty-two feet (seven metres) in diameter, known as a 'pitstead', was cleared and levelled. The cut wood was then stacked in a circular clamp with a flat dome and covered with turf and bracken. This restricted the airflow and enabled the charcoal burners to exercise control, thereby preventing the wood burning too quickly. The burn lasted up to two days and the charcoal was ready when the smoke stopped coming out of the small central flue. There were two types of charcoal: 'soft and small' charcoal used in forges, but 'hard and big' charcoal was required for smelting to prevent the stack collapsing. The type of charcoal produced depended on the type of wood used and the speed of burn, which in turn depended on the experience of the charcoal burner. Since it was necessary to keep 'the burn' under observation night and day, the charcoal burners lived in temporary huts close to the smouldering clamp.[7]

As iron smelting prospered in the early eighteenth century, increased demand for charcoal put a strain on the supply of suitable wood, and Yorkshire was no exception. According to John Hobson, the Dodworth diarist, Francis West (c1640–1717) remembered a time when 'Higham Common in the south west of the Parish was covered with many large trees – all gone for charcoal making.' This is not surprising, since it required two-and-a-half tons of charcoal to produce one ton of bar iron, and in the Weald of Kent it required four thousand acres of well-managed coppiced woodland to support one blast furnace and finery forge. Fortunately, for the remaining forests, in 1709, Abraham Darby (1678–1717) developed a method of producing coke by baking coal to remove impurities such as sulphur.[8]

Coke gradually replaced charcoal in the smelting process, and by 1760 most smelting was carried out using coke, but certain specialist applications, such as the manufacture of wire, continued to use charcoal. The changeover was just in time, as the ever increasing production of iron had led to severe deforestation, not only in Yorkshire where wood had been plentiful, but throughout Great Britain and across western Europe. The introduction of coke changed the nature of the iron making industry. Larger and more capital-intensive furnaces were developed, which gradually replaced the numerous small furnaces and forges. All the raw materials were stored in sheds, to keep them dry, since it was very difficult to make wet material burn. In addition, it was wasteful to use fuel to dry out wet raw materials.[9]

Development of Iron Making

At Milnthorpe, iron was produced in a simple bloomery, where ironstone was smelted with charcoal in a bowl or shaft furnace, which acted as a combustion chamber. When air was forced through the mixture, with hand-operated bellows, a temperature of 1,200° centigrade was achieved, a temperature sufficient to melt the iron and separate it from the ironstone. At this temperature the heavy iron sank to the bottom of the furnace, thereby separating it from the lighter slag, known as fayalite. The result was a spongy, porous mass of relatively pure iron, intermixed with bits of charcoal and extraneous matter termed slag. The mixture was then hammered to remove the majority of the slag, resulting in a compacted iron bar called a bloom. Further refining was carried out in a separate string-hearth, similar to a furnace but without the provision for slag tapping. This process involved reheating the bloom, perhaps several times, and hammering until the required shape and purity was achieved.[10]

Blast Furnace Technology

From about the beginning of the sixteenth century, the direct method was gradually superseded by the indirect method. The first stage was similar to the bloomery and involved heating the raw materials, using water power to blow 'blasts of air' into the furnace. In a blast furnace, iron remained in contact with the charcoal at high temperature, long enough for the iron to attract carbon, and in this form it had a lower melting point than pure iron. This process, known as smelting, enabled the molten iron to be run off from the bottom of the furnace to produce blooms of hard, brittle pig-iron with a high carbon content (4 per cent). Cast pig-iron, or 'sowe iron' as it was known, was useful in its own right, since when molten it could be cast into moulds to produce objects such as 'stoves and grates, agricultural ironwork, as well as pots and pans'.

To produce wrought iron, the cast pig-iron was reheated in a charcoal-fuelled finery hearth, which was kept stirred by an iron rod that ensured the molten iron was evenly exposed to the blast of air provided by water-powered bellows. This allowed the oxygen to combine with the excess carbon in the cast pig-iron and reduce it to a relatively pure state. However, a further process of hammering, known as shingling, was required to remove slag trapped in the interstices of the metal and produce a bloom. The result was wrought iron, containing only a small amount of carbon (0.3 per cent) – just enough to make the metal both tough and malleable. Further hammering and shaping, prior to sale, took place in a chafery, the equivalent of the string-hearth phase in the bloomery process.[11]

Probably the oldest forge in Yorkshire that produced wrought iron from pig-iron was Wortley Top Forge. Here, the blooms of cast pig-iron were reheated, and the impurities beaten out using a 'belly helve type' hammer, where the shaft of the waterwheel was fitted with a cam that lifted the underside of the beam.[12]

Spencer Syndicate 1650–1750

In the seventeenth century, small scale Yorkshire furnaces were leased directly with the ironstone deposits, as in the case of Barnaby, where a surviving document records a lease of ironstone from the mid–seventeenth century that included: the right to build a furnace, get wood, make charcoal and smelt iron – all the requirement to produce iron blooms.[13]

Gradually, the numerous furnaces, all situated within a few miles of the Tankersley outcrop of ironstone, came under the control of John Spencer (d.1691) who, by judicious partnership agreements and marriages, built the 'Spencer Syndicate'. This syndicate had interests in 'almost every ironworks from Lancashire to Derbyshire, comprising at least 10 blast furnaces and 15 forges' of which eight blast furnaces and eleven iron forges were in the south of Yorkshire. These included: Barnaby Furnace (in Cawthorne: 4.5 miles (7 km) NW of Barnsley); Kirkstall Forge (near Leeds); Upper Bank Furnace and Nether Bank Forge (Emley near Silkstone); Colnbridge Forge (near Huddersfield); Wortley Forges (near Penistone); Silkstone Forge and Slitting Mill (Silkstone); Bretton Furnace (NW Barnsley).[14]

Making Wrought Iron in the Eighteenth Century

Richard Hayman has pointed out, 'the technology of iron smelting was relatively simple – the difficult part was technique'. The method for producing wrought iron from ironstone was well understood, but the problem for early eighteenth century iron-makers lay with the quality of the raw materials and process control. Gradually, and slowly, high quality low cost wrought iron evolved after many false starts.[15]

Raw ironstone was of variable quality and originally much of it was imported from Sweden, Germany and Spain, since it contained fewer impurities. When the ironstone was heated with limestone using charcoal, the proportion of limestone to ironstone required careful control, and the quality of the charcoal was critical to prevent 'the stack' collapsing.

The New Coke Technology 1770–1850

By 1770, the old charcoal-fuelled iron industry had been rationalised, giving way to operations on a much larger scale, based on the new technologies of coke and the blast furnace. At Wortley, John Cockshutt junior (d.1774) adapted the Wortley Forge to the new techniques of coke-fuelling, puddling and rolling. He took out a patent in 1771 for a blast furnace, which used a water powered blowing engine to force oxygen into the furnace. This method produced malleable wrought iron direct from ironstone, an important improvement in the manufacture of iron.

The next improvement at Wortley was introduced in 1784 by John's brother, James Cockshutt (1742–1819), a civil engineer and Fellow of the Royal Society, who introduced the process of puddling and rolling, based on the patent of Henry Cort (1740–1800). But this process of refining the ironstone into wrought iron remained comparatively inefficient. The puddling furnace required the stirring of the molten metal, kept separate from the charcoal fire through an aperture by a highly skilled craftsman called a puddler; this exposed the metal evenly to the heat and combustion gases in the furnace, so that the carbon could be oxidised out. As the carbon content decreases, the melting point rises, causing semi-solid bits of iron to appear in the liquid mass. The puddler would gather these in a single lump and work them under a forge hammer, and then the hot wrought iron would be run through rollers (in rolling mills) to form flat iron sheets. About 1787, Wortley prided itself on being the first mill with grooved rolls to be erected in Yorkshire.[16]

> *The puddling furnace remained the bottleneck of the industry. Only men of remarkable strength and endurance could stand up to the heat for hours, turn and stir the thick porridge of liquescent metal, and draw off the blobs of pasty wrought iron. The puddlers were the aristocracy of the proletariat, proud, clannish, set apart by sweat and blood. Few of them lived past forty. Numerous efforts were made to mechanize the puddling furnace – in vain. Machines could be made to stir the bath, but only the human eye and touch could separate out the solidifying decarburized metal.*[17]

Slitting Mills

Nail making was one of the most important outlets for the products of the iron foundries. Historically, iron blooms had been hammered into flat sheets and cut into strips by hand, making the process very expensive. However, the process was mechanised by Godfrey Box, with the introduction of the slitting mill in 1590, when he copied similar machines in Liege.

These slitting mills transformed nail making; they were relatively cheap to build, since the iron was only heated sufficiently for it to be malleable and, by the eighteenth century, charcoal was replaced by more economical coal. Wortley Top Forge manufactured bar iron that was 1.5 inches square and sent it to Mr Woods' slitting mill (Till Mill) that was half a mile above Upper Forge. 'At the slitting mill the bar iron was cut into short lengths, reheated and passed through water-powered rollers which formed them into flat strips. These were finally passed through the slitting machine in which the strips were cut into small rods by circular knives. Rods were returned to Wortley works for sale,' where at the beginning of the eighteenth century 'two thirds were sold as rod iron for the nail makers of Mortomley'.[18]

Later in the century, the wrought iron sheets or bars from the forge were again rolled into wide flat sections. They were then passed through a water powered roller, constructed with separate parallel grooves. This produced a number of narrow strips, or rods, each about four feet six inches (1.4m) in length, of differing square sections, suitable for making into the numerous types and sizes of nails.[19]

In Yorkshire, slitting mills were either attached to a forge, as in the case of Silkstone, which was very close to Barnsley, or Colnbridge, which was very convenient for Mirfield. Alternatively, the sheets or bars were sold to independent slitting mills and the nail rods distributed by middlemen.[20]

Health

The manufacture of iron in all its forms was strenuous work and produced its own characteristic lung diseases. In fact, few men were able to continue doing the physically arduous work beyond the age of forty. According to John Percy, writing in *Metallurgy, Section 1, Iron and Steel* (London, John Murray *1864*):

> ...*the majority [of puddlers] die between the age of 45 and 50 years; and according to the returns of the Registrars [of BMD], pneumonia, or inflammation of the lungs, is the most frequent cause of their death. This is what may be anticipated from the fact that their exposure to great alterations of temperature under conditions of physical exhaustion. Mr Field, optician, Birmingham, informs me that puddlers are moreover liable to cataract, induced by the intensely bright light of the furnace.*[21]

Of course, the iron industry was not the only trade with its own specific infirmity. They varied from: 'weaver's bottom', which resulted from sitting for up to fourteen hours a day at a loom, and 'hod carrier's shoulder', caused by continuously carrying heavy weights on the shoulder, to fatal metal poisoning. Lead poisoning was common in potters, painters, plumbers, gilders and glaziers, who all worked with material containing lead. 'Those who actually produced the lead seldom lived more than a dozen years after taking up the trade.' Arsenic, used in refining copper, shortened the lives of these operatives, while it was well known that mercury poisoning drove hatters mad. Tin was equally poisonous and tin miners frequently died in their early twenties. Then there were a range of dust induced diseases: silicosis from coal mining, 'grinder's rot' from cutlery grinding, and lung infections from sugar baking, all had a pernicious effect. Tailors suffered from a high death rate as a result of consumption (tuberculosis), by working bent double in cramped ill-ventilated rooms.

A contemporary comment in *The Gentleman's Magazine* eloquently sums up the situation:

> *Scarcely are we fed, lodged, clothed, warmed, without sending multitudes to their grave. The collier, the clothier, the painter, the gilder, the miner, the makers of glass, the workers in iron, tin, lead, copper, while they administer to our necessities, or please our taste and fancies, are impairing their health and shortening their days.*[22]

Each occupation had its accompanying diseases. In fact, a pamphlet written in 1782 declared that manufacturing was as bad as war in producing 'a mournful procession of the blind and lame, and of enfeebled, decrepit, asthmatic, consumptive wretches crawling half alive upon the surface of the earth'.[23]

Distribution of Nail Rods

There were three distinct methods of distributing nail rods from the slitting mills to the nail makers in the south of Yorkshire. Bulk raw material could be conveyed by horse and cart over the poorly maintained roads, and it is recorded that from 1647 an iron wayne [sic] made a weekly journey from Wortley Top Forge to Barnsley and Sheffield, carrying nail rods and bar iron (for making wire) respectively. This wain, made of stout timber, was repaired many times over the next two hundred years, so that by the nineteenth century there was no part of the original remaining.[24]

Probably the most flexible method was to convey the finished rods to local villages or market towns by a nail chapman, originally carrying goods on his back; but by the beginning of the eighteenth century he usually owned a string of mules capable of carrying the rods in panniers. He delivered the raw material to the local nail master and collected the finished nails in bulk. This was a very lucrative business and many of these chapmen became quite wealthy, as the will of Nicholas Gills of Chapeltown demonstrates. He left nearly two thousand pounds when he died in 1735. Similarly, John Spark (1656- 1726), prior to his death in April 1726, plodded round the muddy narrow lanes and potholed roads in the south of Yorkshire with his packhorses, carrying rod iron from slitting mills to local foggers (factors) or nail shops, and probably returning with finished nails for his regular outlets. He was one of the early chapmen who served the 'village' of Mapplewell, for it was here on the edge of the parish, rather than in the centre of Darton by the church, that the nail makers had established their industry. John Spark probably started life as a nail maker himself, but as the inventory of his 'goods chattels and cattle' listed on his death demonstrates, he died a wealthy man. It was apparent that 'wealth' was accumulated by distributors and foggers, who acted as middlemen, not by the humble nail makers. The foggers were in turn financed by merchant capitalists who took some of the risk, since they had to market the nails produced by a vast army of independent piece workers. They also reaped most of the profits.[25]

Finally, the third method of distribution was for independent nail makers to collect the rods themselves, or choose one person to collect rods for a small group, thereby eliminating the middlemen. These self-employed men would often set out before dawn for Barnsley or Wakefield, where supplies of nail rods could be obtained, returning with four stones (fifty-six pounds) of rod iron ready to start work in the nail shop after breakfast. Setting out before dawn in the Pennine foothills, particularly in winter, was a chilling experience, especially when an east wind blew from the frozen Siberian plains. It should be borne in mind that during the peak of 'the little ice age' (1550 CE to 1800 CE) the average temperature in England was 0.9° centigrade lower than during the period 1920 to 1960. Keeping warm has always been a problem in the Pennine hills, and particularly so during John Lindley's lifetime.[26]

It is not known how John's father, Robert, obtained his nail rods. He may have purchased rods from a chapman, but it seems more likely that when he required more rods he walked to Barnsley for new supplies. Alternatively, he could walk to the nearest slitting mill at Silkstone to obtain rods, but they were less likely to purchase the previous week's output of nails than the nail master at Barnsley or the chapman. Even further afield was the slitting mill at Wortley, but time was money, and only by obtaining his raw material cheaper was it worth his while undertaking long journeys. Once he had obtained his nail rods, he would carry them on his shoulders back to his workshop to provide that week's raw material for the family. When the rods were exhausted, he would return to the nail master with finished nails to receive payment and repay his credit. If there was no work on offer for the next week, he would then have to visit other nail masters in order to obtain work, or go without, and have no income from nail making for that week.[27]

In the eighteenth century, everything stopped for the harvest, as it was critical for every able man, woman and child, regardless of normal occupation, to help in the fields. For nail makers, one of the attractions of helping with the harvest was that it provided a break from the hot smoky nail shop and put coins directly in the nail maker's pocket.

CHAPTER 4
Nail Making in Darton

History of Nail Making in Darton

The 'village' of Mapplewell, in the parish of Darton, was the major centre of nail making in Yorkshire for three centuries. The reasons are both geographical and historical. Darton, a parish of Barnsley, lies close to the Tankersley ironstone seam, which outcrops between Huddersfield and Sheffield.

The nail making industry in the Barnsley area dates from at least the seventeenth century and possibly earlier. The hearth tax returns of 1672 identified ten out of the sixty-five households in Darton township as owners of forges (small hearths – not to be confused with smelting forges) for making nails, with three of them possessing more than one forge. This contrasts with the four forge owners in Kexborough and the two in Barugh. It is estimated that about one hundred nail makers worked in villages, hamlets and isolated districts in the Barnsley area at this time.[1]

Nail making was essentially a rural craft, which required little capital or technical knowledge, it was considered the bottom rung of the iron-trade manufacturing ladder. Production was organised round the family unit, with practical knowledge and technique passed down from father to son and other close family members, who were said 'to be bred up in the trade'. This produced a closed, male-dominated, inherently empirical culture. For much of the eighteenth century, the trade in Yorkshire was normally combined with small scale farming to produce a supplementary income, until the rapid increase in population, which commenced in the late eighteenth century, destroyed this way of life. In 1739, William Murgatroyd of Wortley Forge observed that 'between March and August clasp nails were made for the London market, during harvest time nail making stopped, in the autumn flat points were made for Virginia (USA) until Martinmas (St Martin's day 11 November), then sharp points were made for the Leeward Islands and Jamaica.'[2]

But even as early as 1735, the oversupply of labour, by virtue of apprentices setting up on their own, before they had completed their seven-year term, was depressing wages. As a result, Jonathan Dearden, who was manager for the export side of the Spencer Syndicate at Bawtry, collected signatures for the Ecclesfield Nail Makers Agreement in 1733. This was expanded, so that by 1735 there were 195 hearth masters who had their signatures to an agreement 'that apprentices would serve their full term'. Unfortunately, the successful production methods and marketing network pioneered by the Spencer Syndicate stagnated; and the more enterprising Midland nail makers were able to undercut their prices. As a result, John Spencer, the head of the Spencer Syndicate, wrote on 18 October 1742 'I have now discontinued ye Nail trade and discharge'd John [Jonathan] Dearden, so that a great Number of Nailors are at present unemploye'd.'[3]

Making Nails in Darton

As a child, John grew up to the sound of hammers striking iron. In fact, the peace and tranquillity of Mapplewell 'village' was broken by the constant rhythmical hammering (rapa-tap-tap), particularly in the evenings when the entire able-bodied members of the numerous hand nail making families were hard at work. This ancient craft that once supported over fifty thousand families, mostly in the Midlands, can now only be witnessed in a few museums, and so it may be advantageous to consider in some detail how John's family supported themselves in the last decades of the eighteenth century.[4]

During the Middle Ages, making nails by hand was a specialist trade, which produced a good standard of living for those able to master the required skills and accumulate enough capital to purchase the necessary equipment. However, the introduction of the slitting mill, in the late sixteenth century, divided the process into two unequal stages. Production of nail rods, as described earlier, was relatively capital-intensive, requiring considerable experience in the practice of iron forging in order to produce the different qualities of iron needed for different types of nail. By contrast, all that remained for the nail maker to do was to cut the rod to the correct length, make a point at one end and a head at the other – using inexpensive hand tools. This was a relatively simple task, although both strength and skill were required to make the larger nails. Despite the expansion of the Royal Navy in the reign of William and Mary, when 'a typical warship required five tons of iron nails', income from nail making began to decline as more and more men took up the trade, so that by the end of the seventeenth century nail making had become a low-paid trade. This division of labour – capital-intensive forging and slitting, and cheap hand fashioning of the final product – became one of the first examples of industrial mass production. Breaking down the process of manufacture into its component tasks was extolled by Adam Smith (1723–1790) in his book *An Inquiry into the Nature and Causes of the Wealth of Nations,* published in 1776 (Smith used the manufacture of pins in his example). This system of mass production was to produce misery for millions of men, women and children during the nineteenth century, since the social consequences of this method of working were completely ignored by the new industrial class.[5]

During the seventeenth century, and most of the eighteenth, the low income per capita could be borne, provided that the whole family worked together, each making their own contribution. Nail making fitted in well as a part-time occupation, carried out to complement the seasonal nature of agriculture. Under these working conditions, the nail maker regarded himself as a 'free' man, varying his work to suit himself and his family. For example, in summer when the days were long and the weather hot, he may have chosen to sleep during the day and work at night. This self-imposed flexibility conferred an important status to a working man that continued well into the factory era, when the agricultural element of the nail makers' work had virtually ceased.[6]

With the improvements in blast furnaces, and the change from charcoal to coke in about 1750, the nailing industry blossomed. So, with the rapid expansion of the North American market, prior to independence in 1776 (Britain made between six and seven thousand tons of nails in 1700), and despite the low wages, times were tolerable for John Lindley's grandfather, and probably also during the early working years of his father, Robert Lindley, as there was plenty of work available. But by the time John Lindley started work in his father's nail making shop, at the age of seven or eight, a major slump in demand (resulting from the American War of Independence 1775–1783) meant that hunger was always a real threat. John's father, Robert Lindley, almost certainly rented his nail shop and bought his raw materials on credit, but rents were low, from one shilling to one shilling and sixpence a week for a cottage and a pound a year for a nail shop.

The Nail Shop

As already described, a nail shop was invariably a single-story building, occasionally an extension (outshutt) of the main family cottage, but more usually a small building set apart from the main dwelling house, and often one 'room' in a separate terrace. Typically, a nail shop was about twelve feet square with a single door, of the type where the top half opened independently of the bottom half, and two unglazed windows for ventilation.

In the middle of the room was a central coal or coke hearth, blasted with a large pair of leather bellows operated by the nail maker's foot. Round the hearth were a number of workplaces – the 'standings or stocks', arranged so that four people (and sometimes more) could work independently, using a single fire, but with the minimum practicable distance between hearth and stock, since speed was of the essence. The 'simple and cheap' equipment comprised: a wooden 'spittal' for shovelling coal and a pair of tongs to handle the hot rods. Each nail maker required a 'stock' or bench, equipped with a flat faced hammer, a 'stiddy' (a three inch cube of steel) used as a work block, a 'hardy' (a fixed cold chisel), and a 'nail can' to catch the finished nails. For very large nails a foot operated power hammer, known as an 'Oliver' or 'Tommy', was used, but these were very scarce in John Lindley's day and it is doubtful if Robert Lindley owned one.[7]

Small nails were made by placing three or four nail rods in the hearth, and when the rods were at the required temperature, the nail maker removed a single rod with the tongs and turned to his stock. This was a wooden structure, about two feet square and two feet six inches high, filled with a mixture of clinker from the fire and clay. Fastened to the clay with iron spikes was a block of iron, about fourteen inches square by five inches deep, that provided a stable working surface to which a series of small tools were fixed. Placing the glowing rod on the stiddy, which acted as an anvil, a point was quickly hammered on the end, before placing the rod across the sharp edge of the hardy. There was no time for measurement; the craftsman judged only by 't'rack o'eye', but long experience taught him to make his products with only a slight variation in length. A single deft blow nearly severed the rod at the required length and the break was completed as the nail was inserted point down into the correct hole on the bore, countersunk for different heads. This left a short piece of metal standing proud. A sharp blow with the hammer formed the head to the correct shape, and at the same time caused the finished nail to leap out of the bore into the nail can. All this was done at incredible speed since it only required twelve strikes of the hammer to complete one nail, a process which normally took just six seconds. This rate of six hundred nails an hour could be maintained over long periods, and experienced nail makers could produce a long thousand (1200) nails in two hours.[8]

Types of Nails

A bewildering variety of nails was made, ranging from short square 'sparrables' to $3^{3}/_{4}$ inch nails. They were referred to as 'twopenny', 'threepenny', 'fourpenny', 'sixpenny', 'eightpenny', 'tenpenny' and 'twelvepenny' nails, corresponding in size to half an inch, one inch, one-and-a-half inches, two inches, two-and-a-half inches, three inches and three-and-a-half inches with flat, rose or diced heads. The names of the nails had nothing whatsoever to do with the price of the nails – rather it related to the weight. The standard unit of weight for nails referred to the weight of one thousand nails of that type. So, one thousand twopenny nails weighed two pounds, where the word penny is a corruption of the word pounds. For example, one thousand 'tenpenny' nails weighed ten pounds – simple if you are a Yorkshireman!

In addition, many specialist nails were made, such as: 'spikes' and 'brags' in sizes of five inches, six inches, and seven inches, in addition to special varieties of tenterhooks, gate nails, mop nails, bellow nails, plate nails, corf nails, horseshoe nails, horse clinkers, billed clinkers and mock clinkers. Boys and girls made the smaller nails up to 'sixpenny'. Women made 'fourpenny' to 'eightpenny' nails, while 'tenpenny' nails usually required the skill and strength of a man, as did the spikes, brags, tenterhooks and gate nails.[9]

Prices and Wages

As has been indicated earlier, the real problem for the nail makers was the over-supply of labour. During John Lindley's lifetime, the population of England and Wales increased from an estimated 7.2 million in 1771 to 17.9 million recorded in the 1851 census. Decline in the handloom weaving industry also drove many women and children onto the labour market. This depressed prices and meant that one 'long thousand' (1,200) 'sparrables', weighing 4lb (1.8 kg), sold for between four and seven pence (before 1973, 240d = £1 = 20s).

Since a skilled nail maker could produce one 'long thousand' sparrables in two hours, going flat out, at four pence for a 'long thousand', his rate of pay was two pence an hour, which did not include time out for fetching coal, stoking the fire, operating the bellows and the numerous other 'housekeeping tasks' required by an independent 'business'. Many of the simple ancillary tasks were carried out by young children. As a result, a skilled nail maker could earn up to twelve shillings for a 72-hour week. This was better than that of an agricultural labourer, and the average weekly income for a family of five (an average family was normally calculated on the basis of two adults and three productive children) was between fifteen and twenty shillings. Some men, by taking their meals at the stock, could earn forty shillings a week by working a 16-hour day for five days, making an 80-hour week. If demand was very high, the average family income could rise to between twenty and thirty shillings a week, but when demand was low, the same output often produced only seven shillings. As a result of this reduction in income, many small nail masters had to become wage earners, thereby losing their artisan status, and, as a consequence, destroying their 'independent' way of life. The result produced fertile ground for radical ideas.[10]

A Working Day

As was the custom, John would have started work as a nail maker at the age of seven or eight. No doubt John's place of work was 'like a coal-hole' (as described in the Midland Mining Commission Report of 1843), but it was here that he was first taught to make a square point on a piece of cold iron. After about three months, when he was proficient with a hammer, he would then have started to make sparrables, the simplest form of nail, and would have been quickly expected to make about one thousand a day. The day started at first light or even earlier. John's mother Jane would get up, clean and light the hearth, then she would make as many small nails as possible before breakfast time. Breakfast was normally taken at 8:00am, lunch at midday, tea at 4:00pm and supper at 8:00pm, allowing a couple of hours more work before bedtime at 10:00pm.

A standard week consisted of working five such days of up to twelve hours (excluding meals) with little work being done on Sunday and Monday. However, during the French and Napoleonic Wars (1791–1815) nail makers worked between seventy-two and eighty hours a week, for up to 347 days a year. They were 'free men' but were ruled by the tyranny of piecework and received starvation returns for their labour.[11]

Shortage of Coins

During the eighteenth century, there was a shortage of coins, gold, silver and copper; and those that remained in circulation were frequently deficient in weight, since sweating down and clipping were widespread. In fact, by the mid-century, there was little silver coin in circulation, except for a quantity of worn shillings and sixpences. Copper halfpennies and farthings ($^1/_4$d) legally had an official value equal to their face value, but they were so deficient that traders only accepted them by weight. In 1797, new coins with denominations of twopence, a penny, a halfpenny and a farthing were produced of excellent quality, but by the end of the decade the price of copper had risen and many of those coins were also melted down for their metal content. There was much settlement in kind – a forerunner of the truck system – and long pay delays became common. Samuel Oldfield paid his poor spinners fortnightly and his better off workers monthly. They were paid in bills, for which local shopkeepers deducted threepence in the pound for conversion. Some manufacturers made their own copper coins for local circulation, so that by 1792 the country was flooded with unofficial local currencies. The practice was banned in 1821, but the improvised currencies kept the everyday economy functioning.[12]

From this precedent it was a small step to exacerbate the problem with the 'truck system'. Following the Truck Act of 1821, a new, despised class of middlemen, often owners of 'Tommy' shops and publicans, moved in to cream off the profits. They supplied raw material on credit and bought back the finished nails, not with coins of the realm, but with tokens that had to be spent on goods, or beer, from their own outlets. This truck system further exacerbated the poverty of the nail makers and the practice was eventually banned by parliament – but nevertheless continued unabated with local magistrates turning a blind eye.[13]

Marketing

The demise of the Spencer Syndicate in 1742 was remarkable, as only a few years earlier they were exporting nails down the river Don and along the coast to Deptford, where London merchants collected them for distribution to southern England and America.[14]

Markets for goods were imperfectly understood by the merchants of the eighteenth century, as they followed the mercantile method of trade. In one sense they had a grasp of the economics of a supply of raw material and the need for a market for manufactured products. This was the rationale behind 'the Empire of the Seas' but they had no concept of the economics of trade cycles. During John's early life, in addition to the domestic market – particularly farmers and builders – there were two insatiable markets for nails, the Royal Navy and the thirteen American colonies. Both were dependant on government policy, and, during this period, the navy went through several phases of expansion and cutbacks, what economists in the twenty-first century label 'boom and bust'.

Colonial 'America' was different; they were not allowed to manufacture nails, the purpose of colonies being to supply raw materials to the mother country and then purchase manufactured goods 'with added value' in return. When the thirteen states declared their independence on 4 July 1776, they naturally commenced making their own nails, and the British export market collapsed. The market did recover after the Treaty of Paris in 1783, but never reached its former level, as the new republic gradually began to industrialise.

The domestic market followed local economic cycles. Two local families in particular fostered the growth of nail making in Mapplewell, by expanding their businesses to encompass outlets in the rapidly growing major towns in the West Riding. In the eighteenth and early nineteenth centuries, large quantities of nails were marketed through Leeds and Pontefract, the industry benefitting from the family connections of the Shaws and the Ledgers based in those towns. However, a good many nails and other small iron products were hawked, not only locally, but far and wide, to places such as Lincolnshire, the Midlands and Newcastle. They were carried on the backs of pack animals, horses, donkeys or mules, by specialist hawkers or by members of small syndicates of nail makers. Products were sold to farmers, blacksmiths, joiners and plumbers who were the end users. Mapplewell appears to have been particularly associated with mules, and there are accounts of gaily decked wedding parties riding down to the parish church in Darton on the backs of these animals.[15]

The 'yeoman' George Shaw moved with his family to Leeds, where he established a successful business before he died in 1749. He had two sons, Joseph who became a nail maker and George, an entrepreneur, who built up an ironmonger's business which, in 1781, was located in 'White Swan Yard'. During this time, he retained connections with Staincross and its nail shops, supplying raw material and selling finished nails. George died in 1785. Joseph Shaw (1764– 1829), grandson of the founder, developed the business further, so that by 1803 he is described as an iron-founder, and by 1817 the site is identified as Hunslet Ironworks, known as the Knowsthorpe Mills, leased from the Aire and Calder Navigation Company, with access to water power and water transport. Despite its expansion into other products, Knowsthorpe Mills continued to advertise nails as one of its products.[16]

A second family, headed by John Ledger, was operating a business which encompassed both manufacturing and marketing of local products as early as 1770. He was purchasing rod iron at Rotherham, a distance of about twenty-five miles (forty km), and Hunslet, a distance of twelve miles (twenty km), to supply his nail shops in Staincross. He owned cottages with attached workshops at Mapplewell, tenanted by other members of the Ledger family. John Ledger was almost certainly born in Darton, but, by 1770, his home and main marketing outlet was at the Market Place in Pontefract. He had other outlets in Leeds and Wakefield. 'The business prospered for his stock and debts increased in value from less than £1,000 in 1785 to over £3,000 in the space of ten years and his stock of four tons of rod iron in 1780 indicates the scale of operation in Staincross.'[17]

Mechanisation

In America, Jacob Perkins (1766–1849) invented a nail making machine that with one pull of a lever automatically cut and headed the nail. He patented his idea in 1795, but, as a result of a long-drawn-out and expensive lawsuit, his company went into liquidation. However, Perkins met Joseph Dyer (1780–1871), another American, who patented the

'Perkins Process' in England in 1810. The machine proved a commercial success, as Dyer transformed Perkins' idea into a practical working model for producing 'cut nails' as opposed to handmade nails. He went on to found the Britannia Nail Works in Birmingham, which was the first company to make 'cold cut' nails by machinery. Development continued, so that by 1830 it was possible to manufacture 'cut nails' in large numbers, and by the 1840s it reached a stage where machines could cut four rows of nails at a time.[18]

The writing was on the wall for the traditional nail makers, and the livelihood of tens of thousands of men, women and children, who had made nails during the eighteenth and nineteenth centuries, was about to disappear. This duly occurred during John Lindley's lifetime. From then on 'nail maker' became a generic term for 'craftsmen' who made many types of small metal products such as: hooks to secure pipes to the wall, steel teeth to fix to drums for tearing up rags in shoddy mills, or chaplets and studs for foundry men. They were in effect jobbing shop metalworkers but a number of them were still recorded as nail makers. A few genuine old nail makers lingered on, and there are records of Ibbotson Haig, who made 'muck' nails in Mapplewell as late as 1943, and Fred Chappell who made nails in Hoylandswaine until the 1940s.[19]

Alternatively, some like George Lindley junior, the son of John Lindley's nephew George (1806–1882), who joined him in Mirfield as a nail maker, diversified into commerce. This branch of the family eventually opened a hardware store in the Easthorpe district of Mirfield. George junior provides a good example of the upward mobility that became possible when the benefits of industrialisation began to benefit the working classes after the Great Exhibition of 1851.

CHAPTER 5
Radical Awakening 1760–1793

The End of an Era

During the first nineteen years of John's life, the political system in England remained as stable as it had done since the 'Glorious Revolution' of 1688, all achieved without a police force or armed militia. Because society was divided into small communities, subordination of the poor was effected by means of the established hierarchy. In this respect the parish priests of the Anglican Church, who frequently also occupied the position of local magistrate, played an important part in ensuring that the 'birthright' of the aristocracy to rule the nation was not challenged. This was psychological control at ground level, through the medium of religious authority.[1]

Nevertheless, the first stirrings of radical discontent, in the eighteenth century, had already begun with the expansion of 'the middling sort' of people, from around the year 1760 – ten years before John Lindley was born. Both political and religious murmurings were being voiced against the autocratic rule of an 'incompetent and predatory oligarchy', which ran the country in the interests of the landed aristocracy. This elite executive was supported by their placemen in the House of Lords and the House of Commons, which were in effect little more than gentlemen's clubs, whose debates and discussions took no account of the opinion of the general public and brooked no criticism. As Charles Dickens (1812–1870) was to record, when acting as a parliamentary reporter in the early 1830s, 'the House of Commons…when full, was a conglomeration of noise and confusion…it had the atmosphere of a club where most of the members spoke in much the same way, a style learnt at their public schools and colleges, the better ones rising to occasional wit, the majority dull, the worst fatuous.'[2]

Rarely did the majority of people have any say in government affairs, except at election time. This generally amounted to no more than loud vocal protest and riotous behaviour at public meetings, which ultimately had no effect on the measures taken in parliament. The electoral process was corrupt, enabling candidates, often junior members or agents of the ruling families, simply to ignore the protests of the so-called 'uneducated and ignorant mob'. In the majority of elections candidates were returned unopposed.[3]

This is not surprising, since contested elections were very expensive, not only for the candidates but often for those eligible to vote. For example, the 1801 census recorded that the population of the city of Sheffield was thirty-one thousand, but that it had no parliamentary representation at all. Freemen of the city of Sheffield, who were qualified to vote for a county candidate, were required to travel to York to cast their vote.[4]

Chapter 5

Political discontent was fuelled by the growth of provincial news-sheets, which developed into newspapers. By 1760, there were about forty such publications, which resulted in an increasingly informed, but still disenfranchised public – a sure recipe for unrest. Once the fight to publish parliamentary debates had been won, in the early 1770s, pressure groups of unelected men and women formed outside parliament, with the object of influencing legislation. As a result, politics would never again be the exclusive prerogative of parliament.[5]

Furthermore, the Test Acts of 1661, 1673 and 1678 established that only persons professing the beliefs of the established Anglican Church were eligible for public employment – ostensibly to discourage Catholicism. Unfortunately, these acts also prevented the increasing number of 'respectable' Nonconformist dissenters, such as Presbyterians, Congregationalists, Baptists, Unitarians and Quakers, as well as Roman Catholics, from holding government office at any level.

In parallel with the political rumblings, was an intellectual religious challenge to the established Anglican Church. Once again authority was being questioned. The philosophy of 'rational dissent' spread during the eighteenth century, particularly in the new industrial areas of the north of England, with a result that, at all levels of society, the cosy world of national aristocracy and local squirearchy was being questioned and undermined. As the nation gradually prospered through trade, there was an increase in the number of 'middling sort of people' and artisans. These were people who were increasingly comfortably off, but did not qualify as lesser gentry; and as Dr Johnson (1709–1784), the English lexicographer, recognised, 'gold and silver destroy subordination'. He was not quite correct, for as the Yorkshire vernacular bluntly stated 'twere brass' generated among 'the muck' in the mills, factories and mines of Yorkshire, Lancashire and the Midlands that produced wealth (hence the phrase 'where there's muck there's brass'). A major change in the attitude to subordination among the newly independent masters and skilled workers of the industrial age was about to take place.[6]

The seeds of radicalism, sown in the 1760s, germinated during the American War of Independence, when the Thirteen American Colonies protested, refusing to pay taxes, proposed by the autocratic ministers of George III, without representation. The war resulted in an increase in British taxation, coupled with a loss of North American trade. Extra-parliamentary opposition to the war was voiced by the moderate Rev. Christopher Wyvill (1740–1822), a Yorkshire clergyman and landowner, who founded the Yorkshire County Association (YCA) in 1779, encompassing the gentry of Yorkshire. They called for a package of 'economical reforms' that included: cuts in government spending on the American War; a reduction in ministerial nepotism and patronage, and the elimination of wasteful government spending. To help remedy these problems, they proposed parliamentary reforms, including annual parliaments to facilitate accountability, and an extra one hundred county MPs, because they thought that county MPs would be more independent in their scrutiny of government expenditure than borough MPs.

The YCA was copied by twelve other counties, but its major strength was confined to Yorkshire and Middlesex. The County Associations were potentially a most dangerous development for the government, because the county MPs held the balance of power in parliament, and the government relied on the country gentlemen for support, since otherwise they had no effective means of fully controlling the House of Commons. At this time, the country gentlemen formed the bulk of the county electorate, they were the backbone of agricultural England, parliament and popular landed opinion. They represented the conservative element of the constitution.[7]

However, the nascent 'industrial revolution' was beginning to create new social and politically underprivileged groups, which were starting to explore their strength in numbers by forming trade unions. Collectively known as the 'lower orders', but as Francis Place (1771–1854), the radical Charing Cross tailor and contemporary of John Lindley, observed: 'the difference between the most skilled and prudent workmen and the most ignorant and imprudent labourers and paupers… is great indeed.'[8]

But, such was the social structure of Britain during the second half of the eighteenth century, that the country gentlemen were totally insensitive to the aspirations of these new groups for representation and political rights, thereby totally misjudging the strength of the radical sentiment that was growing in their midst.[9]

When, in 1781, at the age of twenty-one, William Pitt the Younger (1759–1806) first entered parliament, for the pocket borough of Appleby, he labelled himself a liberal Whig and spoke in favour of limited parliamentary reform, thereby gaining the support of the County Associations. In 1783, he went on to become the youngest first minister of the United Kingdom at the remarkable age of twenty-four (the term 'prime minister' was not used at this time). As soon as he was established in office, he encouraged Henry Duncombe (1728–1818), a county MP for Yorkshire between 1780 and 1796, to present a reform petition on behalf of the Yorkshire County Association in January 1785. The petition proposed the abolition of thirty-six rotten boroughs, and to extend in a small way the electoral franchise to more individuals. Pitt himself failed to give his full support to the bill, as he knew that the King opposed the new measures; consequently, the bill failed to gain support in the House of Commons. Embarrassingly, Manchester and Birmingham were not among the petitioning towns, which led Lord North (1732–1792), the former first minister, to sneer 'What horrid sound of silence doth assail mine ear.'[10]

This was Pitt's only parliamentary reform proposal during his nineteen years as first minister. In fact, despite his earlier declaration 'In constitutional matters he was conservative and took no new initiatives affecting the royal prerogative, cabinet government, the established church, or political party.' As a result, a great opportunity for peaceful reform was lost. In this respect, the intransigence of George III had much to answer for. It is significant that actions like these, of which John Lindley and his fellow nail makers in Mapplewell were probably totally unaware, exercised a profound effect on their future lives.[11]

Nowhere in the country was the mood of discontent, and demand for reform, reflected more than in the city of Sheffield in the south of Yorkshire. Its early commercial success was based on the invention of Benjamin Huntsman (1704–1776) for producing crucible steel in the 1740s; this was a type of hard cast steel that was ideal for making cutlery and cutting-edge tools. He was the first person to produce steel in ingots and, because he did not patent this technique, the secret of his production process remained exclusively his own for many years.[12]

By the late eighteenth century, Sheffield was fast becoming the cutlery centre of the country and overtook London during John Lindley's lifetime. The trade of small workshops and little 'mesters' was crucial in fostering working-class radicalism in Sheffield. It produced numerous groups of independently minded skilled artisans, who were often rebellious, cantankerous and bloody-minded, a characteristic that developed into a caricature of Yorkshire men. In keeping with their individualism, they worshipped in a wide variety of

Nonconformist churches. The main centre of dissent in Sheffield was centred on Upper Chapel, founded in 1700 by Presbyterians and Independents, and presided over by the radical preacher Rev. Joseph Evans (1728 –1803), who was minister from 1758 to 1797. According to Joseph Hunter, the Sheffield antiquarian and historian, 'Evans' opinions were extreme on the side of freedom. He had been a zealous friend of the Americans…He was a hearty well-wisher to the French in their revolution. He gloried in the destruction of the Bastille.' One influential member of Evans' congregation was 'Samuel Shore who belonged to an important family of Sheffield ironmasters'. 'He probably met Tom Paine when he was working in Rotherham on an iron bridge with Shore's relations, the Walkers of Masborough.' In the early 1780s, Shore was a prominent member of Rev. Christopher Wyvill's Yorkshire County Association campaigning for parliamentary reform.[13]

In some ways, Sheffield mirrored the national problem of government, control being in the hands of a self-perpetuating clique, but on a much smaller scale, and was therefore more susceptible to pressure from dissenting citizens. It had no town corporation and was controlled by three bodies: the Church burgesses, the town trustees and the Cutlers' Company. Law and order was in the hands of the justices of the peace, one of whom, Rev. James Wilkinson, vicar of Sheffield, was the only magistrate that resided in the town.[14]

The Cutlers' Company was a self-perpetuating oligarchy, whose members were constantly in dispute with the 'little mesters' employing a handful of semi-independent journeymen. These skilled men were both literate and numerate, and not easily cowed. But small businesses were very vulnerable to adverse trading conditions and sharp practice by factors and master manufacturers. The series of disputes came to a head in 1784, when a group of freemen protested and invoked the Act of Incorporation of the Company, drawn up in 1624. William Wilberforce MP (1759–1833) was brought in to mediate, but although a new act was implemented in 1791, to widen the electorate for officers of the Cutlers' Company, the move came too late and the Cutlers' Company went into decline.[15]

Economically, England had quickly recovered from the downturn in trade that occurred during the American War of Independence, largely as a result of the rapid mechanisation of the cotton industry in Lancashire. This was due to the introduction of the flying shuttle and the spinning jenny, and the north of England experienced a short period of prosperity between the years 1783 to 1789. This was reflected throughout the industrial triangle of Yorkshire, Lancashire and the Midlands, as there was considerable integration between textile production and metal working with coal providing power for both. Nail making, which had suffered a decline during the war, recovered, but it never fully regained the American market once the new republic started to manufacture its own nails. As a result of the general increase in economic activity, new buildings were needed, with a requirement for more building materials, including bricks and tiles and ubiquitous nails. The increased wealth even spawned the beginnings of consumerism, as the discretionary spending of the 'respectable middle sort' was used to buy the new fashionable light clothing made from cotton, while pottery and china from Staffordshire 'replaced wooden platters and pewter trenchers on dining room tables'. Furniture began to make its appearance, for, prior to the Industrial Revolution, most people sat on benches and stools. But above all, the driving force was cotton production, both for the home market and for export.[16]

But the boom was based on very shaky foundations. As the American War demonstrated, export markets were very vulnerable to war conditions, while home markets depended on a constant and thriving customer base. Expansion was powered by mechanisation and the increasing size of the units of production, generating economies of scale. For example, in 1792 John Marshall (1765–1845) built the largest flax spinning mill in England, at Holbeck, and established Leeds as an important centre of the linen trade, competing with Barnsley and Knaresborough. Even more impressive was Benjamin Gott's Bean Ing factory, also built in 1792 in Leeds, powered by the first Boulton-Watt steam engine in the West Riding. By 1797, this factory employed twelve thousand workers making four thousand broad clothes per annum – mostly cheap clothing and army blankets. These two factories were both 'wonders of the age of improvement'. But, as capitalist societies have discovered ever since the Industrial Revolution, while supply can be controlled, demand can be far more volatile and ephemeral. When the first test of the new economics arrived in 1795, with a harvest failure that caused food prices to rise, the majority of working-class spending was diverted to purchasing food. It has been estimated that between forty and eighty per cent of the family budget was spent on bread alone, and the total expenditure on food reached eighty per cent of income, often at the expense of clothing and rent. In the northern counties, the poorest workers consumed oats, with boiling milk or water added, reverting to the traditional diet of oats, barley and rye of the early eighteenth century, but as the *Leeds Intelligencer* reported on 13 and 20 July 1795, the public 'loathed and resisted' this fare.[17]

Government spending on munitions and military clothing and blankets sustained demand until 1797, when suddenly the market for textiles collapsed and mass unemployment was added to the misery of inflated food prices. To compound the problem, the 'better off sort of people' were also being squeezed by the high taxation needed to pay for the large gold subsidies paid to continental allies. The British Army did little fighting during this period.[18]

A major shift also occurred in the traditional structure of society, as the new large factories required far more capital than could be supplied by small owners. Previously, they had often ploughed most of the 'profits' back into their businesses, even paying themselves wages on occasion. The advent of the capitalist entrepreneur completely changed the relationship between employers and employed. People became 'input costs', to be obtained at the lowest possible price, with women and children replacing men wherever possible. They were hired and fired as demand rose and fell, so that gone were the days when 'small masters prided themselves on keeping their journeymen employed during short depressions'.[19]

The French Revolution

On 14 July 1789, a mob of French citizens stormed the Bastille and the French Revolution began in earnest. The news was favourably received throughout Britain, but nowhere more enthusiastically than in Sheffield, for it was here that the germ cell of Yorkshire radicalism had taken root.

The outbreak of the French Revolution broke the pent-up dam of resentment, which had been building during the previous decade, and a national campaign for parliamentary reform erupted. For the nail makers of Darton, the example of the steel makers of Sheffield was close at hand, for outside London it was these tough, independently minded men that spearheaded the challenge to the ruling hegemony in industrial Yorkshire. Perhaps a little prematurely, Sheffield was dubbed the potential 'Faubourg Saint Antoine' of the English Revolution by Gwyn Williams, but Bradford, Halifax, Leeds and Rotherham were also known to have had reform societies at this time.[20]

The ground for a Yorkshire revolution had been inadvertently prepared by Joseph Gales (1761–1841), who founded the *Sheffield Register* in 1787 with his wife Winifred Marshall. 'His paper originally set out to be impartial and independent, catering for a wide audience covering events in Yorkshire and the neighbouring counties of Derbyshire and Nottinghamshire. It also included national and international news with political comment.'

With the advent of the French Revolution, Pitt and his government began to adopt repressive measures against any who threatened 'the constitution'. This was interpreted as the right of the Monarch, Lords and Commons to rule the country as they thought fit. As a result, the *Sheffield Register* became increasingly radical in its opinions, abandoning its non-partisan stance. As editor, it was Gales' inspired writings, more than any other single factor, which spread the 'radical message' in west Yorkshire. He began reprinting extracts from the works of radicals, such as Thomas Paine (1737–1809), Joseph Priestly (1733–1804), Dr Richard Price (1723–1791), William Godwin (1756–1836) and John Horne Tooke, in an attempt to politicise his readers. In this work, he was assisted by his 'indomitable wife, a woman of considerable learning, who contributed political analysis to the paper'.[21]

Gales was a Unitarian who attended the Upper Chapel, where he came increasingly under the influence of the minister, Joseph Evans, and the layman, Samuel Shaw. It was these two individuals who reinforced his radical beliefs and set him on a collision course with authority. Other radical members of Upper Chapel were the Walkers who, in 1789 and 1790, probably introduced Joseph and Winifred to Thomas Paine. A few months after the fall of the Bastille, Gales published the following:

> *French hearts are warmed with the sacred flame of liberty…so that their new statute book is in no danger of being disgraced with Test Acts and penal laws for religious opinions…We have long impersonated the French in dress and dissipation; surely we shall not neglect to imitate them in what is laudable and manly. Many defects remain in our own constitution; to enquire into them and remove them is now absolutely necessary.*[22]

As it turned out, Sheffield was an ideal location from which to ferment rebellion. The problem of establishing government control in Sheffield was clearly set out by the military inspector, Colonel de Lancey, who, in 1798, was sent by the War Office to investigate this belligerent town. He reported:

> *The manufacturers of this town are of a nature to require so little capital to carry them on that a man with a very small sum of money can employ two, three or four men, and this being generally the case there are not in this, as in other great towns, any number of persons of sufficient weight who could by their influence, or the number of their dependents, act with any effect in the case of a disturbance. As the wages given to journeymen are very high, it is pretty generally the practice for them to work for three days, in which they can earn sufficient to enable them to drink and riot for the rest of the week; consequently there can be no place more fit for seditious purpose.*[23]

The high wages that Colonel de Lancey was complaining about were recorded by Arthur Young (1741–1820) in 1790, when he observed that outside London the highest wages were paid in Sheffield and Birmingham. 'In Sheffield, daily earnings of 1s 6d [7.5p] to 2s [10p] were general, while a small number of razor grinders could earn 10s 6d [52.5p] per day, surprising wages for any manual performance…at that time'. It should also be noted that this was a very hazardous occupation due to the inhalation of stone and metal 'dust'.[24]

The conflict between the Cutlers' Company and the freemen of Sheffield continued for several years and although the freemen lost in the end, they gained valuable experience in political agitation, which they were able to employ in the 1790s in response to rising prices set against a background of static wages. Sheffield was to become the first epicentre of Yorkshire radicalism, a storm that was to sweep north to Barnsley, Huddersfield, Halifax, Bradford and Leeds in the succeeding decades.

The War of Words

A battle of words commenced when, on 4 November 1789, Dr Richard Price (1723–1791) delivered a sermon in London, welcoming democracy in France. 'He spoke in glowing eloquence of the way enlightenment was spreading from one continent to another. Mankind was on the verge of a great era of reform and progress.' This produced a backlash, causing the Irish philosopher and politician Edmund Burke (1729–1797) to write his famous *Reflections on the Revolution in France*, published on 1 November 1790. 'Burke believed that the true principles of the Whig creed were being betrayed.' While Burke's predictions regarding the outcome of the Revolution were largely fulfilled, he completely missed the point; namely that the rule of autocratic authority, founded on historic antecedents, was no longer acceptable to common people. Furthermore, he caused Thomas Paine (1737-1809) to respond by writing *The Rights of Man*. The arguments and counter arguments in these two books raised the political consciousness of disenfranchised people to a new pitch, holding out the possibility of electoral emancipation. Already, the American War of Independence and the French Revolution (1789-1799) had opened people's minds to an alternative society.[25]

The Rights of Man part one was published in 1791 and was targeted at people who could hardly afford books, but nevertheless sold two hundred thousand copies in six months! The more republican part two, which also included his ideas on a welfare state, was published in 1792. These books circulated Paine's ideas, and it has been estimated by John Keane 'that one in ten literate people in England owned a copy'. Paine's main argument was that 'a small landowning aristocratic elite had no hereditary right to rule the country in their own interest'.

The publication of *The Rights of Man* sparked off the formation of 'corresponding societies' throughout the country to promote constitutional reform. The first of these was the 'Sheffield Society for Constitutional Information' (SSCI), founded in the autumn of 1791 by five or six artisans; it grew rapidly to between 1,500 and 2,500 subscribers by March 1792. This society was then given permission by Paine to produce fifteen thousand copies of a pamphlet edition of *The Rights of Man* part one at 3d a copy. It was printed by John Cromer of Sheffield and rapidly disseminated throughout the region, facilitated by the fact that the SSCI was allowed to keep the profits. 'The speed with which SSCI got into its stride owed much to the experience gained during the earlier agitation against the Cutlers' Company.' Barnsley is not far from Sheffield, sharing many chapmen and pedlars in common, and it is almost certain that it was one of these copies that was read by John Lindley when they first reached Mapplewell.[26]

However, there was some concern about the formation of the SSCI by local parliamentary reformers, in particular Rev. Christopher Wyvill who wrote:

Chapter 5

...not surprised that many people are very apprehensive of tumulus at that place (Sheffield) and I think fears will increase rather than diminish as the association extends itself more into the neighbouring country. It is unfortunate that Mr Paine took such unconstitutional ground and has formed a party for a Republic among the lower classes of people, by holding out to them the prospect of plundering the rich.[27]

Despite Wyvill's concern, other major British cities rapidly formed a national network of 'corresponding societies', of which the London Corresponding Society (LCS), established in January 1792, was the most famous. By setting the weekly subscription at 1d, the society aimed to represent the 'humble in situation and circumstances'. However, from the earliest days, most corresponding societies did attract a significant minority of respectable members from gentry stock and the professional classes. But these members were concerned more about local issues than national struggles and their debates reflected their parochialism. They were hardly the 'stuff' of a nationwide revolution.

One early example of local action that took place on 28 July 1791, which surely must have reached John Lindley's ears, was the response of the people of Sheffield to the attempt by the Duke of Norfolk (1765–1842), hereditary lord of the manor of Sheffield, and the Reverend John Wilkinson, vicar and local magistrate, with others, to enclose six thousand acres of common land to the west of Sheffield. This included the Rivelin Valley and Hallam Moors, and the village greens of Brookhouse, Newfield, Owlerton and Rivelin. Parliament had been informed by the enclosure commissioners (Wilkinson, Eyre and Ward – the master cutler) that 98.3 per cent of landowners (who stood to gain) had given their consent. Since no one had opposed the act it passed smoothly through parliament. The public was made aware of the new act when Gales put a notice in the *Sheffield Register,* and the vicar put a notice on the church door. Incensed, the men and women of Sheffield broke into the debtors' gaol and released the prisoners, and then proceeded to Wilkinson's grand house, Broom Hall, where they burnt his library and set fire to a number of hayricks. They were only dispersed when the Light Dragoons arrived from Nottingham. The Enclosure Act went through unchanged: The Duke of Norfolk received one thousand three hundred acres, eighty-one acres went to Wilkinson and Gell as tithe holders, the remainder was divided between property owners and freeholders in the area. Just two acres were set aside for the landless poor, who lost their historic rights to grazing for cows and sheep, scrub for poultry, access to footpaths and particularly the right to gather firewood. They also lost access to wild fruit from hedgerows and much else besides.[28]

The Sheffield Clarion Ramblers' handbook of 1941-2, produced by George Ward, calculated that the total appropriation (theft) by the rich landed classes under the Enclosure Acts, in the south of Yorkshire and the Peak District, amounted to 98,314 acres (153.5 square miles).

The hypocrisy of the times can best be gauged by the sentence of death passed on a child in the 1830s for breaking a shop window and stealing (appropriating?) some sweets.[29]

As a result of incendiary incidents, like those in Sheffield, the government adopted a policy of actively persecuting radicals, both in parliament and in the law courts. And so began a long and bitter struggle for wider democratic rights. Initially, the fight was for manhood suffrage, but by the middle of the nineteenth century it had widened to include women. These rights would eventually encompass all levels of society, but were only achieved in the lifetime of John's granddaughter Harriet (1848–1937).[30]

The Fight for Emancipation

The struggle began with '… a wave of popular agitation across the country in 1791-92 and government ministers were alarmed at the rapid spread of Paine's ideas'. They sought to stem the tide of 'seditious' writings, by passing two royal proclamations in 1792, these were popularly known as 'the Two Acts' or 'Gagging Acts'. The SSCI responded that 'they stood for the right of every commoner to have a vote', but they 'abhorred every idea of attempting a Revolution'.[31]

This generated a government-inspired backlash, with rioting by hired ruffians of the 'Church and King Party', most notably in Birmingham, where they burned the house, library and laboratory of the Unitarian Dr Joseph Priestley (1733–1804), the discoverer of the element oxygen, who had moved from Leeds to Birmingham. They also attacked many other notable Presbyterians. 'In two days of rioting they damaged or demolished as many houses of the "damned Presbyterians" as they could find.' The Church and King mob tried to repeat the action in Sheffield, but here they were greatly outnumbered. It was reported that: 'When a meeting of about one hundred people [of the Church and King Party] met in the Cutlers' Hall in June to propose a loyal address, the crowd outside, numbering over a thousand radicals, threatened to pull down the building, and the situation was only defused by the intervention of Joseph Gales.'[32]

Obviously, tensions were rising, and troops were now regularly billeted in Sheffield, as it was considered 'a hotbed of subversion'; as a result, regular clashes took place in the streets. In July 1792, work was begun on a new barracks beyond Shalesmoor, and thus commenced the occupation of Yorkshire by the British Army. Colonel de Lancey reported that:

> *At Sheffield …I found that seditious machinations of Paine and factious people who are endeavouring to disturb the peace of the country had extended to a degree very much beyond my conception; and indeed they seem with great judgement to have chosen this as the centre for their machinations.*[33]

Despite entreaties from close friends, Gales refused to moderate the message of the *Sheffield Register*. Instead, in 1792, he employed the talented writer and poet James Montgomery (1771–1854) as an assistant, and then increased his propaganda campaign by launching a fortnightly journal, the *Sheffield Patriot*, which explored political issues in more depth than the *Register*. Gales' optimism was rewarded and the sales of the *Sheffield Register* rose to two thousand.

CHAPTER 6
War with France 1793–1802

On 21 January 1793, the French revolutionary government executed Louis XVI (1754–1793). In response, Spain and Portugal entered the anti-French coalition in January 1793. Then, on 1 February 1793, France declared war on Great Britain and the Dutch Republic, signalling their interest in the Low Countries, with whom Britain had political and commercial interests; and so, in the space of one month, most of Europe was at war with the new republic. This was to have severe repercussions from Barnsley to Budapest.

Pitt, using the age-old technique of divide and rule, exploited the divisions in the radical ranks by labelling the 'physical force' adherents as Jacobins, attributing to them all the extreme measures adopted by the French Jacobins. When reinforced by a massive government campaign to enthuse the patriotic fervour of the nation, attitudes in Great Britain hardened against radicals and reform, and in the words of Major John Cartwright (1740–1824), 'Pitt was then able to enforce his own system of terror'.

The English Reign of Terror

In Sheffield, Gales' pro-French sentiments were considered treasonable, and he became a marked man. When the Sheffield Church and King Party marched through the town, to celebrate the victory of Admiral Lord Howe (1726–1799) over the French on 'The Glorious First of June 1794', they demonstrated outside Gales' house. Immediately, 'they were opposed by one hundred stout democrats', which rapidly grew to five hundred, as they sang Joseph Mather's version of the national anthem, which commences *'God save great Thomas Paine'*.[1]

Protest grew, and the radical associations of Britain organised a 'convention' in Edinburgh, which was broken up by the local authorities pursuing the government's vendetta against radicals. As a result, most of these associations went into abeyance. In Sheffield, the government action had the opposite effect; it inflamed the people and resulted in a series of mass meetings. In December 1793, there was a public meeting in the local park to call for parliamentary reform. On 28 February 1794, the SSCI organised a mass meeting at Backfields near West Street. It was opened with a hymn, written by James Montgomery, followed by a series of resolutions against war with France. On 7 April 1794, the SSCI held another mass meeting on Castle Hill. On this occasion, they supported an address to the King concerning those radicals imprisoned in Edinburgh. The government response was to imitate the French and introduce the 'English Reign of Terror', with the gibbet replacing the guillotine. It is difficult to know whether the government's reaction was due to genuine fear of a French style revolution in Britain, or an excuse to crack down on radical reform movements. Both views have their adherents, but the second motivation is gaining increasing support from historians.[2]

In May 1794, as a result of reports from government spies, regarding alleged movement of arms, two prominent members of the LCS were arrested in London. In order to legitimise their detention, the Home Office then rushed legislation through parliament to suspend Habeas Corpus (a law that prevents indeterminate detention without trial), an action to be repeated at frequent intervals during the next twenty-six years. With the new legislation in place, a further thirteen members of the LCS were arrested without charge. At the treason trial that followed, William Broomhead explained the motivation behind setting up the SSCI. He said this was:

> *To enlighten the people, to show the people the reason, the ground of all their complaints and sufferings; when a man works hard for thirteen or fourteen hours of the day, the week through, and is not able to maintain his family; that is what I understand of it, to show the people the ground of this, why they were not able.*[3]

In June 1794, Gales, having just avoided arrest on account of being away from home in Derby, decided to leave the country. He travelled to Germany, where he was later joined by his wife and four children. After his fifth child was born, the family emigrated to America, where Gales prospered and eventually became mayor of Raleigh, North Carolina, a post he held for seventeen years.

As a result, James Montgomery took over the *Sheffield Register* and changed its name to the *Sheffield Iris*. He continued Gales' radical policies and was twice imprisoned in York Castle. The first occasion was in January 1795 for three months, and again in January 1796 for six months. Both were on charges of sedition. As with so many sedition cases, charges were brought on the flimsiest pretext. During his second incarceration, he wrote a long poem entitled *The Pleasures of Imprisonment in Two Epistles to a Friend* that was published in *Prison Amusements* in 1797. The second verse reads:

> Each morning, then, at five o'clock,
> The adamantine doors unlock;
> Bolts, bars, and portals crash and thunder;
> The gates of iron burst asunder;
> Hinges that creak, and keys that jingle,
> With clattering chains, in concert mingle:
> So sweet the din, your dainty ear,
> For joy, would break its drum to hear;
> While my dull organs, at the found,
> Rest in tranquillity profound!
> Fantastic dreams amuse my brain,
> And waft my spirit home again:
> Though captive all day long, 'tis true,
> At night I am as free as you;
> Not ramparts high, nor dungeons deep,
> Can hold me - when I'm fast asleep! (Castle of York 14 June 1796)

(John Lindley and his companions were to experience the same feelings twenty-four years later.)

However, the two spells in prison seriously affected Montgomery's health and he moderated the tone of the *Sheffield Iris* until it became quite bland.

The terror that started in Sheffield spread. In Huddersfield, the local landowner and magistrate R. H. Beaumont, of Whitley Hall, ordered the arrest of the *Sheffield News* reporter on 6 June 1794. He was taken to York Castle in handcuffs, possibly for selling seditious pamphlets.[4]

In 1795, a local Huddersfield school teacher and noted Baptist, James Gledhill, was sent to York Castle accused of making seditious statements, namely the act of inciting or causing people to rebel against the authority of the state or monarch. This catchall accusation was frequently invoked to remove troublesome individuals from circulation, and create a 'culture of terror and intimidation'.[5]

However, as demonstrated in Sheffield, moral suasion by radicals was having no effect on the government's attitude to electoral reform – the government argued that all sections of society were represented in parliament and no electoral change was required. As a result of the general frustration in the radical ranks at the lack of progress, an irrevocable split began to appear regarding the question as to whether, in order to achieve their aims, they should continue to use peaceful constitutional means, or resort to physical force. This was a problem that was to beset radicals well into the nineteenth century, for while the middle-class elements of the Corresponding Societies argued for moral improvement of the poor by means of education, the labouring classes were hungry, impatient, and argued for force. Thomas Paine had reasoned that 'the way to end the criminality and barbarity of the poor, was to end poverty itself – education would then follow'.[6]

The Economic Crisis of 1794–6

While the inhabitants of the West Riding were largely insulated from the direct effects of the Revolutionary French War (many inhabitants of Mapplewell probably did not know that there was a war in progress), they were indirectly to experience the full consequences of a pan-European war.

In the year of John Lindley's birth, 1770, Britain became a net importer of cereals in order to feed the growing population, which was increasingly employed in the new expanding industries. Since there was no provision for the storage of one year's grain surplus to be carried over to the next, the nation depended from year to year on the productivity of each harvest. This meant that 'while any particular crisis was national, it was experienced regionally'. As a result, the populous towns and industrial villages of the West Riding of Yorkshire, along with south Lancashire and the Midlands, were among the first to suffer in times of shortage, for they were entirely dependent on the corn markets for their supply of bread.[7]

The first test of the new dependence on imports, to feed the nation in time of war, came at the end of the eighteenth century, when, following the slight recession in the textile industry of 1793-4, the 1794 harvest was 'substandard'. The supply of grain for the densely populated West Riding, with nearly half a million people in non-agricultural employment, came mainly from Lincolnshire, the North Riding and the East Riding. Local prices were heavily geared to the London prices, which responded to market fluctuations. During the exceptionally hard snowbound winter of 1794-5, the price of grain rose slowly, but the knock-on effect of the hard winter, and failure of the autumn sowing, was to produce a very low wheat crop in 1795. Suddenly, in July and August of 1795, absolute shortages were experienced. At Leeds, there was a complete lack of wheat and a bare sufficiency of oats.

Panic set in, but by substituting oats and barley for wheat and, when desperate, giving up cereals altogether, a subsistence diet was achieved. Yorkshire had a long tradition of eating oat cakes and barley bread, and so found it more acceptable than the poor southerners who had grown accustomed to white wheaten bread. But it was recorded in the *Leeds Intelligencer* (13 and 20 July 1795) that the public, forced to eat what they considered animal feed, 'loathed' the diet and 'resisted' whenever possible.[8]

The 1796 harvest was only average, but imported grain supplemented the deficit and prices gradually returned to normal, but the combination of two bad harvests, and the effect of continued war with France, (which restricted trade in British goods, particularly textiles, with the rest of continental Europe), resulted in the labouring classes in the 'industrial triangle of England' experiencing extreme poverty. As the price of grain increased (wheat rose from 43s a quarter in 1792 to 78s 7d a quarter in 1796 and bread from 6d to $9^1/_2$d for a 4lb loaf) there was general deterioration in the diet of the 'lower classes'. In extreme cases, people were reported to be reduced to eating nettles. The following story was not unique:

> *In the depths of the winter of 1794-5 two children were sent from Conisbrough [near Rotherham] to Tickhill, their settlement, to obtain a meal from a subscription charity. [This was a return journey of at least ten miles.] On their return they missed their road in the snow and one died during the night.*[9]

As a result of famine conditions there was unrest throughout the country, particularly in the West Riding. Food riots became commonplace and normally took two distinct forms. In the first case, market traders and shopkeepers were subject to the imposition of 'a fair price' on their goods, known as *taxation populaire*, copying the example of the French revolutionaries. At Shipley and Almondbury, apprentices attacked the premises of corn dealers, while the corn mill at Halifax was surrounded by an angry crowd when it was rumoured that the miller had raised his prices. In June 1795, there were two disturbances in Sheffield, while the people of Wakefield were urged to impose popular prices on commodities brought to market. In Ripon, order was only maintained by means of cavalry patrols.[10]

The second method of protest was to hijack food destined for a different village or town. For example, in early August the bread van from Oldham was attacked as it passed through Saddleworth. Later, the canal at Castleford and Knottingley was closed and the angry crowd seized the contents of the corn barges. These were all acts of desperation, but in fact both methods of protest were counterproductive, as *taxation populaire* only prevented farmers bringing their products to market, while hijacking food in transit only moved the problem from one district to the next.[11]

As might be expected, the ugliest incident occurred in Sheffield. On 4 August, a handbill had been posted which stated '…a plot has been discovered …to starve the poor into the army and starve your Widows and Orphans'. When the new infantry recruits paraded in the evening, a large crowd encouraged them to desert. The Volunteer Infantry was called out and their commanding officer, R.A. Athorpe, furiously rode twelve miles from Earl Fitzwilliam's mansion to take command, killing his horses in the process. 'When Athorpe failed to arrest a man for incitement he lashed out with his sabre…injuring several men women and children. The crowd then stoned the soldiers and continued to do so after Athorpe had read the riot act. Athorpe then ordered the troops to fire into the crowd. As a result two people were killed and many more injured.'[12]

The shootings, on 4 August, resulted in a large meeting a week later at Crooks Moor. The war with France was condemned and the meeting concluded 'with a call for peace, annual parliaments and universal suffrage'.[13]

Experiences such as those described above were to have a profound effect, 'economically, socially and politically', on the people of the West Riding, the memory of which lasted for many years as a 'folk memory', which lay at the heart of the radical working class of that county.[14]

The decline in the living standards of the poorest section of society can be measured by the soaring national death rate between 1795 and 1805, when the annual number of deaths in England increased from 216,000 to 275,000. Large sections of the population were going hungry (in France the peasants were starving); often they migrated from the countryside to the new industrial towns, where they became easy prey to the many diseases that flourished in the unsanitary conditions developing in the new urban slums.[15]

As might be expected, the response of the Home Office to the crisis was to ignore the social distress of the people and concentrate on suppressing the resulting civil unrest by intensifying the 'reign of terror'. Using the unruly meeting in London's Copenhagen Fields, followed by the famous attack on the King's coach on 29 October, as an excuse, Pitt's government introduced further legislation, in the form of the Seditious Meetings Act and the Treasonable Practices Act, commonly known as the 'Two Acts' or 'Gagging Acts'. These acts made actions against the King's person, or his heirs, capital offences and extended the law of treason to include inciting hatred of the King, his heirs, his government or the constitution. Although punishment for this lesser treason was transportation. (This law formed part of the indictment at the trial of the Yorkshire Rebels at York Castle in 1820.)

Francis Place, in the late 1790s, described what this meant for the common people: 'A disloyal word was enough to bring down punishment upon any man's head; laughing at the awkwardness of a volunteer was a criminal offence, people were apprehended and sent on board a [Royal Navy] 'man of war' for this breach of decorum, which was punished as a terrible crime.'[16]

In some cases, the conscience of the nation was touched, and private charity responded benevolently. For example: in 1795, Henry Yarbrough, of Heslington near York, rebuilt the ancient alms-houses and gave land for the village school. That same year, soup kitchens were started, funded by private donations or subsidised from the poor rate. Enormous amounts of private charity went into the relief of distress and more was contributed through the poor rates. One estimate is that in the first half of 1795, the first crisis of the war years, some fifteen to twenty per cent of the population received relief from one form of charity or another. This was the year that the Speenhamland system was introduced, and magistrates agreed to pay relief in proportion to the price of bread.[17]

The food crisis of 1794 to 1796 lasted eighteen months and the country just about survived, but not without much hunger and suffering by the labouring classes. By using direct relief in the form of a variety of expedients, from charitable hand-outs and soup kitchens, to importing grain as a response to riots, the authorities did just about enough to prevent outright starvation and a French-style revolution.[18]

The Economic Crisis of 1799–1801

In order to clamp down on radical agitation, Habeas Corpus was again suspended in 1798, followed in July 1799 by legislation that finally outlawed the LCS. As a consequence, radical discussions became more clandestine and revolutionary activity took on a more 'secret underground' existence. This minor political crisis was to develop into a major national food crisis.[19]

The crisis of 1799-1801 was far worse than that of 1794-1796. The summer of 1799 was cold and wet, with the result that the harvest in the Wolds and Holderness in the East Riding was a disaster. By March of 1800, prices of grain were rising and 'by May most of the West Riding was living from hand to mouth'. The summer in 1800 was hot and dry, promising a good harvest from spring-sown corn, but 'then in the third week in August the country was struck by two weeks of torrential rain'. This foretold disaster, as prices shot up and a second year of harvest failure lay ahead. Since the war with France continued, accompanied by economic depression, the government could and should have anticipated a subsistence crisis. In the West Riding alone, where the industrial population numbered half a million, all were dependent on food grown elsewhere. Hunger and poverty were widespread, and the needs of the poor outstripped the ability of the ratepayers to find sufficient money to support those wretched men, women, and children. As a result, the government had to make loans to the poorest parishes to prevent starvation. In a period of static wages, the price of bread leaped to 15½d a loaf. The historian Roger Wells has observed that 'the poor law was breaking under the strain and that the degree of desperation was a real threat to social stability'.[20]

The crisis started slowly in November 1799, with the women of Huddersfield rioting over the price of potatoes, while 'Hannah Bray with a 'large mob' of angry men and women hijacked a cart of wheat in Huddersfield market and sold it for six shillings a bushel'. For this crime she received a sentence of one year in York Castle.

Then, in April 1800, prices began to escalate, provoking riots in Sheffield, followed by more riots in Leeds which spread to Wakefield in May. However, it was not until there were price increases following the rain in August that the situation began to explode. As could be anticipated, Sheffield again led the way, when 'on August 27 an enormous crowd smashed flour dealers' windows'. It then took Earl Fitzwilliam (1748–1833), with the local volunteers, to prevent an even larger attack on the corn mills at Attercliffe on 2 September; for rioting was proving the most successful method available to the labouring classes of making their hunger known to the authorities. At the local level, the response was to control the crowds with Yeomanry Cavalry, comprised mostly of gentry and farmers, who established a repressive reputation. The use of Volunteer Infantrymen was less successful, for not only were they more unreliable, not wishing to confront their own community, they were subject to reprisals from their workmates, as the following report to the home secretary illustrates:

> ...*on Wednesday morning, one of the men who had paraded the preceding evening [2 Sept.], went to his workshop, the other workmen immediately beset him, took him by the heels and held...his head in a tub of water, till he almost drowned.*[21]

But unrest continued. Following the crisis of September 1800, further attempts were made in the West Riding to organise mass meetings to petition for peace and radical reform; but at Tickhill, Justice Taylor, supported by a troop of cavalry, went to the meeting point at Bagley Green and dispersed the petitioners as fast as they arrived.[22]

Once again, the government's response was to introduce yet further legislation in the form of the Combination Act of 1799 (replaced by an amending Act in 1800). This act restricted public meetings to fifty people, unless magistrates had given permission in advance; it also gave magistrates wide powers over the use of public lecture rooms, thereby curtailing the activities of radical lecturers.[23]

The threat of invoking the Combination Acts severely circumscribed the right of working people to meet together, or 'combine', thereby defending capitalist interests; significantly, they were never used against the employers who frequently 'combined' to create cartels. The Combination Act was a tactical mistake by the government, since by proscribing both political radicals and industrial trade unionists at the same time, they welded both movements into a common cause. This was very significant in the West Riding and was one of the major factors in the class war, which was to continue throughout the remainder of John Lindley's life.[24]

In response to the economic crisis, and in defiance of the Combination Act, a network of popular radical societies under the banner of 'United Britons' sprang up during 1801 and 1802, combining the politics of hunger with radical reform. These were essentially town associations whose formation was promoted and encouraged by Major John Cartwright, the great ex-parliamentary campaigner for universal suffrage. In Christopher Wyvill's words, they were 'more numerous, more zealous and more persevering than the 'Friends of Reform' in the Counties'. In Yorkshire, a more respectable 'Institution of Cloth Dressers' was formed, but the Combination Act eventually drove even this organisation underground.[25]

Union Societies aimed to promote cooperation between skilled workers and middle-class artisans, with the object of instigating parliamentary reform. Initially, they were peaceful radical organisations that aimed to extend the franchise by constitutional means. An extensive network of these unions existed in the industrial towns of northern England. But government intransigence, resisting all change, however small, proved frustrating to many members. As a consequence, the militants, who saw revolution and the use of physical force as the only means of making progress, began to develop a separate identity. The resulting rift between the proposed methods of the 'militants' and 'constitutionalists' caused them to diverge irrevocably, to the detriment of both.[26]

This frustration was expressed by the 'Friends of Liberty', who met on Steeton Moor near Keighley, on 20 April 1801, and rejected the idea of petitioning parliament for the redress of grievances. A handbill asked:

> *...and will you suffer yourselves to be thus imposed upon by a Majority of Mercenary Hirelings, Government Pimps, Corn-dealers, Place Men, Pentioners, Paracites etc. and yourselves starving for Bread.*[27]

Here was the genesis of revolution in the West Riding of Yorkshire.

One of the many clandestine republican groups that existed during this period was in Almondbury near Huddersfield. Members of this group are believed to have formed the instigators of the Yorkshire West Riding Revolt of 1820.

This group has been identified by a letter, dated January 1800, written by 'Citizen' James Gledhill of Battyeford (the district of Mirfield to which John Lindley was to move a few years later), found in the possession of Edmund Norcliffe of Almondbury in 1802. This Edmund Norcliffe is either the same individual, or a relative of John Lindley's close neighbour of the same name in Mirfield.

The letter from James Gledhill was written to 'My Good Friends' and states 'I have sent you my new song for the coming festival. I wish you to be so good as to read it to our friends at Almondbury. I think the composition is a good one and adds new merit to your friend'.

A patriotic song for the 14th July being the anniversary of the French Revolution by Citizen Gledhill

> Again all true patriots rejoice on the Day
> Which gave to fair Liberty Birth
> See the bright Star of freedom i[n]to (Beauties Display)
> View it all stationary on Earth
> Again let us join to extol that great Sower
> With which Gallia from Bondage arose
> So then cast down the Bastille, the Tyrants great Tower
> See them chastise their long cruel foes…

The Treaty of Amiens, signed 25 March 1802, formally ended eight years of war with France, but the peace was not to last and war resumed on 18 May 1803. The national focus on war, patriotism and rearmament, caused the Union Societies to collapse, as their aims became secondary to international concerns, with the government whipping up xenophobia by demonising Napoleon Bonaparte (1769–1821) and his regime. Furthermore, the inspiration furnished by the French republicans began to evaporate, as the 'French revolution' degenerated into a 'Napoleonic dictatorship'.

Characteristically, the British government had not relinquished its repressive stance, as the arrest of two United Britons in Sheffield, for possessing pikes in November 1802, demonstrates. But in general, while legal channels remained open, middle-class reformers were able to retain the support of moderate working-class radicals. At this stage, only a few of the 'physical force' revolutionaries joined the clandestine organisations that met in secret. Pitt's policy of repression against radicals continued, stirring up discontent, but it was the uncharacteristic disagreement with the King, over Catholic emancipation, that prompted his resignation on 14 March 1801, exhausted by seventeen years as first minister.[28]

However, Pitt's policy cast a lasting legacy that left an embittered population and, when he returned to office on 10 May 1804, he found the mood of the country completely changed and the strength of opposition in parliament greatly increased. The popular enthusiasm for war had declined and public opinion was becoming distinctly more antagonistic to reactionary government policy, while the number of 'secret underground' groups and their membership began to increase rapidly.

In the short term the food crisis passed, and the business cycle began an upward trend. This was greatly aided by Admiral Nelson's 'victory', on 2 April 1801, over the Danish fleet in the battle of Copenhagen. This destroyed the threat of an alliance between Denmark, Russia, Prussia and Sweden, thereby guaranteeing that the Baltic Sea would remain open for the export of textiles and import of naval stores, such as timber cordage and tar. This greatly benefitted the country as a whole, and Hull in particular, with its considerable Baltic trade. Hull was the third largest port in the country at that time and the gateway to Yorkshire. Once again, events in distant lands had significant effects on the daily lives of local West Riding communities.[29]

The mass movements of the 1790s in Yorkshire subsided, as food supplies once more returned to normal, but memories of conditions during that period left an indelible legacy of working-class identity that was to erupt during the years to come. In his famous book, *The Making of the English Working Class,* Professor E.P. Thompson identifies this period as one of the elements in the founding of the working-class movement. For John Lindley, in his twenties, living in Darton during this period, we can only guess the effect on his political thinking, but it is almost certain that this was a formative time in his life, which later expressed itself in radical action.[30]

CHAPTER 7
The Move to Mirfield 1802–1803

Mirfield in the First Decade of the Nineteenth Century

John's family could have expected to remain in Darton all their lives, but sometime between February 1802 and March 1806 (possibly during the brief peace of 1802-1803) they moved to the small market town of Mirfield, on the River Calder between Dewsbury and Huddersfield. This represented a move of about eleven miles (eighteen km) from Darton in a north-westerly direction. We know of this move, because parish registers record that John's eldest surviving son, John William, was baptised in Darton in February 1802, while his second eldest surviving son, Robert, was baptised in Mirfield in March 1806. It was a bold move to leave the hamlet of Broadroyd Head where he was surrounded by family and friends. During this period, before the days of welfare, community provided a mutual support system for the poor, and whereas a single person might survive in a new environment, to move with a wife and young family was most unusual.

Mirfield is a very ancient town. It is known that a temporary Roman fort existed at Kirklees, on the road between York (Eboracum) and Manchester, during the Roman occupation (73–410 CE). The site was chosen to dominate the ford crossing the River Calder at what is now Cooper Bridge. Over six hundred years later, it was described in the Domesday Book of 1086 as: 'Mirefelt: Six carucates of land, each as much as two oxen can plough in a year'. The post-conquest village developed around Castle Hall, a fortified manor, and the church of St Mary's, an ancient Saxon church rebuilt by the Normans in stone about 1261.[1]

The town was made up of six hamlets: Towngate, Easthorpe, Lee Green, Northorpe and Battyeford, on the north bank of the River Calder, and Hopton on the south bank. It is not known in which hamlet John's family settled when they first arrived, but in 1838 the family is definitely located at the Knowl in Battyeford, and it is most likely that this was where they settled on their arrival. Battyeford, formerly known as Far Side Moor, is a large sprawling area to the west of the town, as its former name implies. Mirfield was very much part of the West Riding woollen industry and, in 1801, according to the national census, there were 3,724 inhabitants, which was significantly larger than Darton with a population of 1,300 in that same year. Mirfield prospered largely due to its geographical position at the entrance to the Calder Valley, at the junction of the River Calder and River Colne at Cooper Bridge, and with its good access to Bradford and Leeds to the north, by both canal and road. Consequently, it became a centre of transport communication and its manufacturing base began to diversify, providing greater opportunity for employment. The establishment of a bank by Benjamin Wilson in 1799, later to become part of the Mirfield and Huddersfield District Bank, facilitated general commerce.[2]

Reason for Moving

Why did John move to Mirfield? The most probable answer is employment, since this was the principal reason for poor people moving from a familiar environment into the unknown, or perhaps he saw greater opportunities in this much larger town that was not so heavily dependent on nailing. Moving, particularly for families, was a major operation at the beginning of the nineteenth century, when all household goods would need to be carried by hand or hauled in a handcart. Fortunately, for John's family, the newly completed Barnsley Canal would have been available to carry heavy items – if he could afford the higher charge.

The Barnsley Canal linked the Aire and Calder Navigation, near Wakefield, and the Barnaby Basin at Barnsley. It was fourteen and a half miles long (twenty-three km), built in two stages; the northern stage, from the Aire and Calder Navigation to Barnsley, was started on 27 September 1793 and completed on 8 June 1799; the southern section, from Barnsley to Barnaby Basin, was started in 1798 and finished in 1802. The canal's main function was to carry coal from Barnsley to the industry of the West Riding. Also agricultural lime, in the reverse direction, from Knottingley to Barnsley.

It seems highly likely that John did not continue his trade as nail maker in Mirfield but found better paid work related to canal building or barge repair. There were three established boat yards in Mirfield and it is known that he was working on the 'navigation' when he was arrested in 1820. This may have been the canal itself or the 'navigation boat yard'.

Mirfield as a Centre of Communication – Canals

Canals were first built in England by the 3rd Duke of Bridgewater (1736–1803) and the civil engineer James Brindley (1716–1772). The duke used his considerable wealth and political influence to negotiate the acquisition of land. Brindley, a millwright by trade, carried out some of the design (although there is a dispute as to who was the principal designer), oversaw the construction work, and solved the numerous practical problems that occurred in this novel civil engineering project.

Their first canal was commissioned in 1759 to carry coal from Worsley to Manchester, and the aptly named Bridgewater Canal was completed in 1762. Since a canal horse-drawn barge was capable of carrying fifty tonnes, it was soon recognised that they were ideally suited for carrying heavy bulk items such as coal, iron, building materials and grain. As a result, the building of canals developed rapidly in the industrial regions of south Lancashire, the Midlands and west Yorkshire, and canals soon formed a network that covered the country. On the west coast, the Lancashire network found an outlet to the sea at Liverpool, while on the east coast the main outlet for Yorkshire was Hull. There were no less than 125 acts of parliament relating to canals, between 1750 and 1814, with a peak of fifty-one in the period 1790 to 1794. The canal network was the major factor that enabled Britain to move heavy raw materials overland and, as a consequence, 'pioneered the industrial revolution'.[3]

In Mirfield, the River Calder had been made navigable in 1764, when three sections of canal, the Battyeford, Mirfield and Greenwood cuts, were constructed to bypass shallows and loops in the river. This was part of the first phase of the Calder and Hebble Navigation from Wakefield to Brighouse. The second phase, from Brighouse to Sowerby, did not come into commercial operation until 1770, owing to a series of floods; then, by a series of improvements, over the next fifty-eight years, it became a major artery for the woollen towns of west Yorkshire. By the turn of the century, Mirfield was a busy point on the canal network, with as many as forty barges a day passing through the town. The size of the boats operating on the canal was limited to 57 feet 6 inches (17.5 m) in length and 14 feet (4.25 m) beam by the size of the locks. They were known as West Country Vessels and could carry between fifty and sixty tonnes. In addition to the through traffic, there were three boat yards, each with dry dock facilities and all requiring metal workers and nails. The closest yard to the Knowl was Battyeford, while in the middle of town was Ledgard yard (often referred to as Navigation yard) set up in the 1790s, and in the east was Shepley Bridge yard established in 1776.[4]

Of major importance to the prosperity of Mirfield was the construction of the Huddersfield Broad Canal, also known as Ramsden's Canal, which formed a junction with the Calder and Hebble Navigation at Cooper Bridge, Battyeford. The significance of the canal, built by Sir John Ramsden (1755–1839), was the fact that it linked up with the Huddersfield Narrow Canal and the 5,456 yard Standedge Tunnel (three miles completed in 1811) to Ashton-under-Lyne, and then to the network of canals around Manchester, so completing a third trans-Pennine route. Sir John Ramsden invested the income from his canal to buy land, and by 1880 the Ramsden family estate controlled most of the land around Huddersfield. This was typical of the new industrialists who made their money from trade but invested in land.[5]

Turnpike Roads

Historically, goods and people had travelled whenever possible by sea or navigable river, 'the great highways' in pre-industrial Britain. Travel by road for inland destinations was only used if absolutely necessary. However, since the departure of the Romans in 410 CE, maintenance of English roads had a poor record. By the Tudor period, attempts were made to improve the road system to enable waggons to replace trains of packhorses. It was calculated that a horse pulling a cart could transport a much greater load than in panniers on its back.

In 1555, the Highways Act was passed, requiring that every parish should annually select two surveyors to supervise the mending of local roads. Every parish was required to provide two able-bodied men for four days' labour to carry out the task; those who were landless had to do the work themselves or provide substitutes. This act proved unsatisfactory, because frequently it was simply ignored. The act was patently unjust, since it bore heavily and unfairly on parishes with major roads running through them, particularly those which carried heavy waggons (for example the iron wain from Wortley forge), which caused so much damage by gouging out deep ruts that sunk wheels up to their axles. Eventually, a system of payment by tolls was imposed on users, to defray the costs of maintenance.[6]

By the time John moved to Mirfield, road transportation was well developed in the form of turnpike roads (toll roads). These roads were substantial enough to be used by the heavy waggons, which being more efficient justified the extra expense. Turnpikes also enabled coach services to be established – these coaches were lighter and faster than waggons and provided the fastest method of passenger transport at this time. From 1784, a system of mail coaches was instigated, which enabled Royal Mail coaches to carry the mail at an average speed of eight miles an hour and maintain a strict timetable. It soon became a major offence to hinder 'the mail'. For example:

> *On Saturday last [29 November 1828] James Baines, coachman of the Accommodation coach, between Huddersfield and Manchester, was fined £10 by the magistrates of Huddersfield, for wilfully running against, and crossing the mail coach at Marsden, on Thursday 27 November, being the second time he has been fined for so misconducting himself.*[7]

Mail coaches also carried wealthy passengers, and the Post Office supplied guards in scarlet livery to protect the mail and passengers from highwaymen.[8]

Locally, the Dewsbury to Elland turnpike road, which ran through Mirfield, was completed in 1763. This was followed, in 1765, by the widening and improvement of the Nun Brook to Birstall Road, which ran from the turnpike at Nun Brook to the Coach and Horses public house at Birstall. The Three Nuns public house, just north of Cooper Bridge, was to become an important coaching inn. When the Doncaster to Manchester Light Coach route opened in 1790, Mirfield could be said to be on the national coaching network and, by 1830, when John had returned from Van Diemen's Land, four services were in operation, linking Mirfield to Leeds, Manchester, Halifax, Todmorden and Wakefield. Furthermore, he returned to Battyeford in time to see the new road constructed in 1840.[9]

Mirfield as a Manufacturing Town – Industry

In 1770, Mirfield was an agricultural community that supplemented its income by producing woollen textiles, as it had done since the thirteenth century. As with most of the West Riding, the soil around Mirfield was poor and only a dual economy, based on agriculture and local cottage industry, was viable.

The development of Mirfield was initially aided by its location, and the availability of water, both for transporting heavy goods and for powering water wheels. Unfortunately, in common with many other inland rivers, the Calder had a tendency to dry up in summer and frequently formed shallows that boats were unable to navigate. However, there is a limit to the industrial expansion that can be sustained by packhorses and drove roads over moorland. Nevertheless, turnpike roads had produced a satisfactory system for conveying people and light goods during most of the eighteenth century. But what was really needed was the ability to transport heavy goods, and the canal network attempted to address this problem.

Soon after John's birth it became apparent, as a result of inventive applications of James Watt's steam engine (patented 1769), particularly in the cotton industry of Lancashire, that steam power could be applied, not only to pumping water from deep mines, but also to driving machinery that manufactured goods. Gradually, the factory system evolved, which began to change working lives. Wherever coal and water were to be found in advantageous juxtaposition industry flourished.

Unfortunately, the introduction of industry had its downside. The Rev. Ismay (1708–1790), rector of St Mary's Church, reported in his diary that the variety of fish and birds, which had included: salmon, trout, smelt, grailing, daice, perch, eels, chub, barbeles and gudgeon, and in winter, wild duck, widgeon, teal, coots and several varieties of water hen, were seen to disappear from the banks of the polluted River Calder.[10]

Coal

Like Barnsley, Mirfield also lay on the great Yorkshire coalfield, and one of the earliest records of mining dates from 1668, when coal pits on Mirfield Moor were leased to Edward Copley. It was this combination of local coal and river water to produce steam that powered first the Newcomen, and later the more efficient Watts-Boulton steam engines, which came to be used extensively in all stages of manufacture in the textile industry. Importantly, steam engines facilitated the economic pumping of water from deep mines, particularly tin mines, but also coal mines. They were also used to access bulk raw materials and deliver finished products via the canal system, which received a big boost when steam tugs were introduced on the Aire-Calder Navigation in 1831. It is therefore not surprising that Mirfield's woollen and cotton mills flourished in the valley on the banks of the River Calder and Calder-Hebble Canal.[11]

Woollen Mills

In the scattered farms and hamlets around Mirfield, the 'woollen industry' took the form of spinning wool. This was usually carried out by women, and weaving cloth was usually carried out by men, all in their own cottages, which continued well into the nineteenth century. The distribution of raw wool, collection and payment for the woven 'pieces', was the task of middlemen who called on a weekly basis. The woven 'pieces' then required fulling. This is a process by which the cloth is mixed with clay and pounded by heavy wooden hammers to give the cloth its 'body'. This was one of the first processes in England to be mechanised, and Roger the fuller is recorded as early as 1297 in the Wakefield Court Rolls. By 1755, there were three fulling mills in Hopton all using water power. This was the 'putting out system' of manufacture.[12]

The development of new power-driven mechanical techniques, in the eighteenth century, stimulated the growth of the woollen industry and influenced the move from domestic to factory production. For example, hand weaving required two weavers throwing the shuttle from side to side to operate a loom, but the flying shuttle, patented by John Kay (1704–1779), in 1733, allowed one man to weave broadcloth single-handed. The scribbling engine, which carded the wool (straightened it out), was the first of the new developments to have power applied and was easily incorporated into existing fulling mills. By 1802, there were five such mills in Mirfield. Meanwhile, from the 1770s, the hand powered spinning jenny was used for wool spinning, although it was not until the development of the automatic spinning-mule, in the 1820s, that the process could be mechanised. Mechanised power was also introduced into the finishing process (napping) that had traditionally used teasels to raise the nap of the fabric and heavy hand shears to crop the raised fibres to the required even finish.[13]

One of the first woollen mills in Mirfield was Hopton Mill, where Henry Wheatley began manufacturing cloth at Woodlands in 1790 and, by 1815, he was exporting to America. Originally powered by a waterwheel, around 1802, it became one of the first mills in the area to be converted to steam. Coal was obtained from the company's own mine and water from its own reservoirs. They even produced their own gas for lighting. This was typical of the Victorian Self-Help movement promoted by Samuel Smiles (1812–1904).[14]

Corn Mills

In the eighteenth century, the Rev. Ismay wrote that there were three corn mills in Mirfield. They were probably: Ledgard Mill, said to date from the seventeenth century and the oldest of the three, in the east was the mill at Low Bridge, near Shepley Bridge, and (as its name implies) West Mill, at Battyeford, was the third. In the nineteenth century, a fourth mill at the bottom of Bracken Hill was added. When John arrived in Mirfield, the West Mill in Battyeford had been occupied by Samuel Brook since 1801. Brook had insured the mill, which had 'no kiln or steam engine', for eight hundred pounds, and the waterwheel and machinery inside for a further eight hundred, which gives some idea of the capital employed (John's family would have done well to have had an income of fifty pounds p.a.). Brook also occupied the adjacent scribbling, carding and fulling mills, so he was quite a rich man.[15]

Malt Production

As well as being noted for its textile manufacturing, Mirfield was also well known as a centre for producing malt. Mirfield's early maltsters were farmers, who used locally grown and germinated barley to make malt – the raw material of brewing. Brewing ale and beer was a very important industry, whether carried out locally or commercially, as they represented foodstuffs that were safer than drinking water or spirits. With the arrival of the canal in the late eighteenth century, it became possible to produce malt commercially and, as a result, a breed of barley farmers evolved who employed large kilns to produce bulk malt. This enabled the Mirfield maltsters to import barley from other parts of Yorkshire, Norfolk and Lincolnshire. For this reason, the maltsters were located alongside the canal and later the railway. In 1819–20, there were six maltsters in the town. In particular, the firm of J.K. and J. Crowther Ltd dates back to the late eighteenth century, when John Crowther set up in business. After his death, his wife took over running the firm and was later joined by James Firth Crowther. Once again, the ability to transport heavy goods, cheaply, and in bulk, was paying dividends.[16]

John's Family in Mirfield

How did the move to Mirfield affect John's family? There were great similarities between Barnsley, of which Darton was a parish, and Mirfield. The dual economy of Barnsley was based on agriculture and linen weaving with the additional speciality of nail making. Mirfield's was based on agriculture and woollen weaving but arguably had better communications. By 1805, there was a diversity of nascent industry, which allowed far greater employment opportunities in Mirfield than in Darton. Both had the natural availability of coal and the man-made canal system that enabled the transportation of heavy goods. But while Mirfield was at the major junction of the Aire and Calder Navigation and the Huddersfield Narrow Canal, Darton was situated on a blind limb.

Canals were to play an important part in the lives of John Lindley and his family. They provided John's son Robert with the opportunity to escape the family tradition of nail making, first as a bargee, then as a barge owner. Eventually, he became a relatively wealthy artisan, able to provide financial support for his parents when his father returned from Van Diemen's Land.

It is also significant that Ann, born in 1808, and the only surviving daughter, went into domestic service and eventually became a housekeeper. Little is known about the youngest son, Joseph, who was born in Wakefield in 1812 and was employed as a general labourer in 1861.

Education in Mirfield

Were the educational opportunities improved for the children of John and Hannah by moving to Mirfield? Historically it had a free school. Richard Thorpe of Hopton Hall, a local parson of independent means, endowed the school in 1667 with five pounds per year for the education of fifteen poor children 'till they could read English well'. Further bequests from other benefactors allowed an additional five children to be educated. Fee paying children were also accepted when the school was enlarged in 1706. Its first teacher was the Rev. Samuel Peart, curate of the parish church. It is possible that John's children attended this school, since it was close to Knowl Nook where the family are believed to have lived during this period.[17]

Mirfield also had a dame school, situated in Towngate, which was run by Mary Frost until she drowned herself in 1750. No doubt she was replaced by other distressed gentle folk who frequently became teachers.[18]

The great educational difference for John's children was that Mirfield was a larger town than Darton with greater educational opportunities. In addition, by 1805, the Sunday School Movement was well established and John's children were more fortunate than their parents, as they would have been able to learn to read and write at a Nonconformist Sunday school or Bible Society. The Sunday School Movement had been founded by Robert Raikes (1736–1811) of Gloucester, in about 1780, and the movement spread rapidly throughout the country. At these schools, 'children (and adults) could learn reading, writing and arithmetic, with some religious and moral teaching thrown in, for the long morning and afternoon sessions included attending a place of worship during service time.' Sunday schools were the common means for teaching many thousands of poor children to learn to read and write before the Education Act of 1870.[19]

It was an ambitious Tory clergyman, the twenty-two-year-old Rev. Hammond Roberson, who, soon after his arrival as curate of Dewsbury in 1779, introduced what has been claimed to be the first Sunday school in the north of England. He soon had hundreds of children, and a substantial number of illiterate adults, attending his Sunday schools, which were established throughout the district in makeshift premises. So, the spirit of education reached the West Riding at about the time John would have been learning to read and write. But Dewsbury was just too far from Darton (where John was living at that time) for him to be directly influenced by Hammond Roberson. This was probably fortunate for John and his family, as Roberson's aim was to reclaim people, who could not afford schooling, for the established Church of England. The West Riding had been visited many times by John Wesley; for example, he visited 'Sheffield on at least thirty-two occasions between 1742 and 1788' with the result that in the industrial districts of Yorkshire, those people who professed religious beliefs at all were predominantly Methodist.[20]

There were of course public schools for boys, and academies for young ladies, such as Roe Head School in Mirfield, attended by the Brontë sisters, but these were completely outside the educational environment likely to have been attended by John Lindley's family.

It has been claimed by Professor E.P. Thompson that, with the rise of the radical movement, a more egalitarian spirit was engendered among the working class, and the condescension of the eighteenth century became unacceptable. As a result, the radical

Sunday School Movement developed, with one of its main aims to combine literacy and numeracy with political awareness.[21]

Thompson's opinion may have been true in the general community, but in the workplace the implacable ideas of subordination remained. As Francis Place said:

> *I can remember the time when to be able to read, and indulge in reading, would, if known to a master tradesman, have been so serious an objection to a journeyman, that he would scarcely have expected to obtain employment.*[22]

Modern readers who find Francis Place's statement incredible should note that the Northern Star printed the following article from its Huddersfield correspondent on 21 January 1843:

> *About two miles south of Huddersfield a number of young men or youths – in the employ of several mill owners, professedly religious, and pillars of their respective establishments, have preferred of late years literary pursuits to beer house conversation, and for the prosecution of which have contributed to the extent of their means, money to purchase books. They regularly meet, read, converse and improve each other in the best manner they can, and have so far succeeded to astonish not only their parents but all who know them. The surprise spread rapidly among the more influential, among whom were their employers, who instead of being proud to have such men in their employ and supplying them with the means of extending their pursuit, not only condemned their intellectual acquirements, but issued a declaration to their parents that if they allowed their sons to improve themselves, they would not only discharge the youths but them also.*[23]

Religion

The schism of the Christian Church into The Established Anglican Church that supported, and was supported by the landowning classes, and the Nonconformist denominations that voiced dissent, not only in religion but also in politics, because they were excluded by the Test Acts, became very bitter during this period. The origin of dissent stemmed from the translation of the Bible into English by John Wycliffe (1330–1384), who claimed that the Bible was the sole guide for Christian doctrine. This implied that bishops, the clergy and the whole structure of the established Church were redundant. It could also imply that the head of the Church, the King, was also redundant, giving rise to republicanism.

During John Lindley's lifetime, regardless of denomination, the Christian Bible was considered to be literally true, with the Earth created on the nightfall preceding 23 October 4004 BCE, as calculated by Archbishop James Ussher (1581–1656), the primate of all Ireland, and written in his book *Annals of the Old Testament, deduced from the first origins of the world*, published in 1650, and its continuation, published in 1654. It was not until Sir Charles Lyell (1797–1875), a Scottish surveyor, produced *Principles of Geology* in 1830-33 and Charles Darwin (1809–1882) published *On The Origin of Species* in 1859 and *The Descent of Man* in 1871, that an intellectual alternative became credible.

However, it should be remembered that in the nineteenth century most people considered themselves Christian, even if more than half of the labouring classes did not attend either church or chapel. In small towns like Mirfield, the 'church' in all its forms played a central role in both the intellectual and social life of the people, and at the Knowl in Mirfield this was the Wesleyan Methodist Church, built in 1780 and well established by 1805. The alternative social meeting place was the ale house, and it was here that discontent was expressed and radical politics discussed.

A short distance from the Knowl was the Moravian Chapel. The Moravian Protestant Sect, who originated in Bavaria in the late fourteenth century, had first established themselves at Wellhouse in 1743. They then built a new chapel and boarding school in 1801, with places for twenty-five boarders. It was at this school that James Montgomery, the famous editor of the radical *Sheffield Iris*, later poet and hymn writer, spent eighteen months in 1787, before starting an apprenticeship as a baker in Mirfield. In his lifetime, Montgomery wrote over 4,000 hymns, of which the best remembered are *Angels from the Realms of Glory* and *Hail to the Lord's Anointed*. Probably, the most famous scholar to be educated at Wellhouse School was the Liberal statesman Henry Herbert Asquith (1852–1928) who became prime minister of Great Britain (1908–1916).[24]

Health

Any improvement in health during this period is difficult to distinguish. The perception of a healthy environment was growing, with the benefit of clean air and water becoming apparent. At this point, it may be interesting to observe the advertisement for the Moravian school that has just been described:

> *Wellhouse Academy in the extensive and respectable Village of Mirfield, which has long been noted for its beautiful and healthy situation in the picturesque valley of the Calder.*

Of course, vaccination was available but since it was not enthusiastically taken up in England the death toll continued. The vicar of Darton recorded, in 1810, that 'several died of smallpox' that year. Any gain in general health was offset by the growth of disease-ridden slums in the great cities of Leeds, Bradford, and Halifax. In these towns, the death toll of the working masses reached horrendous levels, as agricultural labourers migrated to the towns in search of better paid work.

CHAPTER 8
Growth of Radical Politics 1802 -1810

The Making of a Revolutionary

It was the accident of birth near Barnsley and relocation to Mirfield, both centres of radical militancy, which was to set the pattern of John Lindley's life. To understand how this came about, it is necessary to record something of the seismic change to working practices, and the political upheaval that resulted from those changes in and around Huddersfield during his lifetime. In addition to recorded incidents, a great deal of John Lindley's history can only be implied from the knowledge of his environment. The details of his nail making origin have already been examined at some length, and the traumatic years of the last decade of the eighteenth century have also been explored. It is now time to move on to the first decade of the nineteenth century and examine the general economic situation in the north of England during this period.

As John Lindley approached manhood, in the last decade of the eighteenth century, he found himself living in what proved to be a watershed in both the political and economic life of England. During his lifetime, he witnessed the painful development of what became known as the Industrial Revolution; this revolution was to profoundly change the lives of labouring men, women and children beyond all recognition.

Industrial Revolution

Three great events were to define John Lindley's life, all of which occurred before he was old enough to appreciate their significance. Perhaps it is only with hindsight that people began to realise the impact of the patent of James Watt's steam engine in 1769. This invention, which greatly improved the efficiency of Thomas Newcomen's beam engine, marked the start of the Industrial Revolution, with the world relying on fossil fuels for power, instead of muscle power of men and draught animals. However, despite its inefficiency and unreliability, there were a few Newcomen steam engines operating in Yorkshire in the late eighteenth century. The entire nineteenth century was dedicated to the gradual change from manpower and horsepower to machine power – driven by steam. As a result, centuries of common practice and methods of work were swept away, with resulting social turmoil. A new class of people emerged – the industrialists and the *haute bourgeoisie* – who challenged the power of the landed aristocracy; while agricultural labourers, the handloom weavers, the coal miners and the domestic servants became the new white slaves of the industrial capitalist economic system.

The greatest impact of this 'revolution' was felt in those parts of the country having readily available access to coal and iron. As George Orwell (1903-1950) was to comment more than 150 years later, 'Our civilisation…is founded on coal...the machines that keep us alive, and the machines that make the machines, are all directly or indirectly dependent on coal.…The coalminer is second in importance only to the man who ploughs the soil.' These areas included south Wales, central Scotland, West Midlands, south Lancashire, northeast England and, most significantly for this history, the West Riding of Yorkshire. The new concentrations of population and industry in these areas produced new social relationships, which resulted in a great upsurge in radical thought and action between 1770 and 1850.[1]

The changes began with the introduction of simple pieces of technology into homes and small workshops, which developed into small factories and then ever larger factories – there was a climate of invention and innovation at this time that pervaded the manufacturing districts of England. Suddenly, the eighteenth century ethos of paternalistic decentralised government began to give way to utilitarianism and an unbridled capitalist system of laissez-faire. This followed the economic teaching of Adam Smith, often regarded as the founder of modern economics. His ideas, expounded in *An Inquiry into the Nature and Causes of the Wealth of Nations* (1776), were readily adopted by the new *bourgeoisie*, for it freed them from all restraint and allowed them to exploit their workers in an unprecedented manner, supported by the law of the land when necessary. Laissez-faire swept away customary practice and exposed working people to the harsh discipline of factory environments and unpredictable economic cycles that were alien to them. Agricultural cycles were the wrath of God – economic cycles were the wrath of man.

In the Pennine region of England, where the soil was too poor to sustain the population by agriculture alone, a dual economy had evolved over the centuries, whereby people supplemented their income with that from cottage industries, in particular spinning and handloom weaving. For centuries, this 'domestic work' had been carried on by the 'putting-out' system, a method of subcontracting, whereby the weaver bought his yarn on a weekly basis and made his cloth on his own premises, as and when he chose. In the late eighteenth century, the utilitarian approach to production of maximising efficiency and resulting profits, extolled by Jeremy Bentham (1748–1832), meant that the process of handloom weaving, while still carried out in weavers' cottages (cottages both built and owned by merchant capitalists), left the weavers totally dependent on those who controlled the supply of raw material and bought back the finished product. The manufacturers also frequently owned and rented all or part of the looms the weavers worked. So, while the weavers were poor, hardworking disenfranchised men and women, the manufacturers were rich, often very rich landlords, with a vote in the county of Yorkshire and a say in the running of local affairs.[2]

Enclosure

To compound the problem, the enclosure boom of 1793–1815, a direct result of the French Wars, and the resulting increase in the price of corn, saw three million acres of open fields transferred from common to private ownership. Eighteen hundred enclosure acts were passed between 1796 and 1815. These were private acts of parliament that overrode the opposition of private individuals to the enclosure of common land. Each individual had to be content with land or money. Compensation was awarded by parliamentary commissioners, whose decision was final, and had the force of law. These decisions invariably favoured the rich at the expense of the poor.

Chapter 8

During the latter part of the eighteenth century, agricultural output increased by forty per cent, and was an important factor in sustaining an increased population that was essential to provide labour for the Industrial Revolution. There is continuing debate as to how much of this increased agricultural output was due to enclosure, since there was considerable vested interest in proclaiming the benefits. Not only did the landed gentry gain, much work was generated for land agents and lawyers, and numerous members of the struggling clergy were able to move into the lower gentry, as their tithes were commuted to land holdings.[3]

The social changes were profound. For centuries, every parish had owned common land on which the parishioners could graze their cattle and pigs and allow their poultry to scratch a living. But land that was held in common and was no single individual's responsibility easily became neglected. This was particularly true in parishes of the West Riding, where subsistence increasingly centred on industry, particularly weaving, rather than agriculture. A year before John Lindley's birth, the agricultural pioneer Arthur Young, a great advocate of enclosure, published his *A Six Weeks Tour through the Southern Counties of England and Wales* (1769). This book extolled the virtues of modern farming methods – in particular, the benefit of manure on arable land and the use of seed drills. While this advice had great influence on farming methods in the agricultural south of England, it was often quite inappropriate on the Pennine slopes of Yorkshire and Lancashire.

However, the tragedy of enclosure was not that it changed the old basis of farming and land tenure – which increasingly failed to meet the needs of an expanding population – but that it was done without making provision for that continuing stake in the soil for the majority of people, which in the past had made the English a nation of 'free' men. When the parliamentary commissioners offered a poor commoner a few years' purchase of his hereditary rights of grazing and cutting turf for fuel, they were depriving unborn generations of their economic liberty. This was conveniently forgotten by an aristocracy and gentry who exercised unhindered legislative powers in parliament and who, in their selfish desire to enrich themselves, thereby deprived the common people of their heritage, all under the pretext of eliminating wasteful and obstructive farming methods of the past. The 'theft' of this common land still echoes in the twenty-first century with the fight for 'the right to roam'. Vast areas of moorland were enclosed to produce shooting reserves and game parks for the aristocracy and the very rich. These estates deprived the majority of recreational open spaces and frequently disrupted communities, by severing easy access to nearby villages and towns, since it was not permissible to cross private land.

An example of how the enclosure system operated is well illustrated by the enclosure in Mirfield, where an act was presented in 1796, supervised by three commissioners. They awarded:

> *To Mr Savile, Lord of the Manor, in compensation for his right and interest in the soil of the Commons, one sixteenth part of the said common.*
> *To Reverend Matthew Cookson, Vicar, such land as is equal to the value of the Vicarage Tithes.*
> *To Sir George Armytage, Bart. (1761–1836) all residue, in lieu of, and in compensation for his Greater Rectorial Tithes.*
> *In recompense all tithes were extinguished – this was a general benefit [but all tithes were to be abolished in John Lindley's lifetime regardless of enclosure]. The award was finally made in 1806 enclosing 491 acres, 3 rods, 25 poles of land.*[5]

Enclosure transformed centuries of traditional agricultural practice and turned a 'free' people into dependent peasants. The loss of common grazing rights meant that it was no longer possible for ordinary people to subsist off their smallholdings, thereby causing them to lose their independent means of sustenance. Since the total cost of enclosing land was as much as twelve pounds per acre (five pounds per hectare), many small farmers who could not afford the cost were reduced to becoming farm labourers, working for those who had benefitted from 'the theft' of their common land. A more serious problem, particularly in the Pennines, was the situation of those who lived off the 'wastes' to which they had no title. They were reduced to agricultural day labourers, with a very uncertain wage, or joining the swelling ranks of the destitute urban poor. Not surprisingly, this exacerbated the social unrest of the period, since not only labourers but also craftsmen became entirely dependent on wages.[6]

As a result, crime rose substantially, particularly between 1815 and 1830. By definition, crime was something the poor carried out against the rich. 'While landowners, magistrates, the clergy and poor-law officials committed 'institutional crime' against the poor, the latter resorted to writing threatening letters, maiming of animals, machine-breaking and arson.'[7]

In the wake of enclosure new jobs were created, since there were fences and stone walls to be built, new farmhouses to be erected, ditching and drains to be dug, watercourses to be diverted and roads laid out, all of which resulted in a mini boom for construction workers. However, wages for these 'new jobs' were low, since with so many displaced men and women there was an oversupply of labour, and when the construction work was complete these jobs disappeared. Furthermore, in the Pennines, much of the enclosed land was converted to permanent pasture, so that the actual demand for agricultural labour was greatly reduced on the new enclosed farms.

Since John Lindley and his family moved to Mirfield at the time that the Enclosure Act was implemented there, the resulting 'employment boom' may offer an alternative explanation as to why his family moved from Darton at this time.

A profound effect of enclosure that is not always realised was its effect on leisure. During John's early years, it was customary to hold village festivals, including church processions and feasts, all of which were celebrated in the open air between Easter and the harvest festival, with accompanying fairs on Staincross Common or Darton Common. These fairs would have included travelling showmen, pedlars' stalls, various musicians, menageries, human and animal curiosities, dancing, wrestling, perhaps a football match, and of course a large amount of drinking. With the law turning a blind eye for the duration of the 'celebration', these events acted as a magnet, drawing everyone in the district together, and as such formed part of the local culture, providing a useful safety valve allowing people 'to let off steam'.[8]

With the enclosure of common land, such events became dependent on the whim of the local gentry who now controlled the recreational spaces, and eventually the type of activity permitted. The 'quality' became less inclined to permit and join in traditional juvenile games and pranks; while harvest suppers, clipping suppers and 'hopper feasts' were gradually suppressed as patronage was withdrawn. Now, only the squire's hunt was permitted to ride over private property with impunity (often destroying crops in their wake), as they pursued their quarry.[9]

Riots that took place in Sheffield, resulting from enclosure, were symptomatic of the general decline in the subservience to authority. Many further acts of defiance took place throughout Yorkshire, and there is a tantalising entry in the *Leeds Mercury* 5 June 1809 of a

Mirfield blacksmith who, on being balloted into the militia, refused to take the oath. Could this have been John Lindley, nail maker, who was living at the Knowl in 1809?[10]

Insurrection in Yorkshire

With the return to something like normality in 1802, the Yorkshire magistracy assumed that the improvement in wages and food supply would satisfy 'the lower orders'. But a small group of hard-core Yorkshire Radicals, remembering their experience of the 1790s, went 'underground' and began to develop insurrectionary tactics.[11]

Early attempts to introduce cheap labour and machinery into the woollen district of the West Riding had been discouraging for the owners. In 1799, a gig mill (a water powered revolving cylindrical drum that raised the nap of the cloth prior to cropping) was destroyed at Holbeck, and in 1801 Benjamin Gott (1762–1840) was forced to remove a gig mill in Leeds.[12]

As conditions improved in the summer of 1802, Gott tried to employ two apprentices at his Bean Ing factory in Leeds who were over the age of fourteen, which was the maximum age allowed by the Elizabethan statute. In response, all his eighty croppers handed in their notice, thereby bringing the entire factory employing over one thousand workers to a halt. Here, Gott was up against the shearmen's trade union, the so-called 'Brief Institution', founded in 1796 in Yorkshire and subsequently outlawed by the Combination Act of 1799. The union was formed to aid communication between isolated groups and enable concerted action in the case of disputes. It produced membership cards, available only to fully qualified men, and enforced closed shops. It combined the financial resources of the whole region to back local disputes.[13]

Specifically, it aimed to uphold the Act 5 & 6 Edward VI cap 22 (1505/6) 'An act for putting down gig mills' and the Act 5 Elizabeth cap 4 (1564) 'An act for fixing apprenticeships in the woollen industry.' The first act had the objective of preventing mechanical teasing of cloth, and the second the object of excluding men who had not served a seven year apprenticeship and other unskilled workers from the trade.[14] It is claimed that Queen Elizabeth I (1533–1603) when asked to grant a patent for a new stocking loom, stated:

> *I have too much love for my poor people who obtain their bread by the employment of knitting to give my money to forward an invention that will tend to their ruin by depriving them of employment and thus make them beggars.*[15]

The West Riding cloth workers 'Institution' went on the offensive when trade improved after the Treaty of Amiens. In 1802, there were strikes in Huddersfield against the use of gig mills, but these strikes did not deter the employers from installing more machines as boom conditions returned.[16]

Far more serious was the successful strike, led by croppers, at the totally unionised Bean Ing Factory in Leeds. When Gott openly introduced a few gig mills into this factory he had the windows of his house broken as a warning.

In 1803, gig mills were introduced by William Horsfall into the Ottiwells Mill at Marsden and by Thomas Atkinson into Bradley Mill, near Huddersfield; and both mills were suddenly destroyed by mysterious fires. However, Horsfall and Atkinson both claimed that they were not the result of arson attacks, which may have been true, for greasy wool is very inflammable. In fact, while trade was flourishing and there was plenty of work for croppers, shearing frames and gig mills were insidiously introduced, thereby increasing output and enabling the woollen industry to meet the continuously expanding demand of foreign markets.[17]

However, it was only when the British government introduced the infamous Orders in Council from 1807 onwards, in response to Napoleon's Berlin Decree, that the export trade collapsed and the employers regained the initiative.[18]

The Berlin Decree was introduced by Napoleon in November 1806. The decree closed all European ports to British shipping, and even barred ships of any nationality that had touched a British port. The British government responded by introducing twenty-four Orders in Council that were to affect not only neutral European ports, but also those of America, which was fast becoming Britain's largest export market. Britain's exports to America in 1810 were just over eleven million pounds; in 1811 they fell to just under two million pounds, as America retaliated with the Non-Intercourse Act. It was no consolation to the workers of Yorkshire and Lancashire that the Americans suffered equally through the loss of trade – particularly their merchant fleet, which had grown to the second largest in the world.[19]

These great international decrees had an immediate effect on the local people in and around Mirfield. Within weeks, unsold cloth began to pile up in warehouses, workers were 'laid off' and commerce collapsed. In the following months 1,330 West Riding manufacturers, out of a total of 3,200, were forced to close. To compound the problem, the poor harvest of 1810 was followed by a disastrous harvest in 1811.[20]

William Cartwright first introduced a shearing frame for finishing cloth into his Rawfolds Mill near Liversedge in 1808 or 1809. The mill was powered by water from the River Spen, which was held in a dam running the full length of one side of the building. The shearing frames that he introduced were a late eighteenth century invention, which consists of two pairs of shears, mounted on a wooden frame or carriage, running on wheels, which move across the cloth shaving the nap mechanically. These new machines increased the speed of the process by which woven cloth was 'cropped', and the nap trimmed, by a factor of between five and ten times. Furthermore, they could be operated by unskilled labour. The new machines did not give the cloth such a good finish as the handmade product, but machine-made cloth was far cheaper to produce. This was the foundation of the 'new' factory system with quantity taking precedence over quality. But the crisis of 1811 was to expose the weakness of mechanisation; suddenly Cartwright had a highly capital-intensive productive method of manufacture, but no market. So began the boom and bust cycle that was to expose the great problem of unregulated laissez-faire economies, that of finding a large stable market.[21]

True to the zeitgeist of the late eighteenth century, two Yorkshire brothers, James and Enoch Taylor, found that they could manufacture stronger and cheaper shearing frames to a more exact specification by replacing wood with cast iron. As a result, their foundry in Marsden, situated on the River Colne about seven miles southwest of Huddersfield, became the major source of iron shearing frames in the West Riding. The second product made by the Taylor brothers was a giant sledgehammer, nick-named 'Great Enoch' after their maker. They were often used by the machine breakers to destroy iron shearing frames; giving rise to the Luddite quip – 'Enoch made them [the shearing frame] and Enoch [the sledgehammers] shall break them'. Strangely, although the Taylor 'machines' were the means of putting men out of work, their premises were never attacked and it has been conjectured that the Taylor brothers – who were known to be free thinking radicals – were protected by George Mellor (1789–1813). However, Enoch Taylor suffered continual local animosity until his death in 1837 and it is generally believed that he was the intended victim of assassination, not William Horsfall, in 1812.[22]

Prior to the introduction of shearing frames in 1808, the gig mill had been in operation for some time, although not without incurring resistance. But finishing or cropping the cloth was still done by hand. This was a highly skilled job that involved carefully trimming the nap to give the cloth a neat, smooth finish. The cumbersome cutting shears, used to carry out this process, required both strength and skill to manipulate, since they were four feet long and weighed between fifty and sixty pounds. The quality of the finished product was entirely dependent on the cropper's skill, and it has been estimated that a single cropper could add twenty per cent to the final value of the cloth, depending on the care and skill employed. Consequently, bonuses were paid for high quality finish and the croppers were the highest paid workers in the finishing shops. It was claimed by the *Manchester Exchange Herald* that the croppers could spend 'twice or three times as much money in the alehouse as the weavers or dyers'.[23]

Traditionally, the croppers worked in small workshops, accommodating between four and six men, which had grown up in the Calder and Spen valleys between Leeds and Huddersfield. This method of working produced small, closely knit bands of men, who suddenly found their employment shrinking as local mill owners gradually built larger mills, incorporating an increasing number of gig mills and shearing frames. The manufacturers also found that it was economically more profitable to combine the maximum number of different processes under a single roof. As stated earlier, gig mills had been banned in the sixteenth century, but the manufacturers successfully claimed that the ancient law did not cover new designs, and so disregarded the law. Much to the manufacturers' delight, the government resolved the problem in 1809 by repealing all the protective legislation covering gig mills and numbers of looms. This was followed by repeal of the Statute of Artificers Act in 1813 and the Statute of Apprentices clause in 1814. These statutes had required manufacturers to employ skilled craftsmen who had served an apprenticeship, thereby limiting the number of new entries into any particular trade. As a consequence of the repeal of this legislation, manufacturers were given unrestrained freedom to exploit their workers however they wished, which many of them did. This was one of the earliest examples of government 'removing red tape to encourage entrepreneurs'.[24]

The outcome of this 'new' unregulated factory system, as Friedrich Engels (1820-1895) was to point out in 1844, was that 'the slavery in which the bourgeoisie holds the proletariat chained, is nowhere more conspicuous than in the factory system. Here ends all freedom in law and fact.'[25]

As anticipated, the introduction of new machines resulted in many skilled craftsmen being replaced by unskilled women and children on low wages. By 1811, over 1,000 skilled croppers, about one third of the total workforce in Yorkshire, had been thrown out of work as a result of the introduction of machines and the collapse of the American market. By 1817, when 3,625 croppers petitioned parliament, only 860 remained in full-time work, with the remainder either totally unemployed or working part-time.[26]

CHAPTER 9
Luddite Years 1811 – 1812

The Root Causes of Luddism

The third major economic crisis during John Lindley's lifetime occurred during the period 1811-12, when once again harvest failure coincided with trade depression. The price of bread reached an unprecedented 17d a loaf in 1812, with the result that Poor Law expenditure rose from about four million pounds in 1801 to just over six and a half million pounds in 1811. Private charity amounted to at least as much again. One-fifth of the population of Lancashire towns was estimated to be in receipt of relief. Without this large subsidy of the poor by ratepayers, the social fabric of the country might have crumbled. But the ever-increasing burden of parish rates on the emerging lower middle classes produced increasing resistance to this 'tax'. The time was ripe for the Unitarian philosophy of Jeremy Bentham (1748–1832), building on the work of Adam Smith, to challenge the prevailing religious notion of the duty of the rich to support the poor. In his great work *An Introduction to the Principles of Morals and Legislation* (1789), Bentham promoted the view that 'the government and administration of the country must be made as efficient as possible.' He said hand-outs produced dependency, which in turn encouraged idleness resulting in low wages, and this became the accepted wisdom of the period. This philosophy was to receive political reality with the Poor Law Amendment Act of 1834, thereby 'punishing the countryside for the collapse of social deference in 1830.'[1]

In such an atmosphere of social unrest, secret societies flourished and John Lindley was almost certainly a member of one or more of these groups, as he would not have risen to a delegate role in 1820, at the age of fifty, without prior proof of commitment. He would have attended local meetings, such as the one described by Joseph Tyas who was 'twisted-in' (enrolled) in a 'class' of twenty-five. Members paid a penny a week towards radical publications, which included the *Leeds Mercury*, the *Manchester Observer*, the *Cap of Liberty* and the *Black Dwarf*. The general practice was for literate members to read aloud to their colleagues in small close-knit workshops, or at weekly meetings in friendly public houses. This activity narrowed the gulf between the literate and non-literate and was a powerful force in spreading the radical message. Nationally, the most widely read 'seditious' newspaper of the Luddite period was the *Weekly Political Register*, produced by the famous radical journalist William Cobbett (1763–1835).[2]

Chapter 9

Extract from *The Black Dwarf*, 8 December 1819 edited by T.J. Wooler:

France offers brandies to all the world, at less than three shillings a gallon; but an Englishman is not at liberty to drink it, unless he can pay six or seven shillings and twenty shillings a gallon. And if the plenty of the world were to bring its superfluous corn to the British shores, and offer it at twenty shillings a quarter, the masters of the free born Englishman would insist upon it that he should not have it for less than eighty. His salt costs him six times what it is worth, as salt…his tea pays a hundred per cent duty; in short I am tired of enumerating all his privileges… the real and only freedom of an Englishmen is money and money alone. If rich, what he may buy he may have. If great, what he can take is his; but your poor free-born Briton is one of the most miserable of beings. He labours more, and earns less than any other labourer. His skill and his enterprise are only equalled by his want and misery – his freedom, is the liberty of seeking his only refuge from calamity – the grave.[3]

George Mellor, who became a prominent leader of the aggrieved Yorkshire Luddites, is recorded as reading to his fellow workers from radical newspapers, as well as the *Leeds Mercury*, in private rooms of local taverns such as the Shears Inn, Liversedge. The Shears Inn was almost exclusively used by croppers, and a large room on the first floor above the bar was set aside for their secret meetings and newspaper readings. In the latter half of 1811, *The Leeds Mercury*, bought in 1801, and then edited by the Methodist Whig, Edward Baines (1774–1848), published frequent accounts of machine breaking in Nottinghamshire, Derbyshire and Leicestershire. Since this was the newspaper most widely read by the Yorkshire Radicals, with a circulation of about 3,000, it carried a great deal of influence during this period. After 1797, as a result of government-imposed stamp duty, it cost six-and-a-half pence per copy, or seven pence outside Leeds. This was far more than any working individual could afford, hence the 'clubbing' together to meet the purchase price.[4]

Luddism

The practice of machine wrecking, which later became known as Luddism, a name derived from the semi-mythical apprentice Ned Ludd (variously known as Captain Ludd, General Ludd and King Ludd), was a response to the increasing introduction of machinery into textile mills in the late eighteenth and early nineteenth centuries and the unemployment that resulted from replacing people with machines. Although the single term Luddism came to be used to cover a wide range of activity, in its narrowest sense it should be used to describe the destruction of wide knitting frames that had been introduced into the stocking industry – to produce cheap shoddy products. The new machines created widespread unemployment with resulting poverty, sparking off frame breaking in Nottingham, Leicestershire and south Derbyshire. The fall in demand for high quality stockings was also made worse by the change in fashion, led by the Prince Regent and the English dandy Beau Brummel (1778–1840), for trousers in place of knee britches.[5]

Luddism began in February 1811, in the village of Arnold in Nottinghamshire, when a small group of workmen sabotaged knitting machines by removing jack-wires. When, on 11 March, several hundred people gathered in Nottingham marketplace to protest against the introduction of the new machines, the military were ordered out to disperse them, and the fight began in earnest. Machine breaking continued in this region over a period of the next five years, ending with the execution of James Towle in November 1816, and his brother William Towle, and others at Leicester in April 1817. All this activity might have been unknown in Mirfield but for the frequent reports by the Nottinghamshire correspondent of *The Leeds Mercury*. As a consequence, the topic created great excitement and formed the subject of discussion and debate in the workshops and ale houses of the woollen districts of the West Riding, generating increasing pressure for local action.[6]

Machine breaking was made a capital offence on 5 March 1812, despite the famous speech by the poet Lord Byron (1788–1824) in the House of Lords, pointing out that to implement this law would require 'twelve butchers for a jury and a Jefferys for a judge!' This law was part of 'the draconian measures being introduced by the government to quell the Luddite trouble.' But it was also part of the wider picture of a government unable to control the increased lawlessness resulting from unemployment, poverty and the rapid rise in population, mostly congregating in the new expanding cities of industrial England. The government's response was to extend the Black Act of 1723, until there were well over two hundred crimes punishable by death by the end of the century, thereby equating swearing Luddite oaths with murder! Furthermore, sixty-three crimes against property were made capital offences during the period 1760-1810. Research by Dr Radzinowicz has recorded that 'of ninety-seven executions in London and Middlesex in 1785 only one was for murder, forty-three were for burglary and the remainder for offences against property, which was a Georgian upper class obsession.'[7]

Luddism in the cotton manufacturing district of Manchester, and the surrounding towns of southwest Lancashire, followed the example of the Midlands but was of an entirely different nature. Here, the primary protest was against the introduction of steam-powered looms into the cotton industry, which threatened the livelihood of the increasing numbers of cotton weavers who had flocked to this county during the boom period. As an industry, cotton manufacture had had a fairly short history, commencing around 1770 with the invention of James Hargreaves' (1720–1778) spinning jenny (invented in 1764 and patented in 1770) and Richard Arkwright's (1732–1792) water powered spinning machine (patented 1767). However, the industry had attracted thousands of former agricultural workers from the surrounding countryside and particularly large numbers of poor immigrants from Ireland. Since the power looms in Lancashire were housed in massive multi-story factories, the Luddite attacks were carried out by great crowds of people attacking the buildings rather than the machines. They also frequently developed into riots. Such large numbers of insurgents necessarily had mixed motives – often rioting was more about lack of food than new machinery. The insurgency began with threats against Stockport factory owners in February 1812 and ended on 27 August 1812 with the acquittal of thirty-eight Luddites for taking illegal oaths, as it developed into a political protest movement.[8]

By contrast, Luddism in Yorkshire was essentially a protest by highly paid cloth dressers or shearmen, locally known as croppers, against the introduction of gig mills and shearing frames into the woollen industry, which threatened to create unemployment for these skilled men. The protest was short, bitter and violent. It began on 19 January 1812 with the destruction of Oatlands Mill, at Leeds, and culminated with the execution of George Mellor and sixteen others in January 1813.[9]

The West Riding insurgency was restricted to a small area of the woollen manufacturing districts, bounded by Leeds in the north, Halifax in the west, Wakefield in the east and Huddersfield in the south. Significantly for John Lindley, Mirfield was near the centre of this diamond shaped area. In a period of slow communications and a parochial outlook on life, once the notion of adopting the tactics of the Midland Luddites had taken hold, and the name adopted for anonymous threatening letters, the Yorkshire Luddites were primarily concerned with their own problems and individual acts of retaliation. After all, Manchester was on the other side of the Pennines, and Nottingham at least eighty miles (130 km) away – a journey of four or five days on foot. Nevertheless, some delegates travelled between the major urban centres, maintaining clandestine communications between various secret committees.

It was not the introduction of machinery itself that produced the violent response of the new wage-earning classes. Rather, it was the resulting unemployment and reduction of wages to subsistence level. For example, in the early 1790s, William Cooke converted a mill on the River Spen into a carpet factory, using looms made in Brussels for the purpose. This introduced a new product with no tradition in the area, consequently there was no local resentment and the company continued to make carpets there until 1960.[10]

From the standpoint of the twenty-first century, the actions of the Luddites have been criticised as short-sighted, but in the early nineteenth century, when Poor Law provision was minimal, loss of work by the 'bread winner' often meant starvation for his family. These men were fighting for their lives. As the historian E.P. Thompson has written:

> *Their crafts and traditions may have been dying. Their hostility to the new industrialism may have been backward-looking. Their communitarian ideals may have been fantasies. Their insurrectional conspiracies may have been foolhardy. But they lived through these times of acute social disturbance, and we did not.*[11]

Luddism in Yorkshire

John Lindley lived at the centre of Yorkshire Luddism but as a nail maker by trade, an industry with its own problems, or later as a canal worker, he had no antipathy to shearing frames, and consequently had no reason to be a Luddite. However, recently a document has come to light (Lindley vs Lindley 1883) that claimed that he had not produced a written will, because he had been 'tried for treason and felony' in a Luddite rising in 1817 (this should have read 1820), which he believed disqualified him from such action. Huddersfield was certainly a centre of Luddite activity, but his name does not appear in any of the numerous accounts of machine wrecking that took place in the area between 1811 and 1813. Nevertheless, it is inconceivable that, in an area of small closely-knit communities, he was not acutely aware of all the clandestine activities taking place in Mirfield, since his home at the Knowl was only one-and-a-half miles from the Dumb Steeple, the rendezvous for the famous attack on Rawfolds Mill. Alan Brooke, a noted local Huddersfield historian, has pointed out that Luddite was a general term that included both machine wreckers and radicals. In the West Riding, the movement started out as an industrial dispute, but developed under the leadership of George Mellor into a radical political movement. Colloquially, in the Huddersfield district, Luddite could also mean a rowdy person.[12]

The response by the West Riding croppers to their loss of employment was to follow the example of the framework knitters in Nottinghamshire, Leicestershire and Derbyshire, and embark on a systematic destruction of the hated machines. These were the Yorkshire Luddites. Initially, they gained widespread public sympathy, including that of many small manufacturers and artisans who feared the competition from the new large factories. They also thought that the old social order would be destroyed, as indeed it turned out. Prior to the Industrial Revolution, while everyone knew their place in society, deference and subservience were often compensated for by paternalism and a common community spirit.

Initially, the Yorkshire Luddites decided to concentrate on small manufacturers, because their properties were easy targets. But they got off to a false start when, on Wednesday 15 January 1812 in Leeds, the local magistrate was informed in advance that an attack was to be made that night on a cloth finishing mill. He duly sent a troop of Scots Greys to defend the mill and they surprised a large group of men with blackened faces, armed with various implements, as they were about to cross a bridge on the edge of town. The men scattered but not before James Shaw, who was carrying a hammer and a chisel, was arrested under the 'Black Act' and escorted to York Castle. The case came up in early March, when Sir Simon Le Blanc (1748–1816), a justice of the Court of the King's Bench, gave a long diatribe on the legal meaning of the 'Black Act' and the jury threw out Shaw's case, as he was deemed not to be under arms as defined by the act. James Shaw was released on Wednesday 11 March after two months in York Castle.[13]

The first successful Luddite attack in the woollen industry occurred four days after that failed attack when, at 7:00pm on Sunday 19 January, Oatlands Mill owned by Messrs Oates, Wood and Smithson, near Woodhouse Carr in Leeds, was set on fire in protest against the use of gig mills. Half the upper part of the building was destroyed causing five hundred pounds' worth of damage. Rewards of first one hundred guineas, then two hundred guineas and finally five hundred pounds were offered in *The Leeds Mercury* for information leading to an arrest, but no one came forward.[14]

In early February, a group of masked men ambushed and destroyed a cartload of shearing frames, which were being transported across Hartshead Moor to Rawfolds Mill, only a short distance from its destination.[15]

On 20 February, the government passed a bill making frame breaking a capital offence. Strictly, the bill only covered wide knitting frames used in the Midlands, but it was used indiscriminately to cover the destruction of a wide variety of machines, as the Yorkshire Luddites were to find out. However, with over two hundred capital offences on the statute book, the addition of one more had little effect.

Certainly, the Yorkshire Luddites were undeterred. On the night of 22/23 February, seven shearing frames and twenty-four pairs of shears were destroyed by a group of men with blackened faces, who forced their way into Joseph Hirst's shop at Marsh, west of Huddersfield. A man and two boys were on the premises during the attack but were unharmed, the only casualty being the master's dog that suffered collateral damage from the random firing of pistols. It was noted that the attack was carried out with military precision. The group had divided into two sections. One section, carrying axes and hammers, entered the building and proceeded to destroy all the machinery. The second section, armed with pistols, took up positions outside the building to prevent interference. As soon as the destruction was complete, the men were lined up and numbered off – military style. When all were present and correct, a salvo was fired, and the men marched off to their next target.[16]

The party next marched via Longroyd Bridge, the home village of George Mellor, to James Balderstone's premises near Crosland Moor on the other side of the valley. When Balderstone refused to open the door, it was broken down and the single shearing frame and eight pairs of shears were destroyed, while Balderstone and his wife were held at gun point. Once the shearing frame and shears had been destroyed, the group immediately lined up again, calling out their numbers, and then disappeared into the night. None of the attackers were recognised behind their disguises and none of the local inhabitants came forward with any useful identification.[17]

In response to these attacks, the magistrate Joseph Radcliffe (1744–1819) sent a request for troops to the home secretary, Richard Ryder (1766–1832), who responded by sending a troop of cavalry from Leeds to Huddersfield – about twenty men – to restore confidence.[18]

The next target was Wykenham's Mill, near Huddersfield, where new machinery had been installed and five workers dismissed. This was attacked in February. Here, the leader George Mellor, with great forethought, arranged for the local church bells to be rung if a Dragoon patrol was observed. Thus forewarned, the wreckers were able to evade capture.

Since Ryder had suggested that the magistrates, manufacturers and merchants should look out for themselves, the worthies of Huddersfield duly met on Thursday 27 February, at the George Inn, to form the 'The Committee for Suppressing the Outrages' (CSO). This committee agreed to offer a reward of one hundred guineas for information leading to a conviction, but no one came forward to claim the reward. While it was common knowledge that there was a bitter hostility among the working people in the manufacturing districts of the North and Midlands towards the manufacturers, the failure of large rewards to produce results brought home the gulf between two entrenched positions. Furthermore, the labouring classes were quietly supported in their actions by many middle-class artisans and professional people, who also bitterly resented the capitalist exploitation being carried out by employers, with the tacit approval of magistrates, who upheld their methods.[19]

Before Radcliffe could inform the home secretary of his new committee, a further raid took place at Milnsbridge House, when a shot was fired at William Hinchliffe, a cloth dresser from Golcar. The shot missed, almost certainly deliberately, but about fifty men with blackened faces poured into the building and destroyed all the shearing frames. Hinchliffe was then threatened with worse to come if the machines were replaced.[20]

And so the incidents continued. On the rainy night of 5/6 March, a group of sixteen men were guided to the house of Sam Swallow in Linthwaite, where they demanded entry and smashed four pairs of shears, two shear frames and a brushing machine, while holding Swallow at gunpoint. 'On departing they bade him good morning.' This was typical of the early Luddite attacks, when they showed considerable discipline, and not a little courtesy, in confining the destruction to machinery and avoiding bloodshed.[21]

The party then moved on to William Cotton's premises also at Linthwaite. Here, ten pairs of shears and a brushing machine were destroyed and a gun taken.[22]

On Thursday 12 March, four houses in Slaithwaite were attacked but the victims were not prepared to divulge the details, on account of having received threatening letters.[23]

The raids continued on 13 March, when a party of men, about thirty strong, knocked on the door of George Roberts at South Crosland. He asked what they wanted and was told that they would show him. He opened the door under threats that, if he refused them entry, it would be broken down. The men rushed in, holding him at gunpoint, while they broke his two shearing frames. The party then moved on to Honley, where they hammered on the door of John Garner's premises. Once again, the Luddites gained entrance and then proceeded to destroy two shear frames and seven pairs of shears, along with the tumbling shafts and drums for working the frames. John's pistol was also stolen, and a shot fired before the group departed. By 2:30am, the party had reached Lockwood, where Clement Dyson and his wife Hannah were woken by a great noise of men demanding entrance. The intruders were let in and two frames, seven shears, one brushing machine, and other utensils were broken.[24]

As part of the campaign of machine breaking, a parallel campaign of terror was conducted by means of threatening letters. About 13 March, a note was thrown into Frank Vickerman's premises, which stated:

> *We give you Notice that when the Shers is all Broken the Spinners shall be the next if they be not taken down vickerman tayler Hill he has had is Garde but we will pull all down som night and kill him that Nave and Roag.*

The note was subsequently delivered to the magistrate Joseph Radcliffe by Vickerman himself.[25]

The threatened attack duly took place on 15 March, when, at about 8:30pm, a large group of men, led by George Mellor and William Thorpe, both croppers from Huddersfield, attacked Francis Vickerman's premises, at Taylor Hill. Vickerman was a cloth finisher and member of the notorious CSO committee who, in addition to offering rewards to informers, also coordinated the activities of troops and the civilian 'Watch and Ward' aimed at preventing Luddite depredation. The attack on Vickerman's was both daring and violent. Ten shearing frames and thirty pairs of shears were smashed, but, such was the hatred against Vickerman, that the Luddites abandoned their normal restraint of taking good care only to destroy machines which threatened their livelihood, and destroyed household furniture and broke all the windows in the cropping shop. An abortive attempt was made to burn down the entire premises, but, for once, the military arrived in time to prevent total destruction. Ironically, when the alarm was given, troopers of the 2nd Dragoon Guards, quartered nearby, had to run two miles to Huddersfield where their horses were stabled, before returning to scatter Mellor's men.[26]

On 5 April, three workshops in the Holme Valley, between Honley (four miles south of Huddersfield) and Snowgate Head, Holmfirth (about six miles south of Huddersfield), were attacked by a small band of Luddites who destroyed shearing frames and shears. This included George Smith's property at Snowgate Head who 'had all his dressing-frames and shears broken.'[27]

George Smith could not say that he had not been warned, because about one month earlier, on the 9 or 10 March, he received the following letter:

> *To Mr Smith Shearing Frame Holder at Hill End Yorkshire*
> *Sir*
> *Information has just been given in that you are a holder of those detestable Shearing Frames, and I was desired by my Men to write to you and give you fair Warning to pull them down, and for that purpose I desire that you will now understand I am now writing to you. You will take Notice that if they are not taken down by the end of next Week, I will detach one of my Lieutenants with at least 300 Men to destroy them and furthermore take Notice that if you give us the Trouble of coming so far we will increase your misfortune by burning your Buildings down to Ashes and if you have the Impudence to fire upon any of my Men, they have orders to murder you, & burn all your Housing, you will have Goodness to your Neighbours to inform them that the same fate awaits them if their Frames are not speedily taken down as I understand there are several in your Neighbourhood, Frame holders. ....*

Chapter 9

The letter goes on at some length elucidating their grievances and is signed by the General of the Army of Redressers, Ned Ludd Clerk.[28]

Belligerent threatening letters of this kind were all part of the Luddite campaign of intimidation but were not written by the young men of action who actually carried out the raids. Whereas the destruction of property was obvious to everyone, and the news would be relayed like lightning throughout the woollen district by 'bush telegraph', the letters were probably only known to the manufacturers and the magistrates, which may account for why so many have ended up in Home Office archives.

On 9 April, an attack on a much larger scale than had previously been attempted was carried out by an estimated three hundred men, drawn from several West Riding communities – particularly those of the Wakefield and Huddersfield areas. They attacked Joseph Foster's house and mill at Horbury, about five miles southwest of Wakefield. This was a surprising target, as the unguarded mill was well away from the Colne Valley area normally favoured by the Luddites. Furthermore, as a result of good intelligence work, it was eleven miles away from the nearest detachment of regular troops. They destroyed all the machines, including those in the dressing shop, the scribbling mill, and the woollen warps, they also broke window frames; the estimated total damage amounted to 291 pounds. Two of Foster's sons were tied up and left naked as a further warning.[29]

This event was celebrated in the local alehouses, with the following triumphal song:

> Come all ye croppers stout and bold,
> Let your faith grow stronger still,
> Oh, the cropper lads in the county of York
> Broke the shears at Foster's mill.
> The wind it blew,
> The sparks they flew,
> Which alarmed the town full soon
> And out of bed poor people did creep
> And ran by the light of the moon;
> Around and around they all did stand,
> And solemnly did swear,
> Neither bucket, nor kit nor any such thing
> Should be of assistance there.[30]

It was at St Crispin's Inn in Halifax (called the 'Radical Chapel'), between Halifax parish church and South Parade Wesleyan Chapel, that the elderly radical John Baines passionately expounded his political philosophy. He made no secret of his motives for being a radical; his belief was that 'only the overthrow of the British Aristocracy, which bled the nation white, would bring about the "glorious triumph of democracy"'.[31]

It was at St Crispin's Inn, flushed with success after the attack on Joseph Foster's Mill, that plans were made for an even bolder attack on William Cartwright's Rawfolds Mill at Liversedge, in the Spen Valley. This meeting was attended by representatives from Huddersfield, Leeds and Halifax.[32] After the business of the meeting was concluded, all assembled joined together to sing the 'Croppers Song':

> Come Cropper lads of great renown
> Who love to drink good ale that's brown
> And strike each haughty tyrant down
> With hatchet, pike and gun

Chorus
Oh, the Cropper lads for me
The gallant lads for me
Who with lusty stroke
The shear frames broke
The Cropper lads for me

Who though the specials still advance
And soldiers nightly round us prance
The cropper lads still lead the dance
With hatchet, pike and gun

And night be nigh when all is still
And moon is hid behind the hill
We forward march to do our will
With hatchet, pike and gun

Great Enoch still shall lead the van
Stop him who dare, stop him who can
Press forward every gallant man
With hatchet, pike and gun.

The Oath of Secrecy was then solemnly taken by all present. The following edited version has been attributed to Thomas Broughton, a Barnsley weaver, by the author Brian Bailey:

> *I –, of my own free will and accord, do hereby promise and swear that I will never reveal any of the names of any one of this secret Committee, under the penalty of being sent out of this world by the first Brother that may meet me. I furthermore do swear, that I will pursue with unceasing vengeance any Traitor or Traitors, should there any arise, should he fly to the verge of Statude [Existence]. I furthermore do swear that I will be sober and faithful in all my dealings with my Brothers, and if ever I declare them, my name to be blotted out from the list of Society and never to be remembered, but with contempt and abhorrence. So help me God to keep this my Oath inviolate.*[33]

Attack on Rawfolds Mill

The next target of the Luddites was Rawfolds Mill, a four-storey building employing steam driven shearing machines, situated on the riverside at Liversedge, near Cleckheaton, a small township about eight miles north of Huddersfield. It was chosen in response to the many inflammatory remarks made by the leaseholder William Cartwright. The proposed attack represented an escalation in the campaign of machine breaking; it was the largest mill attacked by the Yorkshire Luddites and marked the climax of their activities in the West Riding.

Rumour circulated that the attempt was to be made on the night of Thursday 9 April, and the picket on duty at the mill observed several signals that indicated an impending attack. But these signals turned out to be decoys, and both Thursday night and Friday night passed without major incident.

On a bitterly cold Saturday night, 11 April 1812, over one hundred men from a wide area of the West Riding met at the ancient Dumb Steeple monument near Mirfield. They were armed with muskets, pistols, hatchets and hammers, under the command of George Mellor. William Thorpe was second in command, with Benjamin Walker and Thomas Smith acting as lieutenants. The men were formed into companies of between twenty and thirty men; they were fortified with tots of rum and marched off in military style on the three-mile journey across Hartshead Moor to Liversedge. Importantly, as will be seen later, the Leeds contingent formed a separate unit and approached the rendezvous from the north.

Dumb Steeple is a prominent early eighteenth century stone obelisk, twenty-six feet high, made of millstone grit, with a stone ball on top. Its origin is mysterious and steeped in legend. An adjacent plaque says that it is a boundary stone that replaced a much earlier wooden landmark for guiding travellers to Cowford, before Cooper Bridge was built. Another legend believes the name to be a corruption of Doom Steeple: a place where a doomed man, fleeing his pursuers, may seek safety. It is the place to which the legendry Robin Hood fled when dying, and his supposed grave lies nearby. However, the late Professor Hamilton Thompson believed that it was set up after some violent dispute, with the meaning Domini Stipulatio (a solemn agreement or covenant). An alternative translation gives Domini Stapulus (the Lord's Steeple). Local legend has it that if a true radical stands in front of the steeple and nods, the stone ball on top of the column nods back. Consequently, it has been proposed that the monument should be dedicated to the 'Radicals of Huddersfield who fought for Liberty'.[34]

At about half-past midnight, two sentries, armed with blunderbusses and posted in the yard outside Rawfolds Mill on picket duty, heard firing from the north side of the mill. This was answered by firing from the south side; and then firing from the west side, again responded to by firing from the east side; this firing was accompanied by numerous other signals, both real and intentionally misleading. The two pickets were thoroughly confused and, in the melee, a number of armed men, led by John Hirst and Samuel Hartley, surprised Cartwright's men, who were then gagged, tied up and bundled away.

As Mellor's men, disguised with blackened faces and jackets turned inside out, stealthily approached the building, the alarm was given by the loud barking of the guard dog installed on the ground floor. Once the alarm had been raised, one company stormed the mill, broke the ground floor windowpanes and discharged a volley of musket fire into the premises, but they were unable to gain entrance as the windows were set high above the ground. A second company began to hammer at the main door and side door with hammers and axes but to no avail.

Cartwright tumbled out of bed in his nightshirt and handed the primed muskets to his small band of defenders, five soldiers and about half a dozen loyal workmen, who hastily took up their prepared positions behind raised flagstones at the first-floor windows. They then proceeded to pour fire down on the attackers who presented easy targets.

The Luddites were taken by surprise and for once their intelligence work had let them down. Rawfolds Mill had been turned into a fortress by William Cartwright; doors had been strengthened and barricaded, spiked rollers put on the stairs, tubs of vitriol (sulphuric acid) had been prepared to pour on the attackers should they gain entrance. In addition to the guard dog, an alarm bell was installed on the roof to summon help.

Undeterred, Mellor's men continued the assault. A fire fight broke out between the two sides with a continuous exchange of shots that lasted, without pause, for about twenty minutes, the defenders using the flashes from the firearms of the attackers to direct their aim.

Under cover of the furious exchange of firearms, a second group of Luddites, armed with hatchets and sledgehammers, repeatedly but unsuccessfully attempted to break down the armoured doors and make a breach. These men suffered heavy casualties, not only from musket fire but also from a quantity of large stones that were hurled from the roof. As a result, many Luddites suffered serious injuries and two were mortally wounded. As the attackers began to run short of ammunition, and with the alarm bell summoning more soldiers, the Luddites gave up the unequal struggle and dispersed, leaving their two wounded comrades, Samuel Hartley and John Booth, behind. An attempt was made to rally the scattered forces to carry off the wounded, but this was not possible, since the fire from the defenders in the mill had been maintained with such perseverance that the attacking force was thoroughly demoralised. During the engagement, 140 balls had been fired from the mill (in twenty minutes); the number of shots fired in reply by the attackers was not known, but the doors and windows were peppered with a large number of pistol and musket balls, though none of them had hit their mark, since not a single defender was wounded. However, Cartwright himself was badly cut by one of his own spiked rollers, when he carelessly walked into one after the fighting had stopped.

Once the firing ceased, the defenders cautiously emerged and medical aid was called in to deal with the two wounded Luddites, who were crying out in agony. Nevertheless, they had to await the arrival of the Queen's Bays (the Second Regiment of Dragoon Guards), which took place about an hour after the attack commenced, before the two men were removed from the field and carried on litters the two miles to the Star Inn at Roberttown for interrogation.

Samuel Hartley was a cropper, formerly in the employment of Mr Cartwright, who had been made redundant by the new shearing frames. He was a fine looking young unmarried man, about twenty-four years old, and a private in the Halifax Local Militia, a regiment in which Mr Cartwright was a captain. Hartley had received a shot in his chest, apparently while making a blow at some part of the mill. The ball had pierced a lung and lodged beneath his left shoulder blade, from where it was extracted with a portion of bone. In this condition, he languished in great pain until about three o'clock on Monday morning when he died.

The other casualty was John Booth, aged about nineteen, who was an apprentice of Mr Wright, a saddler of Huddersfield. Booth's wound was in his leg, which had shattered the bone. It was therefore deemed necessary to amputate his leg; but he lost a large amount of blood while waiting for the surgeon to arrive. As a result, spasms occurred during the operation and he died about six o'clock on Sunday morning.

Despite the extreme pain suffered by both Hartley and Booth, each honoured their code of silence and died without disclosing the names of any of their comrades. None of the other wounded men were ever discovered, which speaks volumes for the solidarity and sympathy of the community in which these events took place.

On Monday, a coroner's inquest assembled to pronounce on the dead bodies and returned a verdict of justifiable homicide.

It is perhaps worth noting that, had the Luddites succeeded in entering the building, a large number of them would have been killed or wounded by the raking fire from the first floor, as there was no cover for the attackers. In addition, a large vat of sulphuric acid had been placed at the top of the stairs to empty on anyone trying to gain access by that route. Perhaps the great mistake that George Mellor's men made, was to continue the policy of destroying machines while leaving individuals unharmed. Cartwright had changed the rules of engagement and the Luddites failed to respond in kind.

The *Leeds Mercury* concluded their article with a solid warning to 'those that are engaged in these violent proceedings, of the fatal consequences that await them in the unequal contest in which they are now waging with the civil and military power of the country.'[35]

After this failure, the mood of the workers became more sombre and the tone of the Luddite songs changed. An echo of Karl Marx (1818–1883) who wrote 'religion is the opiate of the people' becomes evident, as in despair the ballad writers turn to the chiliastic promises of religion to render their misery tolerable:

> How gloomy and dark is the day
> When men have to fight for their bread;
> Some judgment will sure clear the way
> And the poor shall to triumph be led.[36]

Many other large mills had been turned into fortresses and were considered invulnerable to attack, while the presence of over one thousand troops in the Huddersfield district alone enforced the curfew and implemented martial law in that town. The *Leeds Mercury* reported that 'Leeds and Huddersfield have, with their pickets, military patrols etc., assumed more the appearance of garrison towns than the peaceful abodes of trade and industry.' The 'occupation' required the billeting of troops in local public houses, about thirty men per establishment, which caused great resentment by both publicans and the local population, as the troops of the 84th Regiment of Foot did far more damage and caused more civil disturbance than all the so-called rebels put together.[37]

The provocation by 'the Army of Occupation' is well exemplified by the 'Brutal Outrage' on the publican, Mr Fitzgerald, by four men of the Carlow Militia, reported by the *Leeds Mercury*:

> *An assault of the most atrocious and unprovoked nature was committed on Wednesday evening 2 September at about eight o'clock when four private soldiers of the Carlow Militia went into the Union Inn kept by Mr Fitzgerald and ordered a tankard of ale. However they became very clamorous and Mr Fitzgerald asked them to behave with more decorum. This was the only offence he gave them, and the sergeant major of the regiment, who was in the house, took their ale from them and placed it on the bar. Soon after the sergeant major left the house and on applying at the bar the ale was returned to the four men and all unpleasant feelings appeared to have subsided. But this was only the calm before the whirlwind of passion. Having drunk part of the liquor one of them took the tankard in his hand and all four advanced to the bar. The man that held the tankard threw its contents in Mr Fitzgerald's face, and then using the empty tankard, struck him with such a violent blow to the head that Mr Fitzgerald fell to the ground. The other three then drew their bayonets and attacked Mr Fitzgerald with such savage fury as to inflict seven separate wounds on his head and to render him unconscious.*
>
> *A Mr Hinchcliffe, who was in the house, tried to rescue their Mr Fitzgerald from the savage fury of the four soldiers, but in the attempt he received three wounds on*

his head, which prevented him from rendering further assistance. Mrs Fitzgerald who is in an advanced state of pregnancy witnessed the attack and she cried 'Murder' several times. This brought a number of people in from the street including Quartermaster Greasby of the 15th Regiment of Hussars. He seized a bludgeon and fell upon the four soldiers with such vigour that he drove them from the bar and out of the house, and it is to the courageous Quartermaster Greasby that Mr Fitzgerald owes his life. A little while later, Thomas Roden, one of the soldiers, returned for his cap, which had fallen from his head in the affray. He was immediately arrested and taken to York Castle to be tried for this offence. The other three soldiers escaped but are known to the Civil Powers. Mr Fitzgerald though badly lacerated recovered, but a neighbour, the wife of John Thomas, who was in a weak state of health and who witnessed the attack died of shock.

The editor of the *Leeds Mercury* commented 'We have heard persons recommend the process of Military Law in order to tranquillise the disturbed counties. Military Law! They know not what they ask but this transmission may convey some idea of the kind of tranquillity their favoured measure would produce.'[38]

This huge 'army of occupation', estimated at between twelve and fifteen thousand regular troops, were employed to quell the Luddite unrest in Yorkshire, Lancashire and the Midlands. This was at a time when they were desperately needed abroad, both on the continent and in North America. To put this in perspective, when General Arthur Wellesley (1769–1852), later to become 1st Duke of Wellington, landed at Figueira da Foz in Mondego Bay in Portugal at the start of his Peninsula Campaign in 1808, he had under his command only fourteen thousand British troops – comparable to the number of British troops employed to occupy the industrial heartland of England. In fact, if the local militia of Yorkshire, Lancashire and Cheshire are added to the regular force, Lieutenant General Sir Thomas Maitland (1759–1830) had over thirty-five thousand men to occupy and subdue the north of England and the Midlands.[39]

Of course, the Luddites of Huddersfield were not the only radicals challenging authority. John Blackwell, a revolutionary journeyman tailor, led an attack on the local militia armoury in Sheffield on 14 April 1812 in a protest at the price of bread.

The Luddite fatalities at Rawfolds Mill escalated the fight, and George Mellor declared that since the buildings were impregnable the mill owners themselves must be attacked.

The first attempt was made against William Cartwright himself when, on Saturday 18 April, as he was riding home, two shots were fired from opposite sides of the road. Both shots missed and Cartwright, badly shaken, applied spurs to his horse and escaped.[40]

Next came an attempt on Friday 24 April against George Whitfield, a constable at Paddock, when a blunderbuss was fired through his staircase window. The scattered shots caused no physical injuries, but the psychological pressure was mounting against the meagre civilian authorities.[41]

Death of William Horsfall

On Tuesday 28 April, William Horsfall, of Ottiwells Mill Marsden, and Mr Eastwood left Huddersfield together. After they had ridden a short distance, Mr Eastwood took the opportunity to stop and water his horse, while Mr Horsfall rode leisurely on towards Crosland Moor. Soon after he passed the Warren Inn (which lies about one-and-a-half miles from Huddersfield on the Manchester Road), four men, each armed with a horse pistol, were seen in a small field resting the barrels of the heavy pistols in holes in the wall. Horsfall saw two of the pistols and began to turn his horse away, when all four men fired and inflicted four wounds on Horsfall's left side. He instantly fell from his horse, but one foot was caught up in the stirrup and he was dragged a short distance. A number of passers-by, both on horse and on foot, rushed to the spot. They disentangled his foot and took him to the Warren Inn. The assailants began to walk away, then quickly broke into a run and escaped through Dungeon Wood; they were not pursued until the Queen's Bays arrived three quarters of an hour later. One assassin was described as over six feet, a second portly and the other two of medium height, 5ft 6in or 5ft 7in, and slim. They all wore dark coats of coarse woollen cloth and appeared to be workingmen. An unnamed gentleman, who saw Horsfall at the Warren Inn, described three of the wounds 'as slight' but a fourth, made by a musket ball, had entered his right thigh and was severe. The musket ball struck the lower part of the abdomen on the left side but did not enter the abdominal cavity. It passed obliquely downwards, behind the skin, towards the right groin and then penetrated the right thigh, passing behind the bone, from where it was eventually extracted. Initially, Horsfall was exhausted by the loss of blood, but on Wednesday he improved and it began to look as if he might recover, but overnight fresh bleeding and some infection occurred and he died at between seven and eight in the morning.[42]

This event proved to be a turning point in the Luddite campaign. From this point, public support began to decline, as the sympathy of the 'respectable' general public for the machine wreckers stopped short of condoning murder.

Robber Bands

With the change in tactics, attacks on mills and machinery became very infrequent; instead, the Luddites concentrated on stealing arms and money from householders over a wide area. The *Leeds Mercury* reported attacks at Almondbury, Wooldale, Farnley, Netherton, Honley and Marsden with over one hundred stands of arms stolen during the first week of May.[43]

To compound the fear of property owners that was running through the country, the prime minister, Spencer Perceval (1762–1812), was assassinated on 11 May in the lobby of the Houses of Parliament at Westminster. There was rejoicing among the labouring classes throughout the land – in Nottingham, frame knitters built a huge bonfire and riots took place in many northern cities. But the celebration proved premature as the assassin was John Bellingham, a businessman who had been imprisoned by the Russians and felt that he had been let down by his own government. It was an act of personal revenge and not the signal for the start of the revolution as feared. Bellingham was tried at the Old Bailey, found guilty and executed on 18 May.[44]

If the labouring classes were going to overthrow the government, this was the golden opportunity to strike. A revolution might just have succeeded at this moment, but there were no leaders with sufficient experience to take advantage of the spontaneous discontent, and turn working men into a disciplined fighting force, able to take on trained troops. War during the Napoleonic era was essentially a matter of training and discipline. The ability of the infantry to load and fire while taking casualties and to form squares, as protection against cavalry, were the hallmark of the regular army. Guerrilla warfare, as employed by the rebels, produced fear and instability, but did not overthrow governments.

The moment passed. On 21 May, a new administration under Lord Liverpool (1770 – 1828) was formed, with Lord Sidmouth (1757–1844) as home secretary. But the defining event for the Yorkshire Luddites had already taken place when, on 14 May, a meeting had been convened in Wakefield called by the lord lieutenant of the West Riding, Earl Fitzwilliam, and including all the military commanders and local magistrates. At this meeting, Lieutenant General Sir Thomas Maitland, the senior general, rather presumptuously in the presence of the lord lieutenant, assumed overall command of the entire north of England. He then acted swiftly and vigorously. First, he moved his headquarters from Manchester to Wakefield; he sent his second in command Major General Acland with one thousand troops to Huddersfield. He used Captain Francis Raynes to implement clandestine night patrols, arresting anyone who was out after the curfew hour of 9:00pm. He employed the spymaster John Lloyd and his team of spies to identify and bribe possible informers, and authorised the magistrate Joseph Radcliffe to carry out interrogations and committals. In the tradition of the late Prime Minister Pitt, a reign of fear and terror was instituted and the entire region became 'a police state', with arrests and interrogation for the most minor offences – such as damming the King or even Joseph Radcliffe in the ale-house. As a result, the accumulated circumstantial evidence enabled the authorities to send over one hundred men to York Castle and, as a consequence, disrupted the organisation of the Luddite groups. Although George Mellor had been questioned several times during the summer, it was not until 10 October that the authorities felt they had enough evidence to prosecute, and he was finally taken into custody on the 'oath' of his cousin Joseph Mellor.[45]

The 'reign of terror' by the police constables and military produced some bizarre events. On Monday 22 June, James Oldroyd, a clothier of Dewsbury, was drinking in the Black Bull in Mirfield, when he confessed (more likely boasted) that he was at Rawfolds Mill on the night that it was attacked, and that he was engaged in the attack with his comrades when he fell. Oldroyd was duly arrested and taken to York Castle to add to the swelling numbers of detained suspects. Why would he confess unless he was very drunk? While it is unlikely that John Lindley was drinking in the Black Bull that night, the news would have spread like wildfire in the tiny township of Mirfield, and he would certainly have known by early morning.[46]

Even more bizarre was the confession of Corporal Barraclough of the local Upper Agbrigg Militia, who confessed to having assisted in the attack on the shearing mill of William Cartwright at Rawfolds, and also to having been involved in the murder of William Horsfall. On investigation, it was found that he had been with his regiment in York at the time of the murder. He was judged to be simple-minded and returned to his regiment. Perhaps this gives an insight into the quality of the rank and file of the British Army at this time.[47]

Finally, on 20 October, Benjamin Walker, a cloth dresser from Longroyd Bridge, was arrested and taken to Milnsbridge House, under suspicion of being involved in the attack on Rawfolds Mill. Within twenty-four hours of his detention he had succumbed to John Lloyd's 'interrogation methods' (generally interpreted as torture) and confessed that he was one of the four involved in the murder of William Horsfall, along with George Mellor, William Thorpe and Thomas Smith. This statement resulted in Thorpe and Smith being arrested, clapped in irons, and taken to York Castle to join Mellor for trial.[48]

John Lloyd was originally the solicitor and clerk to the Stockport magistrate, Rev. Prescott. He became a zealous spymaster and persecutor of suspected agitators, extracting information by threats and sometimes by torture. General Maitland admitted that much of Lloyd's work was 'out of the strict letter of the law'.[49]

At this time John Lloyd, with the consent of the Treasury solicitor, Henry Hobhouse (1776–1854), and the home secretary, Lord Sidmouth, instituted a policy that affected all

Luddites immediately, and John Lindley and the Yorkshire Rebels eight years later. It came about when a Special Commission was arranged for the end of May, to be held in Chester Castle, to try the cotton workers arrested for rioting in April. Lloyd persuaded a cotton weaver, Thomas Whittaker, to make a written statement that was then passed to Hobhouse, who was amazed, not by the contents, but that a poor weaver should have a basic education and be able to make a written statement in his own hand. This alerted the authorities to the dangers of literate members of the labouring class and they became marked men, singled out for special treatment, as these were obviously the ringleaders to be executed or transported.[50]

A further Special Commission was set up and a show trial of 'Luddites' orchestrated to quash the spirit of dissent in Yorkshire. The belief that the verdict was a foregone conclusion was confirmed by discussions held, one week before the trial commenced, between Hobhouse and General Acland, about the problem of how best to dispose of the bodies after execution, without creating riots. The centre-piece was to be the trial of Mellor, Thorpe and Smith for the murder of William Horsfall, while a further sixty-one prisoners, also being held at York Castle, were to be tried on charges ranging from burglary, and administering illegal oaths, to taking part in the raid on Rawfolds Mill.[51]

The mass arrests and incarceration of the suspects in York Castle brought machine breaking in Yorkshire to an end. But, while the Special Commission was being set up, a series of robberies with violence, of both money and weapons, was reported by the Huddersfield correspondent of the *Leeds Mercury*.[52] On 27 November at 9:15pm, William Walker, a cloth manufacturer of Newhall, Fartown, was robbed by a number of armed men of a gun, a pistol, powder horn, and fifteen pounds in notes and five guineas in gold, while all the time a pistol was pointed at his head. Next, the gang proceeded to the house of George Scholes, a shopkeeper at Fartown, from whom they took a gun, between thirty and forty shillings in silver and one five-pound note. Also, nine or ten provincial pound notes, together with a pair of silver tea tongs and two silver teaspoons. Not content with this booty, they went into the cellar and carried away a bottle of rum and some provisions. The family was told not to leave the house for two hours. The thieves then departed, leaving behind a blunderbuss and a hatchet. They then proceeded to the house of Joshua Thornton, a farmer of Gilley Royd near Fixby, where they arrived at about 10:30pm. Four armed men entered the house and were told that there were no guns or money inside, whereupon they ordered 'Enoch, Captain, Sergeant and Hatchet-men to enter'. On Mrs Thornton's promise to find them some money, they withdrew at the word of command (indicating that they were disciplined). She then took from a drawer a pocketbook with five one-pound notes, which was snatched from her. As they left, one of the men struck Mrs Thornton a blow on the head while another 'fired' a pistol at Mr Thornton, which was either not loaded or failed to ignite.

Next, they went to the house of James Brook of Bracken Hall in Fartown and stole a watch, a one-pound note, and four shillings in silver. From there they went to John Wood's house and broke down his door and window to gain entry, but they did not find anything, so numbering off one to nine they marched off. The next victim was William Radcliffe at Woodstock, where they obtained eleven ten-shilling notes and six guineas in gold and between two and three pounds in silver and copper, besides a quantity of tea, some loaf-sugar and liquids. Finally, the party went to Moses Ball of Gilley Royd where they stole two pounds' worth of silver in change.

A report, dated 10 December, in the *Leeds Mercury* said that Magistrate Radcliffe was questioning a number of suspects in connection with the above robberies. The suspects claimed to be reformers, but the paper thought that they were state Luddites who had fallen on corruption and existed by public plunder. As a result, Joseph Crowther, James Hey and Nathan Hoyle were committed to York Castle on 18 December. The conspiracy of silence that had protected the Luddites earlier in the year had broken down. The change in tactics from disciplined machine breaking, which commanded tacit support, to assassination and robbery of private individuals, deprived the Luddites of both artisan and middle-class radical support. The 'army of redressers' was beginning to look more like a band of thieves.[53]

A brief respite from the bitter struggle occurred when, in the middle of August 1812, the press announced the victory of Salamanca (fought 22 July 1812). The Huddersfield correspondent of the *Leeds Mercury* described how the populace 'had rejoicings and the ringing of bells all the days of Monday 17 August and Tuesday 18 August, for the glorious victory gained by Generalissimo Wellington over Marshal Marmont'.[54]

CHAPTER 10
York Castle 1813

Trial of the Yorkshire Luddites

On Saturday 2 January 1813, great crowds of people, mostly from the industrial towns of Lancashire and the West Riding, converged on the Assize Courts at York Castle to witness the trial of the Luddites. A grand jury was sworn in and Sir Alexander Thompson addressed the twenty-three members who agreed that there was a case to answer with respect to the murder of William Horsfall. The plan was to commence with the trial of George Mellor, William Thorpe and Thomas Smith, and on the following Monday, a jury of twelve men was sworn in. However, Henry Brougham (1778–1868), counsel for the defence, asked for a postponement and this was granted until Wednesday. As a result, the trial of John Swallow, John Batley, Joseph Fisher and John Lumb was brought forward to fill the gap. The four men, three of them coal miners, were accused of robbing Samuel Moxon on 4 July of two pounds and some food.[1]

The trial started with a threatening warning to the prisoners by J.A. Park for the prosecution (Park was to appear later as a judge at the trial of John Lindley) that all prisoners before the Special Commission were to be treated as Luddites. It was quite unjustifiably claimed that all the prisoners were Luddites by association. The unscrupulous Park also made a large number of damning statements in his opening remarks to the jury, which his witnesses failed to support when they gave evidence. In fact, the evidence presented by witnesses bore little relation to the longwinded opening statement by Park. Judge Thompson was culpably negligent in his summing up, when he failed to point out to the jury that Park's statements had no corroborating evidence. Even worse was the fact that counsel for the defence, Henry Brougham, failed to challenge Park's wild suppositions. Since the law did not allow accused prisoners to speak in their own defence they were badly let down by their legal team. All four men were found guilty and sentenced to death.[2]

The delayed 'star attraction' opened on Wednesday 6 January when Mellor, Thorpe and Smith appeared. They were charged with the murder of William Horsfall, machine breaking and attempting to destroy Rawfolds Mill. A number of witnesses were called for the prosecution. The only eyewitness to the murder was Mr Parr, a manufacturer riding home to Marsden. He was about one hundred yards behind Horsfall when he heard a loud discharge of guns and saw Horsfall slump forward in the saddle. A man in a dark coat, carrying a pistol, jumped on the four-foot plantation wall and was about to continue his assault when he saw Parr galloping up. The man then turned and fled accompanied by three other men, also dressed in dark clothes. Parr could not identify any of the prisoners in the dock as being present at the shooting.

Identification rested with Benjamin Walker, the chief prosecution witness, who claimed to be one of the four men at the scene of the crime. He had turned King's evidence to save his life, but proved a most unreliable witness, changing his story several times. He claimed, during the trial, that he was hiding in a nearby wood with Smith when the shots were fired. He said, 'I do not know what Mellor and Thorpe did, I could not see them for the wood.' There was a strong suspicion that he had been bribed by Lloyd and Radcliffe, which if proven would have invalidated his evidence. Walker's evidence was in contradiction to the earlier report in the *Leeds Mercury* of 2 May that reported 'four men fired and four men ran away'.

To further confuse the forensics, all four Luddites were armed with pistols, only two of which – it was claimed – were actually fired. The report by the surgeon, Rowland Houghton of Huddersfield, read as follows:

> *[A] Musket ball on left side of belly [M1], two on top of left thigh [F1 & F2] and one in the scrotum [F3] of the same side. Another slight wound in the lowest part of the belly [F4] and another near the top of the right thigh [P1] within about 4 inches of which wound, towards the outside, a leaden ball was extracted, flattened on one side about the size of a pistol ball. From under part of the right thigh [M2] another round leaden ball of full musket size was extracted near to the joint. The skin over the right groin, also the inside of the thigh had a dark bruised appearance. The ball in the right thigh did the damage.*[3]

From this report, it can be seen that Horsfall sustained seven wounds. It can be interpreted as comprising three main wounds: two caused by musket shots and the other by a pistol ball. The other four wounds may have been caused by fragments. The statement by Joseph Hall that he had witnessed Mellor 'loading his pistol with two pipe-heads of powder and two or three pistol balls hammered into slugs' (perhaps distorting them so that they looked like musket balls) could resolve the confusion, as the damage could have been caused by the discharge of a triple loaded pistol with fragmentation. Or two pistols. The surgeon's conclusion is clear, namely that the ball in the right thigh did the damage, causing fatal bleeding and death.[4]

The case for the defence rested on the alibis of the three men, and a number of witnesses came forward to declare that the prisoners had been seen elsewhere during the crucial period. Unfortunately, there were disparities in the various stories and they were not believed.

On close examination, the conduct of both judges and barristers during the trial for William Horsfall's murder caused concern to some of the legal observers present. In particular, the conduct of the prosecuting attorney J.A. Park fell far short of the professional legal standards expected, even in the early nineteenth century. Furthermore, the witness statements, despite Park's leading questions, did not add up to a conclusive verdict of guilt.[5]

The jury, one of whom was Joseph Radcliffe, took twenty-five minutes to find all three guilty; and at 9:00pm on Wednesday evening the assisting judge, Mr Justice Le Blanc, sentenced them to be hanged by the neck until dead and their bodies to be 'delivered to the surgeons and anatomised'. No time was wasted, and thirty-six hours later, on Friday 8 January, the three men were hanged at 9:00am. The vast crowd significantly remained silent, thereby demonstrating their support for the condemned men. By acting with great speed,

Chapter 10

the authorities had made sure that there was no chance of an appeal. Interestingly, none of the witnesses who provided alibis were charged with perjury.[6]

On the day after the execution of Mellor, Thorpe and Smith the trial of those charged with the attack on Rawfolds Mill took place. Of the eight men accused, five: Thomas Brook, Jonathan Dean, James Haigh, John Ogden and John Walker were convicted and sentenced to death.[7]

Two groups of men were accused of robbery in separate incidents. William Hartley, Job Hey and John Hill were convicted of stealing a gun and a pistol. James Crowther, James Hey and Nathan Hoyle were convicted for robbery at Far Town near Huddersfield. All six were sentenced to death. Of the ten men found guilty of robbery, only John Lumb's application for mercy was granted. But it is perhaps significant that the total value of goods taken in the three robberies carried out by these men was negligible, the arms taken were few and no victim had been bodily harmed.[8]

A number of other cases were tried at this assize, the most notable being that of the veteran radical John Baines, who had been trapped by John M'Donald and John Gosling, two police *agents provocateurs* of very dubious character, who had tricked him into administering the Luddite oath. As a result, he was sentenced to be transported for seven years. He never saw his family again.[9]

On 16 January 1813, the fourteen remaining condemned men were executed behind York Castle in two groups of seven, the largest number ever hanged there in one day, while a further seven were transported to New South Wales. 'So these draconian measures maintained the reputation of England's criminal code as the most barbarous in Europe. There was a general feeling that the Law of Moses warranted not the taking of life for any crime but murder.' As a result, the population was cowed, but not crushed, and a smouldering resentment was generated against the ruling class and all forms of authority. This resentment was to erupt again as armed rebellion in Yorkshire during 1817 and more significantly in 1820.[10]

On 28 January 1813, someone fired warning shots into Milnsbridge House, but the owner Joseph Radcliffe was unhurt in this attack and once again the motive appeared to be to frighten the owner, not to kill him. Milnsbridge House was a small neo-classical mansion, situated about three miles south west of Huddersfield on the banks of the River Colne. It was to his 'Justice Room' in this house that Radcliffe brought suspects that he wished to intimidate and interrogate. He was particularly vindictive in his methods and relentlessly pursued the Yorkshire Radicals during his time in Huddersfield, generating an intense hatred of the man and his methods. As a result, Radcliffe and his family lived in fear and never left Milnsbridge House without an armed guard. He commenced his vendetta in December 1795, but finally in 1813 he was instructed to 'abate his zeal' by the Treasury solicitor, as he was inflaming the local population. Radcliffe prudently took his family on a grand tour of Europe before retiring to Rudding Park near Harrogate. Perhaps he took notice of the threat by Thomas Riley, a tailor of Crosland Moor, advocating the assassination of this 'tyrant upon the earth'.[11]

In the short term the Luddite insurrection was a failure – it did not prevent machinery being introduced into woollen mills; it did not save the jobs of handloom weavers and croppers. But it did foster a general discontent that fuelled the radical politics of the nineteenth century and helped to produce the Reform Act of 1832, which widened the franchise. This act fell far short of the militant reformers' aims and was considered a betrayal of the exploited working class by the property-owning middle class. But the fight was continued by the Chartists and electoral reform progressed slowly with the Reform Acts of 1867 and 1884. These acts increased the male electorate in towns from twenty per cent to sixty and in the counties to seventy per cent. The long-term effect resulted in the Representation of the Peoples Acts that enfranchised women over thirty in 1918 and over twenty-one in 1928, and finally the Labour government led by Clement Attlee (1883–1967) abolished the Business and University (extra) vote in 1948. Reform of the unelected House of Lords continues in the early decades of the twenty-first century.[12]

The executions at York did not end government harassment of the reform movement, as the following incident clearly demonstrates. In 1811, the veteran reform campaigner Major John Cartwright began work to establish a popular Union for Parliamentary Reform, 'to promote universal suffrage'. To facilitate the growth of these clubs he went on extensive tours of the country. On his second tour, in 1813, he travelled more than nine hundred miles and visited thirty communities in twenty-nine days. One of the towns he visited was Huddersfield, where on 21 January he met with a group of local radicals, who were mostly 'working mechanics'. This private meeting was unceremoniously interrupted by the local military commander, supported by a detachment of soldiers, who confiscated his papers and a petition that was being prepared. All those present were taken before the magistrate, Joseph Radcliffe, and fined for tippling (drinking), and only Major Cartwright's knowledge of constitutional law prevented further detention and prosecution. Fortunately, this harassment did not prevent Major Cartwright from collecting over 130,000 signatures in support of a taxpayer franchise and annual parliaments.[13]

CHAPTER 11
Post War Years 1815 – 1819

Price of Peace

The conclusion of the Napoleonic Wars, with victory at Waterloo on 18 June 1815, and the end of the Anglo-American war (1812-1815), produced a national feeling of euphoria but reality soon set in. The government no longer needed the munitions of war and adopted deflationary policies. Agricultural prices fell and the demobilisation of between three and four hundred thousand service personnel soon glutted the already depressed labour market. Added to the unemployment problems, many of the under-funded country banks (these were banks outside London) failed in 1816. The outcome was a catastrophic fall in manufacturing output that lasted from 1815 until 1822 and was made worse by a series of very poor harvests in 1816, 1818 and 1819. The entire country was in a state of severe economic depression.[1]

The government under Lord Liverpool (1770–1828), as ever favouring the landed interests at the expense of the manufacturing districts, responded by introducing a new 'corn law' in 1815 that only compounded the problem. This law prohibited foreign corn being imported until the domestic price reached 80s (£4) a quarter (28lb). It was aimed at keeping marginal farmers in production, at the cost of raising the price of bread to almost famine level. The average price of a 4lb loaf of bread reached nearly 17 pence in 1816, falling to 13 pence in 1817 and $11^1/_2$ pence in 1818 and 1819, compared to an average price of between six and seven pence between the years 1790 to 1794.[2]

Blanketeers

On 4 March 1817, the government again suspended Habeas Corpus, by which means magistrates were able once more to incarcerate anyone of whom they disapproved, holding them indefinitely in custody without trial. To reinforce this draconian measure, the government passed a Seditious Meetings Act – forbidding meetings that magistrates deemed incited people to disobey their authority. This measure was frequently used during the Jacobin period of 1792 to 1824. Notwithstanding, on 10 March a group of about twelve thousand people gathered outside St Peter's Church in Manchester, with the object of marching to London to present a petition to the Prince Regent – later George IV (1762–1830).

Well aware that the normal response of government was to ignore radical petitions, John Bagguley, their leader, was careful to ensure that the protest would be peaceful and that the marchers complied with the correct procedure for presenting petitions. However, beneath the surface was an underlying threat of violence if the Prince Regent did not receive their petition.

When the marchers reached St Peter's Field in Manchester, Bagguley and twenty-seven other ringleaders, including the Manchester tailor and reform 'missionary', John Johnston, were arrested. The plans for the march had been leaked by government spies, and two of the leading organisers had been arrested the previous day. As a result, the authorities had no difficulty dispersing the crowd, who quietly and perhaps a little sullenly went home. Only about three hundred marchers, with blankets strapped to their backs, carrying walking sticks and known as the 'Blanketeers', actually left Manchester. They got as far as Stockport where the military caught up with them. The Yeomanry Cavalry, mostly farmers and landed gentry, in their usual style treated the occasion as if it were a fox hunt, but with human beings playing the part of the prey. This callous use of excessive force dispersed the small band of marchers, wounding several people in the process. One bystander, an innocent old man, who was watching the excitement from his cottage door, was shot dead! Only one person, Abel Couldwell of Stalybridge, was allowed to proceed to London and present his petition to the Prince Regent.[3]

In the same month that the march of the Blanketeers took place, the home secretary, Lord Sidmouth, instituted a crackdown on the radical press, by taking action against 'hawkers and peddlers' without a licence to sell books. Mass arrests of members of provincial reform societies under the guise of the Suspension Act took place. As a result, many prominent radicals, including William Cobbett, went into exile in America.[4]

After the march of the Blanketeers, there was a short respite for the government, probably attributable to the assault on the radical press. Fortunately for the government, the economic situation improved and trade revived; furthermore, the 1817 harvest was better than the previous year and the price of bread dropped back to thirteen pence a loaf. But, despite this apparent improvement of domestic living standards, the underlying political unrest continued. Numerous plots were hatched, only to be foiled by rapid arrests, largely as a result of information supplied to local authorities by the network of well-paid government spies and informers.

The Folly Hall and Pentridge Risings 1817

Despite the failure of the 'Blanketeers' petition', political agitation in Lancashire continued, with Manchester Radicals agreeing to meet at Ardwick Bridge on 28 March to plan a revolt – they had abandoned the ineffectual use of petitions by this time – but once again their meeting place was leaked by spies to the authorities and twenty-three delegates were arrested.

With the Lancashire leaders in gaol, Huddersfield, the 'Radical Capital of Yorkshire' during this period, took up the fight. A political Union for Parliamentary Reform had already been formed there on 13 October 1816 and surrounding townships soon followed suit. In particular, meetings of delegates were held at Thornhill Lees, a small village halfway between Dewsbury and Mirfield, where the inaugural meeting was held on 27 January 1817. This was situated about one mile from John Lindley's home and was to become the centre of operations for 'The Folly Hall' insurrection.

Sometime in late April 1817, four men, John Dickinson, linen draper of Dewsbury, Walker the painter, William Oliver (1774?–1827) claiming to be a delegate from the London 'Hampden Club', and Joseph Mitchell, a prominent Lancashire radical who was to act as 'the principal agent of communication', all met in a public house in John Lindley's home town of Mirfield. Oliver and Mitchell had arrived via Sheffield on the 26 April, and Wakefield on the 27 April. They declared that they were promoting parliamentary reform, but as the Blanketeers' protest had demonstrated, petitioning was ineffective so, like the Manchester Radicals, they agreed that force was the only option. By falsely exaggerating the mass support for revolution in the country, particularly in London, Oliver was able to assume an important role in the local arrangements that were being organised. The plan in Huddersfield was that Tom Vevers' group would raid Milnsbridge House and seize thirty stand of arms (a complete set of weapons for one man). At Hightown, Ben Hepponstall's party was to capture William Cartwright and Rev. Roberson and take them prisoner, and John Smaller's company was to attack Breton Hall, capture the arsenal of one hundred stand of arms, and then proceed to storm the town hall and house of correction. At Sheffield, Wentworth House and the Doncaster arms depots were the targets. Although dubbed a 'weak and impractical scheme', the plan to secure all the military in their quarters (usually public houses), seize their arms, and arrest all the magistrates, was to be repeated throughout the country.[5]

In the meantime, two meetings were held in Sheffield. The last of these, on 30 May, was raided by magistrates on a tip-off from the informant Bradley. Although only four of the leaders out of thirty delegates were arrested, the loss of their leader, William Wolstenholme, seriously affected Sheffield's contribution to the revolution.[6]

Undeterred by the Seditious Meetings Act (1795), which had been revived on 14 March, ten delegates agreed to meet on Friday 6 June, at the *Sportsman's Arms,* Thornhill Lees, to make final arrangements for the rising. Once again, due to intelligence from Bradley, this information was leaked to the authorities and all ten delegates were arrested. They were examined by the authorities with Earl Fitzwilliam in the chair and all were subsequently released on a promise to keep the peace; but on leaving the court house, John Smaller of Holbury and James Mann of Leeds were re-arrested and conveyed to London for further questioning.[7]

Nevertheless, the men from Huddersfield, Holmfirth and Honley decided to proceed with 'the revolution', and on 8 June about three hundred men marched via Knowl Hill to Folly Hall, near Huddersfield. However, Oliver, who was later unmasked as a government spy and *agent provocateur*, was reporting back 'the plans' to the home secretary by passing information to General John Byng's coachman.

It was therefore not surprising that a troop of six men of the Huddersfield Yeomanry Cavalry, under Captain Armytage, just happened to stumble upon about sixty or seventy men guarding Engine Bridge over the River Colne near Folly Hall. Challenges were made on both sides when Private Alexander, either deliberately or accidentally, discharged his pistol into the crowd. This was returned with a full volley and one ball struck Alexander's horse in the head, but the grey was not seriously harmed. Since they were heavily outnumbered, the Yeomanry Cavalry rapidly rode off to warn magistrates in the town centre of the coming assault. With the element of surprise lost, the insurgents decided that their meagre forces were too small and returned to their beds. They did not wait for the contingent from Honley and Holmfirth, led by George Taylor, to join them. This 'southern party', of less than one hundred men, was delayed because initially they had only seven guns between them and it was felt necessary to acquire more firearms before proceeding.[8]

Over the following weeks numerous arrests were made. A detachment of 13th Dragoons was stationed at Huddersfield to reinforce the Yeomanry, and 130 men of the 33rd Regiment of Foot carried out a methodical sweep for arms.[9]

On 14 June, the *Leeds Mercury* publicly exposed Oliver as a government spy, but the unmasking was really due to John Dickinson, who had recognised Oliver in Wakefield when all the rest of his party were in custody. Oliver had escaped from Wakefield gaol with the connivance of General Byng. The result of the exposure was that all those arrested in the aftermath of Folly Hall were acquitted, since the jury would not convict on an informer's evidence. The released men returned to Huddersfield on 27 July to a hero's welcome.[10]

A similar rising took place at Pentridge in Derbyshire, on 9 June 1817, when four hundred revolutionaries were confronted by cavalry and fled. And so, the 'great' national uprising of 1817 petered out and came to nothing, revealing in the process a high degree of organisational inexperience and over-confidence among the participants. This was part of the learning experience of revolution, and some of these problems would be addressed in the future, but there was a widespread belief at the time that an armed uprising and a march on London would overthrow the government and lead to a democratic political system. Rather naively, it was thought that this alone would alleviate poverty and starvation.[11]

Another poor harvest in 1818 produced strikes in Lancashire, along with general unrest, caused by the continuing high price of bread (a 4lb loaf cost $11^1/_2$ pence in 1818 & 1819). This was exacerbated by mass unemployment, particularly in the manufacturing areas of Yorkshire and Lancashire, and continued into 1818 and 1819. As may have been anticipated, the Home Office under its repressive head, Viscount Sidmouth, and his bloodthirsty undersecretary, Henry Hobhouse (1776–1854), responded by clamping down on radical activities using extreme measures, in particular the gallows and transportation. Both proved savage and effective means of cowing resistance.[12]

To compound the problem in Mirfield, a tragedy occurred at Colne Bridge on the night of 14 February 1818. A foreman, going out, presumably for a drink, locked seventeen girls in the factory where they were working. A fire broke out in his absence and all the girls burned to death. Three girls were only nine years old and a further eleven were under fourteen. They were all buried together in Kirkheaton Churchyard. While in general, the lives of children in 1818 may have been of little consequence, this personal loss struck deep into the heart of the community, reinforcing the sense of injustice endured by the working people. This incident and many others like it were to galvanise Richard Oastler, steward of Fixby Hall (between Halifax and Huddersfield), to start the long fight for the Ten Hours Bill to limit the hours of employment for women and children to a maximum of fifty-six hours per week. This was not achieved until 1847, when John Fielden's Factory Act was finally passed, after a gruelling sixteen-year campaign. But it was not until many years later that a bill was passed fixing ten as the minimum age at which children could begin work in a factory.[13]

Peterloo 1819

Mass discontent surfaced yet again in 1819 and demonstrations continued throughout the country. The horrendous climax to this series of demonstrations occurred in Manchester, with an event that was to reverberate across the Pennines and cause the radicals of Yorkshire to take up arms when their turn came to continue the fight.

On 16 August 1819, a huge peaceful demonstration of between sixty and eighty thousand men, women and children (representing about six per cent of the population of Lancashire) assembled at St Peter's Field to hear the famous radical orator, Henry Hunt

(1773–1835), address the meeting. However, as soon as Hunt arrived, the local magistrates signed an affidavit for his arrest and ordered the deputy constable, Joseph Nadin (b.1765), to carry it out. Nadin reported that he could not carry out his orders without military assistance and, as a consequence, William Hulton (1787–1864), high sheriff of Lancashire and chairman of the magistrates, duly sanctioned his use of the available military forces.

The magistrates had certainly come 'prepared for war' and had at their disposal six hundred professional mounted troops of the 15th Hussars, plus several hundred infantrymen of the 88th Regiment of Foot, four hundred mounted men of the Cheshire Yeomanry, four hundred special constables, one hundred and twenty mounted Manchester and Salford Yeomanry and a Royal Artillery force with two six-pounder guns.

The action was initiated by the chief constable who ordered Hugh Birley (b.1778), a local factory owner commanding the mounted Yeomanry, to advance his cavalry to the hustings so that Hunt could be removed. However, the crowd was so dense that the inexperienced troops became fragmented and, as they approached the platform, they lost their composure and began indiscriminately hacking, beating and trampling the crowd out of the way. The following is an eyewitness account by Samuel Bamford (1788–1872) who was on the platform.

> *[the cavalry] were in confusion: they evidently could not, with all the weight of man and horse, penetrate the compact mass of human beings; and their sabres were plied to hew a way through naked held-up hands, and defenceless heads; and then they chopped limbs, and gaping skulls were seen; and groans and cries were mingled with the din of that horrid confusion.*[14]

When all the speakers were off the platform, the Yeomanry went on the rampage. The demonstrators began to respond by throwing sticks and stones at their oppressors, whereupon William Hulton ordered Lieutenant Colonel Guy L'Estrange (b.c1780), who was in charge of the professional soldiers, to assist the Yeomanry. In true military fashion, he formed the 15th Hussars in a line across the eastern end of the field, and then ordered them to charge the crowd. The Cheshire Yeomanry attacking from the south carried out a similar manoeuvre. The fleeing crowd, trapped between these two cavalry formations, tried to escape through Peter Street, only to find their way blocked by the bayonets of the 88th Regiment of Foot. Samuel Bamford continued his description of the final scene as follows:

> *The sun looked down through a sultry and motionless air…over the whole field, were strewed caps, bonnets, hats, shawls and shoes, and other parts of male and female dress: trampled torn and bloody. The yeomanry had dismounted, some easing their horses' girths…some wiping their sabres. Several mounds of human beings still remained where they had fallen, crushed down and smothered. Some of these still groaning – others with staring eyes, were gasping for breath and others would never breathe no more. All was silent save those low sounds and the occasional snorting and pawing of steeds.*[14]

The casualties from Peterloo were horrendous and have been recorded in detail after painstaking research by Michael Bush in *The Casualties of Peterloo*. 'In fact fifteen people were killed or died from their wounds and 654 people were recorded as injured – the majority seriously.' However, the figure for the number of injured was probably well over seven hundred, as some casualty lists have been lost and many cases were not reported for fear of reprisal. Furthermore, it has become obvious from the casualty lists that women, of whom there were a great number, were singled out for particularly brutal treatment by the Yeomanry. 'This was class war at its most bloody, a spiteful one-sided war.'[15]

A contemporary account *The Peter Loo Massacre* was written by P. Wroe in 1819, and this publication was immediately labelled seditious by the local magistrates, and banned on the grounds that our 'gallant troops' and 'worthy citizens' in the Yeomanry would never behave in the despicable manner described in the pamphlet. Common people found themselves in trouble with the authorities for simply discussing such literature, while in the town of Salford in Lancashire, John Chorlton was found guilty of sedition as a result of selling Wroe's pamphlet. This was only one of seventy-five cases of sedition brought in 1819.[16]

Peterloo turned out to be a public relations disaster for the government, as the radicals seized the moral high ground. It provided the springboard for the Yorkshire Revolution of 1820 in which John Lindley was to play an important part, while John Gale Jones recalled the following reaction:

> *From the fatal day when the sword was drawn and war declared against the people of England, by the bloody and unavenged massacre of the defenceless men, women and children of Manchester, I was one of those who made up their mind that all further praying and petitioning ought to be at an end, that the time for reform was past and the hour of revolution come.*[17]

Home Secretary Sidmouth's uncompromising attitude to the incident can be judged from the fact that when the phlegmatic Earl Fitzwilliam, the Whig lord lieutenant of the West Riding of Yorkshire, supported a county meeting to protest against the treatment of civilians, which led to the Peterloo Massacre, he was summarily dismissed from his post on 18 November. This was typical of the response from London. The aristocratic Whig, Earl Fitzwilliam, was one of the greatest landowners in England who lived for a substantial part of the year in his mansion, Wentworth Woodhouse, near the south Yorkshire border, and so had excellent local knowledge of conditions in the West Riding.[18]

Stirrings of Insurrection

The response of the people in the west of Yorkshire to Peterloo was to hastily convene a mass meeting on 19 August 1819. Held at Almondbury Bank, it was attended by thousands, who listened to a report by an unnamed speaker 'from over the Pennines' (Lancashire). This was followed by a mass demonstration at Skircoat Common on Monday 2 October 1819. At a further meeting on 8 November 1819, a crowd of over eight thousand marched to Almondbury Bank, carrying a flag inscribed 'Rouse Britons and assert your rights'. This stormy meeting was chaired by John Dickinson, a Dewsbury draper. With Peterloo fresh in people's minds, the main issue revolved around the perennial question of whether to proceed by constitutional or violent means to achieve a Bill of Rights.[19]

Meanwhile, in the surrounding villages, numerous meetings were held such as to alarm the vicar of Sandal, Rev. T. Westmoreland, who wrote to the home secretary, Lord Sidmouth:

> *I find that the greater part of the people called Methodists are united with the radicals; they assemble in the evenings in certain cottages in the country, under the*

pretence of religious worship but…at these meetings they are in the constant habit of reading the works of Wooler, Cobbett &c. At these meetings also they form plans for advancing the wages of operative manufactures, by means of association.[20]

In the face of mass discontent, demonstrations and rioting, the government responded in December 1819 to the judicial massacre at Peterloo by introducing the notorious 'Six Acts'.

The Six Acts

The first act (60 George III c.1). The Unlawful Drilling Act 1819: prohibited drilling and military training by private individuals on pain of arrest and transportation.

The second act (60 George III c.2). The Seizure of Arms Act: authorised local magistrates to enter and search private houses on suspicion of there being arms, without warrants. If weapons were found they were to be seized and the owners arrested, followed by severe penalties.

The third act (60 George III c.3). The Misdemeanours Act: was ostensibly to prevent delay in the administration of justice. This allowed local magistrates to try people charged with political offences without waiting for the local assizes with a judge and jury, thereby reducing the opportunity for bail. (This was to circumnavigate the reluctance of juries to convict on the evidence of informers).

The fourth act (60 George III c.6). The Seditious Meetings Prevention Act: was to prevent seditious meeting by prohibiting meetings exceeding fifty persons (with certain exceptions such as county and parish meetings). It stipulated that meetings to present petitions must be confined to people of the parish where the meeting was taking place.

The fifth act (60 George III c.8). Blasphemous and Seditious Libels Act: sought to prevent sedition by increasing punishment for blasphemous and seditious libels. The maximum sentence was increased to fourteen years transportation. It gave magistrates the power to search houses, without warrants, for seditious literature.

The sixth act (60 George III c.9). The Newspaper and Stamp Duties Act: subjected certain (radical) newspapers, pamphlets and periodicals that had escaped tax by publishing opinions and not news, to stamp duty, thereby raising their cost to at least 6d. Publishers were required to post a bond for their behaviour with the object of restraining publication of blasphemous and seditious libel. (It was hoped that this would reduce the circulation of radical publications, in particular Cobbett's *Political Register*.)[21]

But, in the wake of the 'Peterloo Massacre', all the Six Acts achieved was to strengthen the resolve of 'the people' to overthrow the government. At a meeting in Leeds, in December 1819, held to protest against the Six Acts, James Brayshaw of Leeds, a Paineite republican and Christian freethinker, proposed a motion in favour of arming. The motion was carried, and the Yorkshire rebellion was instigated. Brayshaw later tried to attribute the rising to James Mann, another Leeds radical and owner of a bookshop, which was used as a meeting place for his fellow conspirators.[22]

There was an increasing belief among the working class and artisans, throughout the land, that the country should not be run by 'the small, wealthy, and mostly unelected aristocratic elite' who ruled in their own interest. Locally, this sentiment was expressed in a resolution passed by the Barnsley Union Society in July 1819, a month before the Peterloo Massacre:

> *The sole design of forming civil government was for promoting the welfare and happiness of the body politic, and whatever authority any man possess is derived from the community at large; consequently, if any government cease to answer the purpose for which it was appointed, or violate the rights of those who are governed, those from whom their power is derived have a right to call their government to account.*[23]

On 29 January 1820, George III died at Windsor after a reign of fifty-nine years. He was hardly missed by the people of the West Riding. Far more important was the price of bread (10d for a 4lb wheaten loaf) and the deepening economic hardship suffered by the labouring classes. At the end of January, the *Leeds Mercury* reported:

> *In Huddersfield and the populous villages by which it is surrounded, a very laborious investigation has been made into the condition of the poor, and the result has been to exhibit a picture of human misery and distress which has astonished those who were before well convinced that the labouring classes were suffering severe privations.*[24]

By the spring, there was still no sign of any increase in the level of employment, discontent was rife and rebellion was in the air. But hunger was not the sole reason for rebellion – the origins went much deeper. The anger at the callous barbarity of the authorities during the 'Peterloo Massacre' was rekindled in the following February, when the trial of the organisers of the Manchester meeting was transferred to York, and the prosecution witnesses passed though Huddersfield on 14th March to the barracking and hisses of the crowd.[25]

This was the background to the Yorkshire West Riding Revolt of 1820 by 'The Radicals', in which John Lindley played his part in the long and desperate fight against tyrannical rule and so earned a place in history.

CHAPTER 12
The West Yorkshire Rebellion of 1820

West Yorkshire Rising 31 March – 1 April 1820

The origin of the Yorkshire Rebellion of 1820 can be traced to a series of meetings held at Joseph Pilling's house near the Red Lion, Huddersfield, sometime in the weeks following the Almondbury meeting of 8 November 1819. The purpose of the group was to discuss political reform and plot revolution to bring about a universal male franchise. It included radical clothier Joshua Hirst of Deighton and a number of other Huddersfield radicals. At the same time, a number of the Leeds radicals were meeting secretly in different locations, with James Mann's bookshop in Leeds acting as a contact point.[1]

In order to ascertain the extent of their support, James Brayshaw, a Yeadon schoolmaster, adopted the guise of a commercial traveller and visited a number of northern towns. He reported back that only Carlisle was making any significant preparations for an uprising. In Leeds, support for revolution had dwindled, probably due to the rigour adopted by the authorities to suppress all signs of dissent. As a consequence, their fortnightly meetings were consolidated with those held in Huddersfield, but close contact was still maintained with other local groups, such as those at Barnsley, Sheffield and Wakefield. In addition, delegates attended meetings in more distant towns such as Birmingham, Glasgow, Manchester and Nottingham, where it is recorded that John Pilling was the Huddersfield representative. It is certain that a much more extensive network of revolutionary cells existed in 1820 than in 1817 and 'at the local level there was far more detailed planning'.[2]

On 23 February 1820 Arthur Thistlewood (1774–1820), who had famously challenged Home Secretary Lord Sidmouth to a duel, and for his temerity had been imprisoned without trial for a year, was arrested in London. He was the leader of a small group in London, who planned to assassinate the entire cabinet at a dinner held at the home of the Earl of Harrowby (1798–1882), in what has been labelled the Cato Street Conspiracy. Thistlewood, James Ings (c1785–1820), John Brunt (c1790–1820), William Davidson (1781–1820) and Richard Tidd (c1775–1820) were executed by hanging outside Newgate Prison on 1 April; after hanging for half an hour they were cut down and their heads severed from their bodies and held up to the proclamation 'the head of a traitor'. It is worth noting that the method of hanging employed (the short drop) resulted in death by strangulation, typically after ten to twenty minutes. The execution at Newgate put an end to any possible support from the capital for the Yorkshire, Lancashire and Glasgow revolutionaries and served as a dire warning as to their possible fate in the event of failure.[3]

The Huddersfield radicals were not deterred by this setback and continued to arm themselves as the following incident records. About three months before the uprising, Joseph Smith, a joiner, called at the blacksmith's shop of Joseph Barker, near his home at Colne Bridge, and asked him to make a pike head. Apparently, there was a problem with the design and so, a week later, Joseph Smith returned with a wooden pattern demonstrating the required design. Barker and his two stepsons, Ben and George, then manufactured around seventeen pike heads at two shillings each. John Lindley ordered three pikes with screw heads and then a further three, but it is not clear if these were the same design as Smith's.[4]

This is the first appearance of John Lindley in the radical records. However, it seems almost certain that he also played a major part in the events leading up to this procurement of arms, as he would not have purchased a number of pike heads on his own initiative.

The next record relies on the testimony of Samuel Norcliffe, who claimed that about 9 March he found John Lindley, the Mirfield delegate, and two others visiting his uncle Edmund Norcliffe at his house in Mirfield. The reason for the visit was the need to collect money to finance travelling expenses of delegates employed in organising the uprising. These delegates were required to visit other towns in the network in order to co-ordinate activities in what was planned to be a national uprising and installation of an alternative government. Since Edmund Norcliffe was a committed supporter of the uprising, he was an obvious person to ask for a donation.[5]

On Sunday 12 March 1820, a meeting was held at Berry Brow School in Huddersfield, attended by Joshua Hirst, Peter Lever, Joseph Pilling and delegates from different parts of the country. Revolutionary progress was discussed and the mood was optimistic; 'they had every reason to hope that all parts of the country were getting on rapidly for a revolution and that it would shortly be affected'. The lesson of over-optimism still had not been learned from the 1817 debacle at Folly Hall![6]

On Sunday 19 March 1820, a second meeting was held at Joseph Strakey's house at Cowcliffe. It was attended by Joshua Hirst, William Hirst, Peter Lever and Joseph Smith from Colne Bridge and about a dozen other delegates. It was at this meeting that it was decided to implement Peter Lever's idea that, in order to coordinate action by the various groups, an official signal to commence the attack should be given by the committee; it would take the form of cards with 'democracy' written on them. To ensure that the message was genuine each card was cut into two, with demo– on one half and –cracy on the other half. One half was given to each of the delegates, with instructions not to mobilise their men until they received the matching half from the accredited messenger.[7]

On Sunday 26 March 1820, delegates 'the greater part of whom had been military men' met again at Joseph Strakey's house for the purpose of formulating a plan of attack on the town of Huddersfield. It was then taken by William Hirst to other members of the Huddersfield committee for their agreement. After this meeting John Lindley returned to Mirfield, implying that, although not being mentioned by name, he had been present at the two previous Sunday meetings. On his way home, he called at Edmund Norcliffe's house where he met Joseph Hirst, John Peacock, John Winter and a carpenter called Thomas Winn. John Tyas of Rastrick was also present. Samuel Norcliffe asked, 'how were they to be sure a general rising was to take place' and that they would not be deceived. The Folly Hall debacle of 1817 was obviously still very much in mind. John Lindley then explained to his group about the 'democracy' cards, assuring them that the signal would be genuine. The big difference on this occasion, resulting from much greater security on the part of the plotters, was that the local magistrates and military had no intelligence about the impending uprising.[8]

The final Cowcliffe meeting, before the uprising, was held on Thursday 30 March 1820, again at Joseph Strakey's house. About twenty delegates attended this meeting, including Peter Lever, Jackson, Joshua Hirst, William Hirst and men from Berry Brow, Honley, Marsden, Lindley, Elland, Rastrick, Ripponden and Liversedge. Lever addressed the meeting, 'the whole country is ready for revolution'. He claimed Manchester, Sheffield and Glasgow were fully prepared. It was noted by the prosecution at the subsequent trial 'that John Lindley did not seem to have taken an active part in this meeting'.[9]

The Plan of Attack

The plan of operation was to march on the town of Huddersfield in four divisions, and to give battle if resistance was shown by the military or magistrates.

The eastern division, comprising sections from Mirfield, Hartshead, High Town and Colne Bridge, with contingents from Dalton and Deighton, was expected to provide between five hundred and one thousand men under John Lindley and Joshua Norcliffe. They were to rendezvous in Kirklees Lane, adjoining the park of Sir George Armytage, which was about four miles from the centre of Huddersfield.

The northern division, comprising sections from Brighouse, Elland, Rastrick and Thornhills, with contributions from Netheroyd Hill and Cowcliffe, was to assemble at Fixby Park, about two miles from Huddersfield. They were expected to provide substantial numbers.

The western division from Lindley, Ripponden, Barkisland, Quarmby and Out Lane was expected to provide one thousand men and assemble at Lindley Moor, about two miles from Huddersfield town centre. In the event, this was the only division to approach its estimated strength and was by far the most numerous group.

The southern division, with contingents from Kirkheaton, Skelmanthorpe, Thornhill, Grange Moor, Kirkburton, Almondbury, and Moldgreen, with an expected strength of over one thousand, was to assemble at Almondbury Bank, within a mile of the centre of the town.

The assembly points for all divisions had a clear view of Castle Hill, the prehistoric hill fort to the south east of the town. The signal for all divisions to commence their march on Huddersfield Town would be given by lighting a beacon on Castle Hill. Having thus surrounded the town, all parties were to advance at the same moment. The northern and western divisions, attacking the upper end of the town, were to capture the horse barracks and secure the cavalry, while the eastern and southern divisions were to take possession of the barracks occupied by the infantry, who were to be secured.

A fifth group, the Huddersfield men residing in the town, were to act as a fifth column and seize the magistrate's quarters at the George Inn. All civil authorities were at the same time to be made prisoners and the principal inhabitants confined to their dwellings. A provisional government would then be declared.

Once Huddersfield had been secured, the signal for a general rising throughout the West Riding and the rest of the country was to be carried out by the stoppage of coaches passing through Huddersfield. The plans were drawn up by Abraham Jackson of Moldgreen using initials to hide the identity of the participants.[10]

The rebellion got off to a bad start when the delegates from Berry Brow, Honley and Holmfirth refused to take part in a night attack and said that they would wait until morning to see the outcome.

At Colne Bridge, there was frantic activity as Ben Barker and his two stepsons were kept busy up until the last minute completing 'late orders' for pikes. 'At the Knowl, Mirfield, John Lindley and Edmund Norcliffe spent much of the day splitting ash poles for shafts and straightening scythe blades in the fire, for pike heads.'[11]

The expected signal to muster arrived at seven o'clock on Friday 31 March, when a messenger from Huddersfield arrived at Cowcliffe. This unnamed person gave Joshua Hirst his half of a 'democracy' card and said he was going on to Liversedge and Mirfield and other places, and asked Hirst to go to Bradley Mill, Lower Road. Joshua Hirst immediately informed his people, about six in number, to be prepared.[12]

John Lindley's matching half 'democracy' card was delivered to him at about eight o'clock, by a young man who told him to take his men to Bradley Mill, Lane End, by half past twelve, and join the contingents from Dalton, Deighton and surrounding townships. John Lindley asked Samuel Norcliffe to go and tell the men to get ready as soon as possible. Samuel Norcliffe first called on John Peacock to mobilise his men. Peacock then proceeded to Lee Green, where he told several people that 'It seems the Revolution is to begin this evening'. Finally, after crossing some fields, he arrived at the turnpike road and met up with John Lindley at the blacksmith's shop of Joseph Holmes. John Peacock, Nathaniel Buckley and George Crabtree arrived equipped with pikes, William Hill and George Hirst carried scythes, and only William Illingworth and George Crabtree had guns. They returned to the Knowl and found that Edmund Norcliffe had gone to bed, which presumably left John Lindley in charge. Pikes were recovered from the mistal (cowshed and milking parlour) and leant against the house wall for anyone who arrived without a weapon. John Lindley spent most of the evening rushing round Mirfield, 'until his shirt was wet on his back' trying to rouse participants. Finally, at eleven-fifty at night, he went to the Kings Head public house in Cripplegate and persuaded four members of the Gill family, Tom, George, Sam and James to accompany him to the Knowl.[13]

Sometime between eleven and midnight, Hannah Schofield, the local nosy parker, observed about a score of men 'with spears' march off under the command of Samuel Norcliffe, who now seemed to have been acting as lieutenant. She observed that they were accompanied part of the way by Edmund Norcliffe's two little daughters. There seemed to have been a distinct lack of weapons, in particular firearms, and if the four to five hundred Mirfield men had turned up, as forecast at the meeting held the previous day, it is difficult to know how they would all have been provided with weapons.[14]

After they left Edmund Norcliffe's house, the Mirfield men proceeded via the Wasps Nest to Battyeford, where they were joined by Samuel Hirst. They then marched on to Dumb Steeple at Cooper Bridge, the historic site of the rendezvous for the attack on Rawfords Mill in 1812.

While waiting at Dumb Steeple for reinforcements, they were joined by Ben Armitage of Clifton. At this point in time an unfortunate incident occurred. Five men, including John Hinchcliffe a farmer from Bradley, Robert Tolson a fancy manufacturer from Dalton, Job Harrison a gamekeeper of Bradley, George Brierley a carpenter of Clifton and an unidentified man were on the way home from an evening out at the Horseshoe Inn, situated at the bottom of Mirfield Moor. Suddenly, they came upon a group of about fifteen unarmed men at the 'weighing machine' near the Dumb Steeple. Hinchcliffe was rash enough to challenge the group and insist that they dispersed. Immediately, forty to fifty men appeared from behind a garden wall. They were armed with five feet long staves, fitted with iron pike heads, which were from nine to twelve inches long. When Tolson asked if they were going to murder them, the men began to prick him with their pikes and he sustained a two-inch deep cut in his back that grazed his ribs. He also sustained a second slight wound in his side. Finally, he was struck on his left arm by a pikestaff and at this point he made his escape. But he had not gone many yards when he heard a pistol shot, and on looking round he saw in the moonlight a man pointing a pistol at Hinchcliffe, at a range of ten to fifteen yards. On his way home, Tolson decided to avoid Dalton Bank, as there was much firing from that direction, and as he passed the house of Thomas Kilner he called in but would not let him accompany him home.

This was the only record of blood being spilled in the entire 'revolution', and it is believed that this was the reason that five members of the Mirfield group were singled out for prosecution at York Castle in June. It is also possible that both John Lindley and John Peacock were marked out for their literacy. This skirmish proved too much for two of the rebels who returned home, while Sam Norcliffe, in order to distance himself from the 'rebellion', claimed that he went no further than Bradley Bar.[15]

It was a greatly diminished force that marched on to Bradley Mill, Lane End, led by John Lindley – they found no one there! Joshua Hirst, armed with a gun and the rest of his party with pikes, had left home at about twelve o'clock and gone to Whitacre's Mill but, on finding that the Deighton men had already dispersed, Hirst said that this was another 'Oliver Job' and took his men home. And so, John Lindley's party turned back along the footpath and met the Colne Bridge men coming from Whitacre's Mill. When asked what was happening, Nathaniel Buckley said in disgust 'that Huddersfield was quieter than it had been for a day or two'. The Barkers and a couple of others decided to call it a night, while some remained for about a quarter of an hour, hoping for a sign that the revolution was still in progress, before returning to their homes between three and four in the morning.[16]

The northern-western division met at Fixby Park where, sometime after midnight, it was estimated that between fifty and three hundred men had assembled (estimates vary widely). Later, they were joined by 'a few men from Fixby' led by Henry Wrigley and Henry Lee, and finally a separate group of about fifteen men arrived under Joseph Tiffany, a cropper from Cowcliffe.[17]

At the township of Lindley, to the west of Huddersfield, there was a determined effort to raid houses for arms. George Pilling, a Birchencliffe cropper, Tom Rhodes, cropper, Tom Schofield, master cropper of Marsh, and Job Barker of Birchencliffe were identified as members of the group that numbered about twenty to thirty men. Later a group of about one hundred men, in three companies with sticks (the witness said they could have been pikes) over their shoulders were seen marching towards Huddersfield.[18]

The Lindley men, when reinforced by others from Ripponden and Barkisland, eventually numbered several hundred. The size of this group gave the men a determination and confidence lacking in other divisions. An advance party went as far as Trinity Church, Greenhead, where they drew up across the road in ranks six deep. When they learned that the other divisions had not mustered as agreed, the Lindley leaders decided to call off the attack, but it was only with the greatest reluctance that the men of the western group dispersed. They were seen returning home in twos and threes by Thomas Wilson at about four o'clock in the morning.[19]

The southern division was due to assemble at Almondbury Bank. At about one in the morning, several men – the advance guard – passed through the tollgate at Dogley Lane coming from the direction of Kirkburton. An hour later, about one hundred men passed through the tollgate, followed at intervals by two further groups of fifty, all marching in well drilled companies. Another witness claimed to have seen a number of people pass his house in Almondbury, two or three having pikes, some having guns, and many wearing white hats, the symbol of the radical movement.[20]

According to the testimony of John Whitacre, the signal beacon on the famous Castle Hill was lit for about five minutes at two in the morning, but by that time it was too late; many men had gone home and enthusiasm had dwindled.

Once alerted, probably by the two to three hundred pistol shots discharged during the evening, the Huddersfield magistrates established their headquarters at the George Hotel. The Yeomanry were mobilised along with a troop of the 4th Dragoon Guards and three companies of the 85th Regiment of Foot. They remained on the alert all night, but the expected attack never came. Over the next few days patrols were sent out to reconnoitre, but all they found were a few pikes and pikestaves.

Depositions from a large number of witnesses were taken by the local Huddersfield magistrate B. Haigh-Allen on 2 and 3 April 1820. These are recorded as follows:

Marmaduke Banson, George Barker, Mark Brook, Charles Chapman, John Crabtree, Thomas Crabtree, Thomas Crother, John Elam, Richard Fox, Joseph Firth, John Hardcastle, Job Harrison, John Hinchcliffe, Joshua Hirst, Thomas Kilner, George Mellar, Elizabeth Milner, Samuel Norcliffe, Jonathan Parrot, Thomas Schofield, Thomas Swift, Richard Thornton, Joseph Tiffany, Robert Tolson, Joseph Tyas, John Waterhouse, John Whitacre, John Wilson.[21]

Some people on this large list were prepared to talk, often very circumspectly, as they had to live in a community that sympathised with the rebels. Often one name and a small number of unidentifiable others were reported. The night attack meant that it was dark and conveniently many witnesses could not see clearly. As a result of all these statements a number of arrests were made, largely on the unsubstantiated claims of these frightened witnesses. The Barkers, John Lindley, John Peacock, Nathaniel Buckley and Joshua Hirst were among the first batch 'charged with being under arms'. *The Times* of 5 April 1820 reported that John Lindley was taken into custody soon after the incident on 31 March.[22]

Strangely, of all the two thousand rebels involved, and the large number of named individuals disclosed to the authorities as participants, many identified as carrying arms, only five men from the Mirfield contingent who met at Dumb Steeple were brought to trial. Most were not even questioned. However, a few men like the Barkers turned King's evidence to avoid prosecution.

The magistrates quickly held a meeting, on Wednesday 5 April, and informed about one hundred of Huddersfield's leading citizens that between one thousand six hundred and two thousand rebels had been under arms the previous Friday 'whose object was to change by force the existing order of society...they had been frustrated by the vigilance of the magistrates and the lack of coordination by the disaffected.'[23]

West Yorkshire Rising 11 – 12 April 1820

The majority of Huddersfield rebels escaped to return to their beds undetected. The following day, James Wilson went to Barnsley and made contact with Richard Addy, a member of the Barnsley Union Society, imparting the news that there was to be a second attempt to capture Huddersfield on 12 April. As a result, Craven Cookson and Stephen Kitchener, two senior members of the secret Barnsley committee, went to Huddersfield to check the plans. They returned to Barnsley, where they reported that the rising was genuine, and recommended that the Barnsley men should join in this second attempt by assembling on Grange Moor on Wednesday 12 April. They should therefore assemble on the night of Tuesday 11 April.

Members of the secret committee met at the house of Thomas Farrimond on the Tuesday morning, to discuss the latest plans from Huddersfield. The leaders, Richard Addy, William Rice, John Burkinshaw and Benjamin Rogers were present with a number of other unnamed members. Instructions were then given that all were to rise and 'meet in arms' at Bank Top at twelve o'clock that night (those that had no arms were to procure them as best they could), before proceeding to Grange Moor to demand their rights. Once the various parties had concentrated in a single body, the plan was to advance and take Huddersfield, then march to Leeds and Wakefield, returning through Barnsley and south to Sheffield. Finally, all parties would converge on the capital and take London. It was announced that the Scots would meet them at Leeds. Those who did not join them would have no mercy shown but would be put to the bayonet by the main body when they passed through Barnsley. With these preliminaries settled, it appears that the news of the intended rising was spread throughout Barnsley and the surrounding district, with the rumours becoming more exaggerated as the day progressed.

March to Grange Moor

Consequently, at about eleven o'clock on the night of 11 April, the men of Dodworth, which is a village about two miles to the south west of Barnsley, were seen on the move. Led by John Pickering, a twenty-six-year-old weaver who had served in the infantry, about forty or fifty men armed chiefly with pikes proceeded to a place called Jackson's Square in Dodworth, where they roused the inhabitants and called on them to join the general rising. From here they went to the house of James Seddon, a weaver, woke up his family and gained admission into his house. Some of them went upstairs to a bedchamber where William Seddon, the son of James, and George Beevers, his apprentice, were in bed. The insurgents forced them to get up and tried to persuade them to join the party, saying that 'they were going to Grange Moor to obtain their rights' and threatening the lives of any that refused.

At about eleven o'clock the Barnsley men, principally of weavers, began to assemble in a field at Bank Top, which is about a mile south of Barnsley. They arrived to the beat of a drum, with flags flying, armed with pikes, guns and other weapons. Some came singly, others in straggling groups to the agreed assembly point. One party, on its way to Bank Top, while passing the house of Mrs Hall, woke up the family and demanded and obtained a gun.

As the small groups arrived at Bank Top the men were formed in ranks by Richard Addy, a former Waterloo man who had served in the Rifle Corps and who was acting as second-in-command of the company. Soon after midnight, their numbers having increased to about two hundred, the men marched off under the leadership of William Comstive, a local weaver in his late twenties who had also fought at Waterloo as a sergeant in the 29th Regiment of Foot.

At Union Street, the Barnsley men were joined by the Dodworth party and the combined force marched through Union Street over Wilson Piece along the Pease Hills to the Callendar House, and then by the coal pit into the turnpike road leading to Grange Moor. This route led the main body of men round the outskirts of Barnsley. However, in a show of bravado, six men, each armed with a pike, marched through the centre of Barnsley defying the patrols sent out by the local inhabitants.

The first place that the men stopped, after reaching the turnpike road, was the house of William Pickard which lay a short distance from the town. Here, they knocked and shouted until Pickard came to the bedroom window and asked what they wanted. They demanded his firearms and, on being told that he had none, they endeavoured to break down the door, but without success; and frustrated they broke many of the bedroom windows instead.

At Bench Lane End, which is near Darton, a party roused George Hirst, innkeeper of the Rose and Crown, and demanded firearms, threatening to break down the door if it were not opened. Here they obtained a gun, which the revolutionaries said they would return.

Upon reaching Darton, sometime after two o'clock, they stopped at the house of Thomas Richardson, an innkeeper, and demanded his firearms. The landlord refused either to open the door or deliver up his arms, so the party attacked the door and broke one of the panels – this induced the landlord to hand over five guns. Since the insurgents were not satisfied that he had handed over all his arms, they issued further threats and obtained from him another gun.

At the house of Thomas Hill at Cold Henley, which they reached sometime after four o'clock, they again demanded firearms and obtained a gun and a small quantity of powder and shot, which was mixed together in a lead box.

By the time the company reached the village of Flockton, which is about half a mile from Grange Moor, daylight was breaking. Here, two or three hundred men were observed by several inhabitants marching towards Grange Moor to the beat of a drum with flags flying, carrying pikes, guns, and hay forks, while many had knapsacks on their backs.

The company arrived at dawn after a six-mile march at the designated meeting point, the Blacksmiths Arms on Grange Moor. This was open moorland situated about halfway between Huddersfield and Barnsley. To their dismay, the Barnsley men were greeted by twenty or so local radicals, rather than the thousands of Huddersfield men that they had expected. Thomas Farrimond declared that they had been betrayed and panic set in. As a result, most of the men quickly returned in small groups back to their respective homes. Shortly after the dispersal, a small detachment of cavalry from Huddersfield, comprising sixteen members of the local Yeomanry and ten men of the 4th Dragoon Guards, under the command of Major de Bath, arrived on the scene. There was no revolutionary army in sight, only a scattering of over one hundred pikes and various flags for the military to collect as trophies. No military engagement took place, and the troops sent to confront the insurgents simply arrested seventeen men.

When the men began to fall into disorder, Comstive said that they had been 'brought into an oven' and they must not go back again, for if they did they would be sure to be hanged. After a fruitless attempt to rally the men, Comstive, Addy and Stansfield joined Hanson in the Blacksmiths Arms. After some consultation, the four decided to set off to Huddersfield to find out the reason why their men had not turned up, but before setting off, all four gave their knapsacks to two followers, Fenton and Thompson, asking them to keep them until they returned. In addition, Addy gave Fenton a green silk flag to take care of.

Chapter 12

Later the same morning, Comstive, Addy, Stansfield and Hanson were seen together at a public house called Hill House near Huddersfield, apparently in an exhausted state. And in the afternoon, they were arrested as they were returning together over Grange Moor. They were escorted to a public house called the Kaye Arms at Grange Ash where they remained that night. While they were at the Kaye Arms, Comstive and Addy each made a voluntary statement to the landlord about the insurrection. Next day they were removed to Huddersfield.

One of the stragglers, Joseph Tyas, was arrested near Huddersfield, three days after the rising. In his pocket was a letter addressed to 'Our brethren in Lankaster Shire' which said 'Our musick in Yorkshire as played twise where yours in Lankashire has never struck at all, is your Musicians sick?' Another straggler, Joseph Chapiel, was apprehended sometime later at Ashton under Lyne, at the house of a shoemaker where he had found employment.

The failure of the numerous radical risings in the early nineteenth century was largely due to the slow and unreliable communications at that time. No one wanted to move first, and the problem of co-ordinating a revolution, on the scale required, proved beyond the organisational abilities of those involved. For this, John Lindley must carry some of the blame, because the small band that assembled at the Dumb Steeple bore no relationship to the hundreds of men promised. As the Mirfield delegate he was culpable of over-optimism. Furthermore, he should have known that working men had no legal access to firearms and still less the ability to use them.

It must be said that the government skilfully played its part with an efficient network of spies and informers, thereby keeping the potential powder keg under control. The official line was that the government feared an 'English Revolution' with similar results to the 'French Revolution', but it has also been suggested that the government played upon this fear to justify its repressive measures.

Incarceration at York Castle

Conditions in York Castle were notoriously grim. On 29 May, the prisoners wrote to the home secretary, Lord Sidmouth, as follows:

> *My Lord*
> *We the undersigned Prisoners in his Majesty's Castle of York, solicit your Lordship for your permission for the Fathers Mothers, Brothers and sisters of we the undersigned to be permitted to see us as we are not all married men, and some of our wives being dead, the present order does not authorise magistrates to grant permission to any but wives and children and we that are not married have not the indulgence of seeing our parents and relatives as above stated. We are your Lordships humble and obedient prisoners.*
> *The following signed their names:*
> *Richard Addy, Benjamin Anson, John Burkinshaw, George Bryan, Joseph Chapiel, William Comstive, John Farrimond, William Holland, Abraham Ingham, Abraham Larksass, John Lindley, Thomas Morgan, John Peacock, William Rice, Benjamin Rogers, Charles Stanfield, John Vallance.*
> *The remainder made their mark:*
> *Thomas Blackburn, Nathaniel Buckley, George Burkinshaw, Michael Downing, James Flowers, John Hobson, John Johnson.*[24]

The fact that seventy per cent of the prisoners could sign their names indicates the degree of literacy of the prisoners. This may reflect the general level of literacy of the radicals in general, or it could be that literate participants were 'selected' for trial because they were regarded as the most dangerous. The signature of Abraham Larksass looks like a joke!

Those who could write letters were permitted to communicate with friends and relatives. On 26 May, William Rice wrote to his brother; firstly, he wanted to convey his 'sincere but humble thanks for the kind treatment of his wife' who was staying under her brother-in-law's roof, and asked that his brother should continue to support his wife. He also complained of those people who administer oaths, as they did not know what distress they caused. William Comstive also wrote an undated letter to his brother or sister, while Michael Downing wrote a long letter to two friends on 28 May; since he could not sign his name on the above petition it must have been written for him, probably by a professional letter writer as the handwriting was good and the letter literate.

When conditions became even worse, a second petition – undated – was written to Sidmouth. In the margin someone has written 'coals found, shaving paid for, soap paid for, clothes found if required'.

> *My Lord*
> *In consequence of our present means being insufficient to support us we the undersigned send their petition to your Lordship imploring your Lordship to be pleased to consider the same. The following is what we are presently allowed; 4s 6d in money 10¹/₂ lb of bread for 7 days each man and we have our washing to pay for out of that money. If your Lordship would be pleased to consider the same, it will be found insufficient to meet the demands of nature and we are all poor and have nothing but the above to subsist on; which is in reality insufficient for men in our most deplorable situation and under a charge of that very great magnitude as we severally are. We are your Lordships very humble obedient Prisoners.*

Treason Trial

As with the Luddite trial of January 1813, the authorities chose to stage a 'show trial' in order to make examples of the identifiable rebel leaders. In this case, however, leniency was shown in order to avoid making martyrs, who would act as a rallying call for further revolt.

The trial commenced on 15 July 1820, at York Castle, before Sir John Bagley and Sir James Allen Park, with a jury of two hundred and fifty, comprised largely of gentlemen and yeomen with over half from the East and North Riding. The prosecutor was John Saville. The trial was presented in two parts. First: The King vs Lindley and others, namely Nathaniel Buckley, Thomas Blackburn, John Peacock and Joseph Smith (who was not in custody), in respect of the disturbances on 31 March and 1 April. And secondly: The King vs Comstive and others (these numbered twenty, but two were not in custody) with respect to 11 and 12 of April.

In the case of The King against John Lindley there were three counts: 'Levying War; Compassing and Imagining to Depose the King; and Compassing to levy War against the King, in order to compel him to change his Measures.'

The prosecution evidence against John Lindley and others was presented by John Saville who stated that: 'Two to three months before the rising, John Lindley who is a nail maker by trade but who was at that time working on the navigation [canal], which runs by Colne Bridge, brought several pikes to Joseph Barker a blacksmith with directions "to make them screw" [the heads screw to the shaft] and when that was done he took them away. John Lindley and John Peacock were frequently seen together at Edmund Norcliffe's [house]. John Lindley was actively engaged during the night in an attempt to raise the Mirfield people, but without much success. He was afterwards seen with a small party, mostly armed with pikes, he himself bearing one, on the Turnpike Road between Colne Bridge and Huddersfield.'

'Nathaniel Buckley appeared on the night of the rising about dark at the shop of Joseph Barker the blacksmith at Colne Bridge and brought with him a piece of iron and ordered a pike to be made from it. A pike was made for him and he waited for it and took it away paying two shillings for it. He was afterwards seen with Lindley's party on the Turnpike Road armed with a pike.'

'Thomas Blackburn who lives at Wasps Nest in Mirfield appears to have joined Lindley's party there, and to have received a pike and proceeded with them to Dumb Steeple and thence to the turnpike road, where he was seen armed with a pike.'

'John Peacock who lives in Tan House in Mirfield was frequently in the house of Edmund Norcliffe as above stated. On the night of the rising when he was informed that the messenger had brought the card and was desired to bring his force to Edmund Norcliffe's house. He agreed to get them as soon as he could and was seen going towards Norcliffe's house with a pike and on his way enquired if any person were there. He was afterward seen with John Lindley's party.'

'Joseph Smith was a joiner who lived at Colne Bridge. He was one of the persons who attended the meeting at Cowcliffe when the DEMOCRACY cards were distributed. He likewise ordered a pike from Joseph Barker to be made according to a wooden pattern, which he supplied, and the pike was made accordingly. On the night of the rising he brought a pistol to Barker's [house] to be cleaned and took from his pocket the two corresponding pieces of card saying that he had orders to meet at Whitacres Mill and he spoke of the intended rising that evening. He was afterwards seen armed with a pike and a horse pistol leading a party to Whitacres Mill. He returned home about six am.'

Reason for Delayed Trial

The judges Mr Justice Bayley and Mr Justice Park, recalling the protracted trial of James Hunt at the previous Spring Assizes and the inconvenience that arose from the delay to succeeding cases, agreed that 'the pleas of the prisoners should be recorded, but their trial postponed until the 9 September.'[26]

The trial duly continued at York Castle before Bayley and Park on Thursday 9 September 1820 at two o'clock. The Crown Prosecution case was presented by Mr Raine, Sergeant Hullock, Sergeant Cross and Mr Littledale; while the accused were represented by Mr Starkie, Mr Blackburn and Mr Williams, who was not in court at the commencement of the trial.

The trial of Comstive and others, included in the second indictment, began with a charade. When all eighteen prisoners were directed to approach the bar, it was found impracticable to place so large a number in front of the bar, and the judge directed that they should be divided into two groups. The following prisoners were then placed at the bar: Richard Addy aged 29, John Burkinshaw 28, Joseph Chapiel 25, William Comstive 28, James Flowers 19, Benjamin Hanson 24, William Rice 40, Benjamin Rogers 30, Charles Stansfield 28, and the indictment was read.

The following is an abstract of the indictment, which contained three counts:

> **The first count** charged the prisoners with levying public war against the King in his realm.
> It alleged that the prisoners, with diverse other false traitors, assembled in the Parish of Silkstone, in the county of York on 11 April, arrayed in a warlike manner, armed with guns and other offensive weapons, and did then levy public war against the King, in his realm, for the purpose of endeavouring by force and violence to change the constitution in Church and State as by the law established.
> **The second count** charged the prisoners with compassing and imagining to depose the King from his imperial state and dignity.
> **The third count** charged the prisoners with conspiring to levy war against the King in order to compel him to change his measures.

The following overt acts were alleged to have been committed by the prisoners, to carry into effect the treasonable purpose in the two latter counts:

> 1. The prisoners met together to make and devise plans to change and subvert by force and violence the constitution as by law established.
> 2. Conspire to levy war for like purpose.
> 3. Providing arms and ammunition for the purpose of attacking the King's soldiers and others, his liege subjects and levying war in order to subvert the constitution.
> 4. Manufacturing pikes shafts For the purpose of attacking soldiers of the King and levying war against him.
> 5. Compelling persons to give up their arms and ammunition for the purpose of using the same to attack and destroy the soldiers and levying war against the King to subvert the constitution.
> 6. Using threats to compel other persons to join them and give up their arms to be used for the purpose.
> 7. Parading arms, with great noise and violence through divers villages, attacking houses and seizing arms and ammunition in order to arm themselves and other false traitors for the purpose of attacking soldiers and subjects of the King and to levy war against him, to subvert the constitution.
> 8. The ordinary making and levying of public war against the King.

The indictment having been read out, the Clerk of the Arraigns asked each prisoner in turn (William Comstive being first) the following questions which he repeated to the others in succession:

> 'How say you William Comstive, are you guilty of this High Treason whereof you are indicted, or not guilty'?
> Prisoner: 'Not guilty'
> Clerk of the Arraigns: 'How will you be tried?'
> Prisoner: 'By God and my country'
> Clerk of the Arraigns: 'God send you a good deliverance'.

The remaining eight prisoners also pleaded not guilty and the process was repeated with the second batch of prisoners: George Bryan aged 33, George Burkinshaw 25, Michael

Chapter 12

Downing 48, John Farrimond 25, Joseph Firth 26, John Hobson 20, William Holland 20, Abraham Ingham 27, John Vallance 24.

The prisoners from the neighbourhood of Huddersfield, included in the first indictment were then placed at the bar. John Lindley aged 50, Nathaniel Buckley 40, Thomas Blackburn 33, John Peacock 45. Joseph Smith, a person not in custody, was included in the same indictment.

Mr Starkie requested that the arrangement of these prisoners might be deferred until Monday, as their attorney, Mr Williams, had not arrived and it might be thought advisable to plead in abatement. The deferment was not allowed. The prisoners were then arraigned and severally pleaded not guilty.

The indictment against the Huddersfield prisoners was in every respect similar to that of the Barnsley prisoners, with the addition of the following overt act: Conspiring to devise plans to attack the town of Huddersfield. The assembling of arms was said to be on 31 March in the parish of Huddersfield.

Mr Starkie objected to the indictment as being deficient in a point of precision, as the overt acts were stated to be committed in the parish of Huddersfield, which includes several townships. It was upon these grounds that the plea in abatement was contemplated.

Mr Justice Bayley then directed William Comstive to be placed at the bar, and his lordship informed him that the court had referred to the statute, which requires the admission of prisoners charged with high treason, and found that they had not the power to make the order requested by the prisoners, they could only accept the attorney and counsel, who were to have free access to them at all reasonable times.

Mr Justice Bayley then stated that it was to be the order of the court that no part of the proceedings, with the speeches of the counsel or the evidence of the witnesses, should be published, either in newspapers or any such mode until after the termination of the trial, as the publication of them during the trial might be attended with prejudice to the prisoners, and the court expected this order to be punctually attended to.

Mr Hargrove, the printer of the *York Herald*, asked the judge whether the proceedings of the opening day were considered as included in the prohibition, and Justice Bayley replied that it would be better to abstain from any publication whatever.

The written case against the Barnsley men was then considered, in order to demonstrate what part the several prisoners took in the insurrection.

The prisoners William Comstive, Richard Addy, Charles Stanfield, Benjamin Hanson, Joseph Chapiel, Benjamin Rogers, Joseph Firth, John Vallance and John Farrimond were at this time living at or in the neighbourhood of Barnsley and, with the exception of Joseph Chapiel who was a cordwainer, were employed as linen weavers. Michael Downing lived at Monk Bretton and had formerly been a soldier. The other prisoners all lived in Dodworth and with the exception of William Rice, who was a cordwainer, were also employed as linen weavers.

The case against the Dodworth party was that after it assembled at the house of William Rice, that William Rice, John Pickering, William Holland, George and John Burkinshaw, George Bryan, Abraham Ingham, John Hobson and James Flowers were all present at the house of James Seddon at the time that the party endeavoured to force Seddon's son and his apprentice to join them. That Pickering was armed with a pike and a blunderbuss and acted as leader of the party. The case against William Comstive, a journeyman, was that he was seen equipping himself at his master's house with a knapsack on his back and a pike in his hand and, thus equipped, he left the house in company with

Thomas Ferrimond, saying that he was going to Bank Top. At Bank Top, Comstive was seen actively engaged in putting the men in ranks as they arrived and conducting himself as their leader. He was afterwards seen with the insurgents on the road near Darton. Richard Addy was seen at Bank Top, apparently acting under orders of Comstive as a subordinate officer or sergeant, and he was again seen with a gun in his hand at Darton, where he reported to some of the men that they had taken three guns.

Charles Stansfield was also seen among the insurgents at Bank Top. Joseph Firth was seen among the insurgents at Old Barnsley and was overheard to say that he would go and fetch a flag from his father's house. And he was afterwards observed between that place and Darton with a flagstaff in his hand. There also, Michael Downing was seen carrying a gun and bayonet. At Bretton, John Vallance was in the ranks with a pike in his hand. At Midgley, Joseph Chapiel was seen with a short gun and he was very busy pointing out the houses where they had firearms. He was also seen at Flockton. At Grange Moor, William Comstive, Richard Addy and Charles Stansfield were seen to be the persons most actively engaged in forming up the men in ranks. Among them were seen Benjamin Rogers, Joseph Firth, Benjamin Hanson, John Vallance, Joseph Chapiel and James Howes.

The judge advised the prisoners that their trial would commence on Monday morning at nine o'clock and the court adjourned. Nothing of significance happened on Saturday evening but, on Sunday, an offer was made to both the Huddersfield men and the Barnsley men by one of the law officers of the crown, to the effect that if they would consent to plead guilty to the charges preferred against them, their lives would be spared.

Sentenced to Death

Promptly at nine o'clock on Monday 11 September the trial commenced.

The prisoners had been given time to reflect on the offer by the court official. So it was not surprising that when Mr Williams, the leading counsel for the prisoners who had at last arrived in York, went to the bar and held a short conference with several of the prisoners for the purpose of ascertaining if they were still desirous of acceding to the proposal, which had been communicated to them the previous day, they all agreed to plead guilty. Having satisfied himself on this point, Mr Williams addressed the court. He stated that since the previous Saturday the prisoners had reconsidered the subject of their plea and were now desirous of withdrawing the plea of not guilty, and to plead guilty to the indictment.

Once Justice Bayley had satisfied himself that all the prisoners had agreed to plead guilty, as confirmed by Comstive (who always seemed to act as the spokesman for the other prisoners), he then launched into a lengthy speech that, by alluding to the influence of the radical press, left a legal loophole to commute the mandatory death sentence to transportation.

> *The Government is bound carefully to attend to each particular case, and it must be a matter of the highest gratification to extend mercy where it can be done consistent with the public good. Yet they have the most painful of all duties to perform, that of exacting justice. I most cordially thank God that in your case mercy may be extended and you may hereafter have an opportunity by your future good conduct to make amends for misconduct already gone by.*
>
> *The offence to which you have pleaded guilty is the highest offence which subjects can commit, and it has in every country been treated as such, and if you look to*

Chapter 12

the consequences to which it naturally leads you must feel them right that it should be thus considered. No man can contemplate the consequences without feeling thankful to God that your offences stopped before these calamitous effects had been produced. If there be an armed insurrection and rising in a country, how calamitous must be the results, who can calculate the amount of the sufferings and evils which it may produce? How many lives might have been sacrificed? How many women might have been made widows? How many children made orphans, deprived of those parents who are to instruct them early in life, and above all to set before them good and virtuous example!

What has been the cause, which has drawn probably with respect to many of you, I may say which has deluded you into commission of this offence I cannot state. But as it is impossible to be in this world without being aware of the seditious and blasphemous publications, which have been everywhere disseminated. I may say this, that if from these publications you have imbibed these principles which have led you to the commission of these acts which have placed you in your present unhappy situation, how much must they have to answer for who have been the instruments of introducing these publications into your hands! It is indeed impossible not to see that seditious and blasphemous publications go hand in hand with treason and rebellion, and in those who seek to excite the latter it is worldly wisdom to endeavour to reserve the influence of religion.

The best security of the peace is the fear of God, and the real way to train men up to sedition is to make man forget his Maker and obliterate all sense of religious obligation. I hope and trust that if any of you should have been thus deluded into a forgetfulness of your Maker, that this delusion will not be permanent. If you should have for a moment forgotten him from whom your health and all your blessings proceed. I trust it will be a delusion of short continuance, and that you will return to that being who is the author of all good.

I trust that the awful situation in which you are now respectively placed will be a warning to you and to others to abstain from those practices which tend to endanger the Government and consequently the lives and security of individuals who live under its protection, you perhaps may all of you have felt the pressure of the times some of you may have been drawn into dangerous practices by the distresses which have been so generally felt. It is the lot of human nature occasionally to meet with distress of different descriptions. It may be employed by Divine Providence as a means to make men look up to him who is the fountain of all health peace and prosperity and who is the giver of all things that man can enjoy. In every different station men meet with suffering and privation, doubtless from the wisdom of him without whom not a sparrow falleth to the ground - we are in his hands and it will be wise for you and for all who hear me submissively to bear the afflictions he imposes and to look up to him in thankfulness for all the blessing we are permitted to enjoy.

It now becomes necessary for me to discharge the most painful part of my duty and to pass upon you the sentence of the law. It is a sentence, which no one can hear without feelings of great solemnity. It is a sentence, which has a tendency to excite abhorrence of the crime against which it is denounced. I have already stated and I feel gratitude in repeating the assurance, that this sentence will not in any part of it be carried into effect with respect to any of you. There will be that commutation of punishment, which his Majesty's Government upon a due consideration of the circumstances of each case may see fit to inflict. It is with them and not us that that commutation rests.

The sentence of law is that you William Comstive [his Lordship here read out the names of all the prisoners] be taken from hence to the place from whence you came and from thence be drawn to the place of execution on a hurdle, there to be hanged by the neck until you are dead – that your heads be afterwards separated from your bodies, and your bodies be divided into four quarters and remain at the disposal of the King – and whenever death shall come may Almighty God extend his mercy to each and every one of you.

The prisoners seemed much affected with the address of Justice Bayley and many including Comstive more than once shed tears. 'The prisoners were removed from the bar and subsequently subjected to various terms of imprisonment and transportation.'[27]

Of the twenty-two men convicted at York, only twelve were actually transported 'beyond the seas' to Van Diemen's Land: John Lindley and John Peacock from Huddersfield; Richard Addy, John Burkinshaw, Joseph Chapiel, William Comstive, Michael Downing, Joseph Firth, Benjamin Hanson, William Rice, Benjamin Rogers and Charles Stansfield from Barnsley.

John Lindley and John Peacock both received sentences of fourteen years, while the Barnsley men all received life. There is an implication in the fact that John Lindley and John Peacock received fourteen years transportation, as opposed to life, that the real leaders of the Huddersfield rebellion had not been apprehended. The Crown kept their word, for in England the general policy with political prisoners was to quietly remove them to the far side of the world and forget about them. This was considered preferable to creating martyrs who might inflame the populace.[28]

James Flowers, who was very deaf, was pardoned 18 January 1821. John Vallance (1792 –1882) a devout Christian, who was said to attend church every day, was also pardoned and released a short time after reaching the hulks at Sheerness, as a result of public agitation and protest. On his release, Vallance continued working for his political beliefs and was arrested in 1839 and committed for trial at York Assizes a second time, when the local magistrates pronounced Chartist demonstrations to be illegal.

Nathaniel Buckley, Thomas Blackburn from Huddersfield, and George Burkinshaw, George Bryan, John Hobson, William Holland, Abraham Ingham from Barnsley were all released on 11 October 1822 after two years' incarceration in the hulks. On release, each man receiving £3 4s towards his travelling expenses from Woolwich, with a certificate of having been pardoned on account of his good behaviour. Thomas Farrimond remained in the hulks at Sheerness until 1828.[29] Thomas Morgan, an accomplice who had been admitted as King's evidence against the Barnsley men, was discharged by proclamation.[30]

Perhaps the 'Yorkshire Rebels' were lucky, as the 'Scottish Weavers', who were all part of the same 'cause', had three members beheaded and twenty-five members transported to Van Diemen's Land. Nevertheless, there was a feeling that the brutality of the justice system, as demonstrated by the mass execution of Luddites at York in 1813, had moved on – for the practical reason that it was seen to be counter-productive. As William Leman Rede observed:

Chapter 12

> *The extension of mercy in such a case was purely prudential; the people had seen enough of the blood of their fellows, and a gory scaffold would have formed a fresh incentive to revolution. An execution of twenty-two was a spectacle that in 1780 was endured but it would have been a dangerous experiment in 1820. Men have learnt that the indiscriminate slaughter of a few dozen prisoners charged as state criminals does not make the peasantry love that state better; and that a minister, whose unpopularity first caused such public risings can quell them more easily by changing his measures than by punishing those who oppose them.*[31]

Rede seems to have forgotten the Luddite, Pentridge and Cato Street executions but his sentiments are correct.

CHAPTER 13
Transportation 1821 – 1828

Journey to Van Diemen's Land

The *Leeds Mercury*, Saturday 18 November 1820, reported that on Sunday and Monday last, a number of prisoners that included John Lindley were removed from York Castle, where they had been detained following their trial, to the York hulk lying upriver at Portsmouth. Hulks were old warships used as prison accommodation when all the gaols were full. They were invariably overcrowded and unsanitary.

On Sunday 30 December 1820, John Lindley and thirty-nine other prisoners were transferred to the 394-ton convict vessel *Lady Ridley*, under the command of Master James Weir, anchored off Spithead. Then, on Sunday 14 January, the *Lady Ridley* sailed along the south coast to Dartmouth, arriving on Monday 15, where she remained until Tuesday 23 January on account of bad weather. Finally, late on 23 January 1821, she set sail on the long voyage to Van Diemen's Land. The political prisoners were kept separate from the other 126 prisoners and hobbled in irons from ankle to ankle. On Thursday 25 January, two days after setting sail, the ship's journal records that six prisoners, including John Lindley, John Peacock and William Comstive 'whose conduct had been orderly', had irons removed from one leg. Five days later, on 30 January, Richard Addy and seven others had irons removed from one leg, but William Rice, Ben Rogers and Joseph Firth had to wait until 21 February to have their leg irons removed. Removal of one leg iron must have been a great relief for the prisoners as it facilitated movement around the ship and represented a significant reward for good conduct. It has been noted by the historian, John West, that the surgeons were usually popular with the prisoners. As 'educated men they were able to distinguish moral imbecility from perverseness, and both from disease'.[1] Certainly, James Wilson took good care of the ship's crew, marines and convicts. He also acted as midwife, for on Monday 5 February the wife of John Freeman was delivered of a baby girl who was subsequently christened Jane. This was not the only birth on the voyage, for on Sunday 18 February the wife of Peter Macauley gave birth to twins christened Andrew and Jane. It is an interesting comment on the status of women during the nineteenth century that the first names of the mothers are never recorded.

On Thursday 8 February, convicts were bathed, bedding aired, clean shirts issued and hair trimmed. Bathing and airing of bedding were to become almost daily occurrences during the tropical part of the voyage. On Tuesday 13 February, lemon juice with sugar was issued. This was very popular with the convicts, but its real purpose was to prevent scurvy. Nevertheless, despite these preventative measures, five cases of scurvy were recorded during the voyage.

Chapter 13

Life on board ship followed a predictable routine. The master's log starts each day recording that prisoners 'scraped the deck and cleaned the prison'. Exercise was taken in groups which varied from five to twenty depending on the situation. A gill of wine was issued to each prisoner on Tuesday 27 February and this became a frequent occurrence as the drinking water became brackish.

On Friday 2 March *Lady Ridley* crossed the equator. There is no record of celebrations on board to mark this as a great occasion.

At the beginning of the voyage (Saturday 6 January) New Testaments and prayer books were issued to all convicts. Frequent religious services and prayers were held for both crew and convicts, usually on deck if the weather was suitable. After one service on Sunday 11 March, Master James Weir declared: 'I think that I never saw an audience listen with more attention to any discourse than these unfortunate men seemed to pay during the reading of the day's sermon'.

Lady Ridley arrived in Rio de Janeiro on Wednesday 21 March where she remained until Tuesday 10 April, replenishing her stores and carrying out necessary repairs.

The journey across the south Atlantic and Indian Oceans was a monotonous repeat of scraping decks, exercise, religious services and issues of wine.

It must have been with great relief that the *Lady Ridley* approached Hobart, the principal town of Van Diemen's Land, sailing up the River Derwent to anchor off Sullivan's Cove. Before the new arrivals, lay a small town with a rather English aspect, consisting of 426 houses with 2,700 inhabitants. The houses were dwarfed by the spire of St David's Church and this in turn looked tiny against the backdrop of Mount Wellington, which at 4,000 feet overshadowed the tiny settlement.[2]

The most telling remark was made by James Wilson, who concluded his account with a triumphant 'Arrived in Hobart Town, Van Diemen's Land without having a single sick person aboard'.

Certainly, the ship's surgeon could congratulate himself. The medical summary states that only nineteen people had been put on the sick list during the entire journey and, of these, five had scurvy and four venereal disease. Only two men were hospitalised and two people died, one of pulmonary infection and the other of manassomes (general fever).[3]

The *Lady Ridley* arrived at an auspicious moment, as the colony was being visited by the governor of New South Wales, Lachlan Macquarie (1762–1824). He made the following note in his diary:

> *Date Tuesday 26 June 1821.*
> *In the afternoon the ship Lady Ridley commanded by Captain Weir with 137 male convicts on board from England, anchored in the harbour. She sailed from Falmouth [should be Dartmouth] on the 23 of January last.*

The official records all state that the *Lady Ridley* arrived in Hobart Town, Van Diemen's Land, on 27 June 1821, after a journey of 156 days, though this was possibly the date of disembarkation. Governor Macquarie sailed from Van Diemen's Land on 29 June in the *Caroline,* to a rousing send off by the people of Hobart, which presumably included John Lindley.[4]

At the conclusion of the voyage, the following letter was addressed to Surgeon Superintendent James Wilson RN. It is taken from the diary of the *Lady Ridley*. This is almost certainly a collective composition, handwritten by one of the prisoners, as there were a number of very literate men among the eleven prisoners (letters of William Rice and Richard Addy testify to this statement). It was neatly 'written up' in the ship's log, probably by the captain's secretary – as befits a medical man, the surgeon's handwriting is almost undecipherable. (The letter was signed by only eleven prisoners because the twelfth, Michael Downing, was transported separately on the *Phoenix*.)

> *To James Wilson Esq.*
> *Honoured Sir.*
> *As we have been in mercy preserved in health and Safety through this long tedious, this trying and difficult Voyage. It indispensably becomes our bounden but elysium duty to express our warmest thanks for the many favours, kindnesses and respectability your honour has from time to time been pleased to show us injured and unfortunate men in this our disaster and while we hope that it may not be accounted unbecoming in us. We do most humbly acknowledge our grateful sense of the impressive manner your honour has from time to time delivered yourself to us and your sympathy shown in your view of our case, together with your manifold endeavours in laying down to us such observations and rules as will if strictly followed lead to our future welfare, comfort to this and eternal bliss in the world which is yet for to come and happy indeed we are to say with truth that your efforts have not been without considerable utility and we largely feel your desire condolence and your anxiety to encourage hope to sooth our sorrows in this melancholy, sinister and miserable situation we unhappily are placed in. Were our feelings highly honourable to yourself we are sensible, must long remain a blessing to us and all our offspring and yourself no less so we only further advance on this subject that we sincerely wish that our situations were equally respectable as they to our great grief are now degrading. We might then have soon to hope that we might soon have an opportunity to make manifest in your* **Esteem** *to your Honour. Yet notwithstanding us being in these fettered and unhappy circumstances we trust as men not void of* **Gratitude** *and common sense, we each possess a heart that feels reflection and ones that dare resent but forgive an injury and advocate justice and support truth and know the value of good and the malignity of injury and wrong and we hope while under your Command as conducted ourselves as men and not like brutes or savages or yet shown the least symptoms of that demagogue spirit of disaffection and malcontent or yet been troublesome by making ridiculous simple and unjust complaints or complaining. But we all have endeavoured to strictly execute everyone and all your respective order, which concerned us with respect and alacrity. We conclude by acknowledging or being Grateful for the manifold favours, constant kindness and respect your honour has been pleased to show us and we reverently pray that you may enjoy many long and happy days.*
> *We remain your very Humble and Obedient Prisoners:*
> *Wm Rice, Jos. Chapiel, Ben'm Rogers, Ch's Stanfield, Ric'd Addy, John Peacock,* **John Lindley,** *Joseph Firth, Ben'm Hanson, John Burkinshaw, W'm Comstive.*

On arrival in Van Diemen's Land, the muster roll [5] described John Lindley as 5ft 9¼ inches tall; with grey eyes; and not grey hair. At fifty-one, he was the oldest member of the group and was assigned to public works in Hobart Town. He had the great advantage of being a 'mechanic', one of the small groups of bricklayers, masons, tilers, blacksmiths, glaziers and joiners who were so desperately required in this primitive society. He also carried with him testimonials to his good character, signed by about one hundred residents from the Huddersfield area.[6]

Since political prisoners were less likely to resort to crime than the petty thieves who made up the majority of transported convicts, they were often known as 'gentlemen prisoners'. For the remaining prisoners aboard the *Lady Ridley*, the future was a lottery, as they were assigned to masters of variable temperament. The following poem recalls the experience.

> The day we landed upon the fatal shore,
> The planters stood round us full twenty score or more;
> They ranked us up like horses and sold us out of hand,
> They roped us to the plough, brave boys, to plough Van Diemen's Land.
>
> The cottages we lived in was built of sods and clay,
> And rotten straw for bed, and we dare not say nay,
> Our cots were fenced with fir, to slumber when we can,
> To drive away the wolves and tigers come by Van Diemen's Land.[7]

Life in Van Diemen's Land

The situation that John Lindley and his fellow prisoners found in Van Diemen's Land had been transformed from a state of anarchy by the then lieutenant-governor, William Sorell (1775–1848). Sorell had taken up his post in April 1817 and, within three months, had concluded the work of his predecessor by exterminating the bush rangers, particularly the Brady gang.[8]

At the time of Macquarie's visit, it had been recorded that there were fifteen thousand acres under cultivation, one hundred and seventy thousand sheep, five thousand pigs and five hundred and fifty horses. This prosperity opened up the way for new development, so that in 1822 over six hundred free settlers arrived, and in March 1824 the first bank was opened. These events set a new tone to the colony and were reinforced by the character of the lieutenant-governor. 'He had a relaxed and friendly manner – and was in the habit of standing at his gate and chatting to passers-by, regardless of their social position.' He also had a pragmatic approach to governing his territory, as he controlled the excesses of vice without trying to raise the moral standards of his people above that which was acceptable in this period. However, there was an unsatisfactory aspect to this relaxed control; prisoners were left to their own devices for long periods with the result that theft was endemic. According to the authorities in London, Sorell's great weakness was that he had a wife in London while living openly with his mistress, Mrs Kent, at Government House in Hobart. This was considered unacceptable conduct by his superiors in London during the early nineteenth century, although a very practical arrangement in a new colony. The only record of what John Lindley did during this period is that he was employed on public works in Hobart.[9]

This relaxed mode of living was to change abruptly with the arrival of Sir George Arthur (1784-1854), the new lieutenant-governor, who disembarked from the Adrian on 12 May 1824, when the 'Tasmanian Twelve' had been three years in Van Diemen's Land. George Arthur 'believed that Van Diemen's Land was a penal settlement and should be run on strict disciplinary grounds. He had a formal manner and he delivered his strictures in an austere and reproving tone.' He has been described as a 'dictatorial, God-fearing, nepotist'. He tried to control all aspects of his administration and would crush anyone who opposed him. This made him unpopular with both his staff and the press. Against this, he was a devout Christian man with moral tastes and occasional touches of humanity. He tried to act impartially, and believed in rewards for good behaviour, but severe punishment for bad conduct. He set up seven levels of punishment that ranged from execution on the scaffold at the bottom, to a ticket of leave with complete freedom at the top. It must be said that before a convict was considered for a ticket of leave, he always had to conform strictly to George Arthur's rules for a considerable period of time. Arthur also instituted a balance between the rights of settlers and assigned convicts, who according to his conviction were not to be treated as slaves. These rules probably worked very much to the benefit of John Lindley who, as his record shows, obtained privileges and finally his release.[10]

Conditions were not necessarily bad under Sir George Arthur for those who conformed to his strict rules. Five years after John Lindley's departure from Van Diemen's Land, Peter Withers, a convict from Wiltshire, records in the following letter to his brother in 1833:

> *All the bondage that I am under is to answer my name every Sunday before I go to church, so you must not think that I am made a slave of, for I am not, it is quite the reverse of it. And I have got a good master and mistress. I have got plenty to eat and drink as good as ever a gentleman in this country has, so all the punishment that I have in this country is the thought of leaving my friends, my wife and my dear children, but I live in hopes of seeing Old England again.*[11]

Communication with the prisoners evidently took place, almost certainly at irregular intervals, and John would know that he was not forgotten in Van Diemen's Land for, on 1 November 1824, a covering letter was sent from the Colonial Office in London to accompany a petition from the minister in Darton to Major General Sir Thomas Brisbane (1773–1860), governor of New South Wales.[12]

> *Colonial Secretaries Office 1 November 1824*
> *Sir, John Lindley the convict whose case is brought under the notice of your Excellency in the enclosed letter from the Minister of the Parish of Darton and others, landed along with the rest of the prisoners who came by the Lady Ridley at Hobart. I have the honour to be sir your Excellency's most obedient very humble servant.*
> *Signed T. Goulburn*
> *His Excellency Sir Thomas Brisbane Governor of New South Wales*

Another example of George Arthur's sense of moral duty can be seen in his granting of permission for the 'Tasmanian Twelve' to forward a petition to London, drawing attention to the different treatment of the prisoners tried at York in 1820.

The 'Tasmanian Twelve' had found out that after the *Lady Ridley* weighed anchor, Nathaniel Buckley and Thomas Blackburn from Huddersfield and George Bryan, John Hobson, William Holland and Abraham Ingham from Barnsley had spent only two years in the hulks before they were pardoned and released. (James Flowers and John Vallance were released early and John Ferryman sometime later.) Not surprisingly, the 'Tasmanian Twelve' were not very pleased with the discrepancy in the treatment of the two groups and in 1826 sent the following petition to the King:

> *To the Kings most Excellent Majesty –*
> *This Humble petition of Joseph Firth, William Rice, John Burkinshaw*, Richard Addy*, Charles Stanfield*, Benjamin Anson*, William Comstive, Joseph Chapel, John Lindley, John Peacock, Mich'l Downing**, & Benjamin Rogers.*
> *May it please Your Majesty –*
> *We your Majesty's most humble petitioners, beg leave to approach your Majesty in the anxious hope that your Majesty's well known paternal benefaction towards every class of your Majesty's subjects, and particularly towards the unfortunate, may be extended to us, under the very peculiar circumstances of our case.*
> *We beg leave, most humbly to submit to your Majesty, that Your Majesty's humble petitioners with ten other individuals viz't George Burkinshaw, John Ferryman, James Flowers, George Bryant, Abraham Hanger, John Vallance, John Hobson, William Holland, Nathaniel Buckley and Thomas Blackburn were in the month of September 1820 arraigned at York Castle on a charge of High Treason and having pleaded guilty were sent in the Lady Ridley Transport ship to this country, under sentence of Transportation for our Lives.*
> *We beg leave most humbly to submit to your Majesty that we have been informed that it has been your Majesty's Gracious pleasure to extend your Royal Mercy to the ten individuals above mentioned, who were arraigned and convicted with us Your Majesty's humble petitioners, at the same time and place, and under the same circumstances for the same offence, who are thereby restored to the blessings of Liberty and the enjoyment of the society of their families. –*
> *That your Majesty's most humble petitioners without presuming to offer any thing in mitigation of our offence further than most humbly to submit to Your Majesty that we were the Dupes of artful and designing men who acted upon our distresses – and our ignorance caused us to be involved in our present unhappy situation. Most Humbly pray of your Majesty to be pleased to take the premises into Your Majesty's most gracious consideration and to extend to [unreadable] Your Majesty's 'Royal Mercy' – as it has been your Majesty's pleasure to bestow it upon our late fellow prisoners. –*
> *And your Majesty's most Humble petitioners, as in duty Bound will ever pray &c.-*
> *Hobart Town, Van Diemen's Land; 13 February 1826*
> *annotations above the names marked* –*
> *John Burkinshaw*, C*** Roo**ing*
> *Richard Addy*, Brodribb*
> *Charles Stanfield*, C. Plains*
> *Benjamin Anson*, Dead*
> *Mich'l Downing**, originally written John, crossed-out for Mich'l;*
> annotated Rec'd Free Pardon
> [These are in a different handwriting, and there is no clue to their authorship or date.][13]

This petition may have been in response to the letter from the minister of the parish of Darton.

It has been noted by Professor Eric Evans that the Radicals were adept at presenting petitions to advance their democratic cause, but this was a legitimate method of influencing parliament before the reform acts of 1832 and 1867. In 1818, it is estimated that one thousand five hundred petitions were received in Westminster. Professor Fred Donnelly notes that 'the Yorkshire rebels' also showed a 'propensity for litigious behaviour'.[14]

The petition failed, but John Lindley's conduct record was good. The report, number L167, states that his gaol record was good, his hulk report (in England) was good and his *Lady Ridley* (ship record) generally good. He had a wife and five children in Mirfield. Two breaches of discipline are recorded during his seven years as a convict.[15]

On 9 November 1825, John Lindley was found fishing round Macy Point in a boat in the River Derwent, at 12 o'clock Sunday last, without permission. On 6 November 1826, John Lindley was absent from muster and church Sunday last. On both these occasions, it was noted that he was the holder of a ticket of leave, which was equivalent to parole, with reporting conditions requiring him to attend muster. Confirmation of the ticket of leave is also recorded in the muster roll of 1826.[16]

Under Sir George Arthur's system of reward and punishment, a man with a fourteen-year sentence could apply for his ticket of leave after six years. This seems to have been John Lindley's case, since on 17 May 1828 he was granted a free pardon, sometimes called a full pardon, – number 46 (TAHO). He was lucky, free pardons ceased soon after that date. Only two other 'Yorkshire Rebels', Downing and Firth, received free pardons, the others received conditional pardons, the condition being that they could not leave Tasmania. However, Firth stayed in Tasmania, prospered, and became a justice of the peace. It is also known that Richard Addy later returned to his hometown of Barnsley and became an active Chartist.[17]

Return Journey to England

Perhaps John Lindley's luck had changed at last. On 15 May, just two days before his full pardon, the fine 317-ton ship *Calista,* under Captain Samuel Hawkins, sailed into Derwent River from Sydney bound for London. There were very few ships sailing directly from Van Diemen's Land to London in 1828 so this was a good omen. *Calista* weighed anchor for London on 6 July carrying fourteen passengers including:

> *Dr Hood, Mr D. Burn, John Robertson, J.C. Cummings , C. Seal and King and nine in the steerage.*
> *The cargo included: 220 pieces of gum plank (from NSW), 448lb wool, 6 logs of huon pine, 6 tons mimosa bark, 18 tons barilla, 63 ox hides, 69 logs she oak, bundle of opossum skins.*[18]

According to Lloyd's List, *Calista* anchored in Greenwich, the port for London, on 22 November 1828. In the absence of definitive evidence, it has been assumed that John Lindley was one of the nine steerage passengers. As an artisan he would have saved his fare by working on his own account, during his captivity, after completing his public works at 3:00pm each day.

The possibility that John Lindley travelled home on the 185-ton brig *Tranmere*, under Captain Alexander Wales, which sailed from Hobart on 27 June 1828, has been discounted, as the passenger list of: Mr R. Towers, James Major, W. Phillips, W. Baitty, Mrs J. Brown and Cath. Steele does not include his name.

However, a complication arises as a result of the following notice in *The Hobart Town Courier* Friday 16 October 1835, under Trade and Shipping:

> *Passengers per [the sailing ship] Lang for London: Mr and Mrs Hector, 3 children and servant, Miss Butcher, Mr and Mrs Tanner, 3 children and servant, Mr David Andrew, Mr Ball, Mr John Lindley, also Lieutenant Lamotte of the 21st Regiment, with 9 invalid troops.*
> *Cargo of the Lang: 132 bales wool, 239 casks spermaceti, 60 ditto head matter, 32 ditto sperm oil, 149 bundles whalebone, 3 packages opossum skins, 7 bundles 2 packages ditto skins, 1 cask seal skins, 2 cases stuffed birds, 9 cases curiosities, 2 boxes seeds, 1 cask wheat, 80 cases sago, 2 ditto thread, 4 casks old copper, 1 box official papers, ...*[19]

In those days, the title Mr signified a gentleman, a status for which John Lindley hardly qualified. Consequently, the question arises, was this Mr John Lindley of Mirfield? If so, why did he wait seven years, an inordinate length of time, after receiving a full pardon with no conditions attached, before returning to his family in Mirfield? It has been suggested that he needed to work for this period of time to earn the money for his passage home, but as explained earlier, he could have saved this money during his captivity.

CHAPTER 14
Tasmanian Twelve

Fate of John Lindley's Comrades

While we know that John Lindley was one of the few convicts (less than ten per cent) transported to New South Wales and Van Diemen's Land who returned to the United Kingdom, it may be of interest to consider the fate of his companions – ten of whom remained in Van Diemen's Land after his departure.

Michael Downing

First, it should be noted that Michael Downing had already left Van Diemen's Land by the time John Lindley received his free pardon. Michael Downing is something of an enigma as his mini biography demonstrates.

Michael Downing was born in Bombay around 1772 and had an Irish father. In 1820, he was a weaver of Monk Bretton and possibly an ex-soldier. Surprisingly, he was the only member of the 'Twelve' unable to sign his name on the petition to the home secretary. Despite his illiteracy, he sent a long letter to two friends on 28 May 1820 from York Castle, presumably written for him. He was transported separately in the *Phoenix*, which sailed from Portsmouth on 5 January 1822 and arrived in Hobart on 20 May 1822. His convict record, number 259, stated that he left a wife and three children in Barnsley. He had severe damage to several fingers and was subject to fits, which may account for the reason that he was employed in Hobart Hospital. His only recorded misdemeanour occurred on 11 February 1825, when the watchman at the hospital stated that he was drunk all the previous Wednesday – for which he was fined five shillings. He received a free pardon (number 14) on 13 January 1826 and the petition from the Tasmanian Twelve to the King dated 13 February 1826 confirms that he had received a free pardon by that date, as his signature is absent. He departed Van Diemen's Land on the *Providence* for Port Jackson on 13 June 1826. *Providence* sailed on from Sydney to Bombay, but it is not known if Michael Downing continued his journey or remained in New South Wales. He was the first of the 'Tasmanian Twelve' to obtain his release, a little surprising since his convict record states that his death sentence had been commuted to transportation for life, but no explanation for his special treatment is known.[1]

Richard Addy

Richard Addy), born about 1791 in Barnby Dan, was a weaver by trade and master of a shop in Wilson's Piece, Barnsley. He was a member of the Barnsley Committee and was delegated to meet members of the Huddersfield Committee on Easter Monday (3 April) to assess the possibility of a second attempt at insurrection. He acted as second in command of the Barnsley Company that marched to Grange Moor on Wednesday 11 April. This was presumably on account of his military experience, having been a member of the famous 95th Rifle Brigade in the Peninsula war. He also served as a member of Captain McNamara's company in the second battalion of the 95th at the battle of Waterloo in June 1815. His name appears on the medal roll of Waterloo Medals issued in 1816. Not only was he able to sign his name on the petition to the home secretary, he had a remarkable command of both written and spoken English.

His convict record, number 102, states that his gaol record was good, his hulk record was good, and his *Lady Ridley* record generally good. He was 5ft 4in (163 cm) tall with hazel eyes and dark brown hair. He left a wife in Barnsley who was a linen weaver. In 1823, he was recorded as being assigned to Oyster Bay. On his release, Addy returned to his native Barnsley and continued his active support of radical causes. In October 1839, following the sentencing of several Chartist leaders he wrote the following letter addressed to the Barnsley magistrates:

> *I cannot but regret that human nature should be so debased as to produce men and fathers of families so reckless of the misery they bring upon their fellow creatures by grasping with odious avidity at any pretence that offers to glut their insatiable political rancour, in incarceration of men who have not committed any offence against either common or statute law of the country [he later continues]…are not the prayers of an impoverished people treated with utter contempt by our rulers? Do not misery and distress stalk through the land? And have you not seen the heaving bosom of the tender mother ready to burst with anguish when the thought of her destitute children flitted across her bosom? Yea! Have you seen hundreds pale and emaciated with ceaseless toil, on the verge of the grave with their souls filled with dreadful imaginations when the recollections of their starving children has rushed upon the mind?*

This does not seem the same man who signed the obeisant letter to the ship's surgeon at the end of the voyage to Van Diemen's Land in 1821![2]

John Burkinshaw

John Burkinshaw was christened at Silkstone on 13 August 1792, the son of William Burkinshaw, a carpenter, and Mary (Darwent). In 1814 his wages, as a linen weaver, were fourteen shillings a week but these fell steadily over the following years. On 15 February 1814 he married Margaret Ashton of Dodworth, whose father Joseph Ashton was also a linen weaver. Their first child was born on 18 April 1814 and christened George but only lived a few days. A daughter, Mary, was born on 26 April 1815 and a second daughter, Ann, on 27 August 1817.

John and his brother George were both apprehended after the Grange Moor fiasco. After the trial on 9 September, his death sentence was commuted to transportation for life and, as was the custom for life prisoners, his wife and family were encouraged to join him. His wife Margaret, and his two daughters, Mary and Ann, were conveyed to Van Diemen's Land, at the government's expense, and arrived around 1822 after a horrendous voyage in which their ship lost a mast. Since he was able to sign his name on the petition to the home secretary, he can be considered to be literate. On arrival in Van Diemen's Land, he was assigned to work on a farm at Pittwater on the Derwent River. He was small and wiry, his convict record states that he was only 5ft ½ inches (154 cm) tall with dark brown hair and brown eyes. While living at Pittwater, John and Mary had three further children, Sarah born 1823, Elizabeth born 1825 and William born 1928. Tragically, his second daughter, Ann, was killed in 1827, aged ten, when thrown from an overturning dray.

John received his conditional ticket of leave in 1830, which meant that he was no longer required to work for a master and was able to seek his own employment. He was required to report twice a year at the police office for the general muster. On 13 October 1831, John applied for a first-class building allotment in Hobart, with the intention of erecting 'a brick or stone dwelling house 45 feet long and proportionally deep'. This was duly granted, despite a footnote from the police magistrate, who said that he doubted that John had the financial means to comply with the terms applying to first-class allotments. John was now working as a carpenter and his wife and children assisted the family income by growing vegetables and hawking them around the streets of Hobart in a wheelbarrow. A daughter, Hannah, was born on 5 June 1832 and George, the last of his children, in 1835. John received his conditional pardon on 28 August 1835 and finally his free pardon on 28 July 1839. His oldest daughter, Mary, married Arthur Henry in 1831. As economic conditions deteriorated in Tasmania, the family moved to the mainland and bought land in December 1857 for twenty-two shillings an acre, at Bung Bong on the Bet Bet Creek near Avoca, Victoria. John's youngest daughter, Hannah, later married William Shiell, a miner nine years her senior on 1 November 1860. William had arrived in Australia in 1853, as second mate on the brig *Gazelle*.

John's wife Margaret died in Hobart on 10 July 1860, aged sixty-nine, whereupon her two children Hannah and William sold their market garden and joined the rest of the family in Bung Bong. Finally, John died at Bung Bong on 9 July 1876, aged eighty-four, probably of a stroke, and is buried at the Wareek Cemetery in Victoria, Australia.

John and Margaret's descendants made a great contribution to Australian society. One of his granddaughters, Emma McBeth, married Archibald Blackwood and founded what was to become one of Australia's most notable academic families. This included Sir Robert Blackwood, first chancellor of Monash University, and his sister Dame Margaret Blackwood, the first woman to hold the post of deputy chancellor of Melbourne University. A cousin, Donald Blackwood, was bishop of Gippsland from 1952 and his grandson, John Burns Blackwood, became dean of the law faculty at the University of Tasmania.[3]

Joseph Chapiel

Joseph Chapiel was born about 1795 in Dewsbury and became a shoemaker in Flockton. Prior to the Grange Moor assembly, he lodged in Taylor Row, and is credited with indicating houses, farms and public houses likely to have guns, which could be 'borrowed' for the occasion. It should be noted that many guns were returned anonymously to their owners after the debacle. He was able to sign his name on the petition to the home secretary and can be considered to be literate. On his arrival in Van Diemen's Land he was described as being 5ft 9in (175 cm) tall, with dark brown eyes, red hair, slightly pockmarked, and he was assigned to public works in Hobart. According to Professor Fred Donnelly he committed multiple offences. He was unmarried and died on 17 July 1832 at Mr Jno Alb…at the Brushy River in northeast Van Diemen's Land.[4]

William Comstive

William Comstive was born near Preston in Lancashire and baptisêd on 10 June 1792 at Garstang parish church. In 1811, at the age of nineteen, he enlisted in the 29th Regiment of Foot under Captain Langton, where he rose to the rank of sergeant. He served in Newfoundland and Wellington's Peninsular campaign. He was allegedly at Waterloo in 1815. On his discharge from the army in 1818, he became a journeyman weaver in Barnsley, and it was here that he became involved in radical politics. His military experience made him the natural military commander of the Barnsley Company at Grange Moor. After his capture he became the spokesman for the West Riding convicts accused of high treason. His death sentence was commuted to transportation for life. On arrival in Van Diemen's Land, he was recorded in the muster roll as being 5ft 9in (175 cm) tall, with hazel eyes and dark brown hair, and was assigned to George Town, where in 1822 he married another convict, Eleanor Louisa Anderson, alias Egerton. They lived in Launceston (Tasmania) and had two sons, Thomas and Daniel. In 1834 he was found guilty of forgery, along with Thomas Horton, a fellow convict from the *Lady Ridley*, as a result of which he was sent to the notorious Norfolk Island, but his sentence was commuted in 1842 and he was given conditional freedom in New South Wales. Louisa died at Launceston on 13 October 1843, without seeing William for the last nine years of their married life. In 1845, William suffered a stroke and, unable to support himself, ended up at the Parramatta Benevolent Home where he died in 1858.[5]

Joseph Firth

Joseph Firth was born about 1794 in Barnsley and was a labourer in his native town. He was able to sign his name on the petition to the home secretary. His death sentence was commuted to transportation across the seas for life. On his arrival in Van Diemen's Land, he was recorded as 5ft 11in (180 cm) tall, with light brown hair, and was assigned to public works in Hobart. His convict record, number 144, stated that his gaol record was good, his hulk record was good, while his *Lady Ridley* record states that his conduct was exemplary. He left his wife and two children with her father in Barnsley and it would appear that they joined him some time later. After he received his free pardon he remained in Van Diemen's Land where he prospered, becoming the owner of a public house called 'York House', which stood on the corner of Waimea Avenue and Sandy Bay. The riverside location with an excellent view was situated in one of the most expensive suburbs of Hobart. Certainly, Joseph Firth used his literacy to good effect, because he became a justice of the peace and well-respected member of the community, despite being fined two pounds for keeping his public house open on a Sunday. By 1829, he owned nine hundred acres at Brown's River, as well as a farm and four houses in the Hobart area. He died at Sandy Bay in 1865, the father of nine children.[6]

Benjamin Hanson

Benjamin Hanson was born around 1796 (possibly in Kirkheaton) and was a weaver from Leeds. He clearly signed his name ANSON on the petition to the home secretary, so perhaps he was only semi-literate, as he normally appears as Hanson in official documents. His death sentence was commuted to transportation for life. On arrival in Van Diemen's Land, he was recorded as 5ft 4in (163 cm) tall, and assigned to Upper Clyde. His convict record, number 317, states that in October 1827 he was accused of robbing Mr Styney of various articles and a number of sheep, but the charge was not substantiated, and the case was dismissed. However, the petition from the 'Tasmanian Twelve' to the King, dated 13 February 1826, incorrectly states that he did not sign the petition because he was dead![7]

John Peacock

John Peacock was born about 1775 in Little Frinton and became a farmer and clothier. His death sentence for high treason was commuted to transportation for fourteen years. He appears to have been a close companion of John Lindley during the voyage in the *Lady Ridley* as they both had one leg iron removed, for orderly conduct, on the same day (25 January 1821). On arrival in Van Diemen's Land, he was recorded as 5ft 5in (165 cm) tall, and assigned to public works in Hobart. He seems to have settled in well, for his convict record shows that his only recorded misdemeanour was to be absent from muster and church in March 1826, and that he received a conditional pardon (Number 129) on 3 March 1830.[8]

William Rice

William Rice was born in 1780 in Rotherham, Yorkshire. He became a cordwainer (shoemaker), first in Barnsley and later in Dodworth. He wrote a letter to his brother from York Castle on 26 May 1820 that demonstrates a high degree of literacy.

He was sentenced to be transported for life and on arrival in Van Diemen's Land was assigned to public work in Hobart. His convict record (con 31-1-34) states that his gaol record was good, his hulk record was good, but his conduct on the *Lady Ridley* was marred by the fact that he was always complaining. He left a wife and three children in Barnsley, Rebecca (Land or Lamb) whom he married in Manchester in 1812, and their three sons George, Edwin and Thomas. In 1823, his family joined him in Van Diemen's Land, at the government's expense, as was the policy with life transportation. Here they had a fourth son born in 1824. The family lived in Campbell Street, Hobart, where William became a constable. (It should be noted that constables were detested by convicts and settlers alike.) He remained in that position until 1833.

As a free settler, William's wife Rebecca was entitled to five acres of land, but William also claimed five acres for each of his three older sons, as they qualified as free immigrants, and was able to start a dairy farm of twenty acres. The venture prospered and they bought more land, so that by 1827 Constable Rice & Sons had the largest dairy farm in Van Diemen's Land.

William received a conditional pardon, number 491, on 1 May 1833 and a free pardon on 6 June 1837. He gave evidence on behalf of William Comstive when the latter was tried for forgery in 1834.

Rebecca died in 1852 and William died in 1853 in Hobart. Their children migrated to Port Phillip.[9]

There were many cases like that of William Rice, where convicts 'made good', and the punishment of transportation was criticised on the grounds that this was no deterrent to potential criminals in England.

Benjamin Rogers

Benjamin Rogers was born about 1790 in Barnsley and was a weaver of that town. He was able to sign his name on the petition to the home secretary and can be considered to be literate. He belonged to the radical religious sect, the Kilhamite New Connection Methodists. On arrival in Van Diemen's Land he was assigned to Coal River. His convict record (34-1-34) shows that he really did not settle to convict life. On 2 February 1822, he was found to have received goods knowing them to have been stolen and received fifty lashes. On 17 June 1825, he was charged with neglect of duty and disobedience, for which he was reprimanded and fined ten shillings. On 4 October 1825, he was charged with felony by the constable, having taken a quantity of brandy from the gaol, property of the guard. This time he got away with it because the charge was dismissed. On 6 December 1825, he was charged with neglect of duty and again on 19 December for which he was fined ten shillings – to be taken from his salary. On 4 August 1834, he was reprimanded for neglect of duty, but this seems to be an error, as he was given a conditional pardon, number 461, on 28 February 1833. His family record states that he married Sara by 1824 and they had five children: Joseph born 1824, Eliza born 1828, Theodore born 1830, Martha born 1833, and Benjamin born 1846. He died in Launceston in 1860.[10]

Charles Stansfield

Charles Stansfield was born about 1792, probably in Barnsley, and was a weaver. He clearly signed his name STANSFIELD on the petition to the home secretary, so he was definitely literate. On arrival in Van Diemen's Land, he was described as 5ft 5in (165cm) tall, with hazel eyes and dark brown hair. He was assigned to the Macquarie District and on 8 March 1822 was charged with absconding from his master's premises and being absent for eight days, for which crime he received fifty lashes and worked two months in the Gaol Gang. He received a conditional pardon on 21 August 1835. He was unmarried and seems to have been a bit of a wanderer.[11]

- - - - -

It is self-evident that the outcome of transportation varied greatly for different members of the 'Tasmanian Twelve'; in general, their history supports the view that, despite the 'social death' inflicted on political prisoners by transportation, many English victims had shed their radical politics by the time they received their conditional pardons. Once emancipated, they were able to enjoy the high wages that were available to skilled labour, which was still in short supply both in Van Diemen's Land and on the Australian mainland. Others of course returned to England to continue the fight.[12]

CHAPTER 15
Return to England 1828

Mirfield 1828

We can assume that on completion of his sentence, John Lindley lost no time in returning to England, and to his wife and family in Mirfield. It was a long walk of nearly two hundred miles from Greenwich to Mirfield, but walking was the common mode of transport for working men and women, and the ability to walk forty miles a day was not uncommon. Bernard Wood records that John Laycock of Glusburn in Kildwick would often walk twenty miles just to hear Dr Wesley play the organ at the morning service in the Leeds parish church. The alternative to walking was a bumpy coach ride that was hardly tolerable in the winter mud. A further option was that John Lindley may have sailed from London to Hull, but probably he had had enough of sea travel by that time.[1]

No doubt on his return he hoped to live peacefully, doing a little work and enjoying the comfort of his family. It is not clear how Hannah and the children survived during John's absence, but the letter from Darton in 1824 indicates that she may have returned to her kinfolk in Mapplewell. Certainly, John's hopes for a quiet life were doomed to disappointment. In reality, he returned to a country convulsed with economic oscillations and political uncertainty and the next twenty years were to be some of the most turbulent in British history. Industrial innovation was changing working practices as never before, while the political system struggled to accommodate the new dynamic social culture that was evolving. Most significantly, members of the greedy landed aristocracy, which numbered between three and five hundred families, were under increasing pressure from the emerging artisan class to relax their grip on the monopoly of power and national wealth.

What were John's first impressions on returning to his hometown? One must have been the obvious growth in the number of people. In his absence, the population of Mirfield, which numbered 5,041 in the 1821 census, the year he was transported to Van Diemen's Land, had increased to 6,496 in the 1831 census, two years after his return, an unprecedented growth of twenty-nine per cent in only ten years.[2]

The most striking new building was the 'new' parish church of St Mary's in Towngate, which dominated the north-eastern part of the town. It had been opened on 29 May 1826 at a cost of £1,600. There were also a large number of new houses, mostly of the stone built one up, one down design, constructed to accommodate the increased population.

Perhaps the most surprising was the small number of new factories. During John's absence there had been only a little industrial development in Mirfield, essentially it remained an agricultural market town set in a pastoral landscape with the mills, rivers, canals and roads following the valley bottom. Green fields dominated the slopes, while the moors on the high ground were still covered in purple heather.[3]

Old Ledgards oil mill, which pressed rapeseed brought from Hull, was still providing oil for the town. It was to be destroyed by fire in the late 1830s and was replaced by Bankfield woollen mill owned by James Swift, a woollen manufacturer, who became the first person to install a gas plant at the mill to light his own premises. Although Yorkshire is always associated with the production of woollen textiles, cotton yarn was also produced in Mirfield by Samuel W. Haigh, who introduced cotton spinning as early as 1838.[4]

More significant for John Lindley, Hammerton's wire works situated on Steanard Lane, in Hopton, was founded about 1830, soon after his return. This was important for John and his nephew George, because the raw materials for wire drawing and nail making used the same quality of iron and were sourced from the same foundries. Hammerton's Mill was a two-storied building powered by a water wheel. The firm manufactured a wide range of products such as wire fencing, riddles and sieves. It also supplied the textile industry with items such as crimpwork for wooley gates and drying floors, mesh coal screens and baskets for power looms.[5]

One great advantage of Mirfield, was the way that many of its diverse small industries interacted with one another to their collective benefit. For example, the currier and leather merchant business established by George Walker, in the 1830s at Kitson Hill, produced velvet leathers designed for both the home and export trade. Another of their specialities was designed for card clothing used throughout the woollen industry.[6]

The other great advantage of Mirfield was its position as a communication centre. On John's return, the Calder and Hebble Navigation, which had played such an important part in the industrial development of Mirfield, was as busy as ever, transporting coal, grain and malt. In 1836, over a period of twenty-five days, 535 vessels went upstream and 384 downstream between Wakefield and Halifax. A breakdown of the cargo of these 919 vessels gives a snapshot of the diversity of heavy goods transported during this period. Upstream: 288 vessels carried corn, 109 mixed goods, 59 limestone, 40 malt, 23 timber, 15 potatoes and 1 pig iron. Downstream: 189 coal, 120 baled goods (woollen products), 61 building stone, 9 scrap iron and oil cake and 5 salt.[7]

Perhaps the most static aspect of the social structure of small market towns was exemplified by Mirfield. The new parish church in Towngate was the centre of the social life of the town and it became famous in later years, because it was here that the three Brontë sisters worshipped, when domiciled at Roe Head School. Roe Head was a small private girls' school, situated less than a mile from the Knowl, owned by Miss Wooler. This school concentrated on providing a respectable English education for between seven and ten girls from the lesser gentry. Charlotte Brontë (1816 – 1855) attended this school as a pupil for eighteen months in 1831 and 1832 and for a short period as a teacher in 1835. Emily Brontë (1818 – 1848) was also a pupil there for three months, and Anne Brontë (1820 – 49) was both a pupil at the school and later a governess to five of the Ingram children in Mirfield.[8]

Although John Lindley lived in the same market town as the Brontë sisters, socially their paths would never have crossed. The Brontë family were members of the lower gentry attending the established Church of England at Hartshead when Rev. Patrick Brontë (1777 – 1861) was the curate there. Later, when he became vicar of Haworth, the sisters attended the 'new' parish church in Mirfield.

The Lindley family were Dissenters. The social distinction is aptly described by Charlotte Brontë in *Shirley* – a novel centred on the Luddite struggles of 1812 around Mirfield.

> *Mrs Pryor, a ladies companion, wondered how her daughter could be so much at ease with a 'man of the people' namely William Farren, the gardener. She found it impossible to speak to him other than stiffly. She felt as if a great gulf lay between her caste and his; and to cross it, or meet him half-way, would be to degrade herself. Mrs Pryor gently asked her daughter Caroline – are you not afraid, my dear to converse with that person so unreservedly? He may presume and become troublesomely garrulous. William presume mama? You don't know him. He never presumes: he is altogether too proud and sensitive to do so. William has very fine feelings. Mrs Pryor smiled sceptically at the naïve notion of the rough-handed, fustian clad clown having 'fine feelings'.*

But William Farren was obviously a Yorkshireman in the same mould as John Lindley:

> *Farren for his part, showed Mrs Pryor only a very sulky brow. He knew when he was misjudged, and was apt to turn unmanageable with such as failed to give him his due.*[9]

Just as formidable as the social divide was the religious segregation, as described by Charlotte Brontë in a letter to George Smith (of Smith Elder, her publisher), dated 16 March 1850:

> *...I enclose for your perusal a scrap of paper, which came into my hands without the knowledge of the writer. He is a poor workingman of this village – [a] thoughtful, reading, feeling being, whose mind is too keen for his frame, and wears it out. I have not spoken to him above thrice in my life, for he is a Dissenter, and has rarely come in my way.*[10]

A friend of Charlotte Brontë describes the situation when they were at school together:

> *The bulk of the population were Dissenters. For example in the local village of Heckmondwike, there were two large chapels, one belonging to the Independents and one to the Methodists, both of which were well filled two or three times on a Sunday, besides having various prayer-meetings, fully attended, on week days. The inhabitants were chapel-going people, very critical about the doctrines of their sermons, tyrannical to their ministers, and violent radicals in politics.*[11]

Anne Brontë spent nine unhappy months at Blake Hall:

> *Blake Hall had been purchased by the Ingham's in 1784, and occupied by them in 1802. Blake Hall was a very old house that had originally belonged to the Hoptons as early as 1643 and was surrounded by a large park which dominated the centre of Towngate. Anne was governess to two of the Ingham's five children from April to December 1839. She described her experience in her novel Agnes Grey. She was eventually dismissed, as she was unable to control the unruly children…The Hall was enlarged in 1845.*[12]

As Mirfield grew, the parish was subdivided and Anglican churches were built in Battyeford (1841) and in Upper Hopton where St John's Church was consecrated 21 October 1846.

Religious Dissenters in Mirfield

The West Riding of Yorkshire was a Nonconformist stronghold and John Wesley preached five times in Mirfield alone, the first occasion being in 1742. He was able to see the fruits of his work when he opened the Knowl Wesleyan Methodist Chapel on 8 April 1780. The chapel soon proved too small and was rebuilt in 1837, at a time when John was working in his new forge at Knowl Nook. It is very probable that John and his nephew George Lindley provided nails for the construction of this chapel. There was certainly no shortage of dissenting groups in Mirfield, but they did not always have dedicated buildings. The New Connection Methodists did not have a chapel until 1835, while the Primitive Methodists, who originally met in a barn at Low Littlemoor and later in a cottage opposite the Airedale Heifer Inn, finally acquired their own building in Battyeford in 1863.[13]

Similarly, 'the earliest Baptist congregation met at Blake Hall in 1816. When the weather was fine services were held on the steps of the Hall or in the kitchen. In winter, services were held in the Tithe Barn.' Mrs Ingham obviously had Baptist sympathies as her father Dr Evans was a tutor at the Baptist College in Bristol.

In 1818, they transferred to an old barn in Littlemoor and then in 1820 to the Free School at the Knowl, where Joshua Garside, a noted local mathematician, was the schoolmaster. Consequently, it was in this building that the first Baptist Church of Mirfield came into being on 25 July 1825 with fourteen members. In allowing his school room to be used by this small group for meetings, Garside had acted on his own initiative, but unfortunately for both Garside and the Baptists, the school had a mixed Anglican and Congregationalist board of governors, and as a result of his presumption Joshua was asked to resign. Baptist services therefore ceased on these premises; demonstrating that religious intolerance during John's lifetime was just as heated as political animosity. Fortunately, James Clarkson offered two rooms in his Nab Lane house, so services continued in these premises for two years. A site was obtained for a new building close to Knowl Nook and within sight of the Wesleyan chapel. In 1828, the Rev. Henry Seabrook of Bradford laid the foundation stone, but the building remained a roofless shell through lack of funds, until the enthusiasm of Henry S. Albrecht, the first minister, had the construction finished in May 1830 at a cost of £1,050. However, there was still a debt of £800 on completion, which took until 1852 to clear. Albrecht refused to accept a salary until the debt was cleared.[14]

Return of Crisis

Once again, a severe economic depression hit the country in 1829–1830 which, combined with the poor harvest of 1829 and the extremely severe winter (1829-30) that followed, caused many country banks to fail. There were about nine hundred of these small private banks in 1815, often set up by successful industrialists to provide local finance, in particular cash for wages. Many of these banks were under-capitalised and relied on the Bank of England as a lender of last resort. During the recurrent economic crises that occurred in John Lindley's lifetime most of these banks went out of business. The vagaries of the new capitalist economy had profound effects on local people. For example, *The Times* reported that Mr Norton, of Clayton near Huddersfield, just walked out on his seven hundred hands, saying that he did not know when he would return, while the same edition reported that there had been 'a run' on Chapman's bank.[15]

In addition to the financial problems, the agricultural counties of southern and eastern England were in revolt. There was rick burning and machine breaking in East Anglia, and the famous 'Swing Riots' (1830–31), primarily in Berkshire, Hampshire, Kent, Sussex and Wiltshire. The retribution for these riots was severe, with 252 people sentenced to death of whom nineteen were actually executed. Five hundred and five of the rioters were transported, 644 gaoled, one whipped, and seven fined.[16]

John must surely have wondered what had been achieved during his long absence, since he had just missed the relatively prosperous period of 1821 to 1827, which peaked in 1825. It was obvious that a new trade depression was about to occur and that all was not well with the economy.

The most important political legislation to take place in John's absence was the repeal of the Combination Acts in 1824, brought about by the agitation of Francis Place, the famous radical tailor of Charing Cross, with the support in parliament of two radical MPs: Sir Francis Burdett (1770–1844) and Joseph Hume (1777–1855).

CHAPTER 16
The Great Reform Bill of 1832

New political hope for the radical cause occurred on 26 June 1830, with the death at Windsor of the sixty-seven-year-old George IV. This event was celebrated with great relief by the entire nation, including John Lindley. As *The Times* reported:

> *There never was an individual less regretted by his fellow creatures than this deceased king... Nothing more remains to be said about George IV but to pay, as we must, for his profusion; and to turn his bad conduct to some account by tying up the hands of those who come after him in what concerns the public money.*[1]

However, the ascension of William IV (1765–1837) occasioned a general election. The Tories, under the Duke of Wellington, were bitterly divided over the subject of Catholic emancipation, and when the election was held in the autumn, reform candidates did well. Wellington was soon outvoted and the 2nd Earl Grey (1764–1845) became prime minister of a coalition government of Whigs and liberal Tories under Robert Peel. Suddenly, the door to electoral reform that had been firmly shut by Wellington was now ajar. All that was required was a firm push, and this was provided by Thomas Attwood (1783–1856), leader of the Birmingham Political Union Campaign for reform.

The government of the United Kingdom was in theory a tripartite system run by the monarch, the hereditary peerage in the House of Lords and an elected House of Commons. In practice, the small clique who ran the executive mostly sat in the un-elected House of Lords. Since the power of the king had been greatly reduced during the reign of George III, the resulting executive was an oligarchy of landed interests. However, the monarch continued to exercise control by formally appointing ministers and, before the Reform Bill of 1832, it was almost impossible for a faction to govern without the support of the Crown.

During the general election of 1830, mass agitation for parliamentary reform was a central issue. The anomalies of the electoral franchise were obvious to all. The pocket boroughs were an open scandal. For example, in 1831 just prior to the Reform Bill, Cornwall with a population of 300,938 elected forty-four MPs to sit in the House of Commons, while Yorkshire with a population of 1,371,359 elected only twenty-eight MPs. This disparity was defended by the government on the grounds that the elected members represented all interests. By this was meant all 'landed interests', since only possession of land was deemed to give a person a stake in the running of the country.

On taking office after the autumn election, the coalition government tried to defuse the national unrest by introducing a Reform Bill in March 1831. The bill was piloted through parliament by Lord John Russell (1792–1878), with the aim of doing just enough to remove some of the most blatant electoral anomalies and open up the franchise to the more 'respectable' citizens. However, the bill was defeated once in the Commons and twice in the Lords, and only the determination of Grey and Peel ensured that the Great Reform Bill of June 1832 was passed at the third attempt. This was largely due to pressure from the prime minister on the King, who very reluctantly agreed to create fifty new Whig lords in order to ensure passage of the bill in the House of Lords. In the event this manoeuvre was not necessary, as the Tory opposition abstained rather than see the House of Lords flooded by Whigs.

The Reform Bill was a great disappointment to the radicals, for although it increased the electorate from about 400,000 to 656,000, and abolished many of the most blatant 'rotten boroughs', redistributing the seats to a number of the new industrial cities, by opting for a ten pound property qualification, instead of a ratepayers franchise, the Reform Act actually disenfranchised a large number of working-class men and a few middle-class widows. It certainly did nothing to promote 'Universal Suffrage'.[2]

There were however two subtle gains. Abolishing many of the rotten boroughs, many of which had been controlled in the government's interest, made it more difficult to appoint ministers of the King's choice and so influence the executive. Also, the threat to swamp the Tory dominated Lords with Whig supporters always remained in the background and was used by Prime Minister H.H. Asquith, who introduced a Parliament Bill in 1910 that abolished the Lords' veto over Commons legislation.

The first general election under the new franchise took place the following November. To the labouring classes the new voting system made no difference to their daily lives; Mirfield with a population of over five thousand still had only one hundred and eighteen voters. The landed aristocracy had been supplanted by a manufacturing aristocracy, who were equally indifferent to the plight of the labouring classes. But, by enfranchising the middle classes, the ruling elite had divided the opposition, leaving the labouring poor to continue the struggle alone. In fact, Richard Oastler held the opinion that 'all the effect of the 1832 act was to enfranchise money: it was a truly bourgeois revolution'.[3]

The great Whig betrayal of 1832 was felt very keenly by the labouring classes, as the Whigs had promoted themselves as defenders of the rights of disenfranchised people – until they themselves obtained political power. Nevertheless, most reformers were still in favour of acting peacefully thereby marginalizing the revolutionaries. But when petitions were rejected out of hand, Habeas Corpus suspended, and new acts rushed through parliament to limit constitutional liberties, the 'constitutional radicals' soon lost all credibility. It has been observed that a great deal of activity, which the government attributed to revolutionary elements, and which so alarmed magistrates, was constitutionally perfectly legitimate. The constitution of England did not in theory allow the government arbitrary power, and rule by proclamation. Certainly, the legal rights available to citizens for arming and drilling were uncertain.[4]

The 'Pilgrimage to York' at Easter 1832 was a loyalist protest against Leeds Whigs and factory-owners, particularly Edward Baines editor of the *Leeds Mercury*. This was a working Tory-Radical alliance, in the tradition of Richard Oastler and Michael Sadler (1780–1835), the radical MP, on the subject of factory reform, intended to divert attention from the Reform Bill. When the *Leeds Mercury* published a hostile account on 28 April, a copy of that paper was tied to a pole with black crepe and carried through the town to the offices of the *Mercury* where it was burned in effigy. During the evening, an even larger crowd burned an effigy of Baines himself bearing the words of William Cobbett: 'The Great Liar of the North'.[5]

Between the years 1830 and 1837 there were no fewer than five general elections (1830, 1831, 1832, 1835 and 1837) while Huddersfield also had two by-elections. Elections were traditionally the time when non-electors could participate in politics. The Reform Act of 1832 prompted newspapers, in their search for sensation, to report contested elections, particularly in industrial towns. The new interest generated large meetings, which in turn generated lively participation by crowds of people wishing to express views of their own. The new political system was thereby unintentionally promoting the politicisation of the emergent working class.[6]

Did John Lindley sense a glimmer of light? Or, like most of his contemporaries, feel that the Whig bourgeoisie had betrayed them? At the age of sixty-five John, still working as a nail maker, and his wife Hannah had escaped subsistence poverty, largely due to the support of their children, but they could not be unaware of the surrounding poverty. In fact, much of society was only held together by a sense of obligation by many of the rich and influential towards the poor – carrying on the eighteenth-century Christian tradition of charity. For example, in 1843, the 4th Earl of Dartmoor, as lord of the manor, visited his tenants in the township of Slaithwaite, just south of Huddersfield. The purpose was to celebrate the coming of age of his eldest son, an old tradition, by laying the foundation stone of a new Church of England Sunday school, on land, high on the moors, that he had donated the previous year. This building was provided to serve as a place of worship for his tenants' children, who lived in the scattered communities of weavers and farmers in this remote place. Similarly, in 1840, his wife became patron of a maternal society for lying-in women, started by the vicar's wife. 'He responded promptly and liberally, though with much discrimination, to every appeal made to him, for the spiritual and educational improvement of the tenants of his estates.'[7]

Perhaps of more significance to ordinary people was the Municipal Reform Act of 1835 which, unlike the 1832 Reform Act, gave the local franchise to all ratepayers – at last some working men had a say in local elections in the new municipal boroughs. As a result, the old local oligarchies of gentry, comprised of Tory lawyers, churchmen and scions of the aristocracy, began to lose their stranglehold on power, as they were gradually replaced by middle-class working artisans, such as shopkeepers and schoolteachers. Just as important was the replacement in large urban areas of 'Peterloo-type magistrates', by Nonconformist ministers and solid middle-class citizens. However, the conduct of magistrate W.B. Farrand, in Bingley in 1848, demonstrates that there was still some way to go to achieve equitable justice for the unrepresented.[8]

Factory Reform and the Ten-Hour Movement

On 29 September 1830, Richard Oastler, son of the leader of the Methodist New Connection in Leeds and steward to Squire Thornhill of Fixby Hall near Huddersfield, wrote his famous letter to the *Leeds Mercury* on 'Yorkshire Slavery', bringing to public attention the conditions under which children were employed in the textile mills of Yorkshire. This lengthy and repetitive letter has been paraphrased as follows:

> *Thousands of little children, both male and female, but principally female, from seven to fourteen years of age are daily compelled to labour from six o'clock in the morning to seven in the evening with only – Britons blush while you read it! With*

only thirty minutes allowed for eating and recreation! Poor infants ye are sacrificed at the shrine of avarice without even the solace of the Negro slave – you are no more than he is, free agents. You are compelled to work as long as the necessity of your needy parents may require or the cold bloodied avarice of your worse than barbarian masters may demand...Let Yorkshire hear thee swear "Her children shall be free".[9]

Oastler was well aware of the cruelties of Negro slavery – people torn from their countries, families, language and culture. If they survived the horrors of the 'middle passage', on arrival in a foreign land they were sold as a commodity, and forced to work (in conditions that Europeans could not endure), degraded and treated as less than human. In this letter, Oastler was using the popular nationwide campaign to abolish African slavery to draw attention to similar horrendous conditions in Yorkshire mills.

On 23 October 1830, the *Leeds Mercury* published two anonymous replies to Oastler's letter. The first said that the hours of work quoted for children in Bradford were correct, but the work was light. The second said that he had seen boys playing happily in the street after work and quoted wages as 5s to 6s per week for a child and 6s to 12s per week for a young woman.[10]

Oastler's letter to the *Leeds Mercury* was followed up in April 1831 by his *Manifesto to the Working Classes of the West Riding* demanding a ten-hour statutory working day. This proposal met with strong opposition from Yorkshire mill owners led by the Ackroyds of Halifax, who called a meeting on 5 March 1831 and drew up 'fourteen points against Oastler'. However, Oastler attended meeting after meeting waging a determined war against the rich for their intense selfishness and their cold neglect of the suffering classes, and so earned himself the titles 'king of the factory children' and 'the good old king'. Typical of Oastler's many campaigns were the mass marches that converged on York on Easter Monday 1832, which resulted in a petition with 130,000 signatures that was later presented to parliament. In parliament, Oastler was supported by the Tory, Michael Sadler, and the radical John Fielden (1784–1849), a wealthy mill owner from Todmorden. Unfortunately, Sadler lost his seat in 1832 as a consequence of the Reform Act. Locally, Lawrence Pitkethly, later leader of the Huddersfield Chartists, gave constant support and Rev. Joseph Rayner Stephens (1805–1879), a Methodist from Manchester, whipped up popular indignation with his fiery preaching. The outcry resulted in the passing of Althorp's Factory Act in August 1833.[11]

Tolpuddle Martyrs

In 1834, there was a wave of rick burning and machine breaking in the southern counties of England. The Whig government, under Lord Melbourne (1779–1848), decided to support magistrates who dealt harshly with trade union activity. The most notorious example occurred in the village of Tolpuddle, Dorset, where members of the *Friendly Society of Agricultural Labourers* refused to work for less than ten shillings (fifty pence) a week, although by this time wages had been reduced to seven shillings a week (thirty-five pence) and were due to be further reduced to six shillings (thirty pence).

James Frampton, a local landowner, wrote a letter of complaint to the prime minister. As a result, George Loveless (1797–1874), a local Methodist preacher, his brother James Loveless (1808–1873), George's brother-in-law, Thomas Standfield (1789–1864) and his son John Standfield, James Brine (1813–1902) and James Hammett (1811–1891), all members of the *Friendly Society*, were arrested and charged with administering unlawful oaths. They were tried at Dorchester Assizes and found guilty on 17 March 1834 and were sentenced to be transported to New South Wales for seven years. When sentenced George Loveless wrote the following lines:

> God is our guide! from field, from wave,
> From plough, from anvil, and from loom;
> We come, our country's rights to save,
> And speak a tyrant faction's doom:
> We raise the watch-word liberty;
> We will, we will, we will be free!

They became known as The Tolpuddle Martyrs. They found conditions in the penal colonies appalling. James Brine had to go six months without shoes or bedding, sleeping on the ground each night. The others fared little better, though hunger, hard labour and the constant threat of brutal corporal punishment for minor offences were familiar to all six men.[12]

The Tolpuddle Martyrs become popular folk heroes and eight hundred thousand signatures were collected for their release. Their supporters organised a political march, one of the first successful marches in the UK, and all, except James Hammett, were released in 1836.

Poor Law Amendment Act 1834

In July or August 1834, the Poor Law Amendment Act brought to an end the Elizabethan Poor Law, based on 'the parish' as the unit of administration supervised by justices of the peace. The legislation aimed at reducing the burden of the poor on the parish rate. The Elizabethan system had in fact become an anachronism, as it encouraged large farmers to pay below subsistence wages, in the knowledge that 'the parish' would relieve the resulting destitution from the parish rates. This was known as the Speenhamland system, introduced by a group of Berkshire magistrates in 1795 and widely adopted in southern and eastern England. In extreme cases, the old parish system could be just as harsh as the new 1834 act, but it was often humanely administered, benefitting the genuinely unemployed and destitute. The parish rates were levied on all parishioners with incomes above a certain level, but there was wide variation between parishes, both on the rates levied, and the amounts of relief paid out. The 1834 act was certainly not suitable for the frequent short-term unemployment experienced in the manufacturing districts of Yorkshire and Lancashire.

The new Poor Law Amendment Act (1834) aimed to group parishes together, who were then required to build union workhouses administered by a board of governors and centrally controlled. Payments to the able-bodied poor living in their own homes known as 'outdoor relief' were to be discontinued. The unpopularity of the new act stemmed from the fact that it deliberately aimed to make conditions in the workhouse considerably worse than those outside, so only the completely destitute would consider submitting themselves to such a regime. Furthermore, it was necessary for applicants to have sold everything of value before entering the workhouse, thereby ensuring that they were totally unable to support themselves should economic conditions improve. This idea was based on the misguided economic philosophy of Jeremy Bentham (1748–1832), who completely ignored the fact that at certain times there really was no paid work available, an error which continues in the twenty-first century. For the manufacturing districts of the North, where cyclical unemployment was endemic, the system was totally inappropriate. No single piece of Whig legislation was to produce more resentment than this single act. Many acts of violence were carried out by the Anti-Poor Law movement in the north of England.[13]

> *Most landowners and middle-class members of Parliament believed …that the poor needed tough treatment, and if they could not support themselves, through old age, misfortune or having too many children to feed, or were laid off by their usual employers, rather than being given piecemeal payments by the parish to keep them going in their cottages they should be forced into enlarged workhouses. Here they would be housed, scantily fed and humiliated by being made to wear uniforms, and their families would be broken up, husbands and wives, mothers and children, put into separate dormitories.*[14]

The aim of the Poor Law Amendment Act was to reduce expenditure that was spiralling out of control, and, in the decade after the act was passed, the reduction in expenditure of the new system was about twenty-six per cent. However, the reduction in expenditure has alternative explanations. It may have been due to the upsurge in railway building from the late 1830s that provided constant, well-paid work for hardy men prepared to live a nomadic lifestyle. But railway expansion did nothing to ameliorate the privation during the 'hungry forties'.[15]

An alternative explanation for the reduced expenditure is the export of surplus labour, either by voluntary emigration to the new colonies, or by transportation of 'the criminal classes'. For example, Robert George Gammage (c1820–1888), the prominent Chartist, wrote that the impact of repealing the Corn Laws in 1846 was partly offset by the large number of people emigrating during this period.

In January 1837, the Poor Law commissioners turned their attention to the industrial districts of the North. As a result, on 7 May 1838, the twenty-three guardians of the Huddersfield Union wrote to the home secretary asking him to defer implementation of the new Poor Law. They claimed that the main long-term recipients of relief under the Poor Law in the Huddersfield area were: the aged, the blind, the infirm, and orphans, each costing between half a crown (twelve and a half pence) and one shilling (five pence) per week. Under the old system, those who were truly in distress were known personally to the local magistrates whereas in the new system, which covered such a large area, the true state of any individual was less likely to be accurately known. Finally, 'to confine the able-bodied in a workhouse because they have no work is very likely a means of preventing them obtaining work: and so making them paupers.'[16]

However, Mirfield already had a workhouse, which was situated at the Knowl at the top of what is now Nettleton Road. This was only a few hundred yards from Knowl Nook where John and his wife lived after his return from Van Diemen's Land. 'The workhouse had been purchased in 1757 and enlarged in 1794. The number of inmates varied from twenty adults and twelve children in 1816 and twenty-six adults and twenty-seven children in 1820', the year of the West Yorkshire Revolution.[17]

Poor Law Meeting at Peep Green 1837

On Bank Holiday Tuesday 16 May 1837, a great Huddersfield meeting was held at Peep Green on Hartshead Moor (about two miles to the northwest of John Lindley's home in Mirfield), to oppose the 1834 Poor Law Amendment Act. Peep Green was to become famous during the next few years, being the most central available venue, capable of accommodating vast crowds, convenient for the many towns that form the woollen district of the West Riding. A large crowd of between sixty thousand (*Leeds Mercury* estimate), one hundred and fifty thousand (*Times* estimate) and between one hundred thousand and two hundred and fifty thousand (Professor Royle's estimate) attended with bands and banners to hear many of the most popular public speakers of the time. In particular: Richard Oastler, John Fielden, Robert Owen, Rev. Joseph Raynor Stephens, John Wood, James Bronterre O'Brien (1805–1864) and Feargus O'Connor (1794–1855); many of these speakers were to become Chartist leaders in the following decade. Edward Baines played down the size of the crowd and claimed many of those attending were women and children, while many bystanders were there for the spectacle alone – nevertheless it was a remarkable turnout and would surely have impressed John Lindley when he reflected on the clandestine meetings and small secretive groups that constituted the Luddites in 1812 and the Yorkshire Revolution in 1820.[18]

The great Whitsuntide meeting was followed by a campaign of intimidation against the authorities – led by Oastler. But by far the most successful resistance came from Huddersfield, where Lawrence Pitkethly implemented 'robust measures' that on 5 June successfully prevented the election of a Board of Guardians clerk, and so delayed by over a year the implementation of the Poor Law Amendment Act in that town. Similarly, in October of 1837, the Bradford Poor Law Guardians wavered in implementing the new law as a result of intense local pressure and there were serious riots in November, which required two troops of cavalry to restore order. The guardians were then able to elect a clerk in January 1838. Both these actions demonstrated the power of the crowd to influence events when the voice of working people combined with a measure of support from the local middle class.[19]

Oastler's principal supporter in Huddersfield was Lawrence Pitkethly, a middle-class draper, who had gained the vote in 1832. Two days before the Poor Law Guardians met to elect their clerk, Pitkethly addressed a mass meeting in the town on the subject of the five leaders of the Glasgow cotton spinners, who had been sentenced to transportation on the technical complicity of being involved in the death of a blackleg in west Scotland. During his speech, Pitkethly covered a wide range of topics, from The Poor Law, Tolpuddle Martyrs, Irish coercion and suppression of Canadian rebels, demonstrating that while everyday life was parochial, centred on the West Riding, the political interest of the crowd was both national and international.[20]

Stamp duty on newspapers was reduced to 1d in March 1836, enabling the 'respectable' press to compete with the unstamped press, thus pricing the latter out of the market. Radicals in turn argued for the abolition on all 'taxes on knowledge' and it was from this largely successful campaign that stamp duty on pamphlets was abolished early in 1836 and the People's Charter emerged.[21]

On 20 June 1837 William IV died at Windsor, aged seventy-one. Again, the press was less than ecstatic about his reign. *The Spectator* declared that William was:

> …*though at times jovial and, for a king, an honest man, [William] was a weak, ignorant, commonplace sort of person…Notwithstanding his feebleness of purpose and littleness of mind, his ignorance and his prejudices, William IV was to the last a popular sovereign, but his very popularity was acquired at the price of something like popular contempt.*[22]

William was certainly not an impressive king and the monarchy was considered both unpopular and irrelevant to the needs of the people.

At the general election held in July 1837, which necessarily followed the ascension of Queen Victoria (1819–1901), three radical MPs, Roebuck, Thompson and Crawford were defeated. This proved disastrous for the reform parties, as suddenly radical motions were unable to be presented in parliament through lack of sponsors. At this election, Richard Oastler contested Huddersfield where he was narrowly defeated. The result caused riots in the locality and the cavalry was required to restore order.[23]

CHAPTER 17
Adult Health

While we have been considering the political unrest that was taking place during the decade after John Lindley's return from Van Diemen's Land, it is important to bear in mind that all this discontent was experienced against a background of ill health. During John's entire lifetime, little progress was made in the scientific understanding and treatment of disease. For most working men and women, the period 1770-1853 'was a time of short lives and sudden death'. Until recent times, life everywhere was lived under the threat of disease, which frequently struck without warning. There was no scientific understanding of the cause of most diseases and the therapeutic benefits of available treatments were often no more than guess work.[1]

Poor people in particular had to harden themselves to sickness, pain, disability and premature ageing. Suffering in silence became second nature, but this did not prevent attempts at self-treatment. They endeavoured to care for themselves and their families using herbal medicines, folk remedies and magic.[2]

Widespread ignorance was reinforced by Christian theology, which at that time regarded undue concern for the welfare of the body as vanity. The Church taught that concern for the soul was all important. Biblical quotations were used to support this dogma: 'Remember the lilies of the fields how they grow'; 'take no concern for the morrow'; God would provide and life's thread depended upon grace and the mysteries of His providence.[3]

As the English poet and classicist Elizabeth Carter (1717–1806) wrote:

> Health is a blessing from above, which Riches cannot buy;
> The Life of Life, the Bodies Peace, and pleasing harmony,
> To him, whose kind Support upholds this sinking house of Clay,
> Of cheerful Hallelujah's I'll the grateful Tribute pay.[4]

During the eighteenth century, known as 'the age of enlightenment', many Christians of all denominations were gradually getting rid of the remains of medieval belief and superstitions that required self-mortification as a treatment for disease, but the habit still lingered on. For, as late as 1831, during the cholera epidemic, the national response was to call for a day of fasting.

Fortunately, positive attempts were made to improve treatment and care, in the belief that 'God helped those that helped themselves'. For example, Anglicans were prominent in founding hospitals to treat the sick, while the Methodist, John Wesley, supplemented his book *Primitive Physick* with scores of proverbs that identified health hazards and offered preservatives against pain, such as 'air slayeth sooner than the sword', 'where the sun enters, the doctor does not', etc.[5]

Healthy Constitution

It was generally accepted that good health was very important if daily life was to be bearable during the Georgian period (1714–1820), since 'diseases were agonising, medicine disgusting and commonly useless'. The labouring classes recognised that it was very important to develop a robust physical constitution when young, if one was to lead a tolerable adult life. The rich were not immune, for pandemics made no distinction of class or wealth. The pampered aristocracy also suffered from untreatable conditions and suffered great pain, as vividly described by Amanda Foreman in *Georgiana: Duchess of Devonshire*. Nevertheless, it was the interminable damp, cold, overwork and poor diet that destroyed the health of the labouring classes in large numbers.[6]

The more educated also believed that it was the bodily constitution that produced the inner vitality and strength, which flowed throughout the body when all a person's organs worked together. They also believed that medication only acted as a palliative. If a person lacked a good constitution in the first place, or let it fall into decay, medicine alone would not bring about a cure when infection occurred. Drugs, potions and spells worked by reinforcing a person's internal powers of resistance. In order to develop a good constitution, it was important to develop 'a sound foundation in infancy and consolidate it in youth'.[7]

The principles of good health had been developed from the Greek philosophy extolling the 'golden mean'. Exercise, food and drink were all to be taken in moderation. However, the Georgians had a different view of moderation to that held in the twenty-first century. Excessive exertion was to be avoided, especially if it produced sweating followed by sudden cooling. For the wealthy, 'the eating of plain food was recommended with no more than two pints of wine a day and two chicken legs and a wing for a meal'. Of course, for the poor, too little food produced malnutrition. During John's lifetime cleanliness, specifically the absence of dirt, began to be associated with a reduction in disease (as in cause and effect), as witnessed by the care taken to minimise dirt on board the *Lady Ridley* by the surgeon James Wilson. For the wealthy, hygiene and personal heath were associated with bodily appearance. Of course, how one thinks of dirt and pollution is relative, for any given class of people, in any given period. It must be remembered that even the Georgian aristocracy were quite used to levels of obnoxious smells and filth that seem intolerable in the twenty-first century – bedbugs, hair nits, lice and fleas were common, with privy-pails slopping over in the sideboard of dining rooms and chamber pots under the bed.[8]

In a provincial town like Mirfield, doctors acted as general practitioners regardless of their training and whether licenced as physicians, surgeons or apothecaries. But university-trained doctors were hardly more effective than the 'quacks' or 'snake oil charlatans' who appeared at fairs, since they also lacked a scientific understanding of disease. In any case there were few effective drugs available at that time. Cinchona (Peruvian or Jesuit's Bark) the basis for quinine, was known to be effective against malaria. Mercury was effective but poisonous, nevertheless it became standard treatment for syphilis at a time when most remedies were vegetable derivatives. This gave rise to the saying 'one night with Venus and a lifetime with Mercury'. Willow bark contains salicylic acid, the main ingredient of aspirin, and in the eighteenth century Rev. Edmund Stone (1702–1768) found that willow bark, usually dissolved in tea or small beer, was an effective remedy for pain and fever. He informed the Royal Society of his discovery in a letter to the president dated 25 April 1763.

An extract from foxgloves (*Digitalis purpurea*) was known to be a useful ancient folk remedy for dropsy. In 1785, Dr William Withering (1741–1799) determined that the active ingredient was digitalis and this extract was effective for treating both dropsy (oedema) and a number of heart conditions. It was one of the most recognisable treatments prescribed by James Wilson, surgeon on the *Lady Ridley,* on the voyage to Van Diemen's Land in 1821.

Laudanum, which contained opium dissolved in alcohol, was an effective, though addictive, pain killer, but most medicines were largely useless palliatives.[9]

As previously stated, drugs were not expected to play a decisive role in healing. Medical practice at this time included regulation of diet and environment (for instance travelling for health) and giving wise counsel. A good drug was not expected to cure a disease on its own account; rather its purpose was to aid the healing power of nature in restoring balance to the system, as were purging, sweating and bleeding.[10]

Malnutrition

Malnutrition among the labouring classes was widespread and increased the risk of infection and infectious disease; for example, it was a major risk factor in the onset of active tuberculosis. In communities or areas that lacked access to safe drinking water, these additional health risks presented a critical problem. Lower energy and impaired function of the brain also reinforced the downward spiral of malnutrition, as victims were less able to carry out the tasks they needed to perform in order to earn sufficient income and acquire food.

Adulteration of food was widespread; while diluting milk with water caused no physical harm, adding chalk and alum to flour to produce 'white' bread certainly did. This meant that disabling and energy sapping diarrhoea and dysentery were commonplace. Food poisoning was common but undiagnosed. The sources were many: particularly ingestion of heavy metals from industrial processes making food containers, or merely transferring by hand to mouth such products as paint, lead pipes, etc., which contaminated food. Many 'physics' prescribed by doctors were poisonous. We have seen earlier that the industry-specific diseases associated with nail making were caused by inhalation of dust entering into the lungs, but some of the particles were also ingested into the digestive system. Infected food was common; an 1863 report to the privy council stated that one-fifth of meat sold came from diseased cattle.

A fungus (*Claviceps purpurea*) infected rye and cereals that caused ergot poisoning, which exhibited convulsive symptoms in the form of painful seizures and spasms, colloquially known as St Anthony's Fire. Ergotism also caused dry gangrene which restricted blood flow to the hands and feet, resulting in the tissue dying and ultimately death.[11]

Sir Edwin Chadwick (1800–1890), in the middle of the century, produced statistics to demonstrate that, while the average life expectance of a lawyer in a rural county of England was fifty-two years, a labourer in Manchester or Liverpool had a life expectancy of seventeen and fifteen respectively.[12]

Intestinal Diseases

These diseases, known as enteric diseases, were transmitted directly from person to person or indirectly through contaminated food and water, but particularly by insects such as dung eating flies. The most common intestinal diseases were diarrhoea and dysentery known as 'the bloody flux'. This condition was not always infectious in origin; it was also caused by metabolic disturbances, due to both chemical poisoning of food and industrial by-products. Many of the drugs in use, particularly herbal medicines, also deliberately caused diarrhoea and were known as 'opening' medicines. Acute diarrhoea was a common affliction of travellers, a great inconvenience, but when persistent, especially when accompanied by chills, fever, abdominal pain and blood in the faeces, the disease was a serious threat to life. Also widespread was gastroenteritis, commonly known as 'food poisoning', caused by any of the thousands of different strains of salmonella which resulted in acute fever. The offending organism was usually imbibed in contaminated food or drink and, after a short incubation period, was followed by the onset of nausea and vomiting, abdominal pain and diarrhoea. Fortunately, it was rarely lethal in healthy individuals.

Contagious Diseases in the early Nineteenth Century

Soon after John Lindley's return to England, there were three massive waves of contagious diseases in the 1830s and 1840s: the first from 1831–1833 included the initial appearance of Asiatic cholera and two influenza epidemics; the second from 1836–1842 encompassed cholera, typhus, typhoid fever, and major epidemics of influenza; and the third epidemic, primarily of cholera, in 1848–49, resulted in ninety thousand deaths in the UK. Highly contagious epidemics affecting the entire population were the unintentional revenge of the working-class slum dwellers on the middle and upper classes. People who sought to isolate themselves from the squalor and filth of urban slums, by living in separate districts, found that disease does not recognise any distinction or boundaries between rich and poor.[13]

Cholera was the most devastating of all the infectious diseases of the nineteenth century. It made its first appearance in Sunderland in the autumn of 1831. The progress of the disease was a horrifying spectacle, beginning with diarrhoea and painful vomiting resulting in thirst and dehydration, the skin soon turned blue, purple and finally brown or black. Eventually, the patient experienced severe breathlessness, followed by rigid spasms of the lower limbs, stomach and abdominal muscles, inevitably resulting in death. The symptoms were mystifying. It was not known at the time that the cholera bacillus was carried in water, and outbreaks of cholera affected most towns, as drinking water was polluted by sewage and effluent from factories. People did develop immunity to this bacillus, but in every generation a serious epidemic affected all major towns.

In their ignorance, parliament suggested a National Fast Day to be held on 21 March 1832, 'as a day of atonement for the sins which were considered responsible for this scourge'. Not surprisingly, this medieval response proved ineffective. The epidemic continued to spread quickly from the northeast of the country to the remainder of the United Kingdom causing over fifty thousand deaths. The outbreak was particularly severe in Yorkshire; Leeds with a population of seventy-six thousand suffered over one thousand eight hundred cases and seven hundred people died of the disease between May and November in 1832. A *Report of the Leeds Board of Health* was produced in 1833 by the surgeon and factory inspector of Leeds, Dr Robert Baker (1803–1880), with an accompanying map by Charles Fowler. This demonstrated conclusively that the highest incidence of the disease was in the most densely populated north eastern part of the town. Dr Baker commented 'how exceedingly the disease has prevailed in those parts of the town where there is a deficiency, often an entire want of sewerage, drainage and paving.' This was over twenty years before the famous study in Soho by the London physician Dr John Snow (1813–1858), which conclusively demonstrated that cholera was carried in the drinking water supply. The outbreak reached Mirfield in 1834, but there the incidence was nothing like as severe as that in Leeds.[14]

Chapter 17

The third cholera epidemic that struck Great Britain in 1848–9 resulted in a horrifying ninety thousand deaths, nearly twice that of the previous epidemic. Once the disease was proven to be linked to the water supply, wealthy people bought spring water from water-sellers, and even this was used to dilute wine (as alcohol killed the bacteria) while preventing intoxication. For the labouring classes there was ale, which was considered a 'temperance drink' as opposed to wine and spirits. Tea (made with boiling water) was also becoming more widely available and became the common beverage of the poor, as this once expensive prestigious beverage became affordable by the working classes.[15]

It was time to discard fasting and initiate public health measures. In particular the Towns Improvement Clauses Act 1847, empowering local authorities to make a series of byelaws on a number of issues relating to public health, and the Public Health Bill passed in 1848 gave local authorities greater powers. Although a great amount of medical knowledge had been accumulated during John's lifetime, it was not until he reached the age of eighty that the benefits began to reach the population at large. Thanks to the work of Sir Edwin Chadwick (1800–1890), public health measures were beginning to transform the health of all; but, as recorded later in the text, they were very slow in reaching Mirfield.[16]

While it is now known that influenza is an infectious disease in its own right (caused by influenza viruses), in the first half of the nineteenth century it was thought to be the early stage of cholera. The most common symptoms of the disease are chills, fever, sore throat, muscle pains, severe headache, coughing, weakness/fatigue and general discomfort. In more serious cases, influenza causes pneumonia, which is an inflammatory condition of the lungs caused by different species of bacteria, viruses and occasionally by chemicals. Typically, influenza is transmitted through the air by coughs or sneezes, creating aerosols containing the virus. Influenza can also be transmitted by direct contact with bird droppings or nasal secretions, or through contact with contaminated surfaces. Influenza viruses, which only replicate inside living cells, are inactivated by sunlight, disinfectants, detergents and soap. Without this knowledge, and given the general hygiene of the period, it is easy to understand why influenza was a major killer.[17]

Typhus was another 'filth' disease, spread from person to person by the body louse (*Pediculus humanus humanus*), which was more widespread than cholera. Once again, lack of adequate washing facilities and poor hygiene encouraged the spread of this louse-borne disease. In one survey of public health, two children were recorded as never having removed the clothes that they were wearing during the previous six months. Typhus was first recognised as a serious disease in the fifteenth century. Very likely sporadic cases appeared before that period, but not enough to attract the attention of physicians or historians. With the expansion of trade and the movement of large numbers of soldiers, typhus became a major epidemic disease. In the sixteenth and seventeenth centuries typhus became known as gaol-fever, because it was commonly associated with those confined within goals, where filth and lousiness abounded. Not until the eighteenth century did improved gaol conditions result in a reduction of typhus victims. This was largely due to the humanitarian Quaker John Howard (1725–1790), who toured British prisons in 1773, and produced a report *The State of Prisons in England and Wales* in 1777, resulting in two acts of parliament that set standards of cleanliness in hospitals and prisons.[18]

Typhoid fever (typhoid), or putrid fever as it was known in the nineteenth century, was also a 'filth disease', caused by ingesting food or water contaminated by the faeces of an infected person. The agent was later discovered to be a bacterium (*Salmonella enterica typhi*). This disease thrived in the overcrowded and unhygienic living conditions of the industrial slums of the nineteenth century. In the West Riding of Yorkshire, Leeds and Bradford were notorious centres of typhoid fever. Nationally, it was controlled through the public health efforts pioneered by Chadwick.[19]

Smallpox was a greatly feared disease, as not only did it disfigure the population (any woman without smallpox scars was considered beautiful), it had a high mortality rate. It is a viral disease (*Variola virus*) that originated in cattle and crossed the species boundary at the time hunter gatherers gave way to farming. It is a systematic illness, usually recognised by the skin lesions, the eruptions closely resembling those of chickenpox, measles and syphilis. A distinguishing feature of smallpox is the permanent facial scarring of the skin upon recovery. The practice of inoculation against smallpox, an ancient eastern procedure, was introduced into England early in the eighteenth century, mostly through the efforts of Lady Mary Wortley Montague (1689–1762), wife of the British ambassador to Turkey. This preventative technique required removing material from a smallpox pustule and introducing it into the skin of a person who had never had the disease. This procedure usually produced only a localised reaction in the recipient but conferred permanent protection against smallpox. However, inoculation was not without its hazards, as it occasionally caused fatal smallpox in some individuals, and was the source of further epidemics.[20]

Later, Edward Jenner (1749-1823), a country doctor living in rural Gloucestershire, pioneered the principle of vaccination. In this part of the country, it was known that the occasional affliction of cattle cowpox sometimes produced what looked like a single pock on the hands of milkmaids, and that this seemed to protect them from the more serious smallpox. Although a farmer called Jesty, and other people, had previously injected the cowpox material into individuals with intent to prevent smallpox, Jenner performed the crucial experiment on 14 May 1796, and published the new preventative. He took some matter from a cowpox lesion on the hand of a milkmaid, Sarah Nelms, and injected it into the arm of a young boy, named James Phipps, who had not had natural smallpox. James developed soreness and a scab on his arm, but, except for a single day's fever remained well. Six weeks later, Jenner inoculated him with live smallpox material. He failed to develop the disease, showing that he was immune. Despite the fact that this was a very dangerous and unethical experiment to perform, Jenner, in 1798, privately published his short treatise on the procedure he called vaccination, after the Latin word for cow. However, during John Lindley's lifetime, vaccination was slow to be implemented in the UK (Napoleon vaccinated his entire army!), and many people died of the disease. The parish record of Darton records that, for 1810, 'several [people] died of smallpox'.[21]

Tuberculosis, known as consumption, was a treacherous, insidious and debilitating disease. It affected more people than any other, with death occurring in the majority of cases after a lingering illness. It is caused by various strains of bacteria (*Mycobacterium tuberculosis*), and usually attacks the lungs, but can also affect other parts of the body. It is spread through the air when people who have the disease cough, sneeze, or spit, and consequently was transmitted from person to person. As a result, it was endemic and became the great killer in the new large towns that were developing in the industrial North. The classic symptoms are a chronic cough with blood-tinged sputum, fever, night sweats, and weight loss. Infection of other organs causes a wide range of symptoms. The environmental cause was the insanitary slum dwellings being erected by speculators and developers to house the growing workforce that was constantly migrating from the English countryside and starving Ireland. Leeds and Bradford were particularly badly affected in this respect. Bradford was described by one inspector as 'the dirtiest, filthiest and worst regulated town in the country'. Consumption was responsible for between a quarter and a third of all deaths during John Lindley's lifetime.[22]

The common cold is and was the most frequent infectious disease in humans, with, on average, two to four infections a year in individual adults, and from six to twelve in individual children. It is caused by a wide spectrum of viruses. Although people had suffered from minor respiratory ailments over the centuries, little prominence was given to discussion of the common cold before the eighteenth century. Common symptoms include a cough, sore throat, runny nose, and fever. There is no known cure, but symptoms usually resolve spontaneously in seven to ten days, with some symptoms possibly lasting for up to three weeks.[23]

Sexually Transmitted Diseases

Syphilis (the great pox) and gonorrhoea are both bacterial infections, usually transmitted from person to person through direct contact. The precise nature of the two diseases was poorly understood before the nineteenth century, when Phillippe Ricord (1800–1889) clarified the clinical features of syphilis in 1838. Gonorrhoea, on the other hand, was recognised in prehistory to be a contagious infection. The origin of syphilis is more obscure, but epidemics occurred throughout Europe during the fifteenth and sixteenth centuries. The most commonly held view is that Christopher Columbus (1451–1506) brought it back from the Americas in 1492, but this theory has been disputed, as earlier dated diseased European skeletons have been found. During these pandemics, syphilis was looked upon as a contagious malady of venereal origin (pox).

The primary cause of venereal syphilis is the organism *Treponema pallidum* that is normally transmitted sexually. A primary chancre appears on the genitals about three weeks after contact, with the simultaneous appearance of enlarged regional lymph nodes. About six weeks after exposure, the first symptoms appear: fever, painful joints, skin rashes, lesions of mucus membranes, and enlarged lymph nodes. These are all due to the spread of the organisms in the blood stream. Then a latent period of many years ensues during which time the *treponema* lurk in the tissues, and from time to time in the blood and spinal fluid, without any obvious evidence of the disease. After a long incubation period the secondary features of the skin lesions appear. The tertiary stage is the most serious when symptoms affect the bones and soft palate and finally inflammation of the heart muscles or the central nervous system, both of which can lead to death. In the eighteenth and nineteenth centuries, gum guaiac and mercury were used in treatment.[24] The modern treatment is penicillin, discovered in 1937 by Sir Alexander Fleming (1881–1955).

Gonorrhoea (colloquially known as clap) is acquired through human contact and is caused by bacteria (*Neisseria gonorrhoeae*). It has a short incubation period of three to seven days. In men there is little systemic reaction, the infection remains localised to the front of the urethra and is observed as a discharge of pus. Symptoms in women are less pronounced and any local discomfort is often attributed to other factors or irritants. Gonorrhoea acquired at birth from the mother can cause blindness in babies. The complications of untreated gonorrhoea can be serious and debilitating. Gonorrhoeal arthritis is a destructive joint disease, producing stiffness or fusion in the large joints. In men there is also the complication of urethral shrinkage, and in women pelvic inflammatory diseases which often lead to sterility.[25]

Diseases Transmitted to Humans from Animals

No infectious disease has been feared more than rabies. It was described as 'one of the greatest of all human calamities' by Dr James Thatcher in 1812. Since Roman times, it was recognised that a person bitten by a mad dog would foam at the mouth and inevitably die. In any community, the death of one individual from rabies created fear in the population at large. It was also known that there were other species of rabid domestic and wild animals, and that the 'poison' transmitted to man was contained in the saliva. The poison turned out to be the rabies virus, either the urban type, existing principally in dogs, and wildlife rabies, which both attack the central nervous system. The treatment was local excision and cauterisation of the injured tissue. Little progress was made on understanding the nature of rabies, until the germ theory of disease had been established.[26]

Parasitic Diseases

Parasitology achieved scientific status in the nineteenth century, concerned chiefly with protozoa and those infections caused by worms. It had been known for centuries that man and animals harboured worms. Their appearance in the intestinal tract and other tissues was assumed to have originated through spontaneous generation. However, Dr Thomas Cameron defined a parasite 'as an organism which at some stage of its life requires some vital factor which can only be obtained from another living organism'.[27]

Care in Old Age

The eighteenth century witnessed unprecedented giving for medical good causes, in particular founding hospitals and dispensaries. Such institutions were meant for the poor (though not poor-law paupers) who would receive care without charge. York saw its first hospital in 1740 and first lunatic asylum by 1800.[28]

The Rise of Pharmaceuticals

Many fields of alternative medicine grew alongside the regular physic, surgery and apothecary trade. After all, regular medicine had no monopoly on effectiveness, and empirics (unqualified practitioners) and nostrum-mongers sold 'cures' that were not necessarily ineffective. For example: opium was prescribed as a painkiller, and antimony was used to cause sweating and reduce fever.[29]

The Industrial Revolution saw the rise of consumer exploitation by means of publicity and advertising. Nostrum-mongers went in for saturation advertising – in the streets, and endlessly in the newspapers. Newspaper agents undertook to distribute drugs, so that country readers often found access to 'mail order' patent medicines easier than to regular doctors. In these ways, eighteenth and nineteenth century medical opportunists cashed in on the self-diagnosing, self-help medical tradition deeply ingrained amongst the laity, while pandering to 'consumerist desires for the miracle cures and something new.' The Victorian lower class and their children swallowed gallons of laudanum, an opium mixture, which eased pain and stupefied infants. Regular doctors were not averse to nostrum-mongering and Dr James's 'Fever Powders' were produced by a bona fide Oxford MD.[30]

By the nineteenth century, things had changed somewhat. Both religious dissenters and political radicals increasingly rejected the values of the titled, the rich and the fashionable. Instead, individualism, liberty, purity and self-help came to express the ideals of self-improvement among the artisans and labouring men of the industrialising Midlands and North. Such people commonly wanted little to do with the commercial nostrums they identified with Mammon. Instead, they embraced a new medical sectarianism, which went hand in hand with religious nonconformity and political radicalism. Herbal remedies, taken straight from nature and often made by the sufferers themselves, excluded professional exploitation and adulteration. Jesse Boot (1850–1931), who helped his mother run his father's herbal medicine shop, in Nottingham, after his father's early death, went on to expand the business and to found the Boots Pure Drug Company. He had his roots in medical botany, and started manufacturing pharmaceuticals, because he was dissatisfied with the impurities of the drugs commonly available.[31]

Some early 'Quack' Remedies

James Graham (1745-1794) touted long life and sexual rejuvenation, to be achieved by mud-bathing, using his special electrified bed, housed in his Temple of Health in London, situated off the Strand.

From the 1780s, the one medicine, *Eau Medicinale,* that would really relieve gout – it contained colchicum – was marketed by a French army officer, Nicholas Husson. Ironically, this 'cure' was derided by the medical profession.

Rose's Balsamic Elixir claimed that it would cure venereal patients at a stroke: 'it removes all pain in three or four doses.' In England (1831), James Morrison (1789–1857) made a fortune with his vegetable pills.

Samuel A. Thompson (1769-1843) developed a people's health movement in America, touting vegetable-based therapies. His favourite was *Lobelia inflata,* whose seeds caused healthy vomiting and heavy sweating. This was brought to England in 1838 by 'Dr' Albert Isaiah Coffin (1790–1866), an American herbalist, who soon had a keen following among self-improving artisans and dissenters, leading to a network of Friendly Botanico-Medical Societies. Medical botany appealed to the self-help mentality.[32]

CHAPTER 18
Chartism 1837–1840

Rise of Chartism

Chartism arose out of the failure of the 1832 Reform Act to satisfy working class demand for universal male suffrage. It was built on three movements, all with origins in the economic depression of 1837 to 1842, namely: the Ten-Hour Movement, pioneered by Oastler and others, which aimed to reduce the length of the working day to a maximum of ten hours; the movement for factory reform; and opposition to the hated 1834 Poor Law Amendment Act, with the delaying tactics of Pitkethly in Huddersfield setting an example. The Chartist leaders were very aware of the grievances of the labouring classes and were politically astute in exploiting popular discontent and hunger, as their prolific journalism makes clear. They sought to solve the national economic and social problems by political means, and rather naively they argued that universal suffrage alone would solve the country's problems. It was said that support from the labouring classes was more a 'gut' feeling, depending on whether their stomachs were full or empty. More politely, the Rev. Joseph R. Stephens said it was a 'knife and fork question' and 'a bread and cheese question' – a natural response to hunger. However, the most famous radical journalist of his age William Cobbett (who prior to his death, in 1835, had relentlessly attacked the Poor Law Amendment Act, demanding an enquiry first into the conditions of the poor) observed that 'it was pointless trying to agitate people with a full stomach.' Consequently, it was no accident that Chartism flourished in the severe industrial depression that lasted from late 1836 to the summer of 1842. The resulting hunger was most severely felt in the Midlands and the north of England.[1]

As we have seen, militant radicalism in the west of Yorkshire had been most active in Huddersfield and Barnsley during the first two decades of the nineteenth century, but by the third and fourth decades militancy had migrated to Bradford, Dewsbury and Halifax. This was because there were great differences in the character of these towns, depending on the economic fortunes of the prevailing industry (Huddersfield concentrating on the fancy trade, such as elaborate waistcoats, while Barnsley specialised in linen weaving supported by nail making and wire drawing), but this migration still left John Lindley at the radical heart of the West Riding. Initially, Chartism was an alliance of many different reform groups, who put aside their differences and combined their efforts, in order to campaign for the six points of the Charter. Under the leadership of the charismatic Irishman, Feargus O'Connor, it was primarily workers in the highly mechanised cotton industry of Lancashire and the worsted industries of Bradford and Halifax who provided the driving force for this first national working-class movement. Undernourished hand-loom weavers and wool combers, the first victims of each trade cycle, became eager recruits to this new hope of a better life. The spectre of Marshall's and Gott's great mills in Leeds, which had haunted the early Luddites, was now casting its shadow over an ever increasing workforce. In Bradford, unemployment and destitution were magnified by technological redundancy, which hit the wool combers of the worsted industry hard. The problem was made worse by the large influx of Irish workers fleeing the potato famine in Ireland.[2]

It is, therefore, perhaps ironic that the greatest electoral success of the Chartist movement in the West Riding took place, not in militant Bradford, with its iron works at Low Moor, but in cosmopolitan Leeds and steel making Sheffield, where Chartist support came from lower-middle- class radicals and artisans. It should be borne in mind that iron working districts always represented a threat to government, with their potential to manufacture large quantities of armaments, such as pikes, and, as a consequence, Sheffield always remained a particular thorn in the side of authoritarian rule.[3]

In Leeds, the first green shoots of democracy emerged when the Chartists stood for election to 'the vestry' where improvement commissioners were elected. In 1840, Joshua Hobson (1810–1876) and John Jackson both stood for election, and Jackson was successful. Two years later, all nineteen Chartist candidates were elected, and they gained control of the vestry. A new Improvement Act did away with the system of improvement commissioners, so the Chartists transferred their attention to the town council. At their first attempt in 1842 they failed to gain a single seat, but in 1843 both Hobson and Jackson were elected for Holbeck Ward. Thereafter, Chartist councillors continued to sit on the Leeds town council until 1853, with a maximum of seven councillors between 1849 and 1850.[4]

In contrast, Isaac Ironside (1808–1870), in Sheffield, used a different tactic and organised a system of ward committees to nominate and support candidates. In 1848, Chartists succeeded in gaining seven seats on the town council and, by the following November, they had twenty-two nominally Chartist members on the council. This enabled Ironside, as leader, to raise topics for discussion such as 'The Charter' and 'National Secular Education'. Ironside's success was attributed to both his personality and the Sheffield radical tradition. But, by using the 1835 act, which introduced household suffrage into local government, he was able to achieve the greatest constitutional success anywhere in the country during the existence of the Chartist movement.[5]

Northern Star

The *Northern Star*, owned by Feargus O'Connor and edited by William Hill, was first published by Joshua Hobson on 18th November 1837, at four pence halfpenny a copy (2p) (equivalent to five pounds in purchasing power in the late twentieth century), which was very expensive for these times. So, the inhabitants of Mirfield shared copies in the time-honoured way, as George Mellor and the Luddites had done twenty years earlier. It has been estimated that at least fifty people had access to each copy. It was an aggressively radical newspaper, 'it spoke the anger of the anti-poor law movement, the frustration of the 10 hour movement and the class consciousness of the unstamped press, and the hopes of the radical reformers'. It was the newspaper through which O'Connor 'preached his beliefs' and received feedback from his readers, who included the full spectrum of radical thought in the country. It was one of the major successes of the Chartist movement that it managed to support the *Northern Star*, 'a very good professional newspaper', for well over a decade.[6]

The major problem that beset Chartism, was the continuing radical problem of whether to use physical force or rely solely on constitutional means. As with all mass movements, opinion was divided, while the emotive speeches of the leader O'Connor were ambiguous and did not provide clear leadership. In one speech he said 'They had a slight taste of physical force in the north. A short time ago members of the Metropolitan Police force were sent to Dewsbury, …but the boys in that noble town sent them home again.' However, he declared that 'his aim was to use moral force as long as possible'. 'Peaceably if we can, forcibly if we must.'[7]

Chartism aimed to relieve economic distress of the labouring classes by political means, and took its name from 'The People's Charter': a long, detailed document drawn up by William Lovett and Francis Place in 1837, and published on 8 May 1838 in London. The full details of the People's Charter are to be found in *History of the Chartist Movement* by R.C. Gammage (c1820–1888).[8]

Its six main points can be summarised as: the right of all men over twenty-one to vote, known as manhood suffrage; all ballots to be secret; abolition of the property qualification for MPs; payment of MPs; constituencies of equal size; and annual parliamentary elections.[9]

The decision to petition parliament to implement the Charter was agreed on 14 May 1838: and it was publicly launched at a mass meeting in Glasgow on 21 May.

The spirit of the new movement was expressed by John Smithson, who wrote in the *Northern Star* on 6 January 1838,

> Rouse working men to each other be true
> Few rich or self styled noble succour you
> 'Tis nature's nobles only that can plan
> And execute in full the rights of man
> Let all men vote and have short reck'nings too
> And then the ballot may some service do
> But if the ballot itself, by itself is got
> Your doom is sealed, contempt will be your lot
> When after this you pray, you'll pray in vain
> Since those you pray to, will have nought to gain
> By granting your request. Take warning then
> Not to trust, the smoothest tongued of men
> We're mortals all, and subject to be frail
> When circumstances change, we change our tale
> Give none the power without a proper check
> Unbounded power has made the world a wreck
> The moment that you will it, you'll be free
> 'Till then, you're slaves to all eternity.

After the launch meeting at Glasgow Green on 21 May, a series of large rallies were organised throughout the country to elect delegates for a national conference to be held in Birmingham, in order to demonstrate the size of mass support for the movement. Meetings were held at Tyneside 27 June; Northampton on 1 August; then Holloway Head, Birmingham on 6 August; Palace Yard, Westminster on 17 September; Kersal Moor, Manchester 24 September; all of which were reported in the *Northern Star*.[10]

While all these other meetings generated interest and excitement, what John Lindley, and many others like him, were waiting for was the West Riding meeting to be held at Peep

Green on Monday 15 October. Peep Green is a natural amphitheatre on Hartshead Moor, about halfway between Huddersfield and Leeds, and two miles northwest of Mirfield. It is conveniently situated to be within easy walking distance (by early nineteenth century standards) of the major conurbations of the West Riding.

West Riding Meeting at Peep Green 15 October 1838

About midday, numerous columns of working people gathered at their respective marshalling points at Leeds, Bradford, Halifax, Huddersfield, Dewsbury and Wakefield, and all the townships and surrounding villages for miles around, ready to march to Hartshead Moor. The column from Millsbridge, led by Feargus O' Connor, was reported by the *Northern Star* to be one-and-a-half miles long. They then set off to march to the rendezvous at Peep Green.[11]

Later, Edward Baines, in the *Leeds Mercury*, poured scorn on the Peep Green meeting, stating that one third were women and children and that the main attractions were stalls selling rum, gin and swipes (a thin cheap beer, poorly brewed, and lacking statutory control). This may have been true, but these great open-air rallies were deliberately held on public holidays and a carnival atmosphere prevailed. Contingents of men, women and children marched with flags flying, accompanied by numerous brass bands. On arrival they found booths and stalls selling pies and refreshments. The flags were an important expression of popular discontent, since they were handmade by local groups and carried messages and slogans written by the grass roots, all duly recorded in the *Northern Star*. While the estimate of some of the numbers of people attending may have been exaggerated, it was not unknown for 'whole townships to empty', as a result of everyone attending such meetings. It is unthinkable that John Lindley was not one of the vast crowd. In fact, every able-bodied person in Mirfield probably enjoyed this notable occasion.[12]

The size of the crowd was certainly large. Estimates varied considerably depending on the source; The *Northern Star* (Chartist) gave a figure in excess of three hundred thousand. The *Leeds Mercury* (Whig) gave an estimate of thirty thousand, while claiming that the *Manchester Guardian* estimated only ten thousand. Perhaps the most accurate estimate is the conservative fifty thousand, by Alan Brooke, a local Huddersfield historian. All are agreed that it was a wet day with a fine drizzle falling, and that the threat of dismissal by many employers of anyone who attended the meeting certainly reduced the numbers.[13]

The meeting opened with a declaration that its purpose was to muster support for 'The People's Charter' and choose delegates for the National Conference to be held in Birmingham. Robert Wilkinson, a leather cutter, was elected to the chair. It was his job to introduce the star attraction, Feargus O'Connor, who was the effective leader of the Chartist movement, both on account of his charismatic oratory and thunderous voice, well suited to outdoor speaking before the days of megaphones, and his ownership of the *Northern Star* newspaper. The platform was shared by many other prominent speakers from Lancashire and Yorkshire, and included: George White (1811-1868), a working man from Leeds; Rev. Joseph Rayner Stephens, the Wesleyan minister from Lancashire; John Fielden MP, a rich manufacturer from Todmorden and a fervent supporter of the Ten-Hour Bill; George Barker of Huddersfield; Joseph Crabtree of Barnsley; Mr John Collins, a working man from Birmingham and well-known public speaker; Mr Richardson of Manchester; Mr James Taylor of Rochdale; Mr Samuel Dickenson of Almondbury; Mr Todd of Dewsbury; Dr Fletcher of Bury; and some other unrecorded speakers.

First an apology for absence from John Powlett was read out. This letter explained that his group could not be present as they had all been threatened with dismissal by their employer if they attended.

The first speaker was Abraham Hanson, of Elland, who spoke of the Whig betrayal over the 1832 Reform Bill. He urged the crowd to let universal suffrage be their rallying point, since they had no representation in parliament, all the tax they paid was so much robbery – echoing the American colonists in 1776.

Peter Bussey (1805–1869), leader of the Bradford Chartists, spoke next, highlighting the turncoat Edward Baines, who had supported the radicals in the *Leeds Mercury*, until the Reform Act brought the Whigs back to power, and then had abandoned the labouring classes. Bussey believed 'Neither the poor man nor the rich man have the natural right to the electoral franchise'. He then struck a militant note with 'What gained the independence of America? It was common sense and American rifles'.

The scene was now set for the star speaker, Feargus O'Connor, who spoke at considerable length and with great effect. He listed a long catalogue of injustices. At this point, the chairman, Robert Wilkinson, proposed the following resolution:

> *That this meeting is of the opinion that the cause of all the corruptions and anomalies in the legislation as well as the distress and difficulties of the commercial, manufacturing trading and working classes is that our representation system is based upon exclusive and unjust privileges, and we therefore believe that the time has arrived for establishing that system on a foundation more in accordance with the principle of justice, brotherly love and with increased knowledge of the people.*

William Thornton of Halifax then proposed a second resolution:

> *The principles of representation defined by the 'People's Charter' are just and reasonable embracing as it does Universal Suffrage, No Property Qualifications, Annual Parliaments, Votes by Ballots, which in their practical operation would in the opinion of this meeting be the means of returning just representatives to the Commons House of Parliament – persons who being responsible to and paid by the people, would be more likely to promote the just interests of the nation, than those who now constitute that assembly. Note A year is long enough to ascertain the value of a servant and too long to be tormented with a knave.*

John Fielden seconded the resolution. He recalled the meeting in 1837 to oppose the New Poor Law. He reminded them that before the Reform Bill, Whigs called upon workers for support. The Reform Act was a complete failure. They had been denied the Factory Bill sponsored by John Hobhouse (1786–1869), which fell with the dissolution of parliament in 1837. He called on people to support universal suffrage, annual parliaments and to abstain from purchasing taxable goods, but not to the detriment of their families.

The meeting then elected by popular acclaim Feargus O'Connor, William Rider, James Paul Cobbett, Lawrence Pitkethly and Peter Bussey to represent them at the National Chartist Convention meeting in February 1839.[14]

At this time, the Huddersfield delegate, Lawrence Pitkethly, came to prominence as the principal associate of Richard Oastler, the leader of the Anti-Poor Law struggle and himself a Poor Law Guardian. He was a prosperous draper from Huddersfield and became a noted local leader without achieving national status. He was a shawl draper, therefore not a working man himself, but a small employer of labour (he employed fellow radical John Leech, who managed his shop). He had gained the vote in 1832 and was a supporter of Richard Carlisle (1790–1843), Henry Hetherington (1792–1849) and the unstamped press. He was also a member of Huddersfield Political Union in 1832, and a leading protester against the sentences passed on the Tolpuddle Martyrs and the Glasgow cotton-spinners. He was Huddersfield's most prominent Chartist, being a delegate to the 1839 and 1842 conventions, and standing with George Julian Harney (1817–1897) as Chartist candidate for the West Riding in the 1841 election. As a supporter of O'Connor, he exemplified the vitality of local radicalism, which gave birth to Chartism.

In the summer of 1842, Pitkethly visited America, where he met a number of former radicals from the West Riding. He serialised his account of conditions in America in the *Northern Star,* with the intention of assisting emigration. Thereafter, he concentrated on running a branch of the British Emigrant Mutual Aid Society from his shop and played little part in the Chartist movement on his return. Of course John Lindley, one of the few local people with experience of the colonies, compared his time in Van Diemen's Land with Pitkethly's account of America, but had no desire to emigrate with his family, as he knew from first-hand experience the harsh living conditions of a pioneering community.[15]

Edward Baines contested the main points of the Charter in the *Leeds Mercury*. For example, he thought that annual elections were too frequent, and people would soon get fed up. Since elections in the early nineteenth century took place over a two-week period, and were often accompanied by serious rioting, he was probably correct.[16]

The reasoning behind annual parliaments was not only the obvious requirement that MPs should be more responsive to the wishes of their electorate, but also to make bribery and corruption, which was rife during this period, too expensive for patrons.

By the autumn of 1838, Chartist meetings began to assume a formidable character, and since it was not possible for the workers to meet by day, great torchlight processions were held at Oldham, Bolton, Stockport, Staleybridge, Ashton, Hyde, Leigh and many other towns in south Lancashire. But the success of the large torchlight meetings so alarmed the upper and middle classes that they responded by displaying a proclamation from the Queen, on the walls of every town, declaring the torchlight meetings illegal.[17]

The arrest of Rev. J.R. Stephens, on 27 December 1838, for addressing a torchlight meeting, produced a great wave of anger throughout the Chartist movement, particularly in south Lancashire, Yorkshire and the Midlands. In January, the *Northern Star* reported that Stephens had been sent to Kirkdale Gaol.[18]

> *Throughout the winter of 1838/39 agitation for the charter made rapid progress. If the Chartists were defeated with one plan another was speedily adopted. The authorities by forbidding torchlight meetings and by arresting the most popular men in the manufacturing districts had dealt a severe blow at the movement; but outdoor meetings continued to be held during the day and indoor assemblies during the evenings, with the rhetoric becoming ever more strident.*[19]

The government's response was to appoint Major General Sir Charles Napier (1782–1853), who was not entirely unsympathetic to the Chartist cause, but 'determined to do his duty', with six thousand troops under his command, to control the unrest in the north of England. Drilling by Chartists was then prohibited. No doubt John Lindley felt that he had seen it all before when General Maitland was appointed to suppress the Luddite insurrection in 1812.[20]

The first Chartist convention was held in London, at the British Coffee House in Cockspur Street on 4 February 1838, but it soon moved to Bolt Court in Fleet Street before adjourning to Birmingham on 13 May and remained in session until the 16 May.[21]

First Chartist Petition

By 7 May 1839 the first petition was ready, signed by one million two hundred and eighty thousand people (fifty per cent more people than had voted in the 1837 election), and was three miles long. It was then resolved to adopt a number of 'ulterior measures' if the petition was rejected; these included withdrawal of bank deposits, a sacred month (that is a month of Sundays), and exclusive dealings (to put pressure on shopkeepers).

The delegates at the convention then set about touring the country to 'sell' the resolutions passed in Birmingham. Mass open air meetings were held on 20 May at Newcastle Town Moor, then at Peep Green on 21 May, and followed at Kersal Moor on 25 May. It was claimed that this latter meeting had been attended by over three hundred thousand people. However, Major General Napier, who was very experienced in estimating the size of large bodies of men, ridiculed O'Connor's overestimate, and kindly attributed it to inexperience. Whereas, in fact, it was almost certainly propaganda.[22]

Chartist Meeting 21 May 1839 at Peep Green

The second Chartist meeting was held at Peep Green, on Whit Tuesday 21 May 1839, and took the form of the traditional Whit Walk. Here Feargus O'Connor, as leader of the Great Northern Union, again addressed a crowd estimated by Ben Wilson, a Halifax Chartist, at over two hundred thousand. The *Leeds Mercury* estimated the crowd at between fifteen and sixteen thousand, playing down the size of the demonstration, as was the custom of this Whig newspaper.[23]

The Earl of Harewood (1797–1857), lord lieutenant of the West Riding, had been asked to convene the meeting, but he declined. Rather, he caused notices to be posted, warning the people against attending illegal meetings, and cautioned all publicans against selling beer or spirits on the site. According to the *Leeds Mercury*, magistrates in Leeds had already declared the meeting illegal.[24]

The authorities, in the form of special constables, yeomanry and the military, were present in great numbers, but the meeting passed off peacefully. Of the many speeches two short passages are noteworthy. O'Connor said that 'I am quite ready…to stand by the law, and not give our tyrants the slightest advantage in attacking us in sections, but should they employ force against us, I am for repelling by attack.' This was his consistent position. While James Bronterre O'Brien said that 'At the next election we must have Chartists as our representatives, and when they have been elected by a show of hands, we must insist on having a formal return to that effect made by the returning officer'. This was a proposal that was never fulfilled.[25]

Exclusive to the West Riding demonstration, the people of Bradford marched in procession to Hartshead Moor with numerous banners. One of them excited great attention; it was a picture of Marcus practising his plan of 'painless extinction' on an infant. The crowd was immense, with Peter Bussey as the principal speaker generating great enthusiasm.[26]

Chapter 18

On 14 June 1839, the petition was introduced into parliament by Thomas Attwood, seconded by John Fielden. The motion was debated on 12 July, when Attwood pointed out that 'wolves could not represent sheep – that hawks could not represent pigeons – nor rich men represent the wants of the poor' and that only universal suffrage could remedy the injustice of the present representation. The young Benjamin Disraeli (1804–1881) was one of those supporting the petition, using the arguments that he was later to use in his novel *Sybil*. Lord John Russell, the home secretary, led the opposition, stating that 'the seven hundred thousand who currently had the vote were more representative of the nation than the one million two hundred and eighty thousand people who had signed the petition'. The motion was rejected by 235 votes to 46.[27]

John Lindley may well have wondered why the Chartists bothered with petitions, given the failure of Major Cartwright's efforts in the 1810s, which he well remembered. The ostensible reason given was that it still remained one of the few legitimate means of activity open to working-class political organisations. However, many Yorkshire Chartists, who were very practical people, thought petitioning a waste of time, since it was no more effective than 'throwing a feather in the wind'.[28]

Inevitably, with the rejection of the petition, the moral force Chartists began to be ousted by the physical force wing. Local plans for strikes and risings were openly discussed, and rumours of rebellion were rife in the West Riding. In fact, unrest continued throughout August, September and October of 1839, with violence and insurrection very much 'in the air'. Wearily, at the age of sixty-nine, John Lindley must have thought, 'not again', for the wisdom of old age must have taught him of the power of the government and the forces it commanded.[29]

On 9 August 1839, a great Chartist march took place in Sheffield, despite it having been banned by the magistrates, and, as it wound its way through the city, the marchers and spectators merged and rioting broke out. The authorities called out the militia and several running battles ensued with considerable damage to property. The Chartists then held torchlight meetings for the next ten days at Skye Edge, a good defensive position overlooking the city. Eventually, more troops were brought in and the meetings were suppressed, but small-scale rioting continued and eventually eighty people were arrested. Also, in August 1839, over six hundred female radicals, led by a band, marched through the main streets of Bradford carrying banners. Bradford had a particularly active women's radical association.[30]

The Chartists then found a novel way of displaying the strength of their support. Hundreds, sometimes thousands, of them assembled at selected churches on a given Sunday, filling all the pews, even the private pews of the gentry, and leaving only standing room in the aisle. Often the organisers would warn the clergy, and recommend that they preach from certain texts, such as 'the husbandman that laboureth shall be the first partaker of the fruits', but usually the clergy responded by preaching about passive obedience and 'the folly of looking to things in this life'.[31]

One well recorded example took place in Barnsley on 4 August 1839, when a 'considerable force of Chartists walked in procession to St Mary's, the principal Anglican Church in the town, filling the building and leaving no room for the usual congregation. The Rev. Williams gave an appropriate sermon, which was listened to with great respect, and the company departed in good order.'[32]

Then, on 3 and 4 November, the powder keg exploded at Newport in Wales, when seven thousand miners and ironworkers, led by John Frost (1784–1877), set out to capture several key towns in south Wales. The first objective was to release Chartist prisoners held in the West Gate Hotel. The building was defended by a large number of constables and, most critically, a small contingent of about thirty regular soldiers. What followed was the most 'fatal clash between radicals and authorities in modern British history'. The Chartist assault became a bloodbath, twenty-four people were killed or died from their injuries, while over fifty were seriously injured. One hundred and twenty-five arrests were made, including Frost and twenty others, who were charged with treason.[33]

The Chartists, like the Luddites before them, still had not learned the lesson of Waterloo; when two ranks of British infantry repelled Napoleon's crack Old Guard with continuous platoon musket fire. There was no way that men armed with pikes, pickaxes and sledgehammers could defeat professional infantry armed with muskets and bayonets.

As a result of the Monmouth Treason Trial in November 1839, and the sentencing of John Frost and his fellow Chartists to death, massive protest meetings and a simultaneous petitioning campaign took place throughout January 1840. Violent confrontations occurred between the civic authorities and the Chartists in Dewsbury, Sheffield and Bradford.[34]

In order to set out the perils of using physical force, an article, with the title *First Essay in Physical Force,* was published in the *Chartist* 12 May 1839, which argued that 'nothing but a simultaneous rising at the same hour all over the country would give the Chartists a chance of success by arms – even that would give them only a slender chance', and that was the reality of the situation. This realisation of the weakness and likely failure of the only physical force likely to be effective, was a sobering thought and restrained the hands of all but the most headstrong. The warning in the *Chartist* was not heeded by a desperate minority of Chartist leaders, including William Ashton of Barnsley and Peter Bussey of Bradford, who took a leading part in organising a further demonstration that centred on the West Riding. Bussey was a former wool comber turned innkeeper, who had risen to prominence in Bradford as leader of the Anti-Poor Law movement.[35]

CHAPTER 19

Law and Order in the Early Nineteenth Century

Rural Police Acts of 1839

In 1829, Home Secretary Sir Robert Peel (1788–1850) formed the Metropolitan Police, a force of one thousand men, to deal with the high level of crime in London. The importance of this innovation was that it was a civilian force, with a sober uniform, armed only with batons. Initially, it ran in parallel with the existing police arrangements of night watchmen and Bow Street Runners and was of doubtful improvement. But, by about 1835, when its strength had risen to just over three thousand, and new ideas of policing had been evolved that combined more discipline with better organisation, it began to make an impact in the capital. Many other cities and towns then copied the 'Met's' example.[1]

Hence, the Municipal Corporations Act of 1835 required corporate boroughs to follow the example of London and set up their own police forces. In 1836, Leeds reorganised its local government and set up a police force immediately. However, most of the other large industrial towns of Yorkshire, which were growing at an alarming rate, were not incorporated until several years later. Sheffield became a municipal corporation in 1843, eight years after the act, Bradford in 1847, Halifax and Wakefield in 1848, and Huddersfield in 1868.

To overcome the restrictions of the 1835 act, it was supplemented by the Rural Police Acts of 1839 and 1840. The West Riding did not adopt the establishment of a rate-supported police force on the grounds of expense and threat to individual and local liberties, since the police were held in low esteem by the emerging middle class. It reasoned 'that for common times the present force is sufficient, and that upon occasions of "outbreak or riot", such as we have unfortunately seen, no additional police force, which can be contemplated, would be sufficient for their protection'. In any case, the insecurity and bad working conditions ensured the 'new' police of the 1830s rarely offered much improvement on the old town watchmen, who were generally ineffective. They were rarely used, except to put down popular recreations in public places. Furthermore, the propertied classes in general, and of Yorkshire in particular, distrusted giving power to local and central government bodies over which they had little control. They preferred to rely on voluntary associations, private police forces and, in the last resort, military force.[2]

The vast county of Yorkshire had been divided into three Ridings in 1660, for administrative purposes, and the existing system of law enforcement in the West Riding rested with the lord lieutenant. He administered justice through a system of magistrates, who were required 'to restrain offenders, rioters and other barrators [fraudsters], and to pursue, and arrest, take and chastise them according to their trespass and offence, and then cause them to be imprisoned and duly punished'.[3]

When he thought necessary, the lord lieutenant could suspend civil law and, by reading the Riot Act of 1715, devolve his power to the military. The Riot Act read as follows:

> *Our Sovereign Lord the King chargeth and commandeth all Persons, being assembled, immediately to disperse themselves, and peaceably to depart to their Habitations, or in their lawful Business, upon the Pains contained in the act made in the first year of King George, for preventing Tumults and riotous assemblies. God Save the King.*[4]

The act could be applied wherever twelve or more persons were 'unlawfully, riotously and tumultuously assembled' and, following this proclamation, anyone remaining after one hour, whatever his or her intentions, was guilty of an offence.[5]

However, the quality of magistrates was variable. General Napier, whose contempt for local magistrates was well known, complained about magistrates 'who chose to go grouse shooting in the middle of the Chartist crisis of 1839,' whether from fear or prudence is not known.

The forces available to magistrates were limited. Parish constables were part-time officials concerned mainly with petty crime and drunken disorder. In cases of major disorder, they needed to call upon the militia, the yeomanry, or regular army for assistance. During the Luddite unrest of 1811-12, an attempt was made to revive the ancient 'Watch and Ward' provision, under which every citizen could be called upon to assist the authorities. But this was very unpopular and, in an emergency, it was found preferable to swear in 'the most respectable members of the community' as special constables. The other resource available to magistrates was the county militia, or trained bands, chosen by lot from every parish to serve for three years in the county regiments. During the French Revolution and Napoleonic Wars, the Supplementary Militia and Provisional Cavalry were formed, but these proved too expensive and were replaced by the local militia and volunteer cavalry. However, recruiting for the militia could itself cause riots, as witnessed in Yorkshire after the 1796 Supplementary Militia Act. In fact, selecting militiamen from the working class was not a success, as their 5d a day food allowance was insufficient during periods of high food prices, and the militiamen acted in the same manner as the starving rioters by stealing food. After 1815, the militia faded away and the cavalry or yeomanry became the preferred troops of the magistracy; they comprised troops of mounted 'tenant farmers and their sons, acting under the command of their landlords and landlords' sons' who frequently behaved as if they were fox hunting. This was exemplified at Peterloo in 1819, when the massacre of unarmed civilians by sabre-wielding yeomanry had serious repercussions throughout the country. The massacre was deeply etched into the collective memories of both the people and the authorities; thereafter the use of the yeomanry was avoided if at all possible. As General Napier was to comment in 1839, 'if the Chartists want a fight they can be indulged without the yeomanry, who are over-zealous for cutting and slashing'. The advantage of yeomanry was that they were only paid when called out, but they were hated by 'the people' and often caused riots by their very appearance.[6]

The mainstay of law and order were the military, both cavalry and infantry, and occasionally the artillery. During the Anti-Poor Law protests and Chartist insurrections, troops were generally used to support large numbers of special constables. The humanitarian General Napier, commanding officer of the Northern District, adopted a policy of keeping his troops in large concentrations and using them to overawe the protesters by demonstrating discipline and firepower, while avoiding direct conflict.[7]

Whenever the military came into direct confrontation with insurgents, the army always won. At Rawfolds Mill in 1812, the rate of fire of a few professionals overwhelmed the attackers. At Folly Hall in 1817, the exchange of shots with a troop of yeomanry caused the protesters to give up and go home, while at Grange Moor in 1820, the knowledge that the cavalry was coming caused the revolutionaries to disperse. Finally, in Bradford in 1840, after some resistance, the Hussars cleared the streets. This was not because of the strength of the army, but was due to the weakness of the insurgents, particularly in weapons, tactics and the fact that they 'were unused to arms'. They were not cowards, just realists who, when faced with overwhelming military power, backed down. There was also reluctance on the part of 'radicals' to kill their opponents. They were protesting – not seeking to destroy the forces of law and order. In many ways, like the army, they were aiming to overawe their opponents by sheer numbers – it was a kind of shadowboxing.

As General Napier observed, 'In urban warfare, the cavalry can do little better than get out of it with all possible speed, and leave it to the infantryman with his rifle', 'but in open warfare the six-foot pike was useless', since it was not long enough. (It was not possible to make it longer without attracting attention. Normally, the shaft was carried as a stave, to which the police could not object. The metal head was only attached at the time of muster. It was for this reason that John Lindley preferred the screw head pike in 1820.)

> *I expect to have very few soldiers and many enemies; hence if we deal with pikemen my intent is to put cavalry on their flanks, making my infantry retire as the pikemen advance. If they halt to face the cavalry, the infantry shall resume fire, for if the cavalry charge pikemen in order the cavalry will be defeated; the pike must be opposed by the musquet [sic] and bayonet, in which the soldiers must be taught to have confidence: it is the master weapon.*[8]

Napier also said he would use buckshot, not bullets, in order to wound but not kill. He was a humane man who sympathised with the Chartists but would not be deflected from his duty.

Electric Telegraph

At that time, the most significant increase in government authority and control was due to technical innovation in the new science of electric communication. This was marked by the introduction into service of the first commercial electric telegraph on 9 July 1839, between Paddington Station and West Drayton Station, a distance of thirteen miles (twenty-one km), pioneered by Sir William Fothergill Cooke (1806–1879) and Charles Wheatstone (1802–1875). The invention was a great success and immediately taken up by the entire railway network as a means of controlling train movements. Once the government realised the benefit of 'instant communication', the telegraph network spread to all major cities in the United Kingdom, enabling ministers to receive prompt information about 'the state of the nation', particularly in those distant rebellious places such as Yorkshire, Lancashire, Cheshire, Wales and Scotland. Much of this information was gathered by paid spies and transmitted by the new system, enabling the government to keep well ahead of the dissidents in the information race. (This technology was the start of the electronic age and it is very difficult, from the perspective of the twenty-first century, to conceive the bewilderment of the vast majority of the population at the nature of electricity and its ability to convey information at almost the speed of light.)

When the speed of information was combined with the ability to move troops and special constables rapidly to troubled spots by train, central government achieved complete military and police control of the country with a minimum of force. For example, it had become possible to transfer an infantry battalion of one thousand troops from London to Manchester in nine hours by train, whereas it would have taken seventeen days to march the same distance.[9]

CHAPTER 20
Chartism in the Hungry Forties 1840 – 1842

The economic depression that occurred in 1842 and 1843 has been described as 'the worst two years of the century'. As a consequence, 'Chartist support increased and once again mass protests became common'.[1]

Discontent in West Riding Towns 1840

In Dewsbury, trade began to get worse towards the end of 1839, and distress continued as the price of bread began to rise from $8^1/_2$d in 1837 to 10d for a 4lb loaf. There were rumours of risings, but nothing significant happened. Then on the night of 11-12 January 1840, the town was taken over by between one and two hundred Chartists. Guns were fired to celebrate success and signal balloons were released, which were answered from Earlsheaton and Hanging Heaton. Since the military were stationed ten miles away at Leeds, there was no immediate force to oppose the takeover. But the Chartist success was short lived for, once the military finally arrived after a delay of a few hours, the leaders were arrested and calm was restored.[2]

General Napier described Dewsbury as:

> *...a curious place. Cavalry should not be here. The town is in a hollow, bounded on one side by the river Calder, it has three entrances, each through a pass, and no messenger could get out of the town save through them, so that cavalry might be blocked up.*[3]

Meanwhile at Sheffield, the situation also began to look ominous. Large groups of people assembled in the open air at night, at these meetings not a word was spoken – just silent gatherings. Nevertheless, they were dispersed by the military. Then about 16 January 1840, several Chartists were arrested on charges of conspiring and administering illegal oaths. One of these was Samuel Holberry (1814–1842), leader of the planned rising in Sheffield. Unlike most Chartists, Holberry was an ex-soldier, having served in the 33rd Regiment of Foot. When stationed at Northampton, he attended night school and had his eyes opened to the degradation of army life, with the result that he bought himself out in 1835. He moved to Sheffield, where he became a rectifying distiller. After a short spell in London, Holberry returned to Sheffield in the autumn of 1838, where he was active in the Baptist church and joined the local Chartists. As a result of the massacre of twenty-two Chartists in Newport on 4 November 1839, Holberry became involved in efforts to mount an armed rising in the West Riding of Yorkshire. In November, the Chartists tested explosive shells in the countryside and then fire-bombed St Mary's Church in Bramall Lane. Holberry then toured the north Midlands and south Yorkshire gathering support. On 9 January 1840, he attended a planning meeting in Sheffield with delegates from Barnsley, Dewsbury, Rotherham and Sheffield, where he used his military experience to draw up a careful plan of action.[4]

> *The rising would begin with diversions on the outskirts of town – firing isolated magistrates houses and the barracks, placing bombs in the police office – and similar diversions in Rotherham. They would assassinate any magistrates seen riding into town. The diversion would draw the military out of town, whereupon two chartist assault groups ... would seize the town hall in Waingate and the nearby Tontine Inn and barricade themselves in these chartist forts.*[5]

Despite precautions using small cells of supporters, called classes, to prevent infiltration, the plan was betrayed by James Allen from Rotherham, with the result that Holberry and associates were arrested. In March 1840, Holberry and seven others were tried in York for seditious conspiracy and found guilty. Holberry was sentenced to four years imprisonment in the Northallerton house of correction, where he was badly and illegally treated; with five weeks on the treadmill and several months of solitary confinement. As a result of pressure from local Chartist groups, he was moved to York Castle in September 1841, but by this time he was suffering from tuberculosis, from which he died in June 1842 at the early age of twenty-eight. He was given a public funeral on 27 June 1842, attended by between twenty and fifty thousand people. A similar fate befell his fellow Chartist from Sheffield, John Clayton (1785/6–1841), who also died in Northallerton Gaol.[6]

In Todmorden, on the border between Yorkshire and Lancashire, there were riots by railwaymen. This was all part of a rising tide of discontent that was potentially leading up to a major insurrection.[7]

Similarly, in Bradford, the continuing depression in the worsted industry reduced the working population to breaking point during the last months of 1839. There was much grumbling and there were rumours of an intended rising, but despite the protests and riots in Dewsbury, Sheffield and Todmorden, Bradford remained quiet. This was, in part, due to the absence of their leader Peter Bussey, who had fled to America after the failure of the Newport rising the previous November. But then occurred what the *Bradford Observer* described as:

> *a wicked attempt to disturb the peace of the town, by the irruption of a number of men from the adjacent county, armed to the teeth at the dead hour of night...*[8]

This 'disturbance' took place on the night of 26 and 27 January 1840, at about one thirty on Monday morning, when Thomas Croft, a night watchman, who had just finished his round, was standing near Bowling Green Inn. He was surprised and taken prisoner by a dozen Chartists armed with pistols and pikes. He was bound and taken to Green Market and placed in the shed at the end of Mr John Crabtree's house, the Market Tavern Inn, where he was guarded by two men with pikes. The rest of the Chartists retired to the Butter Cross, directly opposite Crabtree's house, which had been designated as the rendezvous for the insurgents. A short time later, another party of Chartists entered the Green Market at the top of Rawson's Place, seized night watchman William Illingworth, and conveyed him to Crabtree's shed. In the meantime, small parties of about a dozen Chartists continued to arrive at the Butter Cross. These were the cells into which the organisation had been divided, to prevent infiltration by spies.

The precautions were in vain, as the police had already been alerted by two informers, James Harrison and Joseph Greensmith, and special constables were out patrolling the town during the night. They were supported by troops of 81st Regiment of Foot stationed in the courthouse and two parties of mounted 8th Hussars. All these measures were taken secretly, without alarming the town.

At about one forty-five, magistrates at the courthouse sent a party of special constables to investigate the state of the town and report back on the situation. In going up to Green Market, situated in the centre of town, the special constables were stopped in the middle of Rawson's Place by four men with pistols, who told them that they must not pass that way. But John Slater, one of the special constables, asserted his authority and replied that 'it was their road and proceed they would'. The Chartists followed the police to the top of Rawson's Place and left them. The special constables then divided, one party returning to the courthouse to report, and the other going down Silsbridge Lane to investigate what was going on in the direction of Thornton Road.

When the magistrates received the report from their 'scouts', they sent out William Brigg, the deputy chief constable, with a large party of special constables. While passing the end of the street leading to Market Place, the police were recognised by the two watchmen in custody, and one of them signalled for help by immediately turning the light of his lantern in their direction. This was seen by Brigg, who went to investigate. On recognising Tom Croft, Brigg asked 'Tom, what art thou doing here?' When Croft replied 'we are prisoners', Brigg immediately seized one of the sentries, while the police seized the other. At this, the Chartists hiding in the Butter Cross rushed across the road and rescued the sentry held by the police, but the man taken by Brigg could not be released and was conveyed to the courthouse and locked up.

Yet another large body of constables was sent out to patrol the town and on their arrival at Green Market, just as they were passing the dispensary, they met the main strength of the Chartists armed with pikes, guns and other weapons. The insurgents, faced by superior numbers of police, broke and fled, throwing away their weapons in the process and many were taken into custody. Once again, lack of military discipline on the part of the insurgents meant that they were not prepared to engage in a potentially bloody confrontation with armed police.

By three in the morning, twelve prisoners had been arrested and locked up, while the police and military continued to patrol the streets till daybreak. Four more men were arrested who could not explain why they were abroad at that time of night. It was reported that the insurrection passed 'with so much quietness that scarcely any of the inhabitants were aware of what was happening'. Not a single shot was fired throughout the whole affair and only one special constable was slightly wounded by a pike.

Between six and seven in the morning, news of the arrests spread, and a crowd gathered in front of the courthouse, where the prisoners were to be examined. The courthouse 'presented the appearance of a place in a state of siege, soldiers were on guard, a six-pounder gun in front, and a large number of special constables in and about the place'. None, except well-dressed people, were allowed admittance. The crowd, comprised mostly of working men and women, which was forced to remain outside, became very disorderly, and began covering 'all persons who went in or out of the gates with mud, which they splashed on them with their feet'. Later in the day, eight prisoners were sent to York Castle for trial.

Fortunately, on 1 February, the commutation of John Frost's death sentence, for his part in the Newport Rising, to one of transportation, diffused the situation and ended the likelihood of further uprising.[9]

The reason for the uprising was simple. The blatant social inequality that existed in the country in general, and Bradford in particular, had reached a point where the vast majority of working people were prepared to defy the law rather than starve. As George Flinn, a leader of the Bradford uprising recalled:

> *He was charged by his mill master with having a little more knowledge than most of his fellow workmen; and in the eyes of a mill master that is a crime of no small degree. Well, how was he situated in order to get this knowledge? He lived in a cellar, nine feet by seven. This dwelling was his workshop, his bedroom, his kitchen and his study, and not infrequently his hospital. Could any man live thus and not acquire knowledge? Was he to close his eyes to the fact, that while he was obliged to toil in such a position, the fruits of his labour was filched from him, and splendid mansions arose in every direction around him, inhabited by those who mocked him with expressions of sympathy.*[10]

Perhaps he had in mind the houses of Benjamin Gott, the blanket manufacturer and early victim of Luddism, and John Marshall, the flax spinner, who both built grand mansions on the hills above the River Aire, allegedly in order to dominate the workers toiling in their factories in the valley below. Or Francis Crossley, carpet manufacturer, who built an imposing house called 'Belle View' close to his mill on the edge of Halifax; and Edward Ackroyd, worsted manufacturer, who also built a great house known as 'Bankfield Mansion', across the street from his mill in Halifax.[11]

The Whig authorities responded to these outbreaks of civil disobedience as their Tory predecessors had done before them, by arresting Chartist leaders throughout the country and charging them with treason. In addition, large numbers of local activists (at least 543 between June 1839 and June 1840) were detained for periods of between a few weeks and a few years, thereby depriving the movement of its leadership.[12]

Constitutional Protest

With most of the Chartist leaders in prison, the radical cause threatened to fade away, but new men stepped into their shoes and reorganised the Chartist movement. In particular, James Leach (1806–1869) of Manchester founded the National Charter Association (NCA) of Great Britain on 20 July 1840.[13]

With the formation of the NCA, James Bronterre O'Brien suggested a new tactic of entering Chartist candidates in local parliamentary elections, where they could demonstrate the unrepresentative nature of the electoral system by the show of hands that took place when the candidates were adopted. The show of hands was a formality at adoption meetings, at which all male adults could attend and vote. At the West Riding hustings in 1841, one observer noted that the crowd consisted of nine non-electors for every elector.[14]

On Thursday 21 January 1841, the Leeds Parliamentary Reform Association, a middle-class radical movement, led by Samuel Smiles of *Self-Help* fame, held a 'Great Reform Festival' meeting at Marshall's new mill in Leeds. This caused the Chartists to stage a counter demonstration, by marching through the centre of Leeds before proceeding to an open air meeting at Holbeck Moor, where numerous speakers, led by Robert Lowery (1809–1863), resolved to stand by the six points of the charter. After the meeting on Holbeck Moor, the delegates and many supporters went to Marshall's Mill and hijacked the Reform Festival meeting. As a result, 'it became clear that all attempts to secure a consensus between the middle-class and working-class radicals for anything short of the Charter was not possible, in the charged circumstances that prevailed.'[15]

This was almost certainly a tactical mistake by the Chartists. There was no way that a parliament, dominated by aristocratic landowners and industrialists, was going to hand over power to the working classes or even the middle classes. Certainly, the Charter was ahead of its time in the mid nineteenth century, since it sought to achieve too much in a single step. While a compromise with the less ambitious aims of the middle-class radical movement might have produced some advancement, the betrayal by the middle class in 1832 left a deep suspicion among Chartists (essentially a working-class movement) that all they wanted was a widening of the franchise, to include more middle-class voters, while still leaving the working classes without a vote.

By the middle of 1841, Britain was again moving into a severe depression. The cotton mills of Lancashire were at a standstill and in Birmingham one hundred thousand people were being given poor relief. In the middle of 1841, the Whigs went to the country and were soundly beaten. Feargus O'Connor's instruction to all Chartists was to vote for the Tories as a protest against the Whig Poor Law. This split over voting tactics proved the last straw for the unity of the Chartists; O'Brien spoke against this policy arguing 'Can any good ever come of linking together truth and error, virtue and vice?'

Chartists contested many seats in order to explain and defend the principles of the Charter. For example, Julian Harney and Lawrence Pitkethly contested the West Riding with Lord Morpeth and Lord Milton without success; not a single Chartist candidate was elected in any constituency in the entire country. One of the best results was that of Peter Murray McDouall (1814–1854), at Northampton, who polled one hundred and seventy votes out of a constituency of two thousand. As so often happens in politics, the opposing policy recommendations of O'Connor and O'Brien caused a major spilt and much disunity in the Chartist movement, inevitably with disastrous consequences at the poll.[16]

The general election of 1841 and release of Chartist prisoners, particularly of O'Connor and O'Brien at the end of August, brought new impetus to the Chartist movement which had been rather moribund during the arrests of 1839 and 1840. On his release, O'Connor walked through the streets of York followed by thousands cheering the 'Lion of Freedom'.[17]

> The Lion of Freedom comes from his den,
> We'll rally around him again and again,
> We'll crown him with laurels our champion to be,
> O'Connor, the patriot of sweet liberty.
>
> The pride of the nation, he's noble and brave
> He's the terror of tyrants, the friend of the slave
> The bright star of freedom, the noblest of men,
> We'll rally around him again and again,
>
> Though proud daring tyrants his body confined,

They never could alter his generous mind,
We'll hail our caged lion, now free from his den
We'll rally around him again and again,

Who strove for the patriots? Was up night and day
And saved them from falling to tyrants prey?
It was Feargus O'Connor was diligent then!
We'll rally around him again and again.[18]

Second Chartist Petition 1842

On 2 May 1842, the second Chartist petition was drawn up, still stressing the six points of the Charter. With the individual sheets joined together, it stretched for six miles and contained 3,317,752 signatures; it was accompanied to the House of Commons by one hundred thousand people, with brass bands playing and flags waving. It was wheeled into the House with great ceremony. The prayer for the petition was introduced by Thomas Duncombe (1796–1861) and seconded by John Fielden. The motion to hear the petition was opposed by the famous historian Thomas Macauley (1800–1859), who said that universal suffrage amounted to nothing short of the confiscation of the property of the rich. The motion was defeated in the House by 287 to 49.[19]

CHAPTER 21
Plug Plot of 1842

Industrial Unrest

In the summer of 1842, spontaneous violence erupted throughout the north of England, the Midlands and Scotland. This followed the rejection of the second Chartist petition, which demonstrated the government's complete disregard for the plight of the manufacturing operatives in the country. Violence arose as a result of a series of strikes which had been caused by the continuing economic depression and the consequent reduction in wages by employers in the metal and coal industries of Scotland; the textile industries of Cheshire, Lancashire and Yorkshire; and the pottery and coal industries of Staffordshire. Fortunately, in many of the distressed towns, where unemployment resulted in widespread hunger, the response of local communities was more humane. The local press recorded sizeable donations to the many charitable funds organised for relief of the starving poor.[1]

Unrest started with the coal miners of Staffordshire in July 1842, with the intention of bringing the pottery industry to a standstill, but the real centre of the problem lay in the textile industries. The wave of strikes that were to severely disrupt the cotton and woollen towns started in Lancashire, after the decision by the cotton masters of Ashton-under-Lyne and Stalybridge to reduce wages. Two companies, under protest, agreed to rescind the cuts, but Bayley Brothers, who had reduced the average weekly wage of its workers from 10s 9d (54p) to 10s 3d (51p), refused to restore the 6d (2.5p) cut and their workers went on strike, marching through the town and bringing the whole of Ashton-under-Lyne to a standstill. Then on 8 August, a meeting at Stalybridge agreed to 'turn out' all the factories in that town. The strikes spread rapidly so that, by 11 August, about fifty thousand workers were idle, often due to the fact that the strikers had drawn the boiler plugs in their factory, so that steam power could not be generated. Inevitably the strikes became known as the 'Plug Plot'. As the industrial North came to a standstill, there were serious food shortages and rioting took place in many Lancashire towns. In Manchester, several policemen were killed and food shops looted. The explosive situation came very close to precipitating a general strike.[2]

The strike soon spread across the Pennines, but the events in Lancashire had given the West Riding authorities advance warning, and time to mobilise the forces of law and order. The 17th Lancers were brought to a state of readiness; six hundred men of 73rd Infantry, under Colonel Love, were despatched by train to Bradford; and six hundred and fifty-three men of 32nd Regiment of Foot, under Colonel Maitland, were sent to Leeds from Portsmouth. Three troops of the 17th Yorkshire Hussars under Lt Colonel Beckett were mobilised. When Beckett called for more troops, sixty men of the Royal Irish Fusiliers under Colonel McInnis were promptly dispatched from Hull to Leeds.[3]

Riots in the West Riding

Huddersfield: On Saturday 13 August, between five and six thousand 'turn-outs' (strikers) from Oldham and Ashton-under-Lyne crossed the county border and marched down the Colne Valley, picking up support in Saddleworth. They then passed through Marsden, where they stopped every mill. Flushed with success, a few bold men went and instructed the management to stop work at Sykes' and Fisher's Mill, also in Marsden. When the management derisively refused, a large mob (estimated at over one thousand) appeared from nowhere, surged through the gate and overpowered the occupants. The strikers then proceeded to pull out the boiler plugs, put out the boiler fires, open the shutters to empty the dam, and threatened to level the site if work resumed. They then went to Taylor's Mill and repeated the process.[4]

After passing through Slaithwaite at about noon, they arrived at Milnsbridge, where the water powered fulling mill was stopped, but a water powered corn mill was left working, as it was reasoned that the people would need bread. At Armitage Brothers they met some resistance, but this was soon overcome and the mill was stopped. The 'Lancashire Lads', growing in number, then proceeded in the direction of Huddersfield, turning out every mill on the way, until they came to Starkey Brothers' Mill at Longroyd Bridge. Mr Starkey, a magistrate, would not be intimidated and locked the gates, but the large crowd forced the gates and proceeded to bring his mill to a halt. The strikers finally arrived in Huddersfield at about three in the afternoon. One group went to Schofield's scribbling mill in New Street, where they pulled the boiler plug and emptied out the water. A second group went to Paddock, Marsh and a number of other places, while a third party went to Lockwood and Upperhead Row, before tackling Brook's Mill at Newtown. Here they met some resistance, so they unceremoniously threw Magistrate Brook and his son on the coal heap and drew the boiler plug. Yet another party went along Leeds Road, calling at every mill, extinguishing boiler fires, and turning out the hands. Where they met resistance, they threatened to return on Monday, and if they found any mill still working they would tear it down.[5]

The 'turn-outs', numbering about five thousand, then adjourned to Back Green, where speakers from Ashton-under-Lyne and Saddleworth declared that they were fighting for 'a fair day's wage for a fair day's work'. The *Times* reporter commented on the discipline of the strikers. No breach of peace took place and they were given bread at a few provision shops in New Street, as well as from some private individuals in Castle Street and Dock Street. Many shopkeepers also supplied them with small sums of money, as they were reluctant to offend their working-class customers. It was certainly in their interest to show benevolence to these destitute men and women, in the midst of their own community. Surprisingly, nearly all the men remained sober, even though it was an excessively hot day and 'not ten quarts of ale were drunk'.[6]

On Sunday 14 August, a troop of 43rd Lancers, under Captain Palmer, arrived in Huddersfield at about one in the afternoon, but the town was quiet and they were not required. As a further precaution, four magistrates at the guild hall swore in a large number of special constables (estimated at between three and four hundred). The rioters signalled the arrival of the Lancers by carrier pigeons, which flew off in the direction of Oldham about fifteen miles away. In contrast, the magistrates employed the new electric telegraph to communicate with the military and request reinforcements.[7]

On Monday 15 August, the only mills to ignore the threats and resume work in Huddersfield were Starkey Brothers, George Crossland, Swain and Webb, and Brook, but, as a result of the intimidation by 'the Lancashire Lads', they were all forced to cease work by five in the afternoon. At about four-thirty, the magistrates, ensconced in the George Inn, which was serving as the headquarters for both the magistrates and military and protected by infantry, read the Riot Act for the third time. But when the disaffected strikers refused to leave the town, a charge was made to clear the streets by the 17th Lancers, supported by four hundred special constables. As a consequence, several people were wounded. However, it was only when the infantry was given the order to prepare to fire that the crowd rapidly dispersed before a volley could be fired. Nevertheless, the special constables took eighteen people into custody, one of whom was a woman. The streets were finally cleared by seven in the evening.

But not only were the 'people' getting out of control, so were the military. It was reported that at about a quarter past six, when the omnibus arrived at the Swan Inn in Market Street, from Cooper Bridge, the *Leeds Mercury* and *Leeds Intelligencer* reporters were both attacked by Lancers and only just missed serious injury from sabre cuts. They had to be rescued by special constables, as the military were running amok.[8] Nothing new in this, thought John Lindley as he reflected on Peterloo. By Wednesday 17 August, the *Times* reported that Huddersfield was all quiet.

Holmfirth: On Tuesday 16 August, John Lockwood, aged twenty-two, and two hundred others, stopped the mill of J. Robinson in Holmfirth. The next day, the strikers returned when sixty men, armed with cudgels, attacked New Mill. The 'turn-outs' were soon joined by a large number of local men, women and children, probably primarily bystanders, but adding to the intimidating size of the crowd. This vast assembly then proceeded to Stony Bank Mill, unplugged the boilers and emptied the mill dam. Next, they went to Moorcroft Mill, Ing Nook Mill, Sudehill Mill and Scholes Mill and pulled all the boiler plugs. Finally, the strikers went to Jackson Bridge Mill. where the sixty men from Lancashire, plus about sixty local men, were isolated from their support of the estimated one thousand bystanders by the police. They were then faced down by the magistrates, and special constables, and drifted off to fight another day.[9]

Halifax: On Wednesday 10 August, James Pratt, aged thirty-four, and three men, damaged the mills of Henry Lee Edwards and others, but this was just the start of a frightening three days for the inhabitants of Halifax.[10]

The following Sunday (14th August), the people of Halifax were alerted by the bellman (town crier) that a meeting was to take place the next day, to hear the strike leaders speak. Consequently, at five o'clock on Monday morning, the citizens arose early, and began to assemble peacefully in the market place, only to be interrupted by the magistrates George Pollard and William Briggs, supported by a large number of special constables (estimated at about two hundred). Pollard remonstrated with the crowd for about half an hour, calling on them to obey the law and disperse. But the magistrates were totally ignored, as the crowd unanimously decided to go as a body to Luddenham Foot, where they planned to meet the Lancashire strikers arriving from Todmorden.[11]

The 'turn-outs' from Todmorden approached Halifax down the Calder Valley, passing through Hebden Bridge and Sowerby Bridge, before meeting up with the Halifax dissidents at Kings Cross on the Burnley Road. 'This large body of people, when united together in one large procession, completely filling the road and stretched back a vast length.' Arriving at North Bridge, they were confronted by the military and police, drawn up to completely block the road, with the infantry in front, the cavalry behind, and the special constables at the back. The strikers pressed forward, with the women in the middle for protection, but they were held in check by a wall of bayonets. As tempers flared, the infantry had no hesitation to 'prick' anyone who came too close. One woman cried 'we are not here for bayonets but for bread'; nevertheless, many of the protesters received small bayonet wounds.[12]

An impasse had been reached. But when news arrived that the mills of Norris and Lister at the bottom of Foundry Lane were under attack, some of the military were dispatched to meet this new threat, and there were insufficient troops left to hold North Bridge. The crowd streamed through the gaps, and, when they arrived at Norris and Lister Mills, they found that the military had arrived too late and the boiler plugs had already been drawn.[13]

At the time the Lancashire strikers crossed North Bridge, a large body of men from Bradford, preceded by a troop of 17th Lancers, arrived via New Bank. As the Bradford men tried to enter the centre of town, the Lancers, now supported by infantry and Hussars, tried to block the road. However, the crowd evaded the blockage by the simple device of breaking into small groups and using alternative side streets. Once the reinforcements from Bradford joined the already formidable crowd (estimated at between fifteen to twenty thousand people) all desperately hungry, the situation began to look menacing. So, all shops were ordered to close by ten in the morning and Magistrate Pollard read the Riot Act at eleven. At this point, it must have seemed doubtful whether the two troops of 61st Regiment of Foot (about one hundred men) and two troops of Hussars, one from Leeds and the other from Burnley, plus two hundred special constables and the regular police, would be sufficient to protect all the mills under threat.[14]

Just after twelve noon, a crowd of about ten thousand went to the mill of John Ackroyd and Sons at Haley Hill (Ackroyd had recently reduced wages by twenty per cent). The workers were at dinner, so when two men went to Ackroyd to insist the plugs were drawn Ackroyd, deciding that opposition would result in considerable damage to his plant, agreed to pull the boiler plugs, and to prevent unnecessary damage, even instructed one of his own men to assist.

The crowd then proceeded to Ackroyd's Bowling Dyke Mill, where the strikers attempted to drain the reservoir (since it was supplied by rainwater and would take weeks to fill), but while cutting through the dyke, six men were taken prisoner and were taken into custody by a small detachment of about a dozen soldiers. Several attempts were made to rescue the six men, particularly in the narrow streets close to the police station, but the troops simply faced about and fired a volley into the crowd. A Mr Wadsworth was wounded in the leg. Finally, a passage was forced by the soldiers, by firing a volley followed by a bayonet charge.[15]

By one in the afternoon, the rebels had brought a large number of mills in Halifax to a standstill. The magistrates decided that the crowd was getting out of hand, and so the 17th Hussars were ordered to clear the street as far as Northgate, while two companies of the 61st Regiment of Foot, under Major Burnside, were required to clear a space in front of the police office, and the crowd was driven at bayonet point towards Broad Street. Three people were stabbed by bayonets, one seriously.

At half past two, an unofficial truce evolved and the troops were ordered to return to their quarters to reduce tension. For their part, the strikers decided to retire to Skircoat Moor to discuss further tactics. This meeting was attended by about fifteen thousand people, who resolved to continue their efforts to stop all the mills in Halifax, claiming 'they were driven to excess by poverty and distress that would be made worse by the reduction in wages which they were now resisting'. They also decided to attack Wakefield on Tuesday, and Dewsbury on Wednesday, and delegates were sent to Leeds, Brighouse and Elland to gather support.[16]

Overnight, a large number of the Lancashire contingent camped out on Blackstone Edge, which enabled the Skircoat Moor proceedings to recommence at six o'clock on Tuesday morning, with between two and three thousand people present. The meeting opened with a hymn, after which it was decided to send to Bradford, Huddersfield and Todmorden for further reinforcements. In the meantime, the remainder of the crowd agreed to proceed to Elland, Cooper Bridge, Mirfield, Brighouse, Barkisland and Stainland to stop the mills.[17]

John Lindley certainly witnessed the march through Mirfield, as Frances Stott records 'in August 1842 those involved in the Plug-drawers Riots passed through Mirfield on their way from Stalybridge to Horbury.'[18]

After the early Tuesday morning meeting, a group of strikers proceeded to Ackroyd's Mill at Bowling Dyke, since this was one of the few mills still working. It was defended by about one hundred workmen, armed with staves and guns, and fighting broke out when the strikers attempted to draw the plugs. Troops were called to help defend the mill, and when they opened fire and used bayonets to disperse the strikers, at least one soldier and two civilians were killed. The mill stopped work at teatime.[19]

Other large groups of strikers roamed the streets of the town converging on North Bridge, which gave access to Ackroyd's Mill, known as Shades. This was one of the new factories that employed the hated power looms. The individual groups of strikers united in front of Shades, and between twenty and thirty gained entrance. A number of workmen, armed with staves and sworn in as special constables, closed the mill door and secured some stragglers as prisoners. The defenders immediately hoisted a signal flag to summon help from troops stationed at the Northgate Hotel, which was acting as the military headquarters.

As the relieving soldiers made their way to North Bridge, with the cavalry at a hand gallop and the infantry at a quick run, the crowd was so dense that many of the people in the street could not get out of the way sufficiently rapidly. Consequently, there was a scuffle at Rands Bank and the situation looked as if it was getting out of hand. In one incident, a man unintentionally got in the way of the infantry, upon which one of them pricked him with his bayonet and the man turned and said something offensive to the soldier, who immediately turned round and struck him down with the butt of his musket. The magistrate, Mr Hird of Bradford, and the officer in charge conferred, and then the soldiers fired a few warning shots at the crowd. This was followed by a full volley when between thirty and forty people were hit. A third volley was then fired at the people on the hill, but the ground at Rands Bank rises steeply and the crowd fled for their lives. The troops then continued to fire, the *Northern Star* claimed 'without justification', and more people were wounded. The soldiers then proceeded along the street, driving the people before them. Thirty-six prisoners were taken at Shades Mill. The civilian casualties were considerable and the police station was turned into a hospital to deal with the wounded. Three people were critically wounded, one in the abdomen, one in the groin and one in the back. A further thirteen people were seriously wounded and a large number received slight wounds. The most serious cases were Jonathan Booth, a flax dresser from Northowram, who died the following day, while Samuel Crowther, a nail maker, survived.[20]

Later in the afternoon, a great crowd was milling around and in the town, particularly opposite Northgate Hotel, when they were dispersed by a cavalry charge. Whenever the crowd became unmanageable, the infantry did not hesitate to prick demonstrators with their bayonets, but no serious injuries were inflicted, except for one man who was stabbed through his thick fustian jacket and went writhing down the street. In fact, the only serious injury was to a sergeant, who discharged his own gun and badly damaged his arm.[21]

Finally, as evening approached, the military were ordered to clear everyone off the streets. It was at this point that yet another atrocity was committed, witnessed by Mr Bingley of the *Leeds Times* and Mr Hall of the *Leeds Mercury*. A tall, old man left his house and was deliberately shot by one of the soldiers as he was passing within a few feet of the two reporters. He sustained a dreadful wound to the abdomen and staggered back to his house.[22]

Salterhebble: It was decided by the magistrates that it was safer to confine the prisoners captured on Monday at Halifax, during the affray at Ackroyd's, in the Wakefield House of Correction, before they were examined. Consequently, it was decided to convey them by train on Tuesday afternoon. Headed by Briggs, the magistrate, and guarded by a file of about a dozen Hussars, under their commanding officer, they all rode off at full gallop to Elland station in two omnibuses each drawn by four horses. A rescue attempt was mounted by an estimated three thousand men, as the two omnibuses carrying the prisoners and escorting troops negotiated the exceedingly steep and narrow road at Salterhebble (about halfway between Halifax and Elland), but the ambush failed. At Elland station, the train was waiting and the prisoners were immediately transferred from omnibus to train, which promptly departed at full speed for Wakefield.[23]

At Elland station another omnibus, travelling from Halifax and Leeds to Manchester, with four or five passengers on the inside and the same on the outside, was about to depart when it was attacked by strikers throwing stones. But as soon as it was known that the omnibus contained passengers, and not officials, it was granted immunity. Unfortunately, at that moment, the military arrived and mayhem ensued. Large stones were thrown and scarcely a soldier was unhurt. Three of the eleven Hussars were pulled off their horses and two were made prisoner, leaving them at the mercy of the crowd. Mr Baker, a reporter for the *Northern Star*, had a narrow escape, receiving one or two severe wounds and bruises. Miss Machen of Leeds, sitting between him and the driver, received a cut on the head and was only saved from severe injury by the thick padding of her bonnet. Mr Laycock from Sheffield was badly injured about the legs and he was obliged to leave the omnibus. Fortunately for the two Hussars, Magistrate Briggs finally arrived from Halifax with more troops and freed the prisoners, but Briggs was injured by a stone that broke his left arm and he was forced to retire for treatment.

Leeds: On Wednesday 17 August, at between eleven am and twelve noon, two troops of 17th Lancers, under Prince George Duke of Cambridge, proceeded from Leeds to Bramley (halfway between Leeds and Bradford), but the strikers, with superior local knowledge, evaded the cavalry, causing the Hussars to retrace their steps to Hunslet. Here there was a confrontation, but the strikers decided that the military force was too strong; with the result that both Marshall's Mill and Tilley's Mill escaped damage.[24]

Bradford: On Monday morning, 15 August, Bradford was in a great state of agitation. A large meeting was held at seven o'clock in front of Old Fellows Hall, which lasted until nine. There was an air of expectancy that something was about to happen, for, while most of the shops remained open, all the mills were at a standstill. This was due to apprehension rather than intimidation, as the workers preferred to wait until the situation resolved itself, rather than risk going in to work. Meanwhile, at the courthouse, magistrates were busy swearing in additional special constables, all protected by a detachment of soldiers. Despite the precautions of the magistrates, on Wednesday the Bradford strikers evaded both the military and the special constables, and stopped several mills.[25]

Bingley: On Tuesday 16 August, Robert Leeming, aged twenty-one, with an estimated eight thousand like-minded people, marched from Bradford to Bingley and attacked W & S Nichols Mill in Bingley. They then divided the main group into smaller parties that went to different mills and 'turned them all [the operatives] out' causing all work to cease. One of the parties was led by William Smith, aged twenty-four, who pulled the plugs at J. Leach in Bingley, and another by John Dury, aged twenty-three, and two others, who sabotaged a number of mills.[26]

Kirkburton: On 16 August, John Day, aged twenty-one, sabotaged the mills of J. Roberts & Partners and T. Moorhouse in Kirkburton.[27]

Skipton: Further north in Skipton, an estimated two or three thousand men from Colne in Lancashire crossed the Pennines and went to the mills belonging to Duhert and Sedgewick, and demanded that they stop work. This demand was refused. After about an hour, a number of special constables arrived and began to disperse the crowd, but then the original strikers were reinforced by a very large number of their comrades and, although the Riot Act was read, the strikers pressed home their attack, drew the plugs from the boilers, and brought both mills to a halt.[28]

The Plug Riots were short lived in the West Riding, as by Wednesday afternoon (17th August) the 'riots' were over and life was returning to normal. The mill owners met and agreed to resume work the next day – on Thursday 18th August.[29]

Although strikers in Yorkshire promised 'not to work again until the Charter was established', by the end of August the strikes had dissipated, as the strikers had no food reserves and were reported to be on the verge of starvation. One marcher had been seen to drop dead through starvation, as the strikers passed through Ovenden, a small township between Halifax and Bradford.[30]

CHAPTER 22
Social Reform

During John Lindley's lifetime, he witnessed an agricultural and cottage-based society transformed into a manufacturing and largely urban factory society. The rural community that he was born into in 1770 was far from the idyllic world portrayed by the romantics; working hours were long, from dawn to dusk, and the rewards barely sufficient for subsistence. However, people felt free. They could start and stop work when they pleased, and to a greater or lesser extent decide which task they would perform next. The factory system was more efficient, as capital equipment was introduced to supplement labour. Here, it should be noted, that early machinery was very unreliable and intricate tasks often took decades to mechanise. In particular, adapting machinery developed for the cotton industry of Lancashire often proved very difficult to apply to similar tasks in the woollen industry of Yorkshire. Nevertheless, replacement of people by machines continued throughout John's lifetime. What the early industrialists did not appreciate, or perhaps chose not to notice, was the consequent social devastation inflicted on the majority of inhabitants of the country. The Unitarian philosophy of efficiency at all costs, caused the living and working conditions of those people employed in manufacture to deteriorate. There was a general awareness that the new middle classes were obsessed with making money to the detriment of all else. As factory units became larger and the social conscience could no longer ignore the suffering and degradation of the rapidly increasing labouring classes, it was found necessary to introduce legislation to limit the excesses of capitalist employers. To some extent, social consciousness was raised as a result of the slave trade, but it is interesting to note that William Wilberforce, 'the great humanist', who fought so hard for the black slaves of Africa, opposed the factory acts designed to 'free the child slaves' in his own country. Richard Oastler pointed this out in his famous letter of 29 September 1830 to the *Leeds Mercury*.[1]

Factory Acts

Prior to John's transportation to Van Diemen's Land, there had been a number of attempts to legislate against the evils of the factory system, in particular the 'The Health and Morals of Apprentices Act (1802)' and 'The Factory Act of 1819', but all failed to achieve the desired improvements.

On John's return to Mirfield, he found a new spirit of reform, and during the last twenty-five years of his life a number of factory acts were passed, which gradually improved working conditions in factories. Progress was very slow, resisted at every step by the employers, and, despite constant agitation by Richard Oastler and the Ten-Hour Movement, it took many industrial disasters and critical reports to effect even moderate improvements. Oastler spent his whole life fighting for better factory working conditions and the following tribute is recorded by Lettice Cooper in her book, *Yorkshire West Riding*.

> *When Oastler was an old man, West Riding cloth-makers subscribed a penny each to buy a new suit of clothes for him, and a firm of manufacturers in the Colne Valley gave the cloth free so that the workmen's pennies might be spent on the making, a sign that the masters as well as men were beginning to respect humanity in their trade and could honour a man who had shown a better way to the oppressors as well as saving the oppressed. 'King Richard' had fought a stubborn fight, and more than any other quality the West Riding admires tenacity; and likes a character, even if he is on the other side.[2]*

The Factory Act of 1833 (3 & 4 Will IV c.103)

This act made it illegal for children under the age of nine to work in textile factories (silk mills were exempted). Children between the ages of nine and thirteen were to work no more than nine hours per day (including an hour for lunch), and forty-eight hours per week. They were required to have two hours education per day. Young persons between the ages of fourteen and eighteen were not allowed to work nights and no more than twelve hours per day (including an hour for lunch), but two eight-hour shifts of children were allowed, so that adults could work longer. Most importantly, the act introduced the provision for four paid inspectors to check that the law was being observed. Although the law was widely flouted, the principle that the government had the right to inspect private premises proved to be a watershed in industrial legislation. However, it was not until 1867, fourteen years after the death of John Lindley, that manufacturers were forbidden to employ children under the age of thirteen in factories.[3]

The Mines Act 1842

In 1842, the Mines Act was introduced, partly as a result of the Silkstone disaster in Yorkshire in 1838, when twenty-six children were drowned after a sudden storm flooded R.C. Clarke's Huskar pit. 'One of the boys was seven years old, five children were aged eight and the average age of all children was ten'.[4] As a consequence, a parliamentary commissioner, J.C. Symons, was appointed in 1841 to investigate child labour in Yorkshire coal mines, and reported that:

> *One of the most disgusting sights I have ever seen was that of young females dressed like boys in trousers, crawling on all fours with belts round their waists and chains passing between their legs at day pits at Hunshelf Bank and in many small pit near Holmfrith and New Mills...In two other pits in the Huddersfield Union I have seen the same sight. In one near New Mills the chain passing high up between the legs of two of these girls had worn large holes in their trousers and any sight more disgustingly indecent or revolting can scarcely be imagined than these girls at work – no brothel can beat it... In the Flockton and Thornhill pits the system is even more indecent, for though the girls are clothed at least three quarters of the men work stark naked or with a flannel waistcoat only and in this state they assist one another to fill the corves 18 or 20 times a day.[5]*

Symons' report led to the Mines Act of 1842. The bill was introduced by Lord Ashley. It prohibited the employment of females underground and forbade the use of boys under the age of ten. It appointed one inspector to enforce the regulations. The bill was passed by the House of Commons but was opposed in the House of Lords by Lord Londonderry (1769–1822) and a group of aristocratic mine owners. They succeeded in amending the original proposal, reducing the minimum age at which boys could be employed. A single inspector was totally inadequate for the mountainous task that awaited him, but once again it set a precedent, upon which the government would later build 'The Health and Safety Inspectorate'.[6]

Despite the reduced hours, work underground for both children and adults remained hazardous, and 'accidents', often due to neglect of safety measures, were frequent. By far the most dramatic were the 'pit disasters' that sent shock waves throughout the area, devastating the mining communities. The West Riding of Yorkshire experienced many tragedies, as early as 1803 thirty men were killed by a pit explosion at Barnaby Colliery. But worse was to come; in 1847 an explosion at the Oaks Colliery near Barnsley killed seventy-three men. This mine was also the scene of the 1866 disaster, when 361 men and boys were killed – the worst death toll in west Yorkshire for many years. Two years later, seventy-five men died at Darley Main Colliery. However, the major health hazard and killer was the insidious dust at the coal face. This dust was constantly inhaled by the men cutting the coal, often lying in a cramped prone position. It gave rise to silicosis and pneumoconiosis of the lungs, both of which led to premature death.[7]

Factory Act of 1844 (7 & 8 Vict c15)

When Peel won the 1841 election, he was pressured by the Ten-Hour Movement into introducing a further factory act in 1844, but he was not prepared to reduce the working day below twelve hours for women and young people. Nevertheless, his act represented some improvement. It allowed children to start work at the age of eight rather than nine, which was a backward step. However, to compensate, children aged between eight and thirteen were only allowed to work a maximum of six and a half hours per day. Furthermore, children's ages had to be verified by surgeons, accidental death had to be recorded and investigated, dangerous machinery had to be protected by fences, and meals eaten in a separate place.

1847 Factory Act (10 & 11 Vict c.29)

The fight for factory reform was taken up by John Fielden, MP for Oldham and progressive radical mill owner in Todmorden, who successfully introduced a bill to limit all women, and young people up to the age of eighteen, in textile factories (except for lace and silk production) to a ten-hour working day. The indefatigable Richard Oastler organised massive demonstrations in the north of England, while Lord Shaftsbury (1801–1885) led the campaign in parliament. The triumph was short lived, for, while in 1847 there had been a trade depression and mill owners were happy to restrict the hours of work, as soon as trade picked up they introduced the shift system for young people and women, thereby keeping the mills open from 5:30am until 8:30pm. As a result, adult male workers were still required to work up to fifteen hours per day.

Factory Act 1850 (13 & 14 Vict c.54)

Consequently, it was necessary to produce yet another factory act in 1850. This required that factories should only be open for twelve hours a day, of which one and a half hours should be for meals; the maximum working day for women and young people, aged between nine and eighteen, was to be ten and a half hours; on Saturdays factories must close at 2:00pm, and women and young people should only work seven and a half hours. Surprisingly, production did not fall as many owners expected, as an increase in the health of workers resulted in greater efficiency, while accidents, generally a result of excessive tiredness that caused costly 'downtime', were almost eliminated.

O'Connor's Land Plan

Feargus O'Connor had a different answer to the problem of factory exploitation by profit-hungry employers. After the failure of the second Chartist petition to parliament, O'Connor began to put all his effort into his 'Land Plan'. This was a scheme whereby all Chartists would combine to buy land, which would then be distributed by lot to lucky contributors. Eventually, the profits were to be ploughed back into more land, so that further contributors could be allotted plots of land. In reality, O'Connor was something of a reactionary, looking backwards rather than forwards, as Ernest Jones wrote:

> *O'Connor personified and voiced the demands, not of those in the movement drawn from the new proletarian elements, but of the handloom weavers and the enormous number of immigrants from the Irish countryside who wanted to be led not to a collective socialist society, but back to the old days of pre-industrialism, back to the land and life of their fathers. Essentially they were reactionary in outlook, adding numbers to the movement but confusing its aims and destroying its hope for victory.*[8]

In 1845, a meeting was held in Dewsbury when objections were made to many of the provisions of the 'Land Plan' and the practices of its managers. This plan certainly did not appeal to John Lindley, as, by that time, he already owned his own plot, provided by his daughter in 1838. Nevertheless, O'Connor's Land Plan represented a good example of the popular Victorian virtue of 'Self-Help' expounded by Samuel Smiles, who held the view that 'heaven helps those who help themselves'.[9]

1846 Repeal of the Corn Laws

The Corn Law of 1815, which sought to protect agricultural interests, by forbidding importing foreign wheat when the market price was below eighty shillings an imperial quarter, turned out to be less effective than expected. Consequently, the Association of Agriculturists, representing cereal farming interests, continually pressed for even higher levels of protection. In 1843–1844, a league of farmers was formed to counter the arguments of the well-financed propaganda strategy of the Anti-Corn Law League (ACL), which was gaining support in the country at large. When Peel repealed the Corn Laws in January 1846, largely as a result of continued pressure from the ACL led by Richard Cobden (1804–1865) and John Bright (1811–1889) in parliament, this was viewed as an act of betrayal by many members of his own party. It resulted in a split in the Tory supporters and, eventually, a realignment of political interests in the country.

While the animal rearing and dairy districts of the West Riding, particularly those adjacent to large industrial towns, were not seriously affected by the repeal of the Corn Laws, there was a vast population of operatives and their families, in the manufacturing towns, dependent on the price of bread. So, the abolition of the Corn Laws was of great benefit.[10]

Surprisingly, the Chartists supported the Corn Laws, on the grounds that reduction in the price of bread would depress wages even further, thereby increasing the value of capital. This did not happen. Robert Gammage, chronicler of the Chartist Movement, claimed that two factors prevented the undesirable consequences expected from repeal of the Corn Laws. The first was the mass emigration of the working class to North America, Australia and New Zealand, which drained the labour market of its surplus 'manpower', thereby preventing the lowering of prices and wages, and, consequently, increasing both the value of money and capital. Secondly, the discovery of the Californian and Australian gold mines increased the money supply, maintaining prices and preventing deflation, whereby capital would have gained considerably at the expense of wage earners.[11]

CHAPTER 23
Chartist Disillusionment 1848

Disintegration of the Chartist Movement

As Robert Gammage observed early in 1843, the Chartist movement was in disarray, caused by many political disagreements between various sections of its membership. He believed that this arose from the fact that differences arising from diversity of opinion, and proposed actions, could not be tolerated by one section of the movement: 'hence the dwindling down of the Chartist party from powerful bodies to comparatively insignificant sections'. Certainly, the movement went into decline, but probably a far more important reason for the fall in Chartist activity, and rapid decline in membership, was the revival in trade, which created more employment and less economic deprivation, during 1843.[1]

Chartism - Third Phase 1847-48

Early in 1847, there was yet another trade depression, a recurring problem with market capitalism, and interest in Chartism revived. In Bradford, a tremendous gathering took place with thousands attending from Halifax, Bingley and Keighley. They marched in military order, many brandishing pikes, through the streets of Bradford. They were addressed by David Lightowler (c1795–1875), George White, Peter McDouall, John Shaw and a number of other prominent Chartists. Not the slightest interference took place by the authorities and Bradford was that day in the hands of the Chartists.[2]

The manufacturing depression was, on this occasion, made worse by the number of Irish immigrants in the major towns, contributing to the oversupply of labour. The population census of Bradford in 1841 recorded that ten per cent were born in Ireland, and it was believed that fifty per cent of Bradford Chartists were of Irish descent.[3]

At the general election, held between 29 July and 26 August 1847, the Whig leader Lord John Russell became prime minister, due to a split in the Conservative party. Most significantly, Feargus O'Connor was elected MP for Nottingham, by defeating the Whig minister, Sir John Hobhouse, by 1,257 votes to 893, and became the only Chartist ever to take his seat in parliament. Under O'Connor's leadership, and encouraged by the successful revolution in Paris in 1848, the Chartists set about producing a third petition.[4]

The Third Chartist Petition 1848

On Monday 10th April 1848, a large Chartist demonstration took place when enormous crowds marched from all over London to congregate on Kennington Common, with the object of accompanying the third Chartist petition to the House of Commons. The estimate of the numbers vary, from 500,000 (O'Connor) to 150,000–170,000 (Gammage), down to 12,000-15,000 (Lord John Russell). The procession to present the petition to parliament was banned by the chief commissioner of police. Dramatically, the Duke of Wellington organised the defence of London. He recruited thousands of special constables to perform the initial confrontation, while keeping the military in reserve, should the special constables be overwhelmed. O'Connor decided that discretion was the better part of valour, and took the petition to the Houses of Parliament in three Hansom Cabs.[5]

And so, on the 13 April, the third and final Chartist petition was presented to parliament by Feargus O'Connor MP, claiming that it contained six million signatures. However, on close examination, it was found to include many fictitious names, and despite 1,975,596 genuine signatures, O'Connor was charged with deception and arrested. After due apologies, the matter was dropped, but O'Connor felt that he could no longer persevere with the motion. It has been noted by Edward Vallance, in *A Radical History of Britain*, that many genuine petitioners were disqualified, because literate people signed for illiterate friends; also all the signatures of women were discounted, estimated at eight per cent of the total, despite the fact that the right of women to petition had been established by parliament in 1829.[6]

In April 1848, it was apparent that the physical force wing of the Chartist movement was at loggerheads with their leader, O'Connor, and the split was unbridgeable. There were a number of violent incidents in the Midlands and the North, but the authorities were quick to suppress meetings and demonstrations by introducing martial law. They imprisoned many of the Chartist leaders, most notably Ernest Jones (1819–1869) who was arrested on 6 June 1848, in Manchester, on the flimsy charge of sedition.[7] He received a two-year sentence and was not released until 10 July 1850, thereby further weakening the movement at a critical time.

The Bradford Insurrection of 1848

The severe defeat of the third Chartist petition by parliament did not deter the working men of the North from raising their voice in protest; for, once again, they were facing mass unemployment and starvation. The poor harvest of 1847 resulted in the price of bread increasing from eight and a half pence a loaf in 1846 to eleven and a half pence a loaf in 1847. The inhabitants of Bradford, Bingley and Halifax were particularly badly affected, as the increase in the price of bread coincided with a severe depression in the worsted manufacturing industry, partly caused by the excess of labour, and partly by the introduction of new and more efficient machinery. The net result was exceptionally high levels of unemployment in those particular towns.[8]

Not surprisingly, reports began to reach the Home Office at the end of May, about paramilitary training and drilling in the West Riding of Yorkshire. The labouring classes were once again arming, under the guise of the Life and Property Protection Society (The National Guard), with revolution in mind. Between two and three thousand men drilled openly at Wilsden, about four miles north of Bradford. They marched in military formation, preceded by black banners surmounted by pike heads and armed with clubs; they were in a determined mood and had resolved to resist by force any attempt to arrest their leaders.[9]

When two of these leaders, W. Smith and T. Kilvington, were arrested at nearby Bingley at five o'clock on Friday evening 26 May 1848, they were brought before the magistrate W.B. Farrand and accused of drilling 'The National Guard'. After a summary hearing, lasting only twenty minutes, they were handcuffed and ordered to be conveyed to York Castle for trial.

As they were being marched to the railway station, a large crowd, estimated at about two thousand people, gathered and questioned the constables whether the two men should not receive bail. Smith and Kilvington were then taken back to the magistrate to settle the issue. Farrand was furious that his judgement had been questioned and proposed setting an unreasonably large bail. He ordered the doors of the court to be locked, whereupon a commotion took place, during which the two prisoners were secretly spirited out of the court. A local blacksmith removed the handcuffs and the two men were set free.

At the instigation of Farrand, the special constables patrolled the town until the following Wednesday, when, at seven in the morning, sixty army pensioners (a type of territorial army) arrived by train, armed with guns and sixty rounds of ammunition. A number of 'Noodles' (simpletons – probably bandsmen) arrived from nearby Otley and regular troops from Bradford. The 'Noodles' were sent to guard the station. Then, with Farrand at their head, a number of constables followed by a detachment of regular troops, with the army pensioners bringing up the rear, marched to the local mills and arrested sixteen men at work, ostensibly for assisting in the rescue of Kilvington and Smith. The prisoners were promptly sent by special train, under escort, to York Castle for trial. As a reprisal, the harassed citizens of Bingley set fire to Constable Fould's pleasure boat 'Water Witch', valued at ten pounds.[10]

A correspondent to the Home Office wrote complaining about the Chartists in Bradford who:

> ...perambulated the streets on the Sabbath day marching in military style with their captains in red and green caps and divided into sections and companies, keeping step with true military precision carrying tricolour flags and others bearing abominable inscriptions such as 'more pigs less parsons', 'down with the aristocracy', 'England free or a desert' etc. etc… A ferocious looking blacksmith named the 'Watt Tyler' of Bradford and who openly makes pikes and other deadly weapons for the Chartists is allowed to carry on his nefarious traffic without ever being molested. He is not going to shave his beard until the Charter becomes the law of the land. I enclose a bill that the shopkeepers are forced to put in their windows – those who refuse are told that they will not support them nor will they let others. I will give you a case that came under my own notice. They called upon a shopkeeper to beg something for to purchase flags etc., and he refusing on the market night they surrounded his shop and would not let a single customer enter; so that he was compelled to apologise and give them five shillings and promise to become one of them.[11]

In Bradford the situation became very ugly indeed, as magistrates, on 13 May, attempted to regain control of the town after a week in which the Chartists had marched through the streets unchecked. First, the magistrates issued a proclamation against such proceedings, then, as part of the clampdown, two constables were called out to apprehend David Lightowler and Isaac Jefferson (alias Watt Tyler of Bradford) the blacksmith, who, as the correspondent to the Home Office had complained, manufactured a large number of pikes without hindrance. He is reputed to have had wrists too thick for the police to handcuff. His power base and centre of support was Adelaide Street off Manchester Road, an area densely packed with unemployed wool combers, which the police entered at their peril. When the police constables went to the front door the two men escaped by the back door. The representatives of the law then found themselves surrounded by about a thousand people, who threw stones at them, and a fight ensued, during which the police constables were badly injured.

When on 23 May, Peter McDouall, a notable Chartist leader, made a seditious speech with impunity in the town, it became obvious that a showdown was about to take place. Shops closed in anticipation. The Chartists sent out carrier pigeons requesting help from surrounding towns, particularly Halifax, Bingley and Queenstown.

As a result, on 27 May, two thousand special constables were sworn in and armed with cutlasses. Major General Thorne, in command of all the military forces in the area, then ordered two troops of 5th Dragoon Guards, thirty Royal Horse Artillery from Leeds, two companies of the 81st Regiment of Foot from Hull, and the second West Yorkshire Yeomanry all to converge on Bradford immediately.[12]

On Sunday 28 May, Lord Harewood, the lord lieutenant of the West Riding, and General Thorne conferred and decided to act the following day, as they could not back down having assembled all their forces.

On Monday 29 May, Harewood and Thorne drew up their men in front of Bradford Town Hall. Led by two thousand special constables and police, the 'forces of law and order' marched through the town as far as Adelaide Street, where they were confronted by equal numbers of Chartists armed with clubs. A vicious fight ensued and the police were badly beaten, due to the inept tactics of Harewood and Thorne, as the supporting dragoons were trapped behind the police. Only when the police broke ranks were the military able to get through the crush of people and restore order. Eighteen Chartists; one woman, Mary Mortimer, and seventeen men were arrested and charged with drilling and threatening to shoot the constables when captured.[13]

As a reprisal, the clerk of the court who drew up the order was manhandled by the harassed citizens and, for some time, held over the battlements of a bridge, while it was debated whether to drop him into the water or not – he was finally released shaken but unharmed. The blacksmith, Jefferson, was finally arrested on 16 July, but again he was rescued by his fellow Chartists.[14]

In Leeds, meetings were held nightly, and, to meet the military threat, arming was proposed. Drilling continued, despite the local magistrates issuing a caution against such action. Nevertheless, the *Morning Chronicle* reported that 'a large meeting was held in Leeds to support the insurgents in Bradford, but was controlled by the military before it got out of hand'.[15]

Elsewhere, thousands attended a mass meeting on 18 July at Blackstone Edge, high on the Pennines between Halifax and Rochdale. The weather was wet, as so often it is in this part of the country. A policeman was detected in the crowd, and would probably have been killed, but for the intervention of George White, one of the speakers. After the meeting, a group of delegates agreed that Lancashire would rise on the 15 August, and Bradford the next day to coincide with the London rising. The government was made aware of these plans by the spy Thomas Powell, and three hundred police arrested the leaders in Manchester on the evening of the 15 August. The signal was never sent to Bradford and the revolution was aborted. Finally, Isaac Jefferson was found in his bed in Illingworth and taken into custody near Halifax. At the York Assizes, he was sentenced to four months in gaol.[16]

But as the Chartist cause declined, two new leaders appeared – George Julian Harney and Ernest Jones, both educated men with legal training. The cause was given a boost when, on 11 June 1850, Jones was released from prison, with the result that next day, on Monday 12 June, thousands of Yorkshire Chartists assembled on Toftshaw Moor to hear him speak. Then on 15 July, Jones entered Halifax accompanied by a grand procession, which made for West Hill Park. The meeting was adjourned until the evening. Jones next moved on to

Bingley, where he was met by a procession with music. He was escorted into the town in a carriage drawn by greys. On the following morning (Sunday), he addressed an open-air meeting at the 'Druid's Altar', one of the most romantic spots in Yorkshire. He also visited Doncaster, Sheffield, Hebden Bridge, Holmfirth and Bradford. In Bradford, Jones was met at the railway station, where a carriage was waiting to convey him to the Temperance Hall and seven hundred people joined him in a celebratory tea. A public meeting followed, and Jones addressed the crowd from the steps of the Hall.[17]

In 1852, O'Connor lost his reason in the House of Commons; he was removed by the sergeant at arms, pronounced insane, and was eventually removed to Dr Tuke's Asylum. As Robert Gammage comments, 'How fleeting is the breath of the multitude when that multitude is uninformed ... One day Hosanna; the next Crucify him'.[18]

The third Chartist petition, which had been ridiculed when it came before parliament on 13 April 1848, had quickly degenerated into a farce. This event really spelt the beginning of the end of the Chartist movement. Feargus O'Connor lost his credibility with many Chartists and finally control of the *Northern Star* in January 1852. He died on 30 August 1855. The movement, which had always been a coalition, fragmented into separate sects; led by George Julian Harney, James Bronterre O'Brien and Ernest Jones.

The decline of the Chartist movement after 1852 was rapid, as the various factions that had sunk their differences to campaign for the six points of 'The Charter' began to go their separate ways. However, many writers have pointed out that the long lingering decline, and final death of the Chartist movement, which officially took place at the Chartist Conference on 8 February 1858, when Ernest Jones presided over a meeting that adopted his motion for co-operation with moderate radicals, was to greatly influence the politics of the second half of the nineteenth century.

In July 1852, John Lindley was to witness his last general election – he still had not won the vote that he had fought so hard to achieve. On that occasion, Ernest Jones contested Halifax as a Chartist candidate. At the open air nomination meeting, attended by about twenty thousand people, Jones made one of his best speeches and, at the subsequent show of hands, Sir Charles Wood, the Liberal candidate, received about five hundred votes, while Jones received many thousands. But at the subsequent poll, Wood received five hundred and ninety-six votes and was elected, while Jones received a paltry thirty-eight votes. This demonstrated the iniquitous farce, in terms of fair representation, produced by the 1832 Reform Bill. In fact, the Chartist vote for the 1852 general election amounted to a derisory 0.21 per cent of the total poll, despite the hundreds of thousands of supporters that it commanded throughout the country.[19]

The final word on Chartism goes to Professor Edward Royle, who claimed that 'the Chartists' greatest achievement was Chartism, a movement shot through, not with despair, but hope.'[20]

CHAPTER 24
The Twilight Years in Mirfield 1838–1853

The Coming of the Railway

It is difficult to imagine the emotions of John Lindley and the inhabitants of the Knowl when, in 1840, the first train passed through Mirfield from Manchester to Leeds via Sowerby Bridge, Wakefield and Normanton. The Manchester to Leeds railway line (later part of the Lancashire and Yorkshire Railway network) had been first proposed in October 1830.[1] Perhaps he felt the thrill and excitement expressed by the Yorkshire poet, Ben Preston (1819-1902), in the following poem.

> The Locomotive
>
> The neigh of the dragon, a terrible cry
> Wild, piercing, and shrill, has gone up to the sky;
> He pants for the start, and he snorts in his ire,
> His life-blood is boiling his heart is on fire.
>
> O man, O my brother, how stubborn thy will,
> How dauntless thy courage, how Godlike thy skill:
> The Earth, with its elements, yields to the brave,
> The fire is a bondsman, the vapour a slave.
>
> The vales are uplifted, the mountains are riven,
> And the way of the dragon is shining and even.
> Let us gaze and admire, and declare, if we can,
> How mighty the God that created the man.[2]
>
> ['The man' refers to George Stephenson]

When compared to his journey to Van Diemen's Land in the *Lady Ridley*, only twenty years earlier, at an average speed of between four and five knots, John Lindley would have realised that railways were revolutionising travel of both people and goods by conveying both at unimaginable speeds. What he almost certainly did not appreciate was that this represented a social revolution in itself; suddenly the pedestrian class (all those who had previously travelled by 'shanks' pony') could, for a few pence, travel as far and as fast as the mounted classes (the aristocracy, with their own horse and carriage, and the lesser gentry by horse and stage coach). The age-old class structure based on the horse was suddenly terminally in decline. Of course, the pedestrian class could not sit in the same compartments as 'the quality', but that was a small price to pay.[3]

Throughout Britain 'the age of railway mania' had begun. In John's personal environment, the Manchester to Leeds line, via Huddersfield, was opened in 1848 by the London and North Western Railway. Meanwhile, the enlarged and consolidated Lancashire and Yorkshire Railway opened the Mirfield to Low Moor branch line, via the Spen Valley, on 12 July 1848, and public services commenced a week later on the 18 July. This line crossed the Calder and Hebble Navigation on a wooden bridge before cutting across the Huddersfield Road at Church Lane; it then continued through Northorpe, Heckmondwike and Cleckheaton to Low Moor. The Cleckheaton branch line proved very popular and, on 9 May 1850, the line was extended to terminate at the Bradford Exchange Station, a fast-growing city that had increased its population from 4,506 in 1780 to 103,778 by 1851. The railways cut up the countryside as never before, irrevocably changing the landscape, but they were to provide a major source of employment in Mirfield during the second half of the nineteenth century. There were eventually four stations, extensive goods yards with sidings, marshalling yards and sidings, a locomotive shed and wagon repair shop.[4]

Naturally, the railways were not built without disturbing the peace and tranquillity of Mirfield, as the following anonymous letter testifies:

> *Gentlemen, I beg through the medium of your valuable newspaper to draw your attention to the present disgraceful proceedings in several parts of Mirfield on Sundays from drunkenness and fighting, indeed so proverbial is the fact that of late, numbers from the neighbouring villages resort here on Sundays to witness these most shameful and brutalising exhibitions.*
> *I am well aware of the difficulties of keeping order in a place like Mirfield, infested as it is now with excavators, many of whom are of the lowest grade, but still I am convinced that a little more vigilance on the part of the authorities would in a great measure do away with present state of things.*
> *Some of the innkeepers and beer sellers commit most flagrant offences by selling ale etc. during divine service, out of doors and it is not at all uncommon for groups of persons to be drinking in the outbuildings of the inns etc. even in the fields thus affording every encouragement to drunkenness and disorder.*
> *Should the above remarks be the means of lessening the above vice it would be gratifying. Gentlemen. Your obedient servant. Mirfield 22nd May 1839* [5]

Once the railways became established, the public mail coach network went into rapid decline, as did all the coaching inns that served their customers. The use of private carriages did continue until the advent of the motorcar at the turn of the century, but ownership was more a question of status than transport.

Religion and the Working Class

On 30 March 1851, just before John Lindley died, a national census of religious worship was taken by the civil servant, Horace Mann (1823–1917); his subsequent analysis showed that well over half the population of England did not attend any form of religious worship. Of those in the West Riding that did attend, most were Methodists or Dissenters. In Darton, for example, the parish church of All Saints recorded 104 attending morning service and 47 in the afternoon; but the combined totals for the Wesleyan Association in

Mapplewell, Providence Chapel (New Connection) Mapplewell, and the Wesleyan Methodist in Staincross were 39 for morning service, 142 in the afternoon and 212 in the evening. That is twice as many Methodists as Anglicans. But, although church going was only an occasional activity, particularly for the working classes, most people thought of themselves as Christians and their affiliation tended to follow family tradition.[6] Thomas Frost explained the low attendance as follows:

> *The paucity of worshipers was not due to unbelief or dissent, both of which indicate more exercise of intellect than is compatible with such low material condition as then prevailed upon the masses…whose minds were engrossed almost constantly with one thought – how to get the next meal, to replace some worn-out garment, or pay the rent.* [7]

As one rector from York observed: 'The people have become hardened against all forms of religion and that only is acceptable which can supply the best loaves and fishes.'[8]

John's early years were spent in a very Nonconformist environment, dominated by the Methodist New Connection. As his granddaughter, Harriet Lindley (1846–1937), was married in Wakefield Baptist Chapel in 1868, John may have had Baptist sympathies, if not strong beliefs, but there is no record of this fact during his long period of captivity. No doubt all prisoners were recorded as Church of England, as is the modern practice for anyone without strong religious affiliation.

The Smithy at Mirfield

But while the great national struggle continued, life in towns and villages across the nation progressed as usual, but with quickening pace. In May 1838, at the age of sixty-eight, John Lindley 'purchased from one Joshua Garside, master of the Knowl School, a small plot of ground containing 433 square yards at the Knowl in Mirfield called the Croft or Intake, for the sum of £27'. This money was provided by his daughter, Ann, who may have owned the deeds. On the site, he built a small smithy 'for the purpose of his business'. At the same time Ann 'bought from the same vendor an adjoining plot of land of the same size'. Sometime between 1846 and 1848, Ann had returned from service to look after her aged parents, who could no longer physically cope with day-to-day life. John and Hannah could consider themselves fortunate that they did not have to resort to the local Knowl workhouse, or worse, the Dewsbury Union Workhouse known as 'the Bastille', as did so many of their poor neighbours.[9]

Ann, who had chosen to enter the domestic service of Mr Spence of Tilworth Grange, Sutton, near Kingston-upon-Hull, would have lived in a respectable district and an amply provided household. Initially, her own living and working conditions were probably deplorable, but, as she moved up the domestic ladder to the position of cook or housekeeper, conditions would have improved and her salary increased to the point where she could help support her parents. To be in service was certainly considered socially far more acceptable than working in a mill. In fact, by the time Ann became a housekeeper, she was not only able to help support her parents but could afford to purchase two small plots of land.

There were over one million women in domestic service in 1851, and, despite the meagre wages of between six and ten pounds a year, since all living expenses were included, domestic servants were often able to accumulate small sums of between twenty and thirty pounds, saved over a number of years. In fact, from 1817, penny banks had sprung up precisely to attract the savings of domestic servants and apprentices. Since Ann married late, she was able to accumulate considerably more savings than normal.[10]

When Ann returned to Mirfield, sometime between 1846 and 1848, to look after her parents, as would have been considered the duty of daughters in those days, she kept a shop and took in washing. Finally, she married in 1864 at the age of fifty-five, and when she died she left a will with bequests to her nephews and nieces.[11]

John and Hannah had obviously moved out of the subsistence level of the working class, largely on account of support by their family. This was very common in the nineteenth century, as small local communities, often interrelated by marriage, provided supportive social networks. Neighbours helped one another, lending 'half a cup of sugar' or 'a cup of flour' to be repaid on Friday. Mutual support was essential to survival, especially during 'the hungry forties', and none more so than that provided by sons and daughters. The close-knit community of Mirfield ensured that the community shared a common background in experience and culture – perpetuating local traditions. Had not John's neighbour in Darton, John Peacock, shared his exile?

Retirement

In the 1851 census for Mirfield, John, still living at the Knowl, was recorded as a retired nail maker, a most unusual appellation in an age when most labouring men and women worked until they died.

John died of inflammation of the bladder, ten days short of his eighty-third birthday in mid-November 1853, appropriately in the year transportation to Van Diemen's Land ceased. Since he left no money or effects, except a little furniture in the house, Ann continued to look after her mother, Hannah, until her death on the 23 December 1860, aged eighty-nine. This was a great age in the nineteenth century, when the average lifespan was forty-five years for men and fifty-five years for women.[12]

Hannah lived just long enough to see Mirfield lit by gas in November 1857, supplied by the Mirfield Gas Company from their Ravensthorpe Works. What a long way she had come from the nail maker's cottage in Darton!

A public water supply was not provided by Huddersfield Council until 1876, sixteen years after Hannah died.[13]

Four years after her mother's death, Ann married William Shackleton, a man six years younger than herself. William was born in Dewsbury but living in Bradford when he married. He was employed as a 'hanger on' (a brakeman) at a local coal pit.

John's eldest surviving son, John William, married Mary Booth and had a son, also named John. Young John became a master joiner and inherited the smithy at the Knowl as a result of the court case Lindley vs Lindley in 1883.

John's second surviving son, Robert, married Mary Houlgate, and became a waterman and finally a boat owner. Despite having five children of his own, he greatly helped his sister, Ann, in supporting their parents.

John's youngest surviving son, Joseph, married Ann Race. He is recorded in the 1861 census as a general labourer. They had five children.

John's nephew, George, who had joined him in Mirfield as a nail maker, married Mary Ann Calvert in 1833 at St Mary's Church, Mirfield. They had two sons, Joseph born in 1846, and George junior born in 1851. George junior diversified out of nail making and set up an ironmonger's shop in Easthorpe and bought a large house there, which he named 'Mapplewell' in memory of his birthplace.

A colourful family history of John's nephew, Joseph Lindley (the eldest son of his brother George), with the title *Meet My Ancestor Joseph Lindley (1796-1865)* by Jack Brook, appears in the Barnsley Family History Magazine, April 2011. Joseph was another nail maker from Mapplewell, who diversified out of nail making, in his case into market gardening.

Conclusion

It is good to think that John and Hannah had so many years together after John's return to England. And no doubt John received many free drinks at some of Mirfield's seventeen public houses (recorded in 1825), in return for stories about his time in Van Diemen's Land.

John Lindley suffered great hardship and saw great changes during his lifetime. He belonged to the first generation in the world to experience the effects of industrialisation. As Marx and Engels wrote in the *Communist Manifesto* in 1848:

> *The bourgeoisie, during the rule of scarce one hundred years, has created more massive and more colossal productive forces than have all the preceding generations together. Subjection of Nature's forces to man, machinery, applications to industry and agriculture, steam navigation, railways, electric telegraphs, clearing whole continents for cultivation, canalising of rivers, whole populations conjured out of the ground – what earlier century had even a presentiment that such productive forces slumbered in the lap of social labour?*[14]

Despite the great technical improvements that John witnessed, he personally, and the vast majority of the labouring working class of his generation, were either overworked or under employed, depending on the economic cycle. They lived with the constant threat of hunger. Furthermore, they were always poorly paid and badly housed. They had risked their lives, and many had died, to bring about improvements in the living standards of the working class, but few lived to see the fruits of their struggles.

As for revolution, John Lindley and those who wished to change the system by force of arms, learned from successive failures that it was not possible for working men to free themselves by revolution. The method of gradual reform demonstrated itself as a more practical method of achieving change, albeit very slowly. The realities of government power ultimately taught most reformers the practical, as well as the theoretical, need for reform within the law. By 1853, John Lindley and his many compatriots had learned their lesson by 'dear bought past experience'.[15]

Unfortunately, the economic prosperity that resulted from the first century of the Industrial Revolution and the universal emancipation, for which John Lindley fought so hard, were still some way off when he died in 1853. Although he was only a single strand in the great fight for political and social reform, and improved prosperity for the labouring classes, his life had not been entirely in vain. He had seen his own family prosper and laid the foundation for his descendants to achieve many things: freedom from hunger, education beyond his wildest dreams and universal suffrage for men and women. As one of the beneficiaries – I salute his memory.

EPILOGUE
Posthumous Pardon

The following record appears in Hansard for 22 July 1856 (Commons Sitting):

> Mr T. Duncombe rose to put the following question to the Secretary of State for the Home Department: Whether, under the recent Act of Amnesty granted by Her Majesty to all political exiles, orders had been given for the liberation of the ten following prisoners, convicted of high treason at the York assizes of September 1820, and transported to Van Diemen's Land by the ship *Lady Ridley* in 1821:—William Comstive, William Rice, Richard Addy, Joseph Frith, Charles Stanfield, John Birkenshaw, Benjamin Rogers, Joseph Chapel, Benjamin Hanson, and Michael Downing? [These are the Barnsley men. No mention is made of John Lindley and John Peacock from Mirfield.]
>
> No record of the conviction of those individuals was to be found at the Home Office. They, together with thirteen other persons—making in all twenty-three—had been tried at York in 1820, when Lord Sidmouth was at the head of the Home Department, and had been induced to plead guilty to a charge of high treason, upon the condition that their lives should be spared. Out of the twenty-three who had been placed upon trial, thirteen had been sentenced to only short periods of imprisonment or transportation, and when the recent amnesty to political exiles had been proclaimed, he had made a communication to the Home Office as to whether indulgence would not be extended to the other ten whose names were comprised in his question. The answer to that communication had been, that there was no record of their conviction at the Home Office, or of their present whereabouts, and his object in calling the attention of the right honourable gentleman to the subject now was, that the knowledge that they had received Her Majesty's **pardon** might, by means of the press, be conveyed to those individuals, wherever they might happen to be. The charge made against them had arisen out of a seditious meeting which had been held at Grange Moor, near Barnsley.
>
> Sir George Grey replied that it was not remarkable that no record of the conviction of these men was to be found in the Home Office, because it occurred some thirty-six years ago, and these ten persons were in the following year transported either to Van Diemen's Land or New South Wales, he believed to the latter colony (which was incorrect). From other sources of information, he had ascertained that the offence of which they were convicted was similar in character to those for which pardons had recently been granted. It was right that, if any of these persons were living, they should be included in the amnesty, and instructions had been sent to the colonies that they should be set at liberty.[1]

So, the punishment of transportation had all been a mistake?

It is ironic that, if John Lindley, our Yorkshire Rebel, had not been the victim of this miscarriage of justice, he would not have left his mark on history and this book would not have been written.

LINDLEY FAMILY TREES

John Lindley of Darton and Mirfield (1770-1853)

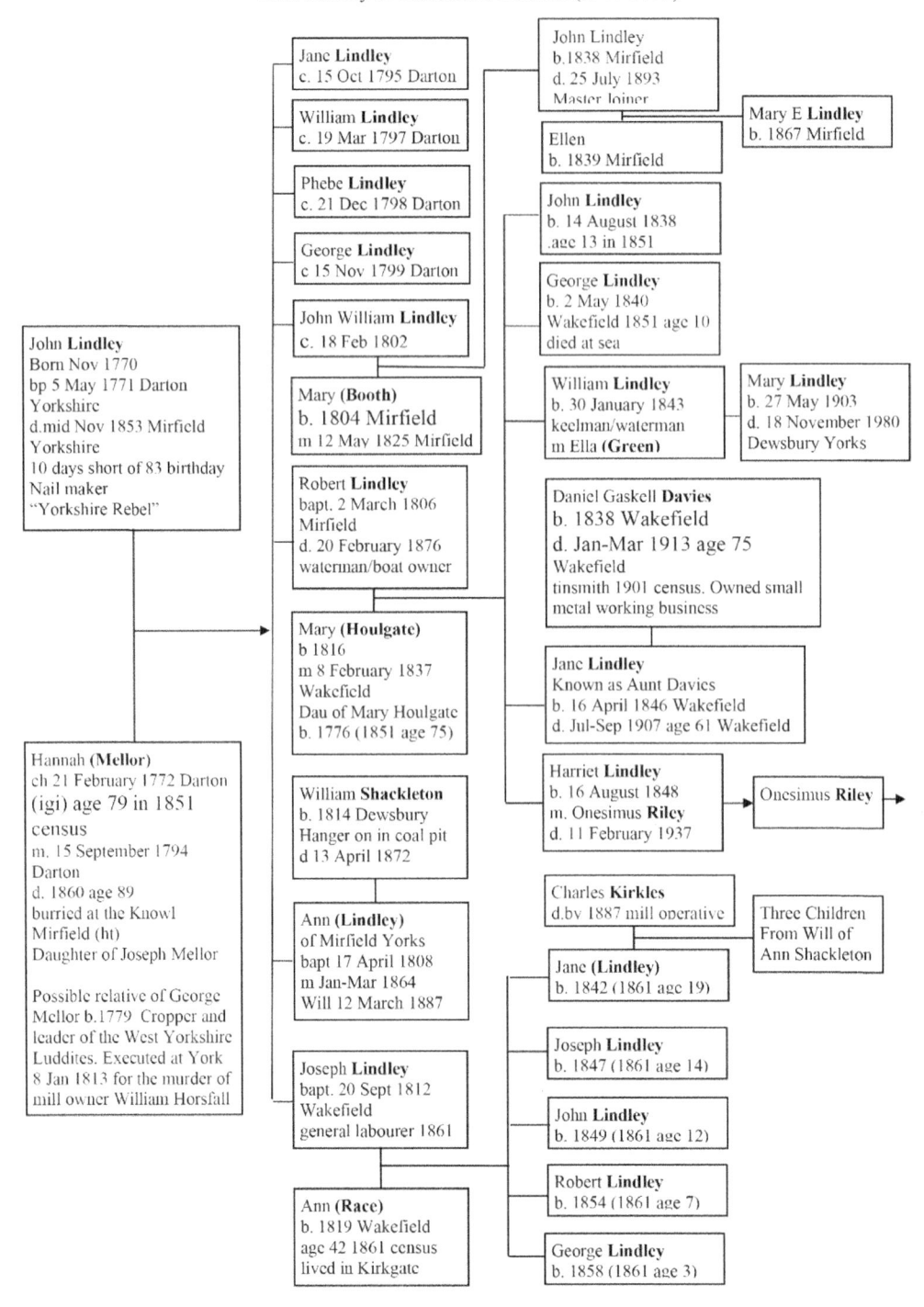

John Lindley
Born Nov 1770
bp 5 May 1771 Darton Yorkshire
d. mid Nov 1853 Mirfield Yorkshire
10 days short of 83 birthday
Nail maker
"Yorkshire Rebel"

Hannah (Mellor)
ch 21 February 1772 Darton
(igi) age 79 in 1851 census
m. 15 September 1794 Darton
d. 1860 age 89
burried at the Knowl Mirfield (ht)
Daughter of Joseph Mellor

Possible relative of George Mellor b.1779 Cropper and leader of the West Yorkshire Luddites. Executed at York 8 Jan 1813 for the murder of mill owner William Horsfall

Jane Lindley c. 15 Oct 1795 Darton

William Lindley c. 19 Mar 1797 Darton

Phebe Lindley c. 21 Dec 1798 Darton

George Lindley c 15 Nov 1799 Darton

John William Lindley c. 18 Feb 1802

Mary (Booth)
b. 1804 Mirfield
m 12 May 1825 Mirfield

Robert Lindley
bapt. 2 March 1806 Mirfield
d. 20 February 1876
waterman/boat owner

Mary (Houlgate)
b 1816
m 8 February 1837 Wakefield
Dau of Mary Houlgate b. 1776 (1851 age 75)

William Shackleton
b. 1814 Dewsbury
Hanger on in coal pit
d 13 April 1872

Ann (Lindley)
of Mirfield Yorks
bapt 17 April 1808
m Jan-Mar 1864
Will 12 March 1887

Joseph Lindley
bapt. 20 Sept 1812 Wakefield
general labourer 1861

Ann (Race)
b. 1819 Wakefield
age 42 1861 census
lived in Kirkgate

John Lindley
b.1838 Mirfield
d. 25 July 1893
Master Joiner

Ellen b. 1839 Mirfield

John Lindley
b. 14 August 1838
age 13 in 1851

George Lindley
b. 2 May 1840
Wakefield 1851 age 10
died at sea

William Lindley
b. 30 January 1843
keelman/waterman
m Ella (Green)

Daniel Gaskell Davies
b. 1838 Wakefield
d. Jan-Mar 1913 age 75 Wakefield
tinsmith 1901 census. Owned small metal working business

Jane Lindley
Known as Aunt Davies
b. 16 April 1846 Wakefield
d. Jul-Sep 1907 age 61 Wakefield

Harriet Lindley
b. 16 August 1848
m. Onesimus Riley
d. 11 February 1937

Charles Kirkles
d. by 1887 mill operative

Jane (Lindley)
b. 1842 (1861 age 19)

Joseph Lindley
b. 1847 (1861 age 14)

John Lindley
b. 1849 (1861 age 12)

Robert Lindley
b. 1854 (1861 age 7)

George Lindley
b. 1858 (1861 age 3)

Mary E Lindley b. 1867 Mirfield

Mary Lindley
b. 27 May 1903
d. 18 November 1980
Dewsbury Yorks

Onesimus Riley

Three Children From Will of Ann Shackleton

John Lindley of Cawthorn born circa 1715

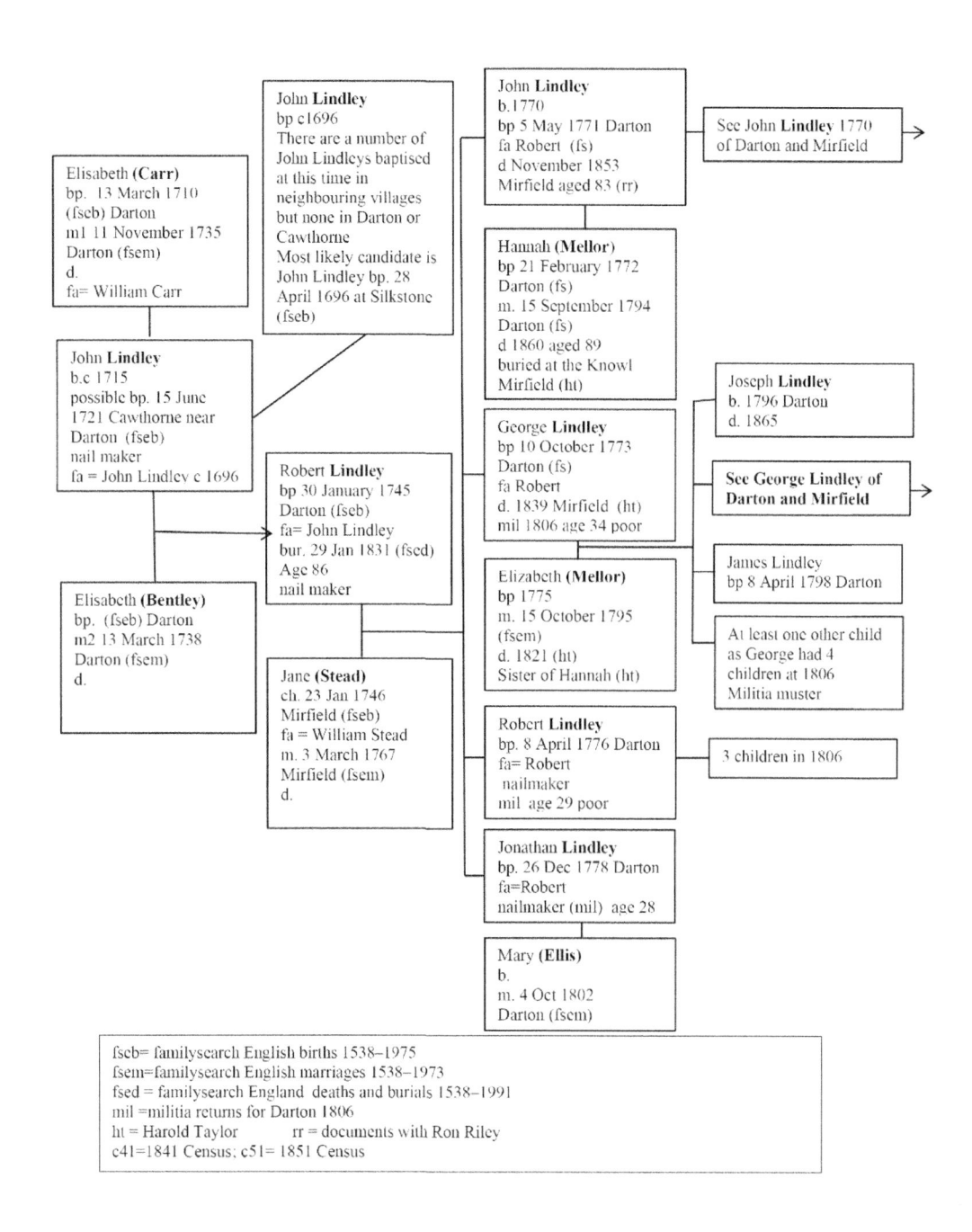

Elisabeth (Carr)
bp. 13 March 1710 (fseb) Darton
m1 11 November 1735 Darton (fsem)
d.
fa= William Carr

John Lindley
bp c1696
There are a number of John Lindleys baptised at this time in neighbouring villages but none in Darton or Cawthorne
Most likely candidate is John Lindley bp. 28 April 1696 at Silkstone (fseb)

John Lindley
b.c 1715
possible bp. 15 June 1721 Cawthorne near Darton (fseb)
nail maker
fa = John Lindley c 1696

Elisabeth (Bentley)
bp. (fseb) Darton
m2 13 March 1738 Darton (fsem)
d.

Robert Lindley
bp 30 January 1745 Darton (fseb)
fa= John Lindley
bur. 29 Jan 1831 (fsed)
Age 86
nail maker

Jane (Stead)
ch. 23 Jan 1746 Mirfield (fseb)
fa = William Stead
m. 3 March 1767 Mirfield (fsem)
d.

John Lindley
b.1770
bp 5 May 1771 Darton
fa Robert (fs)
d November 1853 Mirfield aged 83 (rr)

See John Lindley 1770 of Darton and Mirfield

Hannah (Mellor)
bp 21 February 1772 Darton (fs)
m. 15 September 1794 Darton (fs)
d 1860 aged 89 buried at the Knowl Mirfield (ht)

George Lindley
bp 10 October 1773 Darton (fs)
fa Robert
d. 1839 Mirfield (ht)
mil 1806 age 34 poor

Elizabeth (Mellor)
bp 1775
m. 15 October 1795 (fsem)
d. 1821 (ht)
Sister of Hannah (ht)

Robert Lindley
bp. 8 April 1776 Darton
fa= Robert
nailmaker
mil age 29 poor

Jonathan Lindley
bp. 26 Dec 1778 Darton
fa=Robert
nailmaker (mil) age 28

Mary (Ellis)
b.
m. 4 Oct 1802 Darton (fsem)

Joseph Lindley
b. 1796 Darton
d. 1865

See George Lindley of Darton and Mirfield

James Lindley
bp 8 April 1798 Darton

At least one other child as George had 4 children at 1806 Militia muster

3 children in 1806

---

fseb= familysearch English births 1538–1975
fsem=familysearch English marriages 1538–1973
fsed = familysearch England deaths and burials 1538–1991
mil =militia returns for Darton 1806
ht = Harold Taylor   rr = documents with Ron Riley
c41=1841 Census; c51= 1851 Census

George Lindley of Darton and Mirfield (1806-1882)

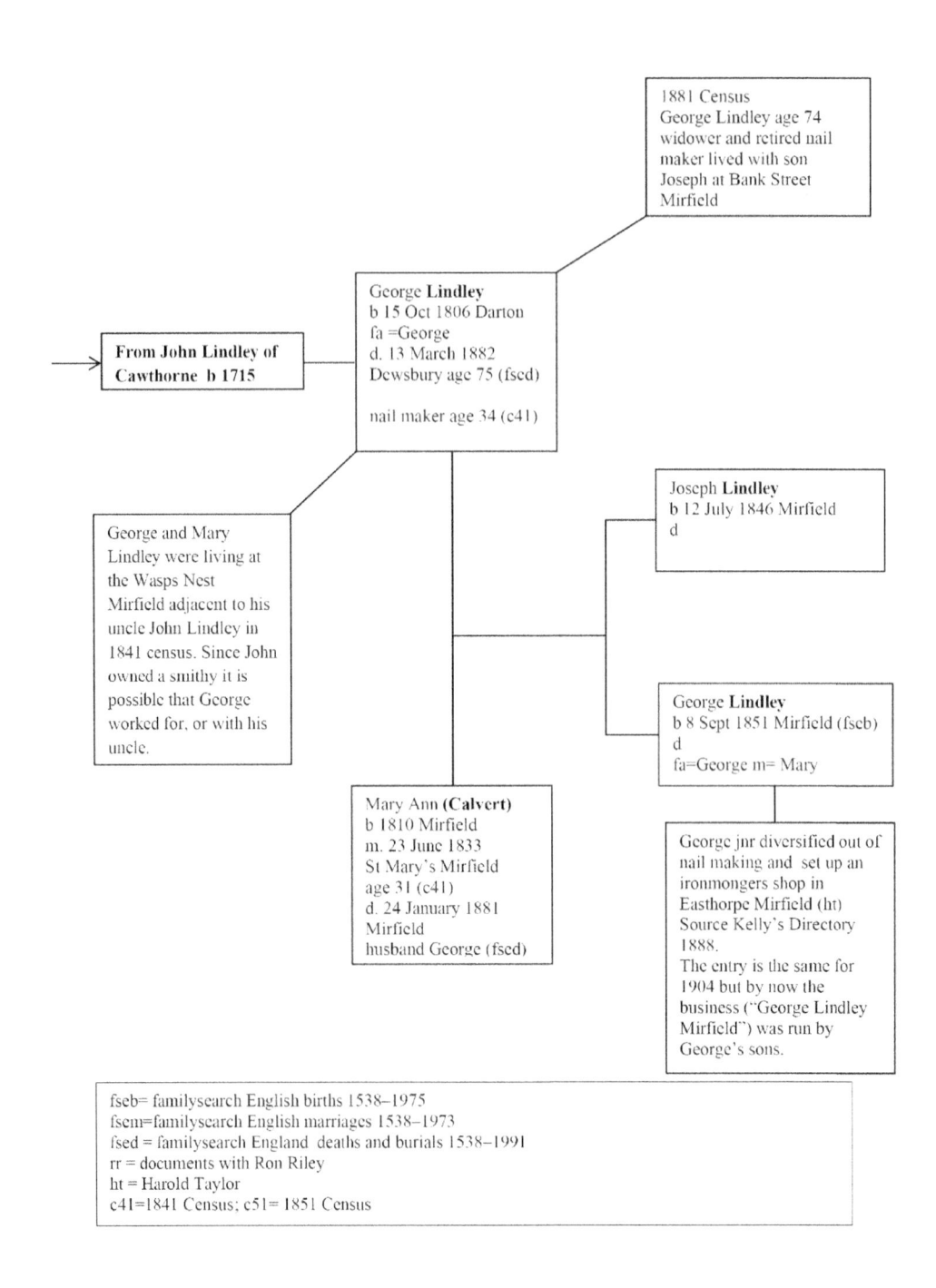

From John Lindley of Cawthorne b 1715 →

George Lindley
b 15 Oct 1806 Darton
fa =George
d. 13 March 1882 Dewsbury age 75 (fsed)

nail maker age 34 (c41)

1881 Census
George Lindley age 74 widower and retired nail maker lived with son Joseph at Bank Street Mirfield

George and Mary Lindley were living at the Wasps Nest Mirfield adjacent to his uncle John Lindley in 1841 census. Since John owned a smithy it is possible that George worked for, or with his uncle.

Mary Ann (Calvert)
b 1810 Mirfield
m. 23 June 1833 St Mary's Mirfield
age 31 (c41)
d. 24 January 1881 Mirfield
husband George (fsed)

Joseph Lindley
b 12 July 1846 Mirfield
d

George Lindley
b 8 Sept 1851 Mirfield (fseb)
d
fa=George m= Mary

George jnr diversified out of nail making and set up an ironmongers shop in Easthorpe Mirfield (ht) Source Kelly's Directory 1888.
The entry is the same for 1904 but by now the business ("George Lindley Mirfield") was run by George's sons.

---

fseb= familysearch English births 1538–1975
fsem=familysearch English marriages 1538–1973
fsed = familysearch England deaths and burials 1538–1991
rr = documents with Ron Riley
ht = Harold Taylor
c41=1841 Census; c51= 1851 Census

END NOTES

Prologue: Captain Cook's Discovery of Eastern Australia 1770

1. Cook p.225 (from Captain Cook's Journal During the First Voyage Round the World. [Guttenberg EBooks])
2. Cook p.225
3. Cook p.230 (from Captain Cook's Journal, 29 April 1770)
4. Finnis p.63, p.112.
5. Stamp p.147
6. Finnis pp.37 & 38
7. Hughes pp.72 &77

Introduction: The life of a Georgian Radical

1. Royle Radical Politics p.3
2. Rule The Vital Century p.1 & p.260 from Max Webber The Protestant Ethic and the Spirit of Capitalism [Unwin 1965 p.59]
3. Hey 2005 p.338, Briggs p.18
4. Armitage pp.3 & 4
5. West p.80

Chapter 1: Childhood in Darton 1770–1775

1. Lindley Papers held by author
2. Porter 1987 pp. 9 & 10
3. Porter 1987 p.31 & Porter 2003 p.100
4. Darton Parish records
5. Spink p.130
6. Porter 2003 p.20
7. Porter 1988 p.29
8. Porter 1988 p.44
9. Porter 1988 p.35
10. Briggs p.28, Porter 1988 p.26 & 27, Royle 1997 p. 303
11. Hey 2002 p.120, Morgan p.500
12. Berridge 1990 p.200
13. Spink 181 &182 & 184
14. Spink 187
15. Spink pp. 191 & 192
16. Spink p.176 from Dr Wade Frost 1936 & Spink p.170
17. Spink p.192 See also Robert Hamilton *An account of a distemper by the common people in England called mumps* [Transactions Royal Society Edinburgh 1790]
18. Spink p.188
19. Porter 1987 p.44
20. Joyce, Cambridge Social History Vol 2 p.138

Chapter 2: Early Years in Darton 1775–1802

1. Caffyn p.1 & p.50
2. Caffyn p.51, Taylor *Aspects of Barnsley* volume 6 chapter 10 p.127
3. Caffyn pp. 51 & 52
4. Dillon p.12
5. Briggs p.28
6. Dillon pp. 16, 55 & 56
7. Taylor *Aspects of Barnsley* volume 6 chapter 7 p.100
8. Caffyn p.49 & p.83 from R Baker 'Report on the conditions of the residences of the labouring classes in the town of Leeds: in the West Riding of Yorkshire.' In: *Local Reports on the sanitary conditions of the labouring population of England* [London 1842] p.358
9. Caffyn p.95 from Builder 1860 p.126
10. Schama volume 3 p.33, Taylor *Aspects of Barnsley* volume 6 chapter 10 p.125
11. Taylor *Aspects of Barnsley* Volume 6 chapter 10 p.125
12. Hey 2005 p.380
13. Dearnley p.28
14. Walton p.163, Berridge p.198, Royle 1997 p.246
15. Sutherland p.129 (quoting Harold Silver *The concept of Popular Education* 1965 p.23)
16. Royle 1997 p.356
17. Dillon p.31
18. Trevelyan p.376
19. Royle 1997 p.356
20. There is a copy of the George Beaumont bequest for maintaining a school at Darton in the 1772-1812 register
21. Sutherland p.129 quoting *Life and Struggles of William Lovett* 1876; 1967 edition. p.111
22. Stamp p.31
23. Royle 1997 p.259, Taylor p.100, Dearnley p.29 both *Aspects of Barnsley* volume 6
24. Schama volume 3 p.44
25. Tranter p.41
26. Briggs p.31
27. Taylor Yorkshire Archaeological Journal p.159
28. Taylor Yorkshire Archaeological Journal p 158
29. Royle 1997 p.303
30. Taylor *Aspects of Barnsley* volume 6 chapter 7 p.102
31. Royle 1997 p.296
32. Royle 1997 p.305
33. Hey 2005 p.353
34. Taylor *Aspects of Barnsley* volume 6 chapter 7 pp. 99–101, Dearnley p.27
35. Royle 1997 p.305, Taylor Aspects of Barnsley volume 6 chapter 7 p.102
36. Taylor Yorkshire Archaeological Journal p.158
37. Porter 1987 pp. 9 & 10, Porter 1988 p.26 Note 29, F. Bottomley *Attitudes to the body in Western Christendom* Lepus Books 1979
38. Stamp p.132
39. Schama volume 3 p.36
40. Royle 1997 p.306
41. Hey 2002 p.85
42. Lindley Papers
43. Hey 2002 p.120

Chapter 3: The South Yorkshire Iron Industry

1. Dillon p.25, Sheffield Trades Historical Society Wortley Ironworks 1961
2. Andrews p.14

3. Sheffield Trades Historical Society Wortley Ironworks 1961, Hayman pp.128 & 129; Details of how the industry developed and expanded in South Yorkshire between the years 1690 and 1750 can be found in *The South Yorkshire Ironmasters* by A. Raistrick and E.Allen.
4. Hayman p.13, Hey 2005 p.340
5. Hayman p.23
6. Raistrick pp. 169 & 170, Dillon p.21
7. Hayman p.131, Raistrick p.174 for a good description of charcoal burning see *Swallows and Amazons* by A. Ransome.
8. *Aspects of Barnsley* volume10 p.127, Andrews p.31, Hayman p.20
9. Hayman p.23
10. Hayman pp. 9, 11, 18 & 19
11. Hayman pp.19, 25, 86, Stamp p.42
12. Hayman p.133
13. Raistrick p.173
14. Dillon p.22
15. Hayman p.11
16. Sheffield Trades Historical Society Wortley Ironworks
17. Landes p.447
18. Andrews p.30
19. Hayman p.29
20. Dillon p.12, Raistrick p.174
21. Hayman p.104
22. Rule *Albion's People* 1992 p.25 [from Gentlemen's magazine LII 1782 p.526]
23. Rule *Vital Century* 1992 pp. 209 & 210
24. Andrews p.62
25. Dillon p.12, Taylor *Aspects of Barnsley* volume 6 chapter 7 p.121
26. Taylor *Aspects of Barnsley* volume 6 chapter 7 p.97, Drake pp.110 & 111
27. Bodey p.16

Chapter 4: Nail Making in Darton

1. Taylor Yorkshire Archaeological Journal Volume 63 1991 p.153
2. Rule *The Vital Century* 1992 p.118, Hayman p.107, Hey 2005 p 329
3. Dillon pp.10 & 11
4. Dearnley p.25
5. Lavery p.82, Bodey p.12, Rule *The Vital Century* 1992 p. 151
6. Bodey p.14
7. Walton p.163
8. Dillon p.12
9. Walton p.164, Willets p.5
10. Dillon p.11, Walton p.163, Bodley p.14, Hey pp. 328/9, E.Thompson pp.217, 287 & 288
11. Bodey pp.12, 14, 16 & 20, Walton p.163
12. Rule *The Vital Century* 1992 pp.303-306.
13. Walton pp.167 & 168
14. Hey p.330
15. Taylor Aspects of Barnsley volume 6 pp.99 & 100
16. Taylor *Yorkshire Archaeological Journal* volume 63 1991 pp.161 & 162
17. Taylor *Yorkshire Archaeological Journal* volume 63 1991 p.161
18. Weightman p.113, Taylor *Yorkshire Archaeological Journal* volume 63 1991 p.166
19. Dearnley pp. 29–31, Black p. 34, Dillon p.58

Chapter 5: Radical Awakening 1760–1793

1. Royle 1971 pp. 3 & 4

2. Tomalin p.69
3. Royle 1997 p.119
4. Price p.9
5. Royle 1997 p.119
6. Briggs pp. 10 & 13
7. Derry p.5
8. Briggs p.10 (from Francis Place Papers, British Library, Add MSS 27,834, f. 45.)
9. Ian R. Christie (1960) 'The Yorkshire Association, 1780-4: A Study in Political Organization' *The Historical Journal*, Vol.3, No.2, pp.144–161
10. Briggs p.70, Royle 1997 p.121, Rule *Albions People* 1992 p.99 (from W. Bowden *Industrial Society in England* p.162)
11. Derry p.41
12. Weightman p.275
13. Price pp.2, 4, 5, 162, Price p.5 (from J.E.Manning *History of the Upper Chapel* 1900 pp.82-83)
14. Price p.3
15. Price pp.7 & 8
16. Wells p.9, Briggs p.24
17. Wells pp.8, 13, 15, Hey 2005 p.340
18. Wells pp.8 & 9
19. Wells p.9
20. Rule *Albion's People* 1992 p.27, Wells p.35 (from G.A.Williams *Artisans and San Culottes* 1968 p.58)
21. Price p.11
22. *Sheffield Register* 4 December 1789
23. Price p.8 (from A. Aspinal *The Early English Trade Unions* 1949 p.4)
24. Rule *Albion's People* 1992 p.173
25. Derry pp. 55 & 68
26. Price pp.14 & 15, Vallance pp. 236 & 237
27. Price p.15 (from Charlton Black E The Association: Britain's Extra-Parliamentary Political Organisations1769-1793 (1963) pp.223-4)
28. Vallance p.238, Price p.13 (from Charlton Black E *The Associations: Extra Parliamentary Political Organisations 1768-1793* (1963) p.61-62).
29. Price p.132 (from *Clarion Ramblers Handbook 1941-2* pp.70 & 71 and p.75)
30. Brooke and Kipling 2012 pp. 2 & 3, Mori p.92
31. Sheffield Register 8 June 1792
32. Briggs p.116, Price pp.15 & 16
33. Price p.16 Price p.10 (Report from Colonel de Lancey Deputy Adjutant to the Secretary of State for War 13 June 1792)

Chapter 6: War with France 1793–1802

1. Price pp.9 &17
2. Price p.18
3. Vallance p.264, Vallance p.239 (quoting Godwin *Friends of Liberty* p.164-7)
4. Brooke and Kipling 2012 p.9
5. Brooke and Kipling 2012 pp. 10 & 11
6. Vallance p.240
7. Wells p.2, Hey p.380
8. Wells pp.2-4 & p.15
9. Wells pp. 19-20 (from *Hull Advertiser* 6 March 1795)
10. Trevelyan p. 478, Brooke & Kipling 2012 p.13, *Leeds Mercury* 1 February 1800
11. Wells pp. 25-27
12. Wells pp. 26-27

13. Wells p.35
14. Wells p.2
15. Wrigley and Schofield
16. Valance p.268 (from Emsley *Britain and the French Revolution*. p.37)
17. Royle 2000 p.160 (from R.Wells *Wretched Faces: Famine in Wartime England 1793-1801* Sutton 1988 p.295)
18. Wells p.44
19. Vallance p.274
20. Wells p.4 & p.7, Royle 2000 p.160 (from R.Wells *Wretched Faces: Famine in Wartime England 1793-1801* Sutton 1988 p.313)
21. Wells p.34
22. Wells pp. 27-28, & p.41
23. Vallance p.272
24. Royle 1997 p.129, Wells pp.35 & 38
25. Brooke and Kipling 2012 p.20, Wells p.36
26. Evans p.23
27. Royle 2000 p 39 (from Wentworth Woodhouse Muniments F45a/12)
28. Brooke and Kipling 2012 p.25
29. Wells p.44, Lavery pp.167 & 168
30. Wells p.45

Chapter 7: The Move to Mirfield 1802–1803

1. Stott p.12
2. Hey p.354, Stott pp.10 & 18, Taylor *Nail Makers and their Successors in the Community of Darton Parish and Township* [Yorkshire Archaeological Journal Volume 63 1991] p.153
3. Tongue p.148
4. Stott p. 62
5. Hey pp.361 & 344, E.Thompson p.38 (from Richard Dennis, *English Industrial Cities of the Nineteenth Century* Cambridge 1984)
6. Plumb P. in An Historical Atlas of Hertfordshire Editor D.Short p.40
7. *Leeds Mercury* 6 December 1828
8. Plumb P. in An Historical Atlas of Hertfordshire Editor D.Short p.40
9. Stott p.7
10. Stott p.58
11. Stott p.51
12. Stott p.6
13. Stott p.7
14. Stott p.51
15. Stott p.50
16. Stott p.57
17. Stott p.38
18. Stott p.16
19. Pobjoy p.168
20. Reid p.13 (from Pobjoy p.135 & Cradock pp. 76–7), Price p.6
21. Thompson E. pp.416, 778 & 785, Trevelyan pp.377–379
22. Place (from F.E.Hyde *Mr Gladstone at the Board of Trade* London 1934 p.131)
23. *Northern Star* 21 January 1843
24. Stott p.43

Chapter 8: Growth of Radical Politics 1802 -1810

1. Orwell p.18, Royle 1996 p.1
2. Donnelly p.10

3. Royle 1997 p.2 & p.294
4. Schama vol 3 p.35
5. Pobjoy pp.141–2
6. Royle 1997 p.2
7. Royle 1997 p.216
8. Royle 1997 p.239
9. Cunningham pp.302 & 303, Royle 1997 p.242
10. Brooke & Kipling 2012 p.25
11. Wells p.45
12. Binfield p.52
13. Reid p.46, Binfield pp.51 & 52 (from *Before the Luddites* by Randle)
14. Binfield p.51
15. Reid p.280 (from Felkin p.51)
16. Brooke & Kipling 2012 p.20
17. Wells p. 45
18. Bailey pp.12 & 13, Brooke and Kipling p.24, Reid p.53
19. Reid p.49 (from F.Darvall p.19 quoting *Accounts and Papers 1812 x. 25*)
20. Reid p.50 (from Fitzwilliam MSS. F47/49 statement in support of the Petitions from the Merchants and Manufactures in the Woollen trade in the West Riding of Yorkshire)
21. Rule pp.363–368, Reid p.27
22. Bailey p.45, Reid p.29
23. Bailey p.26 (quoting *Manchester Exchange Herald* 21 April 1812)
24. Bailey p.27, Reid p.53, Royle 2000 p.39
25. Reid p.28 (from Engels The Condition of the Working Class in England p.205)
26. Hey 2005 p.343, Bailey p.125 (from Parliamentary debate XXXV 1817)

Chapter 9: Luddite Years 1811–1812

1. Royle 2000 p.161, Lowe p.13
2. Evans p.19, Brooke & Kipling 2012 p.91
3. Evans p.119
4. Reid pp.66–67
5. I am indebted to David Pinder for this information.
6. Binfield p.2, Reid pp. 58–59 (from Felkin p.236 and HO 42.120 Conant and Baker to Ryder 9 February 1812)
7. Bailey pp.42–43 & p.xiv, E.Thompson. p.65
8. Binfield pp.3 & 16
9. Binfield p.3
10. Reid pp.26–27
11. Thompson E. p.12
12. Private communication from Alan Brooke
13. *Leeds Mercury* 18 January 1812 & 14 March 1812
14. *Leeds Mercury* 25 January 1812, & *Leeds Intelligencer* 20 January 1812
15. Brooke & Kipling 2012 p.27
16. *Leeds Mercury* 29 February 1812, Reid p.74
17. *Leeds Mercury* 29 February 1812, Bailey p.44, Reid p.74
18. Reid pp.74–75
19. *Leeds Mercury* 29 February 1812, Darvall p.62, Reid p.75
20. HO 40.1/7 deposition of William Hinchcliffe 28 February 1812, Reid p.75
21. Brooke and Kipling 2012 pp.29–30.
22. Brooke & Kipling 2012 p.30 (from H.O. 40 1/1 (174-283) deposition of Sam Swallow)
23. *Leeds Mercury* 14 March 1812
24. Brooke & Kipling 2012 p.30, *Leeds Mercury* 14 March 1812

25. Binman p.211, Brooke & Kipling 2012 p.31
26. Brooke & Kipling 2012 p.31, Bailey p.47, Binman p.211 (from HO 42/121), Reid p.88
27. Binfield p. 208–9 (quoting Thomis *Luddites* p.184), Bailey pp.48-51, Brook and Kipling 2012 p.33
28. The full text is in Binfield p 209–210 (from HO.40/1/1)
29. Brooke & Kipling 2012 p.32, Reid p.100 (from *Manchester Gazette* 18 April 1812)
30. Binfield p.218 (from Peel *The Rising of the Luddites* p.120)
31. Reid p.97 (from Howell p.1161 & Peel p.54)
32. Reid pp.94 & 96
33. Bailey p.83
34. Reid p.98, Pobjoy p.108, personal communication from M. Bates
35. *Leeds Mercury* 18 April 1812, Vallance p.306-7, Bailey pp.54–55, Reid pp.108-117
36. Binman p.226 (from Peel *The Rising of the Luddites* p.120)
37. Brooke & Kipling 2012 p.47, *Leeds Mercury* 4 April 1812
38. *Leeds Mercury* 5 September 1812
39. Mori p.150, Vallance p.306, Robertson pp.32–33, Reid p.152, Lavery p.186
40. *Leeds Mercury* 25 April 1812
41. *Leeds Mercury* 25 April 1812
42. *Leeds Mercury* 2 May 1812: Note the eye witness accounts given by the *Leeds Mercury* differ greatly from the account in Reid pp. 135–136 who has taken his description from E.Baines *Proceedings under the Special Commission at York* [Baines Leeds 1813] who published his part-verbatim report the day after the trial. And T.Howell *State Trials xxxi* 1813 p.959 *et seq*
43. *Leeds Mercury* 9 May 1812
44. Reid p.158, *Leeds Mercury* 23 May 1812
45. Reid p.203 (from *The Times* 1 September 1812), *Leeds Mercury* 17 October 1812
46. *Leeds Mercury* 4 July 1812
47. *Leeds Mercury* 11 July 1812
48. Bailey p.65 (from Greenleaf & Hargreaves), Brooke & Kipling 2012 p.62
49. Bailey p.37
50. Reid p.169 (from HO 42.132)
51. Bailey p.94
52. *Leeds Mercury* 3 December 1812
53. *Leeds Mercury* 12 December 1812, Reid p.228 (from HO 40.2/8 Acland to Beckett 19 December 1812)
54. *Leeds Mercury* 22 August 1812

Chapter 10: York Castle 1813

1. Reid p.238 (from Baines p.52 and Howell p.971)
2. Bailey p.97, Reid pp.238–239
3. TS 11/812 2670 (author's punctuation with interpretation of 'musket' balls M; pistol balls P; fragments F.)
4. Bailey p.105 (from HO 42/128), *Leeds Mercury* 2 May 1812, Reid p.134
5. Reid p.239 (from Rede p.462)
6. Bailey pp.97–98, & 101
7. Reid p.259
8. Reid p.264
9. Reid p.252
10. Bailey p.103
11. Mingay p.28, Bailey pp 105–108, Brooke & Kipling 2012 p.44, Reid pp.19–20
12. H.Matthew *The Liberal Age* (in Morgan p.550)
13. Brooke & Kipling 2012 p.69, E.Thompson p.668, Vallance p.396–7

Chapter 11: Post War Years 1815–1819

1. Evans p.18
2. Watson p.572, Royle 2000 p.199
3. Vallance p.313–4
4. Vallance p.315
5. Royle 2000 p.49, *Leeds Mercury* 14 June 1817, Brooke & Kipling 2012 p.78
6. Brooke and Kipling 2012 p.78
7. Brooke & Kipling 2012 pp.78–79, *Leeds Mercury* 21 June 1817.
8. Royle p.58, Brooke & Kipling 2012 p.84
9. Brooke & Kipling 2012 p.85
10. Royle 2000 p.51, Brooke & Kipling 2012 p.86, *Leeds Mercury* 14 June 1817
11. Brook & Kipling 2012 p.87
12. Evans pp.20–21
13. Pobjoy pp.183–5
14. Bamford p.153
15. Vallance pp.327–342, Thompson E.pp.752–754
16. Vallance p.340
17. *Republican* 28 June 1822
18. Hey p.369, Reid p.21
19. TS 11/1013-4134 Joshua Hirst's statement, Brooke and Kipling 2012 pp.93–95
20. Thompson E. p.922 (from Rev T Westmoreland Vicar of Sandal nr. Wakefield 10 December 1819 H.O.42. 200)
21. Aspinal and Smith p.335, Lowe pp.22–23, Thompson E. p.768
22. Royle p 55
23. Donnelly (quoting *Wakefield and Halifax Journal* 16 July 1819)
24. Brooke & Kipling 2012 p.99
25. Brooke & Kipling 2012 p.99

Chapter 12: The West Yorkshire Rebellion of 1820

1. Brooke & Kipling 2012 p.100
2. Brooke & Kipling 2012 pp.98–99.
3. Brooke & Kipling pp.99–100, Evans p.28
4. TS 11/1013 4131 (George and Ben Barker's statements), Brooke & Kipling 2012 p.100
5. TS 11/1013-4131 (Samuel Norcliffe's statement), Brooke & Kipling 2012 p.100
6. Brooke & Kipling 2012 pp.100–101
7. TS 11/1013-4131 (Joshua Hirst's Statement), Brooke & Kipling 2012 p.101
8. TS 11/1013-4132, Brooke & Kipling 2012 p.101
9. TS 11/1013-4132
10. TS 11/1013-4132, Brooke & Kipling 2012 p.102, Rede p.649
11. Brooke & Kipling p.104
12. TS 11/1013-4134, Brooke & Kipling 2012 p.104
13. TS 11/1013 4132 (George Barker's statement).
14. TS 11/1013-4132 (Hannah Schofield's statement), Brooke & Kipling 2012 p.105
15. TS 11/1013-4134 (Evidence of Robert Tolson, John Hinchcliffe and Thomas Kilner)
16. TS 11/1013-4134 (Joshua Hirst's statement), Brooke & Kipling 2012 p.108
17. Brooke & Kipling 2012 pp.105–106
18. Brooke & Kipling 2012 p.106
19. TS 11/1013 - 4132, Brooke & Kipling 2012 p.108
20. TS 11/1013-4132 (statements by Jonathan Parrot and John Hardcastle), Brooke & Kipling 2012 p.107
21. TS 11/1013-4131
22. Brooke & Kipling 2012 p.109

23. Brooke & Kipling 2012 p.110
24. TNA HO 20/1 (Home Office papers Petition to Sidmouth 29 May 1820).
25. TS 11/1013-4131
26. Rede p.649
27. Rede p.656
28. Evans p.29
29. *Leeds Mercury* 5 October 1822
30. *Leeds Mercury* 14 September 1820
31. Rede p.656

Chapter 13: Transportation 1821–1828

1. West p.347
2. West p.60 & p.541
3. The account of the voyage is taken from 'Diary of the *Lady Ridley* TNA ADM 101 42/2
4. West p.61
5. TAHO CS01/1/403 9108
6. TSA. Colonial Secretary's Office 1/267/6396, Donnelly p.8
7. Hughes p.368 (convict ballad ca. 1825-30)
8. West p.58 & p.566
9. West pp.59, 60, 75, 81, 568, & 573
10. West p.144, Hughes p.385
11. Hughes p.200
12. New South Wales Archives
13. *Historical Records of Australia*, series III, volume V, pp. 452 & 453
14. Evans p.23
15. TAHO CON 31/1/27
16. TNA HO 10/46
17. West p.436, Private correspondence from Peter Thomas of Darwin & Harold Taylor
18. *The Hobart Town Courier* (Tas. 1827 – 1839) 12 July 1828 p.3 Nicholson pp. 143–144
19. *The Hobart Town Courier* (Tas. 1827 – 1839) 16 October 1835 p 3 I am indebted to Peter Thomas for this information

Chapter 14: Tasmanian Twelve

1. TNA HO 20/1, & HO 11/979 3573, TAHO Con 31-1-9, Personal communication from Peter Thomas of Darwin
2. TAHO Con Record 31-1-1, Peter Thomas (from Kirk, Harrison and Burland pp. 395 & 399), Donnelly (from TNA HO 10/45 list of convicts in V.D.L 1823), Information supplied by Harold Taylor from local Sheffield newspaper.
3. Anderson & Shiell *Montserrat to Melbourne* [Published by Anderson & Shiell, Melbourne 1984], *Life of Hannah Burkinshaw – Mrs William Shiell – 1832-1892* I am indebted to Peter Thomas for both these articles
4. Peter Thomas (from Burland *Annals of Barnsley* pp.399), Donnelly (from TNA HO 10/45)
5. Donnelly (from TNA HO 10/45), Personal communication from Peter Thomas
6. *Colonial Times* Wednesday 21 May 1834, TAHO Con 31-1-13, Donnelly (from TNA HO 10/45). Visit by Peter Thomas to site
7. TAHO Con 31-1-18, Donnelly (from TNA HO 10/45)
8. TAHO Con 31-1-34, Donnelly (from TNA HO 10/45)
9. Peter Thomas personal communication, Donnelly (from TNA HO 10/45)
10. TNA RG 4/3645, Donnelly (from TNA HO 10/45)
11. Peter Thomas (from Burland *Annals of Barnsley* p.399), Donnelly (from TNA HO 10/45)
12. Hughes p.197

Chapter 15: Return to England 1828

1. Wood p.31
2. Stott p.10
3. Pobjoy pp.34 & 147, Hey 2005 p.350
4. Stott pp.53 & 55
5. Stott p.56
6. Stott p.3
7. Stott p.62
8. Pobjoy pp.37, 96 & 182
9. Brontë C. *Shirley* p.372
10. Gaskell p.300
11. Gaskell p.74
12. Stott p.17
13. Stott pp.18, 35 & 39
14. Pobjoy p.81, Stott p.40
15. Lowe p.32, *The Times* 29 November 1828
16. Armstrong p.108

Chapter 16: The Great Reform Bill of 1832

1. Delderfield p.120
2. Lovell p.357
3. Leeds Mercury 3 January 1835, Driver Tory Radical: The Life of Richard Oastler 1946
4. Rule *Vital Century* 1992 pp. 146–147
5. Royle 2000 p.158 (from *Leeds Intelligencer* 3 May 1832, *Leeds Mercury* 28 April & 5 May 1832
6. Royle p.11, Cook & Stevenson p. 90
7. Royle 2000 p.160 (from C.A.Hulbert *Annals of the Church in Slaithwaite*)
8. Trevelyan pp.541–2, *Northern Star* 3 June 1848
9. *Leeds Mercury* 16 October 1830
10. *Leeds Mercury* 23 October 1830
11. Gammage p.55, Lowe pp.168 & 171, Vallance p.370
12. Lovett p.364, Lowe pp.348–9 (Conditions from Marlow *Tolpuddle Martyr*)
13. Royle 1996 p.54 (from N.C. Edsall, *The Anti-Poor Law Movement 1834-1844* Manchester University Press 1871)
14. Tomalin p.82
15. Tongue pp.235–236, Armstrong pp.99 & 101
16. *Northern Star* 12 May 1838
17. Stott p.38
18. *The Times* 18 May 1837, *Leeds Mercury* 20 May 1837, Royle 1966 p.22
19. Royle 2000 p.97–98 (from Edsall *The Anti-Poor Law Movement*).
20. Royle 2000 p.98–100 (from *Northern Star*)
21. Vallance p.373
22. Delderfield p.124
23. Royle 1996 p.19, Royle 2000 p.97

Chapter 17: Adult Health

1. Porter 1987 pp. 9–10
2. Porter 2003 p.20
3. Porter 1988 p.26 (from F.Bottomley *Attitudes to the body in Western Christendom* Lepus Books 1979)
4. Porter 1988 p.22
5. Porter 1988 pp.26–27

6. Porter 1988 p.26 (from Porter *English Society in The Eighteenth Century* Harmsworth, Penguin 1982)
7. Porter 1988 p.28
8. Porter 1988 p.35
9. Porter 1987 p.34, Porter 2003 p.100
10. Porter 2003 p.100
11. Hayley The Healthy Body and Victorian Culture
12. Lowe p.179
13. Lowe p.178, Morgan p.500
14. Royle 1997 p.344, Gilbert pp.83–84
15. Lowe p.178
16. Caffyn p.88
17. Spink p.209
18. Walton p.369, Spink pp.322-3
19. Spink p.240
20. Spink pp.9 & 149, Bynum p.75
21. Bynum pp.73–74
22. Hey pp.348–351
23. Spink p.207
24. Spink pp. 304–307
25. Spink p.310
26. Spink pp.417–418, For case study see *Leeds Mercury* Jan 1807
27. Spink p.350
28. Porter 1987 pp.45–46 (from Kathleen Jones *A history of mental health* Routledge and Keegan Paul 1972)
29. Porter 1987 p.44
30. *Leeds Mercury* January 1807, Porter 1987 pp.45–46
31. Porter 1987 pp.45–46
32. Porter 2003 pp.45–50

Chapter 18: Chartism 1837–1840

1. Vallance p.369, Royle 2000 p. 94, Royle 1996 pp.6–7, *Northern Star* 29 September 1838 (reporting a speech on Kersal Moor 24 September 1838)
2. Royle 2000 p.96
3. Harrison p 153, Royle 2000 p.95
4. Royle 1996 p.36
5. Royle 1996 p.36
6. Royle 1996 pp.76–77
7. Gammage p.51
8. Gammage pp.411–426.
9. Lowe pp.77–78
10. Royle 2000 p.93
11. *Northern Star* 16 October 1838
12. Harrison pp.130 & 156
13. Brook p.1 (from Whole Hog–Huddersfield Chartism 1838–1855 by Alan J Brooke)
14. Lowe p.82, for list of grievances see Gammage p.64
15. Royle 1996 pp.24 & 82, Brooke p.9, *Northern Star* 12 January 1839
16. *Leeds Mercury* 20 October 1838
17. Gammage pp.94 & 98, *Northern Star* 10 November 1938
18. Gammage pp.100-101, *Northern Star* 5 January 1839
19. Gammage p.105

20. Royle 1996 p.25 (from F.C.Mather *Public Order in the Age of the Chartists* Manchester University Press 1859)
21. Gammage pp.106–109
22. Royle 1996 pp.24–25 & 80
23. Royle 1997 p.251
24. *Leeds Mercury* 25 May 1839
25. Gammage pp.113–114
26. Gammage p.117
27. Lowe p.79, Gammage pp 138-143, Royle 1996 p.26
28. Vallance pp.379–380 (from Pickering *Chartist Petitioning*)
29. Vallance p.383, Royle 1996 p.26
30. Browne pp.62–63, *Northern Star* August 1839
31. Gammage p.153, *Leeds Mercury* 17 August 1839
32. Harold Taylor personal communication
33. Valance pp. 283–284
34. Browne p.48, Vallance p.385, *The Times* 14 January 1840
35. Royle 2000 pp.103 & 108

Chapter 19: Law and Order in the early Nineteenth Century

1. Royle 2000 p.183
2. Royle 2000 p.182 (from PRO HO 45/264 fos 288-9), Walton p. 379
3. Royle 2000 p.176
4. Royle 2000 p.176; (1 George I cap 5)
5. Royle 2000 p.176
6. Royle 2000 p.181 (from *The Journal of Charles James Napier* vol. 2 p.15 August 1939).
7. Royle 2000 pp.177–178
8. Royle 2000 p.186 (from *The Journal of Charles James Napier,* vol. 2 p.4 March 1939)
9. Royle 1996 p.55, Royle 2000 p.185 (from report to select committee 1844)

Chapter 20: Chartism in the Hungry Forties 1840–1842

1. Price p.47 (from P. Mathis *The First Industrial Nation* (1969) p.236)
2. Peacock pp 23–24 & p.38 (from *Leeds Mercury* 18 January 1840), *The Times* 14 January 1840
3. Peacock p.36 (from W Napier *Life of Charles James Napier* London 1857 vol. 2 p.113)
4. Gammage pp.153 & 173, *The Times* 14th January 1840
5. Price p.45
6. Price p.46, Vallance p.385
7. Peacock p.24 (from *Bradford Observer* 23 January 1840)
8. *Bradford Observer* 30 January 1840
9. Browne p.127, Gammage p 173, Peacock pp 23–25 (from *Bradford Observer* 30 January 1840 and 6 February 1840 & *York Herald* 1 February 1840)
10. Valance p.369 (from Chase *Chartism* p.22)
11. Thompson F. p 45
12. Vallance p.384–385, Royle 1996 p.27
13. Vallance p.387, *Northern Star* 1 August 1840
14. Vallance p.397 (from Chase *Chartism* p.183)
15. Gammage p190–192, Vallance p.396
16. Lowe p.72, Gammage pp.193–5
17. Vallance p.393
18. *Northern Star* 11 September 1841
19. Lowe p.81, Gammage p.209, Vallance p.399

Chapter 21: Plug Plot of 1842

1. *Leeds Mercury* January 1842]
2. Royle 1996 p.30, Lowe p.81, Cook & Stevenson p.193, Vallance p.401
3. *Leeds Mercury* 20 August 1842
4. *Leeds Mercury* 20 August 1842
5. *Leeds Mercury* 20 August 1842, *The Times* 16 August 1842
6. *The Times* 16 August 1842
7. *Leeds Mercury* 20 August 1842
8. *Leeds Mercury* 20 August 1842
9. *Northern Star* 10 Sept 1842, *Leeds Mercury* 20 August 1842
10. *Northern Star* 10 Sept 1842
11. *Leeds Mercury* 20 August 1842
12. *Northern Star* 20 August 1842
13. *Northern Star* 20 August 1842
14. *Northern Star* 20 August 1842, *Leeds Mercury* 20 August 1842
15. *Northern Star* 20 August 1842
16. *Leeds Mercury* 20 August 1842
17. *Northern Star* 20 August 1842
18. Stott p.7
19. *Leeds Mercury* 20 August 1842
20. *Leeds Mercury* 20 August 1842
21. *Northern Star* 20 August 1842
22. *Leeds Mercury* 20 August 1842
23. *The Times* 17 August 1842
24. *The Times* 17 August 1842
25. *The Times* 16 August 1842
26. *Northern Star* 10 Sept 1842
27. *Northern Star* 10 Sept 1842
28. Gammage p.224
29. *Northern Star* 20 August 1842
30. Chase *Chartism* p. 223, Vallance p.403

Chapter 22: Social Reform 1802–1850

1. *Leeds Mercury* 29 September 1830
2. Cooper p.68
3. Hey 2005 p.347, Lowe pp.175–6
4. Hey 2005 p.369
5. Hey 2005 p.370, With special thanks to Alan Brooke (p.5) for this information
6. Lowe p.143
7. Hey 2005 p.369
8. Thompson D. p.31 (from R Groves But We Shall Rise Again: a narrative History of Chartism London 1939 p.27)
9. Gammage p.269
10. Armstrong pp.100–101
11. Gammage pp.271–272

Chapter 23: Chartist Disillusionment 1848.

1. Gammage p.206, Lowe p.81, Royle 1996 p.19
2. Gammage p.332
3. Royle 2000 p.128 (from D. Thompson *Outsiders*)
4. Lowe p.82, Gammage p.285
5. Cook & Stevenson p.193, Royle p.44

6. Gammage p.318, Vallance p.422
7. Gammage pp.329–331, Lowe p.83
8. Royle 2000 p.199 (from B.R.Mitchell *Abstract of British Historical Statistics* CUP 1962)
9. Gammage pp.332–333, *The Times* 31 May 1848
10. *Northern Star* 10 June 1848, Gammage p.333
11. Royle 2000 p.132 (from Wright *Chartist Risings in Bradford* p.49)
12. *Northern Star* 3 June 1848 (from *The Times*), Browne pp.103–5
13. *Northern Star* 3 June 1848, Gammage p.333
14. *Northern Star* 3 June 1848, Royle 2000 p.133
15. Gammage p.333, Browne p.135, *Northern Star* 20 May 1848 & 3 June 1848
16. Gammage p.334, Royle 2000 p.134 (from Wright *Chartist Risings in Bradford*)
17. Gammage pp.334 & 354–355, *Northern Star* 10 June 1848
18. Gammage p.390
19. Gammage p.391
20. Royle 1996 p.93

Chapter 24: The Twilight Years in Mirfield 1838 –1853

1. *Leeds Mercury* 23 October 1830
2. Hoyle p.36
3. Pobjoy p.189, Hoyle p.36
4. Stott p.64
5. *Leeds Mercury* 25 May 1839
6. Hey 2003 pp.120 & 123
7. Royle 1997 p.335 (from T.Frost *Forty Years Recollections* 1880 p.225)
8. Royle 1997 p.192
9. Lindley Papers held by author
10. Royle 1997 pp. 93 & 193, F.Thompson vol.1 p.48, Rule *Vital Century* p.23
11. Lindley Papers
12. Mori p.147, Lindley Papers
13. Stott p.24
14. Nolan p.29
15. *Northern Star* 17 November 1849

Epilogue.

1. http://hansard.millbanksystems.com/commons/1856/jul/22/political-exiles-question

BIBLIOGRAPHY

Anderson D. & Shiell R. *Montserrat to Melbourne* [Published by Anderson & Shiell, Melbourne 1984]
Armitage E. *The Way We Lived Then* [Robson Books 2001]
Andrews C.R. *The Story of Wortley Ironworks* [The South Yorkshire Times Printing Company Ltd. 1950]
Armstrong W.A. in *The Cambridge Social History of Britain volume 1* Editor F.M.L. Thompson [Cambridge University Press 1990]
Aspinall A. & Smith E. *English Historical Documents XI 1783-1832* [Eyre & Spottiswoode 1959]
Bailey B. *The Luddite Rebellion* [Sutton Publishing 1998]
BBC The Great Turning Points in British History [Constable and Robinson 2009]
Bamford S. *Passages in the life of a Radical* [Simpkin Marshall & Co London; Abel Haywood Manchester 1859]
Berridge V. in *The Cambridge Social History of Britain volume 3* Editor F.M.L. Thompson [Cambridge University Press 1990]
Binfield K. *The Writings of the Luddites* [John Hopkins University Press 2004]
Black J. An Illustrated History of eighteenth-century Britain 1688-1793 [Manchester University Press 1996]
Bodey H. *Nail Making* [Shire Publications 1983]
Briggs A. *The Age of Improvement 1783–1867* [Pearson Education 2000]
Brontë C. *Shirley* [Oxford World Classics Oxford University Press New Edition 2007]
Brook R. *The Story of Huddersfield* [Macgibbon and Kee, London, 1968]
Brooke A. *The Whole Hog Huddersfield Chartism 1838–1855* [from Brooke A. The Social and Political Response to Industrialisation in the Huddersfield Area c1790-1850 unpublished PhD thesis 1988]
Brooke A. & Kipling L. *Liberty or Death* [Workers' History Publications 1993]
Brooke A. Magdale & Steps: Life and Industry in a Textile Hamlet [Brooke 2008]
Browne H. *Chartism* [Hodder & Stoughton 2004]
Bynum W. The History of Medicine; a very short introduction [Oxford University Press 2008]
Caffyn L. Workers' Housing in West Yorkshire 1750–1920 [London HMSO 1986]
Cook C. & Stevenson J. *Modern British History* [Pearson Education 4th ed. 2001]
Cooper L. *Yorkshire West Riding* [Robert Hale 1950]
Cradock H.*A. History of the Ancient Parish of Birstall, Yorkshire* [Society for Promoting Christian Knowledge 1933]
Cunningham H. in *The Cambridge Social History of Britain volume 2* Editor F.M.L. Thompson [Cambridge University Press 1990]
Darvall F. Popular Disturbances in Regency England: Being an Account of the Luddite and other Disorders in England during the Years 1811–1817 [Scholars Book Shelf 1934]
Dearnley J. *The Nailmakers of Mapplewell and Staincross* [Cutting Edge Journal of the South Yorkshire Industrial History Society written in the 1940s]
Delderfield E.R. *Kings & Queens of England & Great Britain* [David & Charles 3rd ed. 1998]
Dillon C. *The Nail Makers of Hoylandswaine* [Hoylandswaine History Group 2000]
Donnelly F. *The Yorkshire Rebellion of 1820* [Albion Magazine Online Summer 2007]
Drake F. Global Warming: The Science of Climate Change (London Arnold 2000)
Evans E. *Britain Before the Reform Act 1815-1832* [2nd ed. Pearson Education 2008]

Felkin W.A. History of the Machine Wrought Hosiery and Lace Manufactures [Longmans Green 1867]
Finnis B. Captain James Cook: Seaman and Scientist [Chaucer Press 2003]
Freedman A. *Georgiana: Duchess of Devonshire* [Harper Collins 1999]
Gammage R.G.. *History of the Chartist Movement* [Merlin Press Ltd. 1969 reprint of original 1854 edition]
Gaskell E. *The Life of Charlotte Brontë* [Dent & Sons Everyman's Edition 1982]
Gilbert E.W. *British Pioneers in Geography* [David & Charles 1972]
Haley B. *The Healthy Body and Victorian Culture* [Cambridge Mass: Harvard University Press 1978]
Hargreaves J.A. *Methodism and Luddites in Yorkshire* [Northern History Volume XXVI 1990]
Harrison J.F.C. *Early Victorian Britain 1832-51* [Fontana Press 1988]
Hayman R. Ironmaking. The History and Archaeology of the Iron Industry [Tempus Publishing 2005]
Hey D. *The Oxford Guide to Family History* [Oxford University Press 2002]
Hey D. *How our Ancestors Lived* [The National Archives second edition 2003]
Hey D. A History of Yorkshire [Carnegie 2005]
Hoyle F. *Home is Where the Wind Blows* [University Science Books 1994]
Hughes R. *The Fatal Shore* [Collins Harvill 1987]
Hyde F.E. Mr Gladstone at the Board of Trade [London 1934]
Jackson R *Sailing Ships* [private communication]
Jenkins J. and Evans E. *Victorian Social Life* [John Murray 2002]
Joyce P. in *The Cambridge Social History of Britain volume 2* Editor F.M.L. Thompson [Cambridge University Press 1990]
Landes D. *The Cambridge Economic History of Europe*, [Cambridge University Press Vol. VI, Part I 1966]
Lavery B. *Empire of the Seas* [Conway 2009]
Lloyd's List November 1828
Log of Lady Ridley: [Ships Log] [ADM 101 40/2; Reel No 3200 AJCP Microfilm] including: Master James Weir's Log, and Journal of the Surgeon Superintendent, James Wilson RN
Lowe N. *Modern British History* [Palgrave MacMillan 4th Edition 2009]
Mellor G. *George Mellor & the Yorkshire Luddites* [Unpublished lecture 18 Nov. 2006]
Mingay G.E. *Rural Life in Victorian England* [Sutton Publishing 1998]
Mori J. Britain in the Age of the French Revolution [Pearson Education Ltd 2000]
Morgan K. Editor *The Oxford History of Britain* [Oxford Univerity Press 2001]
Newsom Sidney Carleton Editor *Poems from Shelley and Keats* [MacMillan 1923]
Nicholson I.H. Shipping Arrivals & Departures Tasmania 1803-1833 [Roebuck 1983]
Nolan P. Crossroads: The End of Wild Capitalism & the Future of Humanity [Marshall Cavendish 2009]
Orwell G. *The Road to Wigan Pier* [Penguin Modern Classics 2001]
Peacock A.J. *Bradford Chartism* [St Anthony's Press 1969 Borthwick Papers Number 36]
Pobjoy H.N. *A History of Mirfield* [The Ridings Publishing Company 1969]
Pobjoy H.N. The Story of the Ancient Parish of Hartshead-cum-Clifton [Ridings Publishing Co., 1972]
Porter R. Disease, Medicine and Society in England 1550–1860 [Macmillan Education 1987]
Porter R. and Porter D. In Sickness and in Health: The British Experience 1650-1850 [Fourth Estate 1988]
Porter R. Blood and Guts: A Short History of Medicine [Penguin Books 2003]
Price D. Sheffield Troublemakers: Rebels and Radicals in Sheffield History [Phillimore 2011]
Reid R. Land of Lost Content: Luddite Rebellion of 1812 [William Heinemann Ltd. 1986]
Rede W.L. The History of York Castle in the Nineteenth Century [J.Saunders 1870]
Robertson I.C. Wellington at war in the Peninsula [Pen & Sword 2000]
Royle E. Radical Politics 1790–1900: Religion and Unbelief [Longman 1971]

Royle E. *Chartism* [Addison Wesley Longman 3rd edition 1996]
Royle E. *Modern Britain: A Social History 1750–1997* [Arnold, Hodder Group, 2nd edition 1997]
Royle E. *Revolutionary Britannia* [Manchester University Press 2000]
Rule J. The Labouring Classes in early Industrial England 1750-1850 [Longman 1986]
Rule J. The Vital Century: England's Developing Economy 1714-1815 [Longman 1992]
Rule J. Albion's People: English Society 1714–1815 [Longman 1992]
Schama S. *A History of Britain* [volume 3 BBC 2002]
Short D. Editor *An Historical Atlas of Hertfordshire* [Hertfordshire Publications 2011]
Spoerl J.S. A Brief History of Iron and Steel Production [Wikipedia.org]
Spink W. Infectious Diseases; Prevention and Treatment in the Nineteenth and Twentieth Centuries [Folkestone: Wm Dawson & Sons 1978]
Stamp A.H. A Social and Economic History of England from 1700–1970 [Research Publishing Co. 1979]
State Library of Tasmania & Tasmanian Archive & Heritage Office [TAHO]
Stott F. *Looking Back at Mirfield* [Greenfield House Publishing 2000]
Sutherland G. in *The Cambridge Social History of Britain volume 3* Editor F.M.L. Thompson [Cambridge University Press 1990]
Taylor H. Nails, Mules, Music and Miners: Village Life in Mapplewell and Staincross Through the Nineteenth Century [Aspects of Barnsley volume 6 chapter 7 Editor B.Elliott, Wharncliffe Publishing]
Taylor H. *John Spark: South Yorkshire Chapman of Three Centuries Ago* [Aspects of Barnsley volume 6 chapter 10 Editor B.Elliott, Wharncliffe Publishing]
Taylor H. Nail Makers and their Successors in the Community of Darton Parish and Township [Yorkshire Archaeological Journal Volume 63 1991]
Tomalin C. *Charles Dickens: a life* [W F Howes Ltd. 2011 large print]
Thomas P. Dupes of Artful and Designing Men [Ancestor Winter 1992]
Thompson D. Outsiders: Class, Gender and Nation [Verso 1993]
Thompson E.P. The Making of the English Working Class [Penguin 1991]
Thompson F.M.L. in *The Cambridge Social History of Britain volume 2* Editor F.M.L. Thompson [Cambridge University Press 1990]
Tonge N. Industrialisation and Society 1700-1914 [Thomas Nelson & Sons 1993]
Tranter N. Population since the Industrial Revolution [Croom Helm 1973]
Trevelyan G.M. *English Social History* [Penguin 2000]
Turton K. *A Grim Almanac of South Yorkshire* [Sutton Publishing 2004]
Vallance E. *A Radical History of Britain* [Little, Brown 2009]
Walton J. *The Nail Makers of Darton* [Yorkshire Life Volume 2 No 6 October/December 1950 taken from notes by J.R.Wilkinson]
Walton J.K. in *The Cambridge Social History of Britain* volume 1 Editor F.M.L. Thompson [Cambridge University Press 1990]
Watson J.S. The Oxford History of England volume XII: The Reign of George III 1760-1815 [Clarendon Press 1960]
Weightman G. The Industrial Revolutionaries: The Creation of the Modern World 1776–1914 [Atlantic Books 2007]
Wells R.A.E. *Dearth and Distress in Yorkshire 1793-1802* [St Anthony's Press 1977 Borthwick Papers No 52 1977]
West J. *The History of Tasmania* [Launceston 1852 Reprint editor. A.G.I. Shaw Sydney 1971]
'West Yorkshire Rebellion 1820' (From *The Annals of Yorkshire From the Earliest Period to the Present Time*. Vol. 1 Compiler H. Schroeder 1851) [Google eBooks Chapter IX p.226]
Willetts A. *The Black Country Nail Trade* [Dudley Leisure Services 1987]
Wood G.B. *Yorkshire Villages* [Robert Hale & Co. Ltd. 1971]
Wrigley E.A. & Schofield R.S. The Population History of England 1541–1871 [London 1981]

Web Sites http://www.archives.tas.gov.au

CHRONOLOGY

1770 The birth of John Lindley.
1770 April 29. James Cook secures the eastern coast of Australia for the crown.
1770 James Watt patents his steam engine that inaugurated the industrial revolution.
1776. Adam Smith's Enquiry into the Causes of the Wealth of Nations published.
1776. Declaration of American Independence.
1780 Gordon Riots.
1780 Foundation of Sunday Schools Movement by Thomas Raikes.
1789 July 14. French people storm the Bastille.
1790 Edmund Burke's Reflections on Revolution in France published.
1791 Thomas Paine's *Rights of Man* published.
1792. Mary Wollstonecraft's *Vindication of the Rights of Women* published.
1793 January 21. French execute Louis XVI.
1793-1802 Construction of the Air-Calder Navigation (canal).
1794–6 Economic crisis.
1795 Speenhamland system of outdoor relief introduced.
1795 Jacob Perkins patents nail making machine.
1796 Enclosure Act in Mirfield.
1796 Vaccination against smallpox introduced.
1798 T.R.Malthus's *Essay on Population* published.
1799 Combination Act preventing large meetings.
1802 March 25. Treaty of Amiens – a pause in the French Wars.
1803 General Enclosure Act.
1805 October 21. Battle of Trafalgar and death of Nelson.
1806 November. Napoleon's 'Berlin Decree' closing European Ports to British Shipping.
1807 24 Orders in council affecting trade with neutral ports in Europe and America.
1811 February. Luddite disturbances in Nottinghamshire followed by Yorkshire and Lancashire.
1812 April 11. Attack on Rawfolds Mill when two Luddites were killed.
1812 April 28. William Horsfall shot and killed by Luddites.
1813 January 2. Start of the show trial of Yorkshire Luddites at York Castle.
1813 January 16. Execution of 14 Yorkshire Luddites.
1815 June 18. Battle of Waterloo.
1815 Corn Laws introduced setting the price of corn at 80s a quarter–to subsidise small farmers.
1817 The Savings Bank (England) Act.
1817 March 10. Blanketeers from Manchester march on London.
1817 April (late). Folly Hall Rising.
1819 August 16. The Peterloo Massacre in Manchester killing 11 and wounding over 400 people.
1819 August 19. Protest meeting at Almondbury Park Yorkshire 'attended by thousands'.
1820 January 29. George III died but was not missed by the workers of northern England.
1820 The West Yorkshire Rebellion in Barnsley and Huddersfield.
1820 April 1. Arthur Thistlewood (leader of Cato Conspiracy) hanged.
1820 March 31 and April 1. The first Huddersfield Rising.

1820 April 11. The second Grange Moor Rising.
1820 July 15. Treason Trial at York Castle commences.
1820 September 11. delayed Treason Trial of Yorkshire insurgents ended.
1820 November 18. John Lindley and other prisoners moved to Portsmouth.
1821 January 23. Lady Ridley sets sail from Dartmouth (not Falmouth).
1821 June 27. Lady Ridley arrives in Hobart.
1825 Stockton and Darlington railway opens.
1828 John Lindley returns home.
1829-1830 Economic crisis with banks failing.
1830-1831 Swing riots in in southern England against mechanisation of agriculture.
1830-1832 First major cholera epidemic in England.
1830 June 26. death of George IV.
1830 Liverpool and Manchester railway opens.
1832 Great Reform Bill under Lord Grey followed by the great liberal betrayal.
1832 The Easter Pilgrimage to York.
1833 Factory Act restrictions on child labour.
1834 Slavery officially abolished in British Empire.
1834 Parish workhouses instituted – the Huddersfield response.
1834 March 17. Six 'Tolpuddle martyrs' sentenced to transportation.
1834 Poor Law Amendment Act.
1835 Municipal Reform Act.
1837 May 16. Poor Law meeting at Peep Green.
1837 June 20. William IV died.
1838 October 15. Chartist meeting at Peep Green.
1839 May 7. First Chartist petition.
1839 May 21. Second Chartist meeting at Peep Green.
1839 July 9. First public demonstration of electric telegraph.
1839 Rural Police Acts.
1839 November 4. Newport (Gwent) Large demonstration – fourteen killed. Leaders transported.
1840 Penny Post instituted.
1842 Mines Act: Response to the Silkstone coalmine disaster in 1838.
1840-1842. The hungry forties.
1842. All 19 chartist candidates in Sheffield elected for council seats.
1842 May 2. Second Chartist petition.
1842 August 13 Plug plot riots in Huddersfield.
1844 Peels Factory Act reduced working hours but failed to meet the 10 hour demand.
1846 Corn Laws abolished.
1847 Factory Act in response to a trade depression.
1948 Public Health Act.
1848 April 10. Third Chartist petition.
1848 May 26 Bradford Insurrection.
1848 October 15. Peep Green protest meeting.
1850 Factory Act to meet the shortcomings of the 1847 Act.
1851 Great Exhibition in London. Over six million people attend.
1852 July. The last general election of John Lindley's life – he still had failed to win the vote.
1853 November (mid). The death of John Lindley age 83.
1856 July 22. Posthumous pardon.

INDEX OF NAMES

Ackroyd, Edward (worsted manufacturer), 170
Ackroyd, John (mill owner), 176
Acland Major General (second-in-command), 86
Addy Richard (Yorkshire rebel of Barnsley), 106, 107, 113, 114, 124, **126**, 195
Albrecht Rev. Henry S. (Baptist minister of Knowl Chapel), 135
Alexander Mrs Cecil Frances (hymn writer), 21
Alexander Private (Huddersfield Yeomanry Cavalry), 95
Allen James (informer from Rotherham), 168
Andrew David (passenger on Lang), 125
Anson Benjamin (Yorkshire rebel), 109
Arkwright Richard (inventor powered spinning machine), 74
Armitage Ben (Yorkshire rebel of Mirfield), 104
Armytage Captain (Huddersfield Yeomanry Cavalry), 95
Armytage Sir George (Mirfield landowner), 67, 103
Arthur Sir George (Lieutenant-Governor Van Diemen's Land), 121, 124
Arthur Wellesley. *See* Wellington Duke of
Ashley Lord (House of Lords, introduced Mines Act 1842), 182
Ashton Joseph (linen weaver), 127
Ashton Margaret (daughter of Joseph Ashton), 127
Ashton William (Chartist of Barnsley), 162

Asquith Henry Herbert (prime minister 1908-1916), 64, 138
Athorpe R.A (CO Sheffield Volunteer Infantry), 50
Atkinson Thomas (owner Bradley Mill), 69
Attlee Clement (prime minister (1945-1951), 92
Attwood Thomas (Birmingham politician), 137, 161
Bagguley John (leader Blanketeers), 93
Bagley Sir John (Judge), 110
Bailey Brian (author), 80
Baines Edward (editor Leeds Mercury), 73, 138, 143, 157, 158, 159
Baines James (coachman), 59
Baines John (local radical philosopher), 79, 91
Baker Dr Robert (factory inspector of Leeds), 13, 148
Baker Mr (Northern Star reporter), 178
Balderstone James (owner of shearing shop), 76
Ball Moses (of Gilley Royd), 87
Ball Mr (passenger on Lang), 125
Bamford Samuel (Peterloo commentator), 97
Banks Joseph (botanist later FRS), 3
Banson Marmaduke (witness), 106
Bard Samuel (American physician), 10
Barker Ben (blacksmith, son of Joseph), 104
Barker George (Chartist of Huddersfield), 106
Barker Job (blacksmith, son of Joseph), 105

Barker Joseph (blacksmith of Colne Bridge), 102, 111
Barraclough Corporal (Agbrigg Militia), 86
Batley John (coal miner), 89
Bayley Mr Justice (judge), 111, 113
Beaumont George (of Darton Hall), 16
Beaumont R.H. (land owner and magistrate), 49
Beckett Lieutenant-Colonel (17th Yorkshire Hussars), 173
Beevers George (apprentice of James Seddon), 107
Bellingham John (assassin of prime minister Spencer), 85
Bentham Jeremy (philosopher), 66, 72, 141
Bingley Mr (Leeds Times reporter), 178
Birley Hugh (factory owner), 97
Blackburn Mr (defence attorney at York), 111
Blackburn Thomas (Yorkshire rebel of Wasp Nest), 109, 110, 111, 113, 116, 122, 123
Blackwell John (Sheffield Luddite), 84
Blackwood Archibald (Australian academic), 128
Boot Jesse (pharmacist), 153
Booth John (Luddite), 82
Booth Jonathan (Halifax victim of Army), 178
Boulton Mathew (entrepreneur), 5
Box Godfrey (introduced slitting mills), 27
Bradley (informant), 95
Bramwell William (Methodist of Dewsbury), 21
Bray Hannah (Huddersfield housewife), 52
Brayshaw James (of Leeds), 99
Brayshaw James (Republican schoolmaster of Yeadon), 101
Bridgewater 3rd Duke of (built first canal in England), 57
Brierley George (carpenter of Clifton), 104

Briggs William (deputy chief constable of Bradford), 175
Bright John MP (Anti Corn Law), 183
Brindley James (canal engineer), 57
Brine James (Tolpuddle Martyr), 140
Brisbane Major General Sir Thomas (Governor NSW), 122
Brontë Anne (author), 133, 134
Brontë Charlotte (author), 133, 134
Brontë Emily (author), 133
Brontë Rev. Patrick (clergyman), 133
Brook James (of Bracken Hall, Fartown), 87
Brook Mark (witness), 106
Brook Mr (magistrate, owned mill at Brooktown), 174
Brook Samuel (owned West Mill Battyeford), 61
Brook Thomas (Luddite), 91
Brooke Alan (local historian), 75, 157
Broomhead William (lawyer), 48
Brougham Henry (defence lawyer York), 89
Broughton Thomas (Barnsley weaver), 80
Brummel Beau (English dandy), 73
Brunt John (member of Cato Street conspiracy), 101
Bryan George (Yorkshire rebel), 112, 113
Buckley Nathaniel (Yorkshire rebel), 104, 105, 106, 109, 110, 111, 113, 116, 122, 123
Burdett Sir Francis (radical MP), 136
Burke Edmund (philosopher and politician), 44
Burkinshaw George (Yorkshire rebel), 109, 112, 116, 123
Burkinshaw John (Yorkshire rebel of Barnsley), 107, 109, 111, 113, 116, 120, 123, 127
Burn D. (passenger on Calista), 124
Burnside Major (61st Regiment of Foot), 176
Bush Michael (historian of Peterloo), 97
Bussey Peter (Bradford Chartist), 158, 160, 162, 168
Butcher Miss (passenger on Lang), 125

Butler John (bishop), 20
Byng General John, 95, 96
Byron Lord (poet), 74
Cambridge Duke of, 178
Cameron Dr Thomas (physician – described parasites), 152
Carlisle Richard (radical politician), 159
Carter Elizabeth (poet), 145
Cartwright Major John (parliamentary campaigner), 47, 53, 92
Cartwright William (owner of Rawfolds Mill), 70, 79, 80, 81, 84, 86, 95
Chadwick Sir Edwin (public health reformer), 147, 149
Chapiel Joseph (Yorkshire rebel of Barnsley), 109, 111, 113, 114, 116, 128
Chapman Charles (witness), 106
Chappell Fred (nail maker), 37
Chorlton John (seller of Wroe's pamphlet), 98
Clarke R.C. (coal mine owner), 181
Clarkson James (of Nab Lane), 135
Clayton John (Sheffield Chartist), 168
Cobbett James Paul (Chartist), 158
Cobbett William (radical journalist), 72, 94, 139, 154
Cobden Richard (Anti Corn Law), 183
Cockshutt James FRS (civil engineer), 27
Cockshutt John (iron maker), 27
Coffin Albert Isaiah (herbalist), 153
Collins John (Birmingham Chartist), 157
Columbus Christopher (explorer - reached Hispaniola 1492), 151
Comstive William (leader of Yorkshire rebels, a weaver), 107, 109, 110, 111, 112, 113, 114, 116, 118, 123, 129, 130, 195
Cook James Lieutenant (Explorer- later Captain Cook), 2, 3
Cooke Sir William Fothergill (pioneer electric telegraph), 165
Cooke William (owner of carpet factory), 75
Cookson Craven (Yorkshire rebel of Barnsley), 107
Cookson Rev. Matthew (vicar of Mirfield), 67
Cooper Lettice (author), 181

Copley Edward (coal miner), 60
Cort Henry (iron manufacturer), 27
Cotton William (owner of shearing frames), 77
Couldwell Abel (Blanketeer), 94
Crabtree George (Yorkshire rebel), 104
Crabtree John (Bradford Chartist), 106, 168
Crabtree Joseph (Barnsley Chartist), 157
Crabtree Thomas (witness), 106
Crawford (radical MP), 144
Croft Thomas (night watchman of Bradford), 168
Cromer John (printer of Sheffield), 44
Cross Sergeant (prosecutor at York), 111
Crossley Francis (carpet manufacture), 170
Crother Thomas (witness), 106
Crowther James Firth (Mirfield maltster), 61
Crowther John (Mirfield maltster), 61
Crowther Joseph (labourer), 88
Crowther Samuel (wounded nail maker), 178
Cummings J.C. (passenger on Calista), 124
Darby Abraham (coke manufacturer), 25
Dartmoor 4th Earl (Lord of the Manor of Slaithwaite), 139
Darwin Charles (botanist), 63
Davidson William (member of Cato Street conspiracy), 101
Day John (saboteur from Kirkburton), 179
de Bath Major (4th Dragoon Guards), 108
de Lancey Colonel (military inspector), 43, 46
Dean Jonathan (Luddite), 91
Dearden Jonathan (manager Spencer syndicate), 31
Dearnley James (local historian), 14
Defoe Daniel (author), 11
Dickens Charles (author), 38
Dickenson Samuel (Almondbury Chartist), 157

Dickinson John (draper of Dewsbury), 94, 96, 98
Dillon Cynthia (local historian), 6, 13, 16
Disraeli Benjamin (prime minister 1868 & 1874-1880), 161
Donnelly Fred. (history professor Canada), 124, 128
Downing Michael (Yorkshire rebel), 110, 113, **126**
Duncombe Henry (Yorkshire County MP), 40
Duncombe Thomas MP (proposer of amnesty 1856), 172
Dury John (protester from Bradford), 179
Dyer Joseph (American inventor), 36
Dyson Clement (owner of shearing frames), 77
Eastwood Mr (companion of W. Horsfall), 84
Eden Sir Fredrick (statistician), 14
Edwards Henry Lee (mill owner of Halifax), 175
Elam John (witness), 106
Engels Friedrich (factory owner and author), 71
Evans Dr (Mrs Ingham's father), 135
Evans Eric (history professor), 124
Evans Rev. Joseph (radical preacher), 41, 43
Eyre (enclosure commissioner), 45
Farrand W.B. (magistrate of Bingley), 139, 186, 187
Farren William (gardener to the Bronte's), 134
Farrimond Thomas (Yorkshire rebel of Barnsley), 107, 108, 116
Fenton (Yorkshire rebel of Barnsley), 108
Field Mr (optician of Birmingham), 28
Fielden John MP (radical mill owner, social reformer, sponsor of Ten Hour Act), 96, 140, 143, 157, 158, 161, 172, 182
Firth Joseph (witness), 106, 113, 114, 116, 118, 120, 123, 129
Fisher Joseph (coal miner), 89
Fitzgerald Mr (publican), 83

Fitzwilliam Earl (Lord Lieutenant West Riding), 50, 52, 86, 95, 98
Fleming Sir Alexander (discoverer of penicillin), 151
Fletcher Dr (Bury Chartist), 157
Flinn George (leader Bradford insurgency), 170
Flowers James (Yorkshire rebel), 109, 111, 113, 116, 122, 123
Foreman Amanda (author), 146
Foster Joseph (mill owner), 79
Fothergill John FRS (Yorkshire physician), 10
Fould (police constable of Bingley), 187
Fowler Charles (map maker of Leeds), 148
Fox Richard (witness), 106
Frampton James (Tolpuddle landowner), 140
Freeman John (father of baby Jane), 118
Frost John (Welsh Chartist), 161, 162, 170
Frost Mary (school dame), 62
Frost Thomas (commentator), 192
Gales Joseph (founder Sheffield Register), 43, 46
Gammage Robert George (Chartist chronicler), 142
Garner John (owner of shearing frames), 77
Garside Joshua (local mathematician), 135
Gell (Sheffield Tithe holder), 45
Gill George (Yorkshire rebel), 104
Gill James (Yorkshire rebel), 104
Gill Sam (Yorkshire rebel), 104
Gill Tom (Yorkshire rebel), 104
Gills Nicholas (chapman), 29
Gledhill James (Huddersfield school teacher), 49
Godwin William (author), 43
Goodwin George (editor), 13
Gosling John (agent provocateur), 91
Gott Benjamin (Ing factory manufacturer), 170
Graham James (medical quack), 153

Greasby Quartermaster (15 Regiment of Hussars), 84
Greensmith Joseph (Bradford informer), 169
Grey Earl (prime minister 1830-1834), 137
Haig Ibbotson (nail maker), 37
Haigh James (Luddite), 91
Haigh Samuel W. (cotton spinner), 133
Haigh-Allen B. (magistrate), 106
Hall Joseph (witness at York), 90
Hall Mr (Leeds Mercury reporter), 178
Hall Mrs (housewife of Bank Top), 107
Hammerton Mr (wire drawer), 133
Hammett James (Tolpuddle Martyr), 140
Hanson Abraham (Eland Chartist), 158
Hanson Benjamin (Yorkshire rebel of Barnsley), 111, 113, 114, 116, 129, 195
Hardcastle John (witness), 106
Harewood Earl of (Lord Lieutenant of West Riding), 160, 188
Hargreaves James (inventor spinning jenny), 74
Hargrove Mr (printer of York Herald), 113
Harney George Julian (Chartist politician), 159
Harrison James (informer of Bradford, 169
Harrison Job (gamekeeper of Bradley), 104, 106
Harrowby Earl of (of Cato Street), 101
Hartley Samuel (Luddite), 81, 82
Hartley William (Luddite), 91
Hawkins Captain Samuel (Calista), 124
Hayman Richard (author), 27
Hector Mr & Mrs (passengers on Lang), 125
Henry Arthur (market gardener), 128
Henry Hobhouse (Treasury solicitor), 86, 96
Hepponstall Ben (leader at Folly Hall), 95
Herring Archbishop, 19
Hetherington Henry (Chartist politician), 159
Hey James (Luddite), 88, 91
Hey Job (Luddite), 91

Hicks Lieutenant (Second Lieutenant Endeavour), 2
Hill John (Luddite), 91
Hill Thomas (householder of Cold Henley), 108
Hill William (editor of Northern Star), 155
Hinchcliffe John (farmer of Bradley), 104, 106
Hinchcliffe Mr (bystander), 83
Hinchliffe William (cloth dresser), 77
Hird Mr (magistrate of Bradford), 177
Hirst George (innkeeper of Rose and Crown Darton), 104, 108
Hirst John (Luddite), 81
Hirst Joseph (owner of shearing shop), 102
Hirst Joshua (clothier of Deighton), 101, 102, 103, 104, 105, 106, 206
Hirst William (Yorkshire rebel), 102, 103
Hobhouse Sir John (1st Baron Broughton), 158, 185
Hobson John (Dodworth diarist), 25, 109, 113, 116, 122, 123
Holberry Samuel (Sheffield Chartist), 167
Holland William (Yorkshire rebel), 109, 113, 116, 122, 123
Holmes Joseph (blacksmith and Yorkshire rebel), 104
Hood Dr (passenger on Calista), 124
Horsfall William (owner Ottiwells Mill), 69, 71, 84, 86, 87, 89, 90, 216
Houghton Rowland (surgeon of Huddersfield), 90
Howard John (instigated prison reform), 149
Howe Admiral Lord Richard (victor 'Glorious First of June'), 47
Howes James (Yorkshire rebel), 114
Howitt William (author and journalist), 21
Hoyle Nathan (Luddite), 88, 91
Hullock Sergeant (prosecutor at York), 111
Hulton William (High Sheriff of Lancashire), 97
Hume Joseph (radical MP), 136

Hunt Henry (orator), 96
Hunter Joseph (Sheffield antiquarian), 41
Huntsman Benjamin (invention of crucible steel), 40
Husson Nicholas (discovered cure for gout), 153
Illingworth William (night watchman of Bradford), 168
Illingworth William (Yorkshire rebel), 104
Ingham Abraham (Yorkshire rebel), 109, 113, 116, 122
Ingham Mr (owner of Blake Hall), 134
Ings James (member of Cato Street conspiracy), 101
Ironside Isaac (Chartist of Sheffield), 155
Ismay Rev. (rector of St Mary's Church), 59, 61
Jackson Abraham (Yorkshire rebel of Moldgreen), 103
Jackson John (Chartist of Leeds), 155
Jefferson Isaac (alias Watt Tyler of Bradford), 187, 188
Jenner Dr Edward (introduced vaccination), 150
Jesty (farmer who used cowpox), 150
Johnson Dr Samuel (English lexicographer), 39
Johnston John (reform 'missionary'), 94
Jones Ernest (Chartist reformer), 183, 186, 188, 189
Jones John Gale (journalist), 98
Joshua Hobson, 155
Kay John (invented flying shuttle), 60
Keane John (commentator), 44
Kent Mrs (mistress of Governor Sorell), 121
Kilham Alexander (breakaway Methodist), 20
Kilner Thomas (householder of Mirfield), 105, 106, 206
Kilvington T. (Bradford protester), 186, 187
King George III (reign 1760-1820), 3, 39, 40, 99, 100, 137, 215, 216
King George IV (reign 1820-1830), 93, 137, 217

King Mr (passenger on Calista), 124
King William IV (reign 1830-1837), 137, 143, 217
Kitchener Stephen (Yorkshire rebel of Barnsley), 107
L'Estrange Lieutenant-Colonel Guy, 97
Lamotte Lieutenant (passenger on Lang), 125
Larksass (Joke?) Abraham (Yorkshire rebel), 109
Laycock John (a walker of Giusburn), 132
Laycock Mr (riot victim from Sheffield), 178
Le Blanc Sir Simon (King's Bench judge), 76
Leach James (founder of National Charter Association), 170
Ledger John (of Pontefract), 36
Lee Henry (Yorkshire rebel from Fixby), 105
Leech John (shopkeeper for Pitkethley), 159
Leeming Robert (protester of Bradford), 179
Lever Peter (Yorkshire rebel), 102, 103
Lightowler David (Chartist), 185, 187
Lind Dr James (naval surgeon), 3
Lindley Ann (daughter of John Lindley), 192, 193
Lindley George (nephew of John Lindley), 37, 135
Lindley Harriet (granddaughter of John Lindley), 45, 192
Lindley Jane (mother of John Lindley), 7, 8, 34
Lindley John senior (grandfather of John Lindley), 11
Lindley John William (son of John Lindley), 22, 56, 193
Lindley Jonathan (brother of John Lindley), 8
Lindley Robert junior (son of John Lindley), 7, 8, 32, 33
Littledale Mr (prosecutor at York), 111
Liverpool Lord (prime minister 1812-1827), 85, 93

Lloyd John (spymaster), 86
Locke John (philosopher), 8
Lockwood John (of Holmfirth), 175
Londonderry Lord (opposed Mines Act 1842), 182
Louis XVI (King of France), 47
Love Colonel (of 73 Infantry), 173
Loveless George (Tolpuddle Martyr), 140
Loveless James (Tolpuddle Martyr), 140
Lovett William (co-author of People's Charter), 17, 156, 200
Lowery Robert (Leeds Chartist), 171
Ludd Ned (mythical apprentice Luddite), 73, 79
Lumb John (coal miner), 89, 91
Lyell Sir Charles (geologist), 63
M'Donald James (agent provocateur), 91
Macauley Peter (father of Andrew and Jane), 118
Macauley Thomas (historian and member of parliament), 172
Machen Miss (riot victim from Leeds), 178
Macquarie Lachlan (Governor NSW), 119
Maitland Colonel (32nd Regiment of Foot), 173
Maitland Lieutenant-General Sir Thomas (CO 'army of the north'), 84, 86
Mann Horace (civil servant, religious census), 191
Mann James (Leeds bookseller), 95, 99, 101
Marmont Marshal (French general), 88
Marshall John (flax spinner of Leeds), 42, 170
Marshall Winifred (wife of Joseph Gales), 43
Marx Karl (political writer), 83
Mather Joseph (song writer), 47
McDouall Peter Murray (Chartist parliamentary candidate), 171, 185, 188
McInnis Colonel (Royal Irish Fusiliers), 174
Melbourne Viscount (prime minister 1835-1841), 140

Mellor Elizabeth (John Lindley's sister-in-law), 17
Mellor George (leader Yorkshire Luddite), 71, 73, 74, 75, 76, 77, 78, 81, 83, 84, 86, 89, 155, 214
Mellor Hannah (wife of John Lindley), 22, 62
Mellor Joseph (John Lindley's father-in-law), 22
Mellor Joseph (Luddite), 86
Milner Elizabeth (witness), 106
Milton Lord MP, 171
Mitchell Joseph (Lancashire radical), 94
Montague Lady Mary Wortley (pioneered immunisation), 150
Montgomery James (newspaper editor, writer and poet), 46, 47, 48, 64
Morgan Thomas (Yorkshire rebel, turned Kings Evidence), 109, 116
Morpeth Lord MP, 171
Morrison James (quack doctor), 153
Mortimer Mary (Bradford Chartist), 188
Moxon Samuel (victim), 89
Murgatroyd William (of Wortley forge), 31
Nadin Joseph (deputy constable), 97
Napier Major General Sir Charles (commander northern armies), 159
Nelms Sarah (cowpox donor for Dr Jenner), 150
Nelson Robert (educational philanthropist), 16
Nelson Vice Admiral Horatio (victor of Trafalgar), 54
Newcomen Thomas (inventor of steam engine), 5, 65
Norcliffe Edmund (of Almondbury), 53, 102, 104, 111
Norcliffe Samuel (nephew of Edmund), 102, 104, 106, 206
Norfolk Duke of (Lord of the Manor of Sheffield), 45
North Lord (prime minister 1770-1782), 40
Norton Mr (factory owner at Clayton), 135

O'Brien James Bronterre (Chartist), 143, 160, 170, 171, 189
O'Connor Feargus (Chartist leader), 143, 154, 155, 157, 158, 160, 171, 172, 183, 185, 186, 189
Oastler Richard (campaigner for Ten Hour Movement), 96, 138, 139, 140, 143, 144, 154, 158, 180, 181, 182, 208
Oates (mill owner), 76
Ogden John (Luddite), 91
Oldfield Samuel (master spinner), 35
Oldroyd James (clothier of Dewsbury), 86
Oliver William (Informer), 33, 94, 95, 96, 105
Orwell George (author), 65
Owen Robert (radical factory owner), 15
Paine Thomas (radical author), 43, 44, 47, 49, 216
Palmer Captain (43rd Lancers), 174
Park Sir James Allen (judge at York), 110
Parr Mr (manufacturer of Marsden), 89
Parrot Jonathan (witness), 106
Peacock John (Yorkshire rebel of Tan House), 102, 104, 105, 106, 109, 110, 111, 113, 116, 118, 120, 123, 130, 193, 195
Peart Rev. Samuel (curate and school teacher), 62
Peel Sir Robert (prime minister 1834-35 and 1841-46), 137, 163
Perceval Spencer (prime minister 1809-1812), 85
Percy John (author), 28
Perkins Jacob (of America), 36, 216
Phillip Captain Arthur (commander first fleet), 4
Phipps James (recipient of Dr Jenner's cowpox), 150
Pickard William (householder of Barnsley), 108
Pickering John (Yorkshire rebel, weaver of Dodworth), 107, 113
Pilling George (Yorkshire rebel, cropper), 105
Pilling John (Huddersfield representative), 101
Pilling Joseph (Yorkshire rebel of Huddersfield), 101, 102

Pitkethly Lawrence (draper, Huddersfield Chartist), 140, 143, 158, 171
Pitt William the Younger (prime minister 1783-1801), 4, 40
Place Francis (radical tailor), 40, 51, 63, 136, 156, 202
Pollard George (Halifax magistrate), 175
Powell Thomas (Government spy), 188
Powlett John (Chartist), 158
Pratt James (Chartist of Halifax), 175
Prescott Rev. (Stockport magistrate), 86
Preston Ben (Yorkshire poet), 190
Price Dr Richard (radical author), 43, 44
Priestly Dr Joseph (chemist and author), 43
Prince George. *See* Cambridge Duke of
Pryor Mrs (lady's companion), 134
Queen Anne (reign 1702-1714), 16
Queen Elizabeth I (reign 1558-1603), 69
Queen Victoria (reign 1837-1901), 144
Radcliffe Joseph (local magistrate), 77, 78, 86, 90, 91, 92
Radcliffe William (of Woodstock), 87
Radzinowicz Dr (historian), 74
Raikes Rev. Robert (founder Sunday School Movement), 62
Raine (prosecutor at York), 111
Ramsden Sir John (builder of Huddersfield Broad Canal), 58
Raynes Captain Francis (soldier), 86
Rede William Leman (historian), 116
Rhazes (medieval physician), 10
Rhodes Tom (Yorkshire rebel cropper), 105
Rice William (Yorkshire rebel of Barnsley), 107, 109, 110, 111, 113, 116, 118, 120, 123, 130, 195
Richardson (Manchester Chartist), 157
Richardson Thomas (innkeeper of Darton), 108
Ricord Phillippe (isolated the clinical features of syphilis), 151
Rider William (Chartist), 158
Riley Thomas (tailor), 91
Roberson Rev. Hammond (curate of Dewsbury), 62

Roberts George (owner of shearing frames), 77
Robertson John (passenger on Calista), 124
Robinson J. (mill owner of Holmfirth), 175
Roden Thomas (soldier of Carlow Militia), 84
Roebuck (radical MP), 144
Rogers Benjamin (Yorkshire rebel of Barnsley), 107, 109, 111, 113, 114, 116, 123, 130, 195
Royle Edward (professor and author), 189
Russell Lord John (prime minister 1846-1852), 137, 161, 185, 186
Ryder Richard (home secretary), 77
Sadler Michael (radical MP), 138, 140
Savile (Lord of the manor of Mirfield), 67
Saville John (prosecutor at York), 110
Schofield Hannah (nosy parker of the Knowl), 104
Schofield Tomas (master cropper of Marsh), 106
Scholes George (shopkeeper), 87
Seabrook Rev. Henry (of Bradford), 135
Seal C. (passenger on Calista), 124
Seddon James (weaver of Dodworth), 107, 113
Seddon William (son of James), 107
Shackleton William (husband of Anne Lindley), 193
Shaftsbury Lord (social campaigner in House of Lords), 182
Shaw George junior (ironmonger of Leeds), 36
Shaw George senior (Chartist), 36
Shaw Hannah (school dame), 16
Shaw James (Leeds Luddite), 76
Shaw John (Chartist of Staincross), 185
Shaw Joseph junior (iron founder), 36
Shaw Joseph senior (nail maker), 36
Shiell William (miner), 128
Shore Samuel (Sheffield iron master), 41
Sidmouth Lord (home secretary), 85, 86, 94, 98, 101, 109, 195
Slater John (special constable of Bradford), 169
Smaller John (of Holbury, leader at Folly Hall), 95
Smiles Samuel (author of Self-Help), 60, 170, 183
Smith Adam (author and economist), 32, 66, 72, 216
Smith George (of Snowgate Head), 78
Smith George (publisher), 134
Smith Joseph (joiner from Colne Bridge), 102, 110, 111, 113
Smith Thomas (Luddite), 81, 86, 89
Smith William (Protester), 179
Smithson (mill owner), 156
Smyth family (medieval iron makers), 23
Snow Dr John (physician of cholera fame), 148
Solander Dr (scientist on Endeavour), 3
Sorell William (Lieutenant-Governor Van Diemen's Land), 121
Spark John (local chapman), 14, 29, 215
Spence Mr (of Tilworth Grange), 192
Spencer John (head of Spencer syndicate), 26, 31
Standfield John (Tolpuddle Martyr), 140
Standfield Thomas (Tolpuddle Martyr), 140
Stanfield Charles (Yorkshire rebel of Barnsley), 109, 113, 123, 195
Starkey Mr (magistrate and owner of Mill at Longroyd Bridge), 174
Starkie Mr (defence attorney at York), 111, 113
Stephens Rev. Joseph Rayner (fiery Methodist preacher), 140, 143, 154, 157, 159
Stone Rev. Edmund (discovered willow bark – salicylic acid), 146
Stott Frances (Mirfield author), 6, 177
Strakey Joseph (Yorkshire rebel of Cowcliffe), 102, 103
Swallow John (coal miner), 89
Swallow Sam (owner of shearing frames), 77
Swift James (woollen manufacturer), 133
Swift Thomas (witness), 106
Sydenham Dr Thomas (physician father of medicine), 10

Symons J.C. (parliamentary commissioner), 181
Tait Rev. Archibald (Dean of Carlisle), 10
Tanner Mr & Mrs (passengers on Lang), 125
Taylor (justice of Tickhill), 52
Taylor George (of Honley and Holmfirth), 95
Taylor Harold (local historian), 6, 14
Taylor James & Enoch (manufacturers of shearing frames), 70
Taylor James (Rochdale Chartist), 157
Thatcher Dr James (physician – described rabies), 152
Thistlewood Arthur (leader Cato Street conspiracy), 101
Thompson (Yorkshire rebel of Barnsley), 108
Thompson Professor E.P. (Marxist historian), 55, 62, 75
Thompson Professor Hamilton (historian), 81
Thompson Samuel A. (American medical quack), 153
Thompson Sir Alexander (judge at York), 89
Thorne Major General (Yorkshire area commander), 188
Thornhill (squire of Fixby Hall), 139
Thornton Joshua (farmer), 87
Thornton Richard (witness), 106
Thornton William (Halifax Chartist), 158
Thorpe Rev. Richard (of Hopton Hall), 62
Thorpe William (Luddite), 78, 81, 86, 89
Tidd Richard (member of Cato Street conspiracy), 101
Tiffany Joseph (Yorkshire rebel cropper of Cowcliffe), 105, 106
Todd Mr (Dewsbury Chartist), 157
Tolson Robert (fancy manufacturer from Dalton), 104
Tooke John Horne (political journalist), 43
Towle James (executed Luddite), 74
Towle William (executed Luddite), 74
Tuke Dr (owner of asylum), 189

Tupia (Polynesian guide on Endeavour)), 3
Tyas John (Yorkshire rebel of Rastrick), 102
Tyas Joseph (Yorkshire rebel of Barnsley), 72, 106, 109
Ussher Archbishop James (Primate of all Ireland), 63
Vallance Edward (author), 186
Vallance John (Yorkshire rebel), 109, 113, 114, 116, 122, 123
Vever Tom (leader at Folly Hall), 95
Vickerman Frank (cloth finisher), 78
Wadsworth Mr (victim of army volley), 176
Wales Captain Alexander (of Tranmere), 124
Walker Benjamin (Luddite, cloth dresser), 81, 86, 90
Walker George (leather merchant of Kitston), 133
Walker John (Luddite), 91
Walker William (cloth manufacturer), 87
Walton John (local historian), 15
Ward George (Sheffield Clarion Ramblers), 45
Waterhouse John (witness), 106
Watt James (inventor of efficient steam engine), 5, 59, 65, 216
Watt Tyler of Bradford. *See* Jefferson Isaac
Webber Max (sociologist), 5
Weir James (Master of the Lady Ridley), 118, 119
Wellington Duke of (prime minister 1828-1830), 84, 137, 186
Wells Roger (historian), 52
Wesley John (founder Methodist Church), 9, 19, 20, 21, 62, 135, 145
West Francis (resident of Dodworth), 25
West John (historian), 118
Westmoreland Rev. T. (vicar of Sandal), 98
Wheatley Henry (owner of woollen mill), 60
Wheatstone Charles (pioneer electric telegraph), 165

Whitacre John (witness), 106
White George (Leeds Chartist), 157, 185, 188
Whitfield George (constable of Paddock), 84
Whittaker Thomas (cotton weaver), 87
Wilberforce William MP (humanist against slave trade), 41, 180
Wilkinson Rev. John (vicar of Sheffield and local magistrate), 45
Wilkinson Robert (Chartist leather cutter), 157, 158
Williams Gwyn (Sheffield journalist), 42
Williams Mr (defence attorney at York), 111, 113, 114
Williams Rev. (vicar of St Mary's Church Barnsley), 161
Wilson Ben (Halifax Chartist), 160
Wilson Benjamin (established bank in Mirfield), 57
Wilson James (Yorkshire rebel), 106
Wilson James RN (surgeon Lady Ridley), 118, 119, 146
Wilson John (witness), 106
Wilson Thomas (householder), 105
Winn Thomas (carpenter, Yorkshire rebel), 102
Winter John (Yorkshire rebel), 102
Withering Dr William (discovered digitalis – foxglove), 146
Withers Peter (convict from Wiltshire), 122
Wolstenholme William (leader of Folly Hall rising), 95
Wood (mill owner), 76
Wood John (Chartist), 143
Wood Sir Charles (Liberal candidate), 189
Woods Bernard (local historian), 132
Woods Mr (slitting mill owner), 28
Wooler Miss (head of Roe Head School), 133
Wooler T.J. (editor Black Dwarf), 73
Wortley Sir Francis (South Yorkshire landowner), 24
Wright Mr (saddler of Huddersfield), 82
Wrigley Henry (Yorkshire rebel from Fixby), 105
Wroe P. (author of The Peterloo Massacre), 98
Wycliffe John (translator of Bible into English), 63
Wyvill Rev. Christopher (clergyman founder YCA), 39, 41, 44, 45, 53
Yarbrough Henry (of Heslington), 51

ABOUT THE AUTHOR

Ron Riley was born in Bradford, Yorkshire and although he only lived in that county for the first nine years of his life he is one hundred per cent a Yorkshireman. At school, where he also met his wife, Ron developed a passion for history which has never left him. On retirement he became a full time 'historian' with a temporary reader's ticket for the British library. As part of his research for Yorkshire Rebel he visited the Caird Library at Greenwich and the Barnsley Library and Mirfield Library in Yorkshire, but his favourite destination is the National Archives at Kew. While searching for his ancestors he discovered his great-great-great grandfather John Lindley, a nail maker from Darton in Yorkshire. Later he found a mention of John Lindley in a Yorkshire magazine and so began a gradual realisation that this ancestor was more than just another downtrodden victim of the Industrial Revolution. From this small beginning arose the idea for this book, an account of the life of an ordinary yet extraordinary working man spanning the first eighty years of the Industrial Revolution in Yorkshire. Here was an opportunity of recording an important period of British history from a new perspective – the anonymous multitude who made Britain Great.